MARCH OF THE WOODEN SOLDIERS

THE AMAZING STORY OF LAUREL AND HARDY'S "BABES IN TOYLAND"

BY RANDY SKRETVEDT

BONAVENTURE PRESS

*– To Ray Faiola, Rob Falcone, Jonathan DiDonato, Robert M. Grippo and Kevin Butler,
true defenders of Toyland, and Payne Johnson, the smartest of the Three Little Pigs.*

March of the Wooden Soldiers:
The Amazing Story of Laurel and Hardy's "Babes in Toyland"

Published by
Bonaventure Press
Aliso Viejo, CA
USA
bonaventure.press@gmail.com
www.bonaventurepress.com

All rights reserved. No part of this book may be reproduced or transmitted in any form or by any means, electronic or mechanical, including photocopying, recording or by any information storage and retrieval system without written permission from the author, except for the inclusion of brief quotations in a review.

Copyright © 2023 by Randy Skretvedt

Cover Designed by Joe Busam

Colorization by Ron Yungul

Interior Designed by David Koenig

Manufactured in the United States of America

Publisher's Cataloguing-in-Publication Data
Skretvedt, Randy W.
March of the wooden soldiers / by Randy Skretvedt
p. cm.

791.43028

Hardcover: ISBN: 978-1-937878-20-7
Softcover: ISBN: 978-1-937878-21-4

Contents

Introduction	4
1 – The Babes Are Born	5
2 – The Film That Wasn't	14
3 – "The Best Boss I Ever Had"	23
4 – Stan, Babe, Hal and the Two Leos	29
5 – The Boss Shoots the Works	37
6 – Mr. Roach's Story	46
7 – Rewrite	52
8 – Production Starts	56
9 – Adrift	66
10 – "Babes" Back in Business	73
11 – Limping Along	99
12 – Rushing to Conclusion	102
"I Went to Toyland with Laurel & Hardy"	128
Portrait Gallery	130
13 – Ballyhoo, Release and Reception	140
14 – The Producer and the Counterspy	162
15 – New Titles and a New Medium	167
16 – WPIX and a Thanksgiving Tradition	173
17 – Soldiers Marching to Your Home	184
18 – Other Productions, 1949-1961	189
19 – Other Productions, 1980-1997	201
20 – And They Lived Happily Ever Afterward	208
Who's Who in Toyland: The Cast Members	218
Who's Who in Toyland: Behind the Camera	231
Credits	234
Video and Audio Releases	236
Sources	237
Acknowledgements	238
Index	239

Introduction

March of the Wooden Soldiers – the 1934 Laurel and Hardy film originally titled *Babes in Toyland* – has been a holiday classic on television since the early 1950s. The annual showing on WPIX in New York has kept this film alive in American popular culture, when for many years that film was all but unavailable anywhere else.

The film exudes warmth, charm, happiness and a wish for love to conquer evil. The hundreds of people who contributed to making the movie certainly shared those emotions. But, as with any creative collaboration, there were conflicts.

Behind the scenes, there were injuries, a divorce, a not-quite-legal marriage, a secret romance, a barroom fistfight, illnesses and a rift that nearly spelled the end of the Laurel and Hardy team. The film was made at great cost – and not just financial.

The Laurel and Hardy film is an enduring classic, but it's only part of the fascinating story of *Babes in Toyland*.

Chapter 1

The Babes Are Born

The story of *Babes in Toyland* begins with Dorothy, the Scarecrow, the Tin Man and the Cowardly Lion. L. Frank Baum's book *The Wonderful Wizard of Oz*, published on September 1, 1900 by the Chicago-based George M. Hill Company, was so hugely popular that the first edition of 10,000 copies had sold out by October. A second printing of 15,000 was snapped up before that month was out. Publisher Hill initially had been skeptical of the book's success and agreed to print it only because Fred R. Hamlin, who managed the Chicago Grand Opera House, agreed beforehand to stage a musical play to promote the book.

Composer Paul Tietjens, another Chicagoan and only 24, wrote a score inspired by the light-classical style of Victor Herbert, while Baum wrote the script and the lyrics. However, producer Hamlin, along with director Julian Mitchell, wanted a zanier show; Mitchell also wanted songs in a more popular style, breaking away from the book's storyline to include topical comedy songs. Ultimately, many composers and lyricists contributed to the score over the course of the show's run.

Adding comedy material to the script as the show evolved was Glen MacDonough, born in Brooklyn on November 12, 1870. He was from a theatrical family; his father, Thomas, was a theater manager, and his mother was an actress going by the name Laura Don. MacDonough was a feature and human-interest reporter for the *New York World* before the lure of the theater overtook him, too. At the time he joined the *Oz* crew, he had written seven Broadway shows including a musical fantasy called *Chris and the Wonderful Lamp* with music by John Philip Sousa.

The Wizard of Oz – the book's full title wouldn't fit on a marquee – debuted on June 17, 1902 at the Grand Opera House in Chicago, with Anna Laughlin as Dorothy Gale of Kansas, Fred Stone as the Scarecrow, David Montgomery as the Tin Woodman, Arthur Hill as the Cowardly Lion, and Bobby Gaylor as Oz. After touring through the Midwest in the summer and fall of 1902, *Oz* came to Broadway as the inaugural offering of the Majestic Theater on January 21, 1903. It ran for 293 performances through October 3, went back on the road, and returned to Broadway at the Majestic on March 21, 1904. This production moved to the New York Theatre and then the Academy of Music for a total of 171 performances before closing on November 25, 1905. The rousing and surprising reception accorded the *Oz* musical was noted by many in the theatrical community, including composer Victor Herbert.

Herbert was a man of great energy and prodigious output. As one source notes, "Herbert produced two operas, a cantata, 43 operettas, incidental music to 10 plays, 31 compositions for orchestra, nine band compositions, nine cello compositions, five violin compositions with piano or orchestra, 22 piano compositions and numerous songs, choral compositions, and orchestrations of works by other composers, among other music." Standing five feet, eight inches tall, he weighed about 250 pounds for most of his adult life but was not fat. He was quite muscular, being fond of hiking and swimming. He loved food and strong drink and indulged in them frequently despite having poor teeth. His handsome, usually smiling face was adorned with a magnificent mustache, waxed at the tips.

Herbert was friendly and gracious but could burst into anger or tears at a moment's notice. He was his own harshest critic of his work, trying always to surmount what he saw as his musical deficiencies. A musical prodigy, he took to the cello almost immediately and was hailed as a great cellist although he rarely practiced. He was a long-standing member of the New York theatrical fraternity the Lambs Club and produced several of their annual "Gambols," some of which featured entertainments that

Left: The Wizard of Oz stage production of 1902 featured Anna Laughlin as Dorothy and, somewhere under that costume, Arthur Hill as the Cowardly Lion. *Right:* Fred Stone as the Scarecrow and David C. Montgomery as the Tin Man became a popular comedy team on Broadway.

lampooned his own work. He wanted to leave what he called an Irish will, reading "I, Victor Herbert, being of sound mind and body, spent all my money." While he left a modest financial estate, his daughter Ella took what there was and built it into a fortune.

He was born February 1, 1859 on the island of Guernsey, although his mother, Frances "Fanny" Lover Muspratt, told him that he'd been born in Dublin, Ireland, which Victor believed all his life. (He was proudly Irish and – thanks to his mother – was of Irish descent, but never set foot in Ireland.) The high-spirited Fanny was separated from her husband, chemical industrialist Frederic Muspratt. He had spent much of their marriage on research trips to Morocco and Australia, leaving Fanny alone with their infant daughter, Angela. Muspratt divorced Fanny in 1861 after learning that she had borne a son by the mysterious August Herbert, who had long since vanished. Fanny married a German medical doctor, Carl Theodor Schmid, in 1866. Victor joined his mother in Stuttgart the following year and at eight years old began studying piano, flute, piccolo, cello and music theory.

In 1881, age 22, he joined the Royal Court orchestra in Stuttgart and became a featured cellist; five years later, Herbert and his new bride, soprano Therese Forster, came to the United States, having been hired to join the Metropolitan Opera company in New York. In the summer of 1888, Herbert became the assistant conductor of the New York Philharmonic, an association which lasted through 1898, when he was named the primary conductor of the Pittsburgh Symphony. During this time, Herbert was also composing; he wrote an operetta,

Prince Ananais, for the comic opera company The Bostonians.

Herbert's next operetta, *The Wizard of the Nile*, debuted on Broadway on November 4, 1895 and ran for 105 performances through February 1, 1896. This first Broadway production would prove to be Herbert's most successful for several years. His subsequent track record on the Great White Way was perhaps less than stellar:

The Serenade – March 16 through May 22, 1897, 79 performances
The Fortune Teller – September 26 through October 29, 1898, 40 performances
Cyrano de Bergerac – September 18 through October 14, 1899, 28 performances
The Singing Girl – October 23, 1899 through January 6, 1900, 80 performances
The Ameer – December 4, 1899 through January 20, 1900, 51 performances
The Viceroy – April 30 through May 5, 1900, 28 performances

To be fair, *The Serenade* had proven popular in venues beyond Broadway, and was produced by several companies internationally for a few years, but the others had had their moment and then faded. From 1900 through much of 1903, Herbert concentrated on working with the Pittsburgh Symphony.

Fred Hamlin and Julian Mitchell were eager to create a show like *The Wizard of Oz* to occupy their Chicago theater once the production had moved on to New York. Hamlin and Mitchell liked Glen MacDonough's work on *Oz* and wanted a similar show, a musical comedy which would also display the same lavish style of costumes and scenery. John H. Young, who had helped design the magnificent scenery for *Oz*, remained to provide the same magic for the new production, while MacDonough began working on a story near the end of 1902.

MacDonough had collaborated with Victor Herbert in 1896 on a political satire, *The Gold Bug*. Likewise, Mitchell had directed the Broadway productions of Herbert's *The Fortune Teller* and *The Singing Girl* and knew that his continental, light-classical style of composition would be perfect for an opulent fantasy such as this. Mitchell and MacDonough took the train to Pittsburgh, arriving on March 1, 1903, hoping to engage Herbert's services. Since Hamlin, Mitchell, Young and MacDonough were already working on what promised to be a surefire hit in a guaranteed venue, Herbert signed on to the project, his first work for the theater in more than two years. He specifically asked for Max Hirschfeld as the music director, and with that request granted, quickly got to work. He finished writing the last number on June 9, 1903, eight days before the show's scheduled opening in Chicago.

MacDonough clearly used the successful structure of *Oz* as a template for his new story. *Oz* had a child as its heroine, Dorothy Gale. *Babes in Toyland* had two children, Alan and Jane, orphans who have inherited a fortune from their late parents.

Oz opened with an amazing scenic spectacle, the tornado that carried Dorothy from Kansas to Oz, while the prologue for *Babes* displayed a sea storm and a shipwreck, in which Alan and Jane are presumed drowned. Happily, they are rescued by some roving gypsy girls and returned to the garden of Contrary Mary – who is in love with Alan.

Top: Composer Victor Herbert returned to composing for the theater with *Babes in Toyland*. *Middle:* Glen MacDonough wrote the well-remembered lyrics and not-so-well-remembered book. *Bottom*: Julian Mitchell directed and choreographed the show.

Oz had as its primary villain Pastoria, the former King of Oz, whose throne has been usurped by the Wizard; *Babes* had a Toymaker who at first seems kindly, but in fact hates children. He puts evil spirits into his "demon dolls" so that they will kill each child who receives one on Christmas. The dolls turn on him and send the Toymaker plunging to his death in a boiling volcano.

Earlier, the Toymaker had conspired to kill Alan and Jane with the other truly nasty character of the piece, Uncle Barnaby. He is the guardian of the orphaned Alan and Jane, and wants these Babes dead because upon their demise he stands to inherit the riches left to them by their parents. Barnaby lusts after this bounty so that he may support Contrary Mary, whom he hopes to wed, but who sensibly wants no part of him. He has two bumbling henchmen, Gonzorgo and Roderigo, who at Barnaby's bidding had put Alan and Jane aboard the galleon that sank in the storm at sea.

Both shows displayed opulent, sumptuous scenery as the environment of fantasy lands – *Oz* with the Emerald City, and *Babes* with Toyland. The Herbert show also presented that lethal volcano, something which librettist MacDonough had insisted upon in preliminary discussions with director Mitchell.

Each show had a lavish music number in its second act. *Oz* had a "Ball of All Nations" in which the Wizard, having given a brain to the Scarecrow and a heart to the Tin Woodman, celebrates with a spectacular party showcasing songs about the Irish, Italians and Native Americans. *Babes* had the "March of Toy Soldiers" and a "Military Ball" as the finale to the second scene of Act Two.

Each show had an "all is lost" low point in Act Three. In *Oz*, the evil Pastoria, having regained his throne, declares Dorothy, the Scarecrow and the Tin Woodsman to be enemies of the state and orders their execution. In *Babes*, Barnaby frames Alan for the death of the Toymaker. Barnaby promises to exonerate him if Contrary Mary will be his bride. She reluctantly goes through with the wedding, but Barnaby then reneges and names Alan to two officials as the culprit. It looks as though Alan is going to be executed by Gonzorgo and Roderigo.

Both productions had last-minute happy resolutions. *Wizard* had a true *deus ex machina* finale, but instead of a Greek god coming from the sky to set things right, it was the good Witch of the North. She stops the planned execution, liberates Dorothy and her friends, and sends Dorothy home to Kansas. In *Babes*, helpful Tom-Tom discovers an ancient law of Toyland in which a widow "may claim a condemned man for her second husband, and he shall be free as long as he supports said widow and saves her from becoming a charge upon the state." All of this comes true when Barnaby unwittingly drinks a poisoned glass of wine intended to be the agent of Alan's demise. Contrary Mary is suddenly a widow, and claims Alan as her husband.

Besides the many similarities to the *Wizard of Oz* script, *Babes in Toyland* had other narrative tributaries flowing into the river of its storyline. Several characters were from children's rhymes, among them Contrary Mary and her garden, Tom-Tom the Piper's son (and by extension, his mother, Widow Piper), Jack and Jill, Little Bo-Peep, Little Miss Muffet, Little Tommy Tucker, Little Boy Blue, Peter the Pumpkin Eater, Simple Simon, Curly Locks, Bobby Shaftoe, and, from a full-fledged story, Little Red Riding Hood.

MacDonough always insisted that his primary inspiration was an 1859 story by Irishman Fitz-James O'Brien, "The Wondersmith." The title character, a European immigrant named Herr Hippe, is an impoverished toymaker who lives in a bohemian section of New York City and detests the wealthy and privileged families of nearby neighborhoods. He plots to murder their children at Christmas by creating hordes of toy soldiers, dolls and animals, all of whom are possessed by evil demons, and who will prove to be real surprise presents by stabbing the kids to death. Unfortunately for Herr Hippe, his diabolical creations turn on him. Quoting Mr. O'Brien, "To stab and kill was their mission, and they stabbed and killed with incredible fury. They clustered on the Wondersmith's sallow cheeks and sinewy throat, piercing every portion with their diminutive poisoned blades." When Herr Hippe throws his small assailants into the fireplace, they run back out, now aflame, and set his workshop on fire.

Clearly, this jolly yarn has many elements which MacDonough incorporated into his script 43 years later, notably the references to Christmas. The second act of *Babes in Toyland* (eventually) opened with Herbert and MacDonough's song "Hail to Christmas," set in the Christmas Tree Grove. It's also easy to see where MacDonough got the ideas of the toy soldiers, the evil toymaker whose creations destroy him, and his fiery demise.

The centuries-old English ballad, folk tale and subsequent "Christmas pantomime" of *Babes in the Wood* furnished more elements of the *Babes in Toyland* script, which seemed to acknowledge this lineage in its title. Two orphaned children, who have been left a large inheritance by their deceased parents, are put into the care of an uncle and aunt. The scheming uncle hires two thugs to kill the kids, so that he may acquire the loot. The children are brought into a lonely place deep in the woods, but one thug, conscience-stricken and unable to carry out the plot, kills his criminal crony and runs off. Here's where the many renderings of the story differ. In one version of the folk tale, the children wander alone in the woods until they die; sympathetic birds then cover their bodies with leaves. In another, they are taken to Heaven, and God pours his wrath upon the wicked uncle.

In the earliest known stage version performed in 1793, the children survive and are returned to their parents, who evidently weren't really dead at the beginning of this variation. By 1867, theatrical performances had introduced Robin Hood and his merry men, who rescue the kids from a (brief) lifetime of wandering in the forest, and expose the uncle as a villain.

Later Christmas pantomime productions were transformed into wild comedy. An 1897 production at the Drury Lane theatre in London starred Herbert Campbell, who at six feet tall and 256 pounds was a particularly outrageous "dame." His co-star was the diminutive, droll Dan Leno – the comedian who was idolized by young Arthur Stanley Jefferson, later to become Stan Laurel.

MacDonough took the most prominent elements of all these sources and combined them in the *Babes in Toyland* script, adding his own characters (notably Barnaby's clumsy henchmen Gonzorgo and Roderigo, and the Toymaker's clumsy henchman Grumio) and infusing the entire concoction with a healthy dollop of wit. He also may have derived some of his story from *The Toyshop*, a children's operetta written by one Alice Riley of Evanston, Illinois, who in a July 1903 plagiarism lawsuit claimed that she had sent her script to producer Fred Hamlin at the Chicago Opera House in 1902. At the trial, MacDonough stated that he had never seen this script but admitted his other sources of inspiration. The case was settled in favor of Hamlin, Mitchell, MacDonough and Herbert in May 1904.

Babes in Toyland was not quite the smash hit that *The Wizard of Oz* had been, but it was certainly a success. The version that audiences saw in the Chicago Grand Opera House on the opening night of June 17, 1903 – exactly one year after the debut of *The Wizard of Oz* in that same venue – boasted a score consisting of 24 songs, five of which were cut the next night. One of those was "Toyland," which was reinstated by the middle of July.

The cast of 123 people with 24 speaking roles was headed by William Norris as Alan, who was 33 years old but small enough in stature to be believable in his role as a very young man. (His first stage success, *Delmonico's at Six* in 1894, was written by Glen MacDonough.) Mabel Barrison, at 21, was more easily suited to her role as Jane; she had gotten scathing reviews for her performance as waitress Tryxie Tryfle in *The Wizard of Oz*, but after director Julian Mitchell sent her to a company headed by comedians Weber and Fields, she learned her craft and became a fine actress. Uncle Barnaby was played by George W. Denham, who had the unhappy distinction of being in the company performing *Our American Cousin* in Ford's Theater the night Lincoln was shot. Bessie Wynn, who like Mabel Barrison had been a key performer in *The Wizard of Oz*, played Tom-Tom; her solo of "Toyland" became a highlight of the show. She would later become a vaudeville headliner, billed as "The Venus with the Velvet Voice."

After a nearly four-month run in Chicago, *Babes in Toyland* moved to the Majestic Theatre at 5 Columbus Circle in New York, where it enjoyed a healthy residency of 192 performances from October 13, 1903 through March 19, 1904. At this point the score had been whittled all the way down to a mere

Top: George W. Denham was the first of many actors to play Barnaby. *Bottom*: Mr. Denham looked somewhat better out of character.

22 songs, one of which was a new hit, "I Can't Do the Sum." This version was brought back for a limited engagement of 21 performances from January 2 through 21, 1905. Sadly, producer Fred Hamlin didn't savor the success of *Babes in Toyland* long; he died of tuberculosis at his New York home, a week before his 41st birthday, on November 27, 1904.

There were two touring companies, one for large theaters that replicated the New York production as faithfully as possible, and another for smaller venues, with only a 20-piece orchestra and more modest scenery. Both tours ended in May 1906.

We who know *Babes in Toyland* only from its later, much revised incarnations are surprised to learn of the violence in the 1903 original – Alan and Jane being kidnapped and nearly drowned, the Toymaker attacked by his own demonic creations before being burned to death in a volcano, Alan's near execution, and Barnaby's death by the poison which he intended for the kids. Along with that was a frightening scene in the Spider's Forest, in which a spider as big as a man crawled up trees, swung on a line across the stage, and spun a web designed to entrap Alan and Jane, before being stomped to death by a bear.

The spider was played in the original production by Robert Burns, a 25-year-old comedian, acrobat, dancer and contortionist from Philadelphia. He studied live tarantulas in order to mimic their movement plausibly. In November 1905, Burns told a reporter for the *Boston American*, "There is nothing I could do which would better bring into use all the skill of the acrobat and the contortionist. I have to keep my mind constantly on being a spider and move rapidly, for it is only in the rapidity that you would get the smooth crawling motion which is what makes the spider a success." In 1915, Burns would be making movies in Jacksonville, Florida as half of a comedy team, Pokes and Jabbs. A supporting player in some of those films was a Georgia boy named Oliver "Babe" Hardy. By 1930, Hardy was half of a movie comedy team, and Burns was a supporting actor in some of *his* films.

Audiences of the time, including children, seemed to mind the many frightening elements of the original *Babes* not a bit. A *New York Times* reviewer who caught the opening night at the Majestic Theatre enthused, "Taken as a whole, it is a remarkably clean and wholesome entertainment. It is the kind of show that every child will want to take his parents to see, and no child need hesitate to do so for an instant.

"Of course it's quite reasonable to suppose, on the other hand, that some fathers and mothers will see it just the sort of thing to hold over the heads of the little ones, with a 'If you're good you go, and if you're naughty you don't,' but then 'Babes in Toyland' is worth being good for."

Top: William Norris and Mabel Barrison as Alan and Jane donned some fanciful costumes. *Bottom*: Norris, at 33, played Alan, a babe barely into adulthood.

Reading through MacDonough's script, you get the impression that he's created some vivid and colorful characters that would work well in some story, just not this one. The plot meanders into so many diversions, specialty numbers and dance routines that the main point of the narrative is lost. Many of the musical numbers have no bearing at all on the story. With so many main characters, sometimes it becomes confusing as to who is a romantic partner and who is a sibling. (To clarify, Tom-Tom and Contrary Mary are brother and sister, the two eldest children of the Widow Piper. Alan and Jane – who are not babes at all, but of marriageable age – are siblings, Barnaby's nephew and niece. Tom-Tom loves Jane and Alan loves Mary. There.)

In this script, there is no Santa Claus, and Christmas is mentioned only as

George W. Denham as Barnaby consorts with Charles Barry as Gonzorgo and Frank Hayes (probably) as Roderigo.

The life-sized wooden soldiers provided a memorable spectacle, accompanied by "March of the Toys."

— 11 —

Left: Robert "Bobby" Burns played the Spider, and would go on to a long career in movies. *Right*: "Toyland" was sung in the original production by Margaret Sutherland, playing Max, an apprentice to the Toymaker.

a day that the Toymaker hopes will be lethal to children. (The song "Hail to Christmas" would be added later.) "Toyland" is sung here by the Toymaker midway through the show, and he turns out to be a very nasty character indeed, so that negates the wistful sentimentality of the song. Nobody lives in a shoe, although the Widow Piper has many children – and seems eager to get rid of them. She aggressively encourages the marriage of wealthy Barnaby to her daughter Contrary Mary. Mary has never gotten along well with her mother, so she has no qualms about voicing her loathing of Barnaby.

Gonzorgo and Roderigo are prominent throughout the play and anticipate Laurel and Hardy in their personalities. Roderigo is described as "a sentimental ruffian" and cries frequently, unable to carry out the misdeeds he's often called upon to perform.

The wooden soldiers are life-size but have no point in the story other than to provide a showy musical number. There are no villains or Bogeymen to be routed by the soldiers, the only remaining villain at the story's end being Barnaby. The last act is not an epic battle, but a trial for Tom-Tom, falsely accused by Barnaby of murdering the Toymaker.

There are several jokes which are still pretty funny more than a century later. One story element which was cut almost immediately had Barnaby admitting that he had taken Alan and Jane's entire inheritance and invested it in, as Barnaby describes it, "The Eats Heapa Buckwheat Company. A patent health food. It's made of excelsior, it tastes like sawdust, and it looks like buckwheat.

Mixed with Modified Milk and Not Quite Butter, it's a meal fit for a horse." This led into a song by Barnaby, Roderigo and Gonzorgo, "The Health Food Man," which included the lyric, "He ate these things for seven weeks; he really thought they filled him. His health grew better every day, until starvation killed him!" This was probably inspired by the eccentric John Harvey Kellogg and his Battle Creek Sanitarium.

Victor Herbert and Glen MacDonough had another successful collaboration, *It Happened in Nordland*, which ran for 254 performances and nearly a year from December 1904 through November 1905. The composer and lyricist-librettist then worked together on another childlike musical fantasy, *Wonderland*, directed by Julian Mitchell and staged at the Majestic Theatre, but lightning did not strike twice. It garnered only 73 performances from October 24 through December 23, 1905.

MacDonough wrote the books and provided the lyrics for another 15 Broadway shows, the most popular being *Hitchy-Koo* (1917), a vehicle for comedians Raymond Hitchcock and Leon Errol with vivacious Irene Bordoni, and *The Kiss Burglar* (1918) starring Fay Bainter. Sadly, he suffered from depression and nervous disorders for most of his life and died at 53 from what *The Billboard* termed "a complete nervous breakdown" followed by a stroke, in the Stamford Hall Sanitarium in Connecticut on March 30, 1924.

Herbert would contribute music to nearly 40 more Broadway productions. *Babes in Toyland* was the first of several beloved and frequently revived shows featuring his music, among them *Mlle. Modiste*, *The Red Mill*, *Naughty Marietta* and *Sweethearts*. One of his proudest accomplishments was helping to create the American Society of Composers, Authors and Publishers, which to this day ensures that its members will be properly paid for public performances of their works. He succumbed to a heart attack outside his doctor's office on East 77th Street in New York at 65 on May 26, 1924. He died barely two months after the death of MacDonough, for whom Herbert had been a pallbearer.

Babes in Toyland would long outlast its creators, but it would never again be performed in its original form. Evolving tastes and social mores would necessitate many alterations, some of them drastic, in future productions. However, the characters of Barnaby and the Toymaker, and the songs "Toyland," "Don't Cry, Bo-Peep," "Go to Sleep, Slumber Deep," and especially "March of the Toys" would prove to be essential in any configuration, no matter how the story might change.

Top: Sheet music was available in 1903 for 16 of the show's numbers – there were more. *Bottom*: Since *The Wizard of Oz* had been a huge success as a show and a book, Glen MacDonough (with Anna Alice Chapin) created a children's book from *Babes in Toyland*. This was published with several different covers.

Chapter 2

The Film That Wasn't

During the 1910s and early 1920s, *Babes in Toyland* existed mainly in the memories of those who had seen the 1903-06 stage productions, and in phonograph records, lots of them. Medleys of the most popular tunes from the show, always including "Toyland" and "March of the Toys," appeared on discs from Edison, Columbia, Victor and Brunswick, in musical combinations ranging from accordion solos to banjo duets to full orchestras. In 1911, the Victor Talking Machine Company issued three 12-inch 78rpm discs of "March of the Toys," "The Birth of the Butterfly" and "The Military Ball," all selections from *Babes in Toyland*, credited to Victor Herbert's Orchestra. The Victor ledgers show that Herbert himself was the conductor; he was reputed to bring out shades of emotion in performance of his compositions that no other conductor could achieve. Herbert's Orchestra made 103 recordings for Victor between 1903 and 1919, with a further seven sides for Edison in 1910 and early 1911.

In 1915, Herbert and MacDonough's creation was remembered during the Panama-Pacific International Exposition in San Francisco, with a 14-acre section called "Toyland Grown-Up." According to the Exposition's official guide, this featured "fantastic toys, scenery, amusements and entertainments" created by Frederic Thompson (1873-1919), who made a career from designing elaborate rides and attractions for fairs and amusement parks. The 1915 Toyland featured oversized reproductions of building blocks, dolls and other toys, as the stage production had done.

In 1922, a full 19 years after she had starred in the Broadway production as Tom-Tom, Bessie Wynn was announced as the star of a new "Rearranged" version of *Babes in Toyland*, produced by one Francis A. Mangan. Miss Wynn was to be "Supported by a cast of eighteen, in three scenes, for the exclusive use of motion picture theaters." This scaled-down production was set to open in Atlantic City on August 27, and while an advertisement in *Film Daily* noted that "Bookings are now being taken for a tour of the leading motion picture theatres, to commence September 15," there's no evidence that such a tour actually happened.

A revival of *Babes in Toyland* was staged from December 23, 1929 to January 11, 1930 for a total of 32 performances. This was produced by the Jolson Theatre Musical Comedy Company, which had been performing operettas, most of them Victor Herbert shows, since September at Jolson's 59th Street Theatre in New York. (Al Jolson had nothing to do with these productions; they were simply presented at the theater that had been named for him, such was the esteem in which he was held on Broadway.)

The story appears to have been similar to the one used in 1903. The cast included Frank Gallagher as Alan, Betty Byron as Jane, Dean Raymond as the Master Toymaker, Joseph Schrode as the Giant Spider, and William Balfour as Barnaby. Balfour, 55 years old at the time, played in Broadway theaters from 1904 through 1942. He appeared in only one film, *A Son of the Hills*, a 1917 five-reeler for Vitagraph starring Antonio Moreno.

After this engagement, the company traveled to the Keith's Theatre in Philadelphia, with a second company playing at the Majestic Theater in Boston. (*Variety*, the bible of show business, noted that the Philadelphia production was "very disappointing in its second and final week at Keith's, but sensational at matinees. Two extra shows were given last week, one on Friday matinee and the other at 10:30 Saturday morning.") They continued to Poli's Theatre in Washington D.C. in early March 1930, then began a two-week engagement on March 26 at the Majestic in Chicago; business was good enough to warrant a holdover for a third week.

```
                    SYNOPSIS OF
           AGREEMENT RE OPERETTA "BABES IN TOYLAND"
           ----------

DATE            April 9, 1930
PARTIES         Ella Herbert Bartlett )
                Clifford V. Herbert   )  all of New York City   "LICENSORS"
                Clifford C. Potter    )
                Alan Mac Donough      )

                RKO PRODUCTIONS, INC., 1560 Broadway
                                       New York City            "LICENSEE"

FACTS RE
OPERETTA        Composed by Victor Herbert
                Books and Lyrics written by Glen MacDonough

                Copyrighted in U. S. A.

PROPORTIONATE   2/3 interest of Victor Herbert bequeathed by him to
INTEREST OF         daughter, Ella Herbert Bartlett;
RESPECTIVE      1/3 interest of Victor Herbert bequeathed by him to
LICENSORS           widow, Theresa Herbert, now deceased, who be-
                    queathed such 1/3 interest to son Clifford V.
                    Herbert;
                All rights of Glen MacDonough bequeathed to widow,
                Margaret Jefferson MacDonough, who later married
                Clifford C. Potter; Margaret Jefferson (MacDonough)
                Potter died intestate and, under the laws of New York,
                surviving husband, Clifford C. Potter received 1/3
                of her estate, and Alan MacDonough, son of Glen Mac-
                Donough, received 2/3 of her estate.

COPYRIGHT       (Above surviving children entitled to right of re-
RENEWAL            newal of copyright.)
RIGHT                           (Pages 1&2 - Par. 1)

PURPOSE OF
AGREEMENT       Exclusive Motion Picture Rights and Synchronization
                and Sound Picture Rights to said Operetta, throughout
                the world, granted by Licensors to Licensee.
                                (Page 2 - Par 2)
TERM            Ten years from date of general release of first syn-
                chronized and sound motion picture; but not to extend
                beyond eleven years from date of this agreement.
                                (Page 2 - Par 2)
TERM            To include book, score, music language, lines, dialogue
"OPERETTA"      and lyrics of said operetta and of musical numbers and
defined         songs thereof used or interpolated therein. (Schedule
                A, attached to contract, enumerates said material)
                                (Pages 2&3 - Par 3)
TERM "MOTION    Exclusive right to make motion picture versions of said
PICTURE RIGHTS" Operetta, of types now or hereafter known, and to pro-
DEFINED         duce and reproduce as many photoplays, including nega-
                tives and positive prints made therefrom, as may be
                desired by Licensee.
                                (Page 3 - Par. 3)
```

Left: RKO paid $50,000 to the heirs of Victor Herbert and Glen MacDonough for the movie rights. *Top Right:* Producer William LeBaron had written the book and lyrics for a Victor Herbert show in 1917 and was enthusiastic about his music. *Bottom*: Luther Reed, at the pinnacle of his career, was set to direct.

The renewed interest in *Babes in Toyland* attracted the attention of executives at Radio Pictures. (This company would be known in the film industry as RKO, and in September 1932 would formally change its name to RKO Radio Pictures.) The firm was formed in 1928 from a combination movie studio and distributor, Film Booking Office, which had been acquired by Joseph P. Kennedy, father of John F. and Robert F. Kennedy. In May 1928, Kennedy bought a controlling interest in the Keith-Albee-Orpheum vaudeville circuit, a chain of more than 700 theaters. In October, David Sarnoff, head of the Radio Corporation of America, bought Kennedy's stock.

Sarnoff knew that talkies were the wave of the future and planned to implement RCA's new Photophone sound-on-film process in the movies produced by Radio Pictures. He would refurbish the old vaudeville theaters with Photophone projectors, consoles and speakers. This format was much easier for theater projectionists than Warner Bros.' cumbersome Vitaphone, which employed soundtracks on records, separate from the film. Synchronization would not be a problem with Photophone, as it often was with Vitaphone. Radio Pictures' first release, arriving on March 24, 1929, was *Syncopation*, a musical featuring the hot dance band of Fred Waring's Pennsylvanians.

> PAGE SIX SATURDAY, MAY 3, 1930
> INSIDE FACTS OF STAGE AND SCREEN
>
> **RADIO TO PRODUCE 'BABES IN TOYLAND'**
>
> Victor Herbert's operetta, "Babes in Toyland," will be given a lavish production on the talking screen.
>
> The spectacular musical fantasy, for years a favorite on the stage, will be produced as one of the special productions on Radio Pictures' 1930-31 program, according to William LeBaron, vice-president in charge of RKO production.

Top: Movie industry trade papers detailed the production. *Bottom*: Movie stardom was predicted for baritone Everett Marshall, leading man in *Dixiana*.

Radio Pictures had a successful first season in 1929 and early 1930, marked by the musical comedies *Rio Rita*, *The Cuckoos* and *Hit the Deck*. The first two co-starred Bert Wheeler and Robert Woolsey, who had first been paired in the Broadway production of *Rio Rita* and found that they clicked with each other and with audiences. Wheeler's cheerful naivete contrasted with the cigar-smoking Woolsey's more cynical outlook. They would remain a successful comedy team for RKO until Woolsey's health failed in 1937; he died at 50 of kidney disease on October 31, 1938.

The studio was planning an even more impressive second-year program for 1930-31, with the projected budget for 34 feature films totaling $20,000,000. Of these, 12 movies were going to be "Titan" productions, lavish and expensive. The first one would be *Dixiana*, a musical set in New Orleans before the Civil War; it would star Everett Marshall, baritone star of the Metropolitan Opera, with Bebe Daniels as his love interest and Wheeler and Woolsey for comedy relief. The last 20 minutes of the film would be in Technicolor (still in the "two color" process which predominantly registered orange and green); the sets and costumes by Max Rée would be more luxuriant than anything seen before, and the film would literally have "a cast of thousands."

Filming of this season of "only big pictures" would take place on Radio's newly constructed sound stages in Hollywood, including the largest one in the world. The new stages gave Radio three times the production capability than the studio had achieved in its first year of operation.

On March 19, 1930, *Variety* reported, "Radio Pictures has purchased the screen rights to the late Victor Herbert's 'Babes in Toyland.' Price reported at $50,000. Radio has not set a date for production." The agreement between Radio Pictures and the Victor Herbert estate was not finalized until April 9, 1930, although the studio was already releasing details about the forthcoming film to the trade papers.

Herbert's estate was represented by his daughter, Ella Victoria Herbert Bartlett. Born in New York City on October 28, 1890, she had worked as her father's secretary; after his death in 1924, she demonstrated her prodigious skills as a businesswoman, steadily increasing the estate into the millions of dollars by licensing performance rights to his compositions and shows. (In 1925, she managed to sell the rights for Herbert's musical *The Red Mill* to International Film Service – for a silent film of an operetta.)

William LeBaron was going to produce *Babes in Toyland*, just as he'd done for *Dixiana*. Born on February 16, 1883 in Elgin, Illinois to John and Mary LeBaron, he was educated at the Chicago Academy for the Arts and New York University. By 1905 the entire family had moved to New York, where John was a magazine editor and William became assistant editor of *Collier's Weekly*, later becoming managing editor.

He wanted to be a playwright, and achieved this goal in 1910 when his musical play *The Echo*, cowritten with Deems Taylor, was produced at the Globe Theatre on Broadway and ran for 53 performances. He would write the book – and in the case of musicals, the lyrics – for 16 shows on Broadway through August 1925. The most successful was *Apple Blossoms* (October 7, 1919 – April 24, 1920, 256 performances) starring the young Fred and Adele Astaire with comedian Roy Atwell and baritone John Charles Thomas.

A notable collaboration came in 1917, when he wrote the book and lyrics for *Her Regiment*, with Victor Herbert writing the music. The show debuted on

November 12, 1917 at New York's Broadhurst Theatre, and although it only ran for 56 performances through December 29, LeBaron retained an abiding affection for Herbert and his music.

From 1919 through 1924, LeBaron was director of Cosmopolitan Film Productions in New York, and then supervisor of the Famous Players-Lasky Corporation, overseeing films made at Paramount's Astoria Studios in Queens, through 1927. He came to Hollywood that year as vice-president of the Film Booking Office studio, which, as noted, became Radio Pictures late in 1928. LeBaron became head of production for that studio, staying until early 1932, at which point he assumed the same position when he rejoined Paramount.

In April 1930, with a touring stage company of *Babes in Toyland* doing excellent business in Chicago and then Pittsburgh, the trade papers – including *Variety*, *Hollywood Filmograph*, *The Film Daily*, *Motion Picture News* and *Exhibitors Herald-World* – were filled with stories about the forthcoming Radio Pictures extravaganza. William LeBaron announced that Louisville, Kentucky native Irene Dunne, who had appeared on the stage in a road company of *Show Boat* and in seven Broadway musicals between 1919 and 1928, would play Jane. Everett Marshall would be cast as Alan. Miss Dunne was 31 and Marshall was 28, so neither was the youngster that the role of a babe in Toyland would seem to call for.

Top: Having scored a hit in *Rio Rita*, Wheeler and Woolsey were set to provide the comedy. *Bottom*: Broadway veteran Irene Dunne was cast as the leading lady in *Babes in Toyland*.

Wheeler and Woolsey, who seemed to be a good luck charm for Radio Pictures, were again cast as the comedy relief, likely in the roles of Barnaby's bumbling henchmen. Joseph Cawthorn, born in New York in 1868, had made his Broadway debut at 30 in Victor Herbert's show *The Fortune Teller*, and subsequently appeared in Herbert's *The Singing Girl* and *Little Nemo*. Clearly, he was an excellent choice for another Herbert presentation; presumably he was to play Uncle Barnaby.

Luther Reed had directed Radio's smash musical comedies *Rio Rita* and *Hit the Deck*. He had also written their scripts, adaptations from hit Broadway shows. As plans for *Babes in Toyland* were being announced in the trade papers,

Top: Wheeler and Woolsey's perennial companion was Dorothy Lee, also cast in the film. *Bottom*: Joseph Cawthorn, prominent in *Dixiana*, was in the cast...

Reed was directing Radio's most Titanic of its Titan productions, *Dixiana*, which he had also adapted for the screen from a story by author Anne Caldwell. He seemed to be the favorite and most successful director on the lot.

Born Luther Anderson Reed in Berlin, Wisconsin on July 3, 1888, he was educated at Columbia College in Missouri, then spent five years as a music and drama critic for the *New York Herald*. He came to Hollywood in 1915, joining the Jesse L. Lasky Feature Play Company as a scenario writer. His career was interrupted by service in the World War, where he attained the rank of second lieutenant at Camp Upton in Yaphank, New York. Returning to scenarios, he worked for Universal, Metro, Thomas Ince and Cosmopolitan Productions. The latter was William Randolph Hearst's company; Reed wrote *Enchantment* and *Beauty's Worth* for Hearst's favorite actress – and longtime mistress – Marion Davies.

Around 1920, he wrote two musical comedies for the stage, *The Sympathizers* and *On the Level*, and had a third comedy, *Dear Me*, achieve a respectable run of 138 performances at the Theatre Republic on 42nd Street from January through May 1921.

After he'd written 30 film scenarios, he made his debut as a director in 1926 with *The Ace of Cads*, a dramatic feature for Paramount starring Adolphe Menjou. He piloted seven features for Paramount before moving to Radio Pictures, where in 1929 he made good with his writing and direction of *Rio Rita*.

As Reed's new picture, *Dixiana*, was awaiting release, the June 14, 1930 issue of *Exhibitors Herald-World* described the ambitious Radio Pictures schedule for the new season: "Radio Pictures announces it will limit production for the season of 1930-31 to 34 all-talking pictures. Each of these productions is to be filmed as a box-office special, obtaining the full value of Radio Pictures' greatly increased studio facilities, which have been enlarged under a six million dollar construction program... Twenty million dollars is said to have been budgeted for the carrying out of the Radio Pictures program, with more available should occasion call for it. Of the 34 Radios, 24 are to be large scale productions....

"Looming very large in the Radio Pictures announcement is the reference to the imperishable Victor Herbert operetta, 'Babes in Toyland.'... Everett Marshall, Bert Wheeler, Robert Woolsey, Joseph Cawthorn, Irene Dunne, Margaret Padula, Edna May Oliver, Ned Sparks, Dorothy Lee and the Tiller Sunshine Girls have already been cast for this production. Costumes and sets will be by Max Rée, choruses and ensembles by Pearl Eaton, and musical direction by Victor Baravalle. [Max Steiner was brought from New York to work on arrangements.] William LeBaron will have this important production under his personal supervision. Fifty per cent of 'Babes in Toyland' is to be in Technicolor, according to present plans... A great deal will be expected from the Radio Picture, 'Babes in Toyland,' and a great deal doubtlessly will be afforded. This is a type of subject that will bring vast new throngs to the picture theaters."

The RKO executives were counting on the film to bring children back to movie theaters. Joseph Plunkett, vice president of the studio, gave a talk to the studio's combined sales forces at the Blackstone Hotel in Chicago. "Much of the product of the companies during the past year has been such as to keep children away from the theaters," he announced. "We must bring the children back, and Radio Pictures in its production plans for next year is meeting that requirement. For example, we are going to make Victor Herbert's 'Babes in Toyland.' I know of no picture material that could have such an appeal to the young people."

Meanwhile, Luther Reed was singing the praises of leading man Everett Marshall, telling *Hollywood Filmograph* that "public reaction will cause Radio Pictures officials to make young Everett Marshall a star shortly after the release of his first picture, 'Dixiana.'" The *Filmograph* reporter added, "The very pleasing screen personality, appearance and vocal powers of Marshall will by that time have been recognized, according to Reed, and he is willing to wager that Marshall's third RKO film will be in the capacity of a star."

Further bolstering the studio's confidence that *Babes in Toyland* would be a smash was the popularity of movie musicals. This was a type of movie that obviously hadn't existed in the silent-film era, and it was a great novelty. The public clamor for sound films began with Al Jolson's musical drama for Warner Bros., *The Jazz Singer*, in 1927. The second film to win the Academy Award for Best Picture was MGM's *The Broadway Melody*, one of the first "backstage" musicals. In 1929, 69 musical features were released in the United States, and 1930 would bring a further 64 tuneful productions. On August 14, 1930, Hiram S. Brown, the president of RKO, announced that he expected *Babes in Toyland* to be "one of the most spectacular pictures of the year."

This rosy picture began to darken in the next few days. More than one new movie musical per week for over a year was starting to be too much of a good thing. On August 16, *Inside Facts* reported, "Worthwhile musical pictures with dramatic story interest always will be popular. So says Victor Baravalle, RKO Radio Pictures' musical director, against reports that the public is tiring of music from the screen." However, that same issue included another article which was not quite so optimistic about the future of movie musicals:

"Fear has been spread in Hollywood that the musical talking pictures have utterly collapsed, and in the future this form of entertainment would be abandoned as screen fare…

"Universal is offering extra money for stories which do not require musical settings….the new U. slogan is 'Not a song in a carload.'…

"At Paramount, according to the publicity department, there will not be as much singing in their pictures as there has been in the past…

"Pathé's experience has been two musical successes and one flop. They scheduled eight musical comedies for next season but exhibitors squawked and the idea was abandoned.

"RKO are very optimistic about their musicals, however, although they admit not as much enthusiasm as of yore."

The last days of August brought many conflicting stories about the fate of RKO's *Babes in Toyland*. Luther Reed was announcing to reporters that he would be including six previously unpublished Victor Herbert songs in the film. Reed stated that he did not believe that musicals were in a decline, that there would always be a popular demand for well-done musical films. In contrast to this was an article in the August 20 issue of *Variety*:

> 'TOYLAND' CALLED OFF; ANOTHER MUSICAL!
>
> Hollywood, Aug. 19 – A report is about that Radio Pictures has called off its proposed talker production of the stage musical, 'Babes in Toyland.'
>
> Single reason rumored is that 'Babes' is a musical also for the screen, with the present not the ripe time for it.

Top: … as was Edna May Oliver… *Bottom*: … and also Ned Sparks.

Preparations had gone ahead for the making. Indications were the screen musical would have run into a large cost sum for Radio.

This is said to be one of the causes taking Wm. LeBaron, Radio's studio head, to New York just now.

By August 23, 1930 *Motion Picture News* confirmed, "Evidence that producers feel musicals have run their course is borne out by decisions of RKO to postpone indefinitely 'Babes in Toyland,' which was originally slated to be one of the highlights of the company's new program. Irene Dunn [sic], who was to play the lead, has been switched to 'Cimarron.'"

The studio had so much riding on the box office performance of *Dixiana*. The publicity department placed prominent display advertisements in most of the trades in July and August, reading, "In staggering magnificence, in thundering emotions comes *Dixiana* to hold the world spellbound! ALL THAT IS LIFE HAS BEEN ENGULFED IN THIS AMAZING PRODUCTION! COMING WITH A RUSH!... 'BABES IN TOYLAND'... not to mention a grand and gorgeous galaxy of other great attractions in THE NEW PAGEANT OF THE TITANS!"

Dixiana opened with strong returns in major cities in August 1930 but faded quickly. Like Radio Pictures' mammoth new production facilities, the film had been started before the October 1929 stock market crash. It was so expensive that because of the public's waning interest in musicals and the deepening Depression, it returned a loss to the studio of $300,000. *Screenland* called it "An elaborate disappointment… Bebe and Everett Marshall sing, there's occasional color, and Bert and Bobby work hard—but no use." *The New Movie* called it "Pretentious but dull." *Silver Screen* noted, "There's little to recommend."

Everett Marshall, for whom stardom had been so confidently predicted, never made another film for Radio Pictures. Co-star Dorothy Lee, never one to mince words, recalled decades later, "He had a magnificent voice but all of the charm of a cigar store Indian. His role was really important – I mean, he was only the male love interest! And he blew it in a big way. RKO dumped Everett Marshall before the film finished unspooling." In 1931, he was on Broadway in *George White's Scandals*; he would appear in another five Broadway shows, concluding with a starring role in *The Student Prince* in 1943. That show and *Blossom Time* were mainstays of his lengthy stage career. He made only one more film, a Warner Bros. B-picture starring Dolores Del Rio, *I Live for Love*, in 1935.

Luther Reed was likewise toppled from his prestigious position with RKO. Not only was *Dixiana* a prominent failure; his personal life was unraveling. He had been married from 1920 to actress Naomi Childers, and they had a son, Peter. Naomi divorced Reed in 1929 on the grounds of desertion. On June 15, 1930, he married actress Jocelyn Lee in Tijuana. On September 23, Reed sued her for divorce, claiming that she had an uncontrollable temper. During a vacation in Agua Caliente, Reed had been playing poker with Wheeler and Woolsey, when Mrs. Reed asked him for some money. "I gave her half I had won, and she threw it on the floor and called me a cheat," Reed testified. "I picked up some of the silver dollars from the floor and handed them to my wife and she threw them in my face. Mexican officers suggested we go to our bungalow. When I asked Jocelyn to keep quiet, she cut my scalp with an ash tray. Officers came in and told us we would have to leave the hotel."

For her part, during four days of testimony, the former Miss Lee stated that she had found Reed keeping company with a woman unknown to her, both unclothed, in the bed of a friend's house.

Although they had been married for only three months, the couple had somehow managed to produce two daughters – Celeste, age three, and Dana, age two. United Press reported that Mrs. Reed received custody and "asked for alimony of $2,400 monthly, but Reed pleaded the divorce action had made it impossible for him to obtain employment, and that he therefore could not afford the greater amount." Jocelyn wound up receiving $100 a week, and even this sum soon proved difficult for Luther to provide.

Thanks to the failure of *Dixiana* and the sensational divorce testimony hitting the newspapers, Reed never made another film for Radio Pictures, or any other major studio. After two years of inactivity, he wrote an adaptation of *Bachelor Mother* for the low-budget and short-lived Goldsmith Productions company. He fared a little better in mid-1933, collaborating on the script for a two-reel comedy, *Meet the Champ*, distributed by Paramount. Right after this, he co-wrote the screenplay for *The Sweetheart of Sigma Chi*, distributed by Monogram. He directed one more feature, *Convention Girl*, starring Rose Hobart and produced in 1935 by the obscure Falcon Pictures. After that, he made industrial and promotional films in New York for Johns Manville, a Denver-based company which made insulation and roofing materials. He collaborated on one more script, *A Hat, a Coat, a Glove*, written for television's *Matinee Theatre* and broadcast on April 26, 1957. He died at 73 in New York on November 16, 1961.

Radio Pictures held on to the film rights for *Babes in*

RKO ran this lavish two-page, full color advertisement in many of the film industry trade papers.

Toyland but substituted on its program a much less expensive comedy, *Bachelor Apartment*, starring Lowell Sherman, Irene Dunne, and silent-era stars Mae Murray and Norman Kerry. *Harrison's Reports* of April 15, 1931 noted to theater managers, "'Babes in Toyland' was to have been founded on Victor Herbert's musical comedy, with Bert Wheeler and Robert Woolsey in the leading parts… RKO must be commended for having refrained from making 'Babes in Toyland,' because musical pictures no longer draw in the majority of the theatres; but it should at least make the picture with Bert Wheeler and Robert Woolsey before it should ask you to accept it."

In September 1931, *Motion Picture Projectionist* and *Motion Picture Herald* both reported that the studio was planning a Technicolor film of *Babes*, along with *Bird of Paradise* and *Marcheta*. In August 1932, RKO released *Bird of Paradise* – entirely in black and white. The studio never made the other two pictures.

The *New Movie Magazine* of December 1931 reported that "At RKO, William LeBaron announces that 'Babes in Toyland' is again being seriously considered for production," but that it would not be "patterned along the previous operetta lines," and that the studio had "announced that there will not be any large choruses of beautiful dancers. We can remember when there used to be more than 500 girls employed in the various studios as dancers and show girls. Hi-ho, the good old days." That flicker of optimism was the last printed reference to an RKO production of Herbert's operetta, planned with such confidence in March 1930.

Top: *Dixiana* proved to be a very expensive failure, which sealed the fate of *Babes in Toyland*. Bottom: A glut of movie musicals, the ever-deepening Depression, and the failure of *Dixiana* spelled the end of RKO's *Babes in Toyland*.

Our best guess at what RKO's *Babes in Toyland* would have been like is provided by that noble failure, *Dixiana*, with its cast including Everett Marshall, Wheeler and Woolsey, Dorothy Lee and Joseph Cawthorn. It also had amazingly elaborate sets and sumptuous costumes for hundreds of extras by Danish-born designer Max Rée. Max Steiner provided the orchestrations, Fred Fleck was assistant director, and of course Luther Reed was the scenarist and director. All of these people were assigned to *Babes in Toyland*. For an early 1930 musical, *Dixiana* is surprisingly lively in spots, but has long, arid stretches where the actors stand and talk. Everett Marshall has a fine voice but is not exactly riveting as an actor. The movie is still quite watchable, but not as technically adept as it would have been a couple of years later.

Meanwhile, as *Babes in Toyland* reverted to being only a stage property – another production played in Rochester, New York in December 1932 – movie musicals began to revive. While there were only ten musical films produced in the United States in 1932, the number would increase to 25 in 1933, led by Warner Bros.' magnificent trilogy of *42nd Street* arriving on March 11, *Gold Diggers of 1933* on May 27, and *Footlight Parade* on October 21. At the very end of 1933, RKO would release the harbinger of another great musical series with *Flying Down to Rio*, the first movie to team Fred Astaire with Ginger Rogers.

One of those 1933 movie musicals, appearing on May 5, was *The Devil's Brother*, based on an operetta of 1810 by Daniel-Francois Auber, *Fra Diavolo*. MGM released it, Hal Roach produced it, Laurel and Hardy starred in it, Dennis King sang in it, and the world embraced it. Made for just over $200,000, the film grossed about $333,000 in the United States and Canada, but it was a sensation in Europe, where Auber's operetta was well known. It grossed $1,227,819.40, returning to the Hal Roach Studio a net profit of $475,156.97. This was the biggest financial success that Roach had attained with Laurel and Hardy, and he was eager to find another operetta to duplicate its success. Executives at RKO noted its popularity and scrapped a planned Wheeler and Woolsey collegiate comedy, *Frat Heads*, in favor of making a similar period musical, *Cockeyed Cavaliers*; they even borrowed the leading lady of *The Devil's Brother*, Thelma Todd.

RKO's proposed *Babes in Toyland* movie had been so aggressively promoted in the trade papers that Hal Roach must have been well aware of it, and also aware of it being put on the shelf. However, Walt Disney was instrumental in bringing together Roach and RKO. Roach and Disney were both enthusiastic polo players; Roach kept a string of ponies at the Uplifters Club, a 120-acre recreational facility in Pacific Palisades, frequented by the well-to-do men (only) of Los Angeles. RKO, trying to do something with their $50,000 investment, contacted Disney about making an animated feature from the property. When he gave RKO a budget estimate, the studio decided that this was still too expensive. Disney then told Roach that RKO wasn't doing anything with *Babes in Toyland* and might be receptive to selling the rights.

Here was a property that would have the musical charm of *The Devil's Brother*, and would be even better suited for children, a large component of Laurel and Hardy's audience. Roach was determined to make *Babes in Toyland* an impressive feature picture with his starring team. For a small independent studio that mostly made two-reelers, such an expensive undertaking was going to be a risk that might threaten the existence of the studio – but Hal Roach had never shied away from a challenge.

Chapter 3

"The Best Boss I Ever Had"

Those of us who still go to movie theaters, wanting to see films on a truly big screen instead of a home monitor or, worse, a cellphone, are resigned to seeing a lot of advertising, a painfully long procession of coming attractions trailers, and one feature film. In the 1920s and '30s, a moviegoer would see one feature film, but it was bolstered with a supporting program of a cartoon, a newsreel (the only way to see current events in those pre-television days), and a short subject. This would often be a comedy, and if it ran for about 20 minutes it would be known in the movie industry as a "two-reeler," since one reel of 35mm film ran for 10 minutes. (Comedies running for about 20 minutes are still made in great profusion today, except now they're on television and called sitcoms.)

So vitally important were these short comedies to audiences and to theater managers that several studios were devoted solely to producing them. There were dozens of these studios in the Teens and early Twenties, but the most important and longest-lasting producers of comedy shorts were Mack Sennett, Earle W. Hammons of Educational Pictures, Al Christie, the Weiss Brothers, and Hal Roach.

Roach's comedies differed from the other producers' because he emphasized strong, consistent characterization in his star comedians, and wanted coherent, plausible stories. Slapstick was still in abundance in his films, but it had a reason for being. Sennett's films, conversely, emphasized wild gags often at the expense of logic, while Christie's polite farce comedies were almost entirely based on situations.

Harry Eugene Roach was born in Elmira, New York, on January 14, 1892. His longtime friend, actor George O'Brien, once described him as "a rock 'em, sock 'em guy," not because Roach was pugnacious or combative, but because he was confident, assertive, unafraid, and accomplished virtually everything he set out to do in his 100 years on earth.

Family folklore said that when his mother, Mabel Bally Roach, was near the time of his birth, she was hoping for a girl and wanted to name the child Harriet, in honor of her own mother. When the newborn turned out to be a boy, she still wanted to name him Harriet, but wiser heads prevailed and the boy was christened Harry instead. As a young adult, he had it changed to Hal.

He had an adventurous youth; at 17 he went to Alaska and spent a year loading six-horse pack teams. He then took a job in Seattle driving an ice-cream truck, getting fired for driving it "fast and hard." He next found employment with a construction company, which brought him to Los Angeles. One day in 1913, he happened to read a newspaper advertisement offering a dollar a day plus carfare and lunch to anyone who had Western-style clothes and wanted to work in the movies. Roach put on his Stetson and boots and took the streetcar to 1712 Allesandro Street in Edendale, the headquarters of the 101 Bison Company.

The first scene in which Roach worked as an extra was set in a gambling hall. The leading man was supposed to win a fortune at roulette, then lose all of it. Unfortunately, nobody on the film crew knew which way the ball was supposed to spin in the roulette wheel. Roach had seen his share of real gambling halls and solved the problem. (The ball spins clockwise while the wheel spins counterclockwise.) In gratitude, the studio raised his pay to $5.00 a day, and Roach was officially in the movies.

He found even more lucrative work at Universal as a $30-per-week "dress extra." An extra was someone who walked around or stood in the background of scenes; a dress extra provided his or her own clothes and was paid more, because the studio didn't need to rent or fit their clothing. Roach became friends with two other extras

With partner Dan Linthicum, Roach created the Rolin Studios. Cast and crew surround star comedian Harold Lloyd as "Lonesome Luke," with Hal Roach directly above.

When Hal Roach began producing films in 1914, at 22, he sported a rakish mustache.

whom he would later employ – Harold Lloyd and George Marshall, later the noted director of classics such as *Destry Rides Again*. Marshall noted in 1974, "At Universal there were five of us, all about the same size, so we could switch clothes rapidly. Hal and I were very close friends; we were like brothers almost. As things went along, we bought a complete wardrobe – and then Universal would keep us, as we were very handy for them for any particular role."

Roach was a sometime actor in Westerns starring J. Warren Kerrigan, then worked his way up to assistant director in short films starring Jeanie MacPherson, later renowned as a screenwriter. Roach was always skillful at what we now call networking – in later years he belonged to seemingly every club and social organization in Los Angeles – and he met an attorney who had a well-to-do friend who wanted to get into the movie business. Roach told the attorney he was "the best undiscovered director in the business," and with new financing, he was soon making his own films. On July 23, 1914, Roach and partners Dan Linthicum and I.H. Nance formed the Rolin Film Company, with Roach as president. Nance was soon replaced by Dwight Whiting, who became the company's general manager. They began making a series of one-reel comedies starring Harold Lloyd as "Willie Work."

These first films were distributed to theaters by the Sawyer Film Mart, run by Arthur H. Sawyer. Unfortunately, Mr. Sawyer sold Roach's films to another company without giving credit or remuneration to the novice producer. (The 1914 payroll ledgers for the studio, still in existence at the University of Southern California, list the company's first films, with this notation in a margin in Mr.

Roach's hand: "Swiped by Sawyer.") One day in a theater, Roach happened to see one of his own films boasting a credit for the Pathé Exchange, a reputable company whose origins extended to the earliest days of filmmaking in France. Roach contacted the Pathé people, told them that he was the producer of this film, and asked if they wanted more. They did.

By April 1915, Rolin had made a distribution agreement with Pathé for his films, which now featured Lloyd as "Lonesome Luke," a character who outwardly was the opposite of Charlie Chaplin (too-tight trousers and shoes as opposed to Charlie's baggy pants and floppy footwear) but inwardly still an imitation of the Tramp. In 1917, Lloyd tried a new character, devoid of any unusual makeup or costuming except for a pair of horn-rimmed glasses. The first film with this new personality, *Over the Fence*, was released on September 9, 1917, and the immediate popularity of the winsome "glasses character" soon spelled the end of Lonesome Luke.

Roach began making several series of short comedies starring comedian Snub Pollard, a little man with a big mustache; a group of kids who were soon named after their first film, *Our Gang*; a series of two-reelers starring Ziegfeld Follies star, cowboy trick-roper Will Rogers; and some "cliffhanger" serials starring Ruth Roland. He also produced a group of domestic comedies about *The Spat Family*; a few Western features starring Rex, the King of Wild Horses; an unusual series with an all-animal cast called *The Dippy Doo-Dads*, and in February 1923, some comedies starring an English comedian named Stan Laurel.

Early in his producing career, Roach had leased space at a studio in Edendale, California, and then moved to the Bradbury Mansion at 406 Court Street in Los Angeles. In November 1919, thanks to land provided for free by financier Harry H. Culver, who wanted to encourage municipal development, construction began on the new Hal E. Roach Studios, which was completed officially on April 20, 1920. The building would stand at 8822 Washington Boulevard in Culver City until 1963.

The 19-acre lot boasted all the amenities of the major studios, having four shooting stages, a processing laboratory and film vaults. The studio made its own scenery and props at its planing mill and plaster shop. It contained a backlot with a "New York Street" and building façades for other locations, as well as dressing rooms, a makeup department, a research library, and, later, its own music scoring stage.

Roach's studio also had something that others didn't have – a friendly, low-key atmosphere that was ideal for people creating laughter. Because Roach produced comedies, his studio was promoted as "The Lot of Fun." His studio was a special place, a creative oasis where talented people could do their best work with little interference from the boss.

Richard Currier, who was a film editor on the lot from 1920 to 1932, recalled in 1980, "The fact of the matter is, he's the best boss I ever had. I've never heard of anybody that didn't like Hal Roach. He was friendlier than other bosses at the studios. He was the big boss, but he didn't show it. And he was smart, too – he did a hell of a lot of thinking that nobody knew about but Hal.

"No bunch of people could live together as amicably as the gang at Roach's. Nobody was jealous or yelling their heads off – it was a hell of a swell place to work. Over the years, I've dreamt many times about working back there. I have dreams of my same office, same gang around me and all. The people down there made such an impression on me, that my inner soul, or whatever you call it,

Top: In 1917, Lloyd began making films with the new "glasses character," which instantly became very popular. *Bottom*: Lloyd's success brought prosperity to Hal Roach, seen here around 1920.

keeps bringing it back to me all the time."

Anita Garvin, who appeared in many Roach comedies from 1925 through 1940, also retained a special affection for the studio. "The Christie studio was close-knit, but there was something special at Roach's," she recalled. "I don't know anybody on the lot who wasn't easy to get along with. I can't tell you how happy the days were that I spent in that place. I loved every minute of it.

"There was never any pressure to get the pictures done in a hurry. That was one thing about the Roach studio – it wasn't like working for other small studios; they used to take pretty good time in making the films. At most of the other studios, you'd adhere to the script more or less, but on the Roach lot we were quite informal, and everyone could speak their mind. You didn't have to be afraid to open your mouth to the director or anybody else."

Roy Seawright, who began as Hal Roach's office boy in 1919 and ultimately became head of the special effects department, asserted, "There's been no other studio to date like it. MGM, Fox, Universal – they were nothing but machines. The Roach lot was very individual. And the people there had talent with a wonderful sense of humor.

"Mr. Roach would come in in the morning, he'd walk down the street; he'd greet everybody, and everybody would greet him. He expressed so much warmth and love and affection for everybody that it was just contagious – it spread from him to other people within the organization. So much great talent emanated from that lot. It took the Hal Roach Studio to nurture those people's talents and bring them to the fore."

One person whose talents were nurtured at the Roach studio was George Stevens, who was a cameraman at the lot starting in 1923 and graduated to directing in 1930. Ultimately, he would become one of the most respected directors of his era, winning Academy Awards for *A Place in the Sun* (1951) and *Giant* (1956).

Roach found another great talent through his socializing skills. He was an enthusiastic sportsman. He wasn't a good golfer (unlike so many enthusiasts of the game at his studio), but he loved playing polo with friends Walt Disney and Will Rogers, and had a stable of polo ponies at the Uplifter's Club in the Pacific Palisades region of Los Angeles. He also played handball at the Los Angeles Athletic Club, and there he met a young man, of Irish descent like himself, who constantly made him laugh with funny stories. The man's name was Leo McCarey, and he was working as an assistant to director Tod Browning at Universal. Roach told him, "I make my living making people laugh. If you think you can be funny on the screen, stop in and see me sometime. I'll give you a job." Before too long, McCarey's employment at Universal was no more, and he went to see Roach, who was as good as his word.

McCarey started as a gag man for the *Our Gang* series, but as he recalled in 1969, "I had so many ideas for gags that he gave me an actor named Charley Chase and he let me direct him." In December 1923, McCarey was assigned to Chase's new unit, making one-reelers. Chase's real name was Charles Parrott. He was a talented director, having made more than 130 films for Sennett, Fox, Paramount and Hal Roach from 1914 through 1923, but didn't enjoy directing films in which he starred.

McCarey was a total novice as a director but found Chase an illuminating teacher: "He was a great help to me and I hope that I reciprocated to him." In time, McCarey would become the Academy Award-winning director of feature films such as *The Awful Truth* and *Going My Way*, but when Chase died in 1940, McCarey said, "Whatever success I have had or may have, I owe to his help because he taught me all I know." In March 1927, McCarey would be appointed as the Roach studio's supervising director, overseeing all of its releases.

Roach continued to be very involved in the production of each of his films, often suggesting the basic story ideas. However, his management style allowed the talented people whom he hired to do their best work without interference. Roach managed, but he didn't micro-manage.

As Anita Garvin remembered, "You'd see Mr. Roach on the lot walking up and down, but rarely on the set. I think he realized that it made people uncomfortable – if you saw him there, you were bound to stiffen up. You just wouldn't be yourself."

Roach was well aware of this, as he related in 1981. "I would very seldom be on the set, unless I was directing," he said. "In fact, I would slow them down on the set, because they all knew I'd had more experience than anybody else. I knew more about the business, and unless I was directing – it was more of an embarrassment, you know what I mean?"

The main area where Roach would exercise his judgment was in the projection room, where he sat each morning and watched the film that had been shot the day before, called "rushes" or "dailies." The Roach studio had its own processing laboratory, and since there was such a quick turnaround on each day's footage, better ideas could be implemented if needed, while the sets were still standing. "Now, I *always* saw the dailies," Roach asserted. I would criticize the hell out of the dailies; if I didn't like them, I'd tell the people the way I thought the scenes should be. But as far as telling them on the set – I didn't believe in it. And that applied to practically everybody. You saw the results in

Roach's new studio on Washington Boulevard in Culver City was called "The Lot of Fun," and stood from 1919 until 1963.

the projection room. If you didn't have faith in the people that were making the picture, then they shouldn't be there in the first place."

Richard W. Bann, a close associate of Roach's from the late 1960s until his death at 100 in November 1992, sums it up: "The simple fact is that Roach gave the orders. Everyone on the lot was working to please him. If he didn't like something, it was changed. A business trip or a trip to play polo had no impact on his control; he talked, privately, with the key people before he left. He saw the results when he returned. They did it the way he wanted, or they fixed it when he objected."

Bann saw this in action when working and visiting with Roach from the 1970s through 1992. "Hal was always a gentleman, a dignified gentleman, and he would answer your questions with his typical courtesy," Bann said. "If it was a creative film question, suddenly you'd see him come to life as the producer he'd been, and still was. Being such an original thinker, with such a great sense of humor, he could effortlessly see things in a fresh, new way, and fast, like no one else could. And best of all would be to see him interact with Hal Roach Studios alumni; you'd see the enormous respect they held him in, and how he'd tell them what they should do, or what he wanted them to do, giving orders and sizing up a situation with clear thinking and brainpower that amazed me.

Top Left: Charles Parrott, a writer-director-actor who had made films since 1914, joined the Roach studio in 1921 as director general, starred in one-reelers as "Jimmie Jump," and finally became "Charley Chase" in 1924. *Bottom*: Leo McCarey started as a gag man with Roach, became Charley Chase's director, and in 1927 was promoted to supervisor of the studio's entire product. *Top Right*: In 1922, Roach began another popular series, *Our Gang*. Seen here are Ernie "Sunshine Sammy" Morrison, Mickey Daniels, Mary Kornman, Joe Cobb, Jackie Condon and Allen "Farina" Hoskins.

"At every age, even 100, he was still Hal Roach. Everything he'd been and done, it was all still there, even if stratified beneath the layers. Once in a while you'd see the man Will Rogers knew, or Thelma Todd knew. It was easy to see why the people who worked there showed him such fierce loyalty, and I mean everyone I ever met who worked there. But he didn't live in the past, nor did he feel any need to prove anything to anyone. What a great man."

Roach pursued many interests with zest and enthusiasm – flying in his private plane, hunting for quail and bear (his office was decorated with several bearskins), playing polo, and even in old age swimming vigorously every day (but still smoking Winston 100s). He loved thinking up story ideas and seeing them realized on film. He knew that in a comedy studio the atmosphere had to be a happy one, and he was wise enough to hire talented people and then leave them alone. His studio was unique because he was unique, and he cared enough about every one of the more than 1,200 films he produced to rewrite and refilm scenes until everything met with his satisfaction, which is why hundreds of them are still cherished today.

Roach's most popular films, then and now, featured an Englishman and a Southern gentleman, who were teamed by a self-described "crazy Irishman."

Chapter 4

Stan, Babe, Hal and the Two Leos

Leo McCarey was a very busy man.

In March 1927, Hal Roach had appointed him as the supervising director of the studio, overseeing its entire product. "Supervisor meant being responsible for practically everything on the film," he recalled. "Story, gags, screening the rushes, editing, sending out the prints, cutting again when the previews weren't good enough. Also, sometimes it meant shooting sequences over again."

In 1927, the Roach studio completed or had in production 52 films. One was a feature, *No Man's Law*, starring Rex, the King of Wild Horses. The rest were shorts starring Charley Chase, the *Our Gang* kids, Jewish comedian Max Davidson in what the studio called "dialect comedies" although they were silent, and a series called the All-Stars, which often featured actors and actresses whose fame had faded.

Priscilla Dean, Agnes Ayres and Lionel Barrymore – whose career as actor and director would rebound a couple of years later – each did turns in the series, which was bolstered by some very talented supporting comedians.

These included a bald-headed, mustachioed Scotsman named James Finlayson, who could convey displeasure with a menacing squint; Anita Garvin, a statuesque brunette skilled at playing scheming gold-diggers, fearsome wives or good-time girls; little Charlie Hall, who often disproved the notion that good things come in small packages; and a six-foot-one, 284 pound comedian, Oliver Hardy, who could play policemen, hotel detectives, doctors, cab drivers or anything else, always bringing a special flair and humor to his performances.

He was born as Norvell Hardy in Harlem, Georgia, on January 18, 1892. His parents, Oliver and Emily Hardy, ran the Turnell Butler Hotel in Madison, Georgia. Emily had been previously married to a man named Sam Tant who had died, leaving her with two sons and two daughters. She had one son, Norvell, with second husband Oliver – who then suddenly dropped dead at 50 in November 1892. The two-time widow with five children found a new home in Milledgeville, Georgia, managing the Baldwin Hotel, an impressive three-story structure.

Young Novell loved music; when he was eight, he did a brief vaudeville tour as a boy soprano with Coburn's Minstrels, and later sang to slides in a theater. When he was 18 he found that he loved movies, too, as the projectionist and man of all work at Milledgeville's Palace Theater. He screened lots of short films with comedians of dubious talent, and figured that he could be just as good, or just as bad, as they were.

Jacksonville, Florida was 300 miles south of Milledgeville and was a thriving moviemaking center, thanks to abundant sunshine. Just before he turned 22, Hardy headed for Florida. He got a job singing in a Jacksonville nightclub, Cutie Pearce's, and also sang at the Orpheum Theater. Before long, he met a pianist named Madelyn Saloshin, ten years his senior; they married on November 17, 1913.

Little Arthur Stanley Jefferson and Norvell Hardy, both about six years old.

Bottom: Making his show business debut at 16 in 1906, Stan Jefferson appears to have been a very self-confident young comedian. *Top Left*: Stan had many partners in vaudeville. One who became an off-stage partner as well was Mae Cuthbert, who gave Stan his new stage name of Laurel. This advertisement is from the February 23, 1919 issue of the *Des Moines Register*. *Top Right*: Stan made 12 two-reel comedies for producer Joe Rock in 1924-25.

Hardy spent his days getting to know people at the many film companies in Jacksonville – among them Edison, Kalem and Lubin – and would help with props even without pay. One day in the spring of 1914 when he was visiting the Lubin studio, they needed a fat boy for a comedy called *Outwitting Dad*, and from that point Hardy never looked back.

By this time, he had adopted the first name of the father he never knew, becoming Oliver Norvell Hardy. However, he attained another lasting name when he got a shave at a Jacksonville barber shop frequented by the Lubin actors and crew. The barber was an Italian gentleman, whom Hardy described as "a boy who liked boys." He recalled, "Well, he took a great fancy to me and after he finished shaving me, he'd rub powder into my face and pat my cheeks and say, 'Nice-a bab-ee. Nice-a bab-ee.' The gang always used to kid me about it and after a while they started to call me 'Baby' and then it was cut down to 'Babe' – and I've been Babe Hardy ever since."

As Babe Hardy, Oliver Hardy, or even O.N. Hardy, he appeared in more than 300 films from 1914 through early 1927, supporting star comedians like Chaplin imitator Billy West (who brought Hardy to California in 1918), Jimmy Aubrey, and Larry Semon.

On January 27, 1925, Hardy first stepped in front of a camera belonging to the Hal Roach Studios, in a supporting role for a *Spat Family* two-reeler, *Wild Papa*. Over the next year, Hardy would play in another seven shorts, supporting Charley Chase, Clyde Cook and Glenn Tryon in a variety of roles. Roach found him so versatile and useful that he signed Hardy to an exclusive contract on February 6, 1926, ensuring that he would have the services of the genial, portly gentleman for a long time to come.

Someone else who was proving useful to Roach in many ways was an Englishman doing his third tour of duty with the studio.

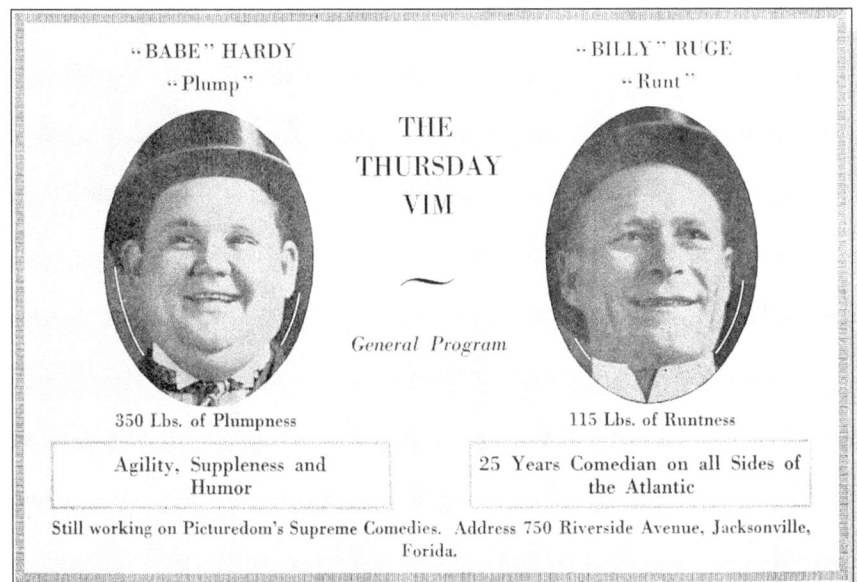

His name was Stan Laurel, although he was born as Arthur Stanley Jefferson in Ulverston, Lancashire, England on June 16, 1890. His father, Arthur Jefferson – known to all as A.J. – was a playwright, comic actor and director, and managed several small theaters in the north of England and Scotland. His mother was an actress and went by the name Madge Metcalfe. Young Stanley always wanted toys associated with putting on shows, and at one point had a miniature theater in the basement of his parents' home. He wrote a play that was suspiciously similar to some of the bloodthirsty melodramas which his father presented. Stan directed and, of course, cast himself as the handsome hero. Unfortunately, this early career ended abruptly when, during an onstage battle, Stan and another young would-be actor knocked over an oil lamp and set the curtains ablaze.

His career began in earnest when the family lived in Glasgow, and in 1906, at 16, he got a booking at a small theater called the Panopticon. His routine was a pastiche of jokes from other boy comedians, plus one original song. Unknown to Stan, his father by sheer coincidence happened to be in the audience, and saw that Stan had borrowed his best checked trousers. Sensing that any protest against a career as a comedian was futile, A.J. got his son a job with a touring company of *Sleeping Beauty*, where he played a Golliwog, a large stuffed doll. By 1910 Stan had enough experience to join Fred Karno's London Comedians, a troupe of young comics who appeared in a variety of knockabout sketches. The star of the company was Charles Chaplin, renowned for playing a rowdy drunk who disrupts a theatre performance, in the sketch *Mumming Birds*. The troupe came to America in 1910 and again in 1912, and Stan decided to stay in the States.

He worked mostly in American vaudeville for the next ten years with a variety of partners. For a few years he imitated his old friend and roommate Chaplin in a sketch called *The Keystone Trio*; he was also part of a comedy magic act, Martini and Maximillian. A turbulent professional and personal partnership began in December 1916 with Australian actress Mae Charlotte Dahlberg Cuthbert. She shortened both of their names when she found a book in a dressing room showing a Roman general wearing a wreath of laurel. Stan and Mae Laurel toured the United States for the next six years, in a sketch called *Raffles, the Dentist* and another one, *No Mother to Guide Her*, in which Stan

Bottom: Stan had three tours of duty at the Hal Roach Studios. The second one, in 1923-24, resulted in many one- and two-reel comedies such as this. *Top Left*: Hardy was half of a movie comedy team in 1916 with diminutive Billy Ruge, as "Plump and Runt." *Top Right*: Hardy was given the nickname "Babe" by an Italian barber in Jacksonville who would rub talcum into his chubby cheeks and call him "Nice-a babee."

Oliver Norvell Hardy began appearing in films in 1914 at 22, in Jacksonville, Florida. In *Ups and Downs* (1915), he menaces Ethel Burton as Bobby Burns and Walter Stull as "Pokes and Jabbs" look on.

Chaplin imitator Billy West brought Babe to Los Angeles. In *His Day Out*, he plays a villain similar to Eric Campbell in the Chaplin comedies.

appeared in drag as a vamp.

Stan was eager to get in films, and in 1917 made a pilot film, *Nuts in May*, for producer Isidore Bernstein. He appeared in a few films at Universal in 1918, followed by five one-reelers for Hal Roach and three two-reelers in support of star comic Larry Semon at Vitagraph.

In February 1921, Gilbert M. Anderson, who had attained fame around 1909 as "Broncho Billy," the movies' first great Western star, financed a pilot film for a projected Stan Laurel series. Titled *The Lucky Dog*, this two-reeler was especially notable because the "heavy," or villain, was played by Babe Hardy. They have two lengthy scenes together, and one can already see how well they react to each other, having an immediate rapport. Stan made a half-dozen films for Anderson (including a parody of Rudolph Valentino's hit film *Blood and Sand*, titled *Mud and Sand* and starring Stan as matador Rhubarb Vaselino), then went to the Hal Roach Studios for a return engagement.

Stan starred in an amazing 25 films for Roach in one year, starting in February 1923; they expanded from one reel to two midway through. Many of them were very good – particularly *Smithy*, which cast Stan as an inept construction worker, and *Kill or Cure*, in which he was an aggressive patent-medicine salesman. At this point, Stan had no defined character, which is probably why audiences and exhibitors didn't take to his films with much enthusiasm.

Still, his box-office performance was good enough for producer Joe Rock to give him a try, and Stan made a dozen two-reelers for him in 1924 and '25. The best of the lot was *Dr. Pyckle and Mr. Pride*, a wild Jekyll and Hyde parody. Rock had told his financiers that he was making one Laurel comedy each month for a certain amount; in truth, he finished all twelve in seven months and pocketed the rest of the dough. Stan could not appear onscreen for at least five months, lest he uncover Joe Rock's scheme, so back he went to the Roach lot, this time solely as a writer and director. "I wasn't too successful as a film comic," Stan admitted in 1957. "I didn't feel I was so hot myself, so I was very happy to get into some other end of the business." Mae Laurel had become a burden to Stan in every way by this time, and Joe Rock did Stan the favor of arranging for her return to Australia.

Stan began writing scripts for other comics and co-directing films with Richard Wallace, ultimately becoming a full-fledged director. Among the two-reelers he piloted were *Yes, Yes, Nanette* and *Wandering Papas*, both of which featured Babe Hardy in the cast. On June 14, 1926, Babe began working on a Mabel Normand short, *One Hour Married*. Midway through the filming, Babe was at home, doing some cooking, and he accidentally tipped a pan full of very hot grease over his arm, burning it badly. He had been scheduled to appear in another short, *Get 'em Young*, starting on June 19, but needed time to heal. Roach offered Stan a bonus if he would step in front of the cameras again and take Babe's place. Since the last of the Joe Rock pictures, *Half a Man*, had already been released, Stan complied – and continued working on both sides of the camera for the rest of his 13 years at the Roach studio.

Babe Hardy just happened to be in the cast of nearly every one of the next dozen films in which Stan appeared. Sometimes, they were teamed through the entire film (as in *Duck Soup* and *Do Detectives Think?*); in others, they were adversaries (as in *Sailors, Beware!* and *Flying Elephants*). Leo McCarey, overseeing every one of the Roach comedies being made, was keenly aware of the special rapport that Stan and Babe demonstrated, and he suggested to Roach that the

Top: Laurel and Hardy first crossed paths in 1921, with Stan as the star of *The Lucky Dog* and Hardy, of course, as the villain. In this first meeting, they worked well together, but wouldn't meet again for five more years. *Bottom*: Scottish comedian Jimmy Finlayson was a mainstay of the Hal Roach Studios. When the talkies came in, audiences could hear his exasperated "D'oh!," which was borrowed much later by Dan Castellaneta as the voice of Homer Simpson.

Top Left: Many of the early films in which Laurel and Hardy appeared had them in very different characters from the Stan and Ollie we know and love, as in *Slipping Wives* (1927). *Top Right*: Leo McCarey suggested to Hal Roach that the studio build a series around Laurel and Hardy. Studio publicity called *The Second 100 Years* their "first starring picture as a comedy duo." *Bottom*: Eventually, the characters grew into the "Stan and Ollie" beloved by millions.

studio should build a series around them.

Roach had just secured a new distribution deal with the most successful of all the major studios, Metro-Goldwyn-Mayer. No doubt the MGM executives would welcome a new series with these two talented comic actors. *The Second 100 Years*, featuring Laurel and Hardy as escaped convicts, was released by MGM on October 8, 1927, with publicity releases proclaiming, "New starring team uncorks riotous performance in first picture as comedy duo."

Laurel and Hardy made another 21 silent two-reelers, immediately receiving enthusiastic acclaim from the New York executives at Loews, Incorporated (MGM's parent company), and from audiences around the world. These included *The Battle of the Century* (1927), in which a minor skirmish between Stan, Ollie and a bakery delivery man culminates with hundreds of people in an epic pie fight. *Two Tars* (1928) cast the boys as sailors on shore leave who get tangled in a traffic jam and wind up dismantling several jalopies. *Their Purple Moment* and *We Faw Down* (both 1928) depicted the boys trying to have some naughty fun away from their domineering wives, to no avail. *That's My Wife* (1929) displayed Stan in drag, masquerading as Mrs. Hardy so that Ollie could claim an inheritance. *Big Business* (1929) saw the boys as door-to-door Christmas tree salesmen, encountering cantankerous homeowner Jimmy Finlayson, and ultimately destroying his house while he dismantles their trees and Model T.

Leo McCarey was supervising director on all of these films, and directed three of the L&H silents; he also contributed stories to many of them and likely directed scenes for others without credit. He left the Roach studio in late December 1928, just as Laurel and Hardy were finishing *Big Business*, having gotten an offer to direct features from the Pathé studio. If McCarey had never made another movie, his contribution to films would still be enormous, for having suggested a permanent Laurel and Hardy team to Hal Roach.

As for that other Leo, the lion that roared at the beginning of every Metro-Goldwyn-Mayer release, he was very beneficial to Roach and his studio. MGM's motto was "Do it big, do it right, give it class," and to that end they were willing to provide substantial funding for Roach's comedies. Although

HE'S PROUD OF LEO, JUNIOR—

Metro-Goldwyn-Mayer, Greatest of Feature Producers, has become Greatest of Short Film Producers

HAL ROACH, THE FAMOUS COMEDY PRODUCER, SAYS:

From letters that come to me, I notice a growing demand for short films in addition to feature length films. Watch these Short Subjects when you go to theatre and see how many of the questions below you can answer. I will give $50 and a handsome cane offered by Charley Chase to the man with the best score. The most successful lady will receive $50 and the tiara head-dress worn by Agnes Ayres in the Technicolor subject "Lady of Victories." For the next 50 best answers, the "Our Gang" rascals will present their photographs.

THE TEST

1. How many of the "Our Gang" comedy rascals can you name?
2. Tell in 75 words why the M-G-M News has become the leader of Newsreels.
3. What company produces the Oddities for M-G-M?
4. In what Technicolor Great Events picture does the Father of our country appear?
5. Of what great living national hero has M-G-M made a special short subject?

Write your answers on one side of a single sheet of paper and mail to Competition Editor, 3rd Floor, 1540 Broadway, New York. All answers must be received by June 15th. Winners' names will be published in a later issue of this magazine.

NOTE: If you do not attend pictures yourself you may question your friends or consult motion picture magazines. In event of ties, each tying contestant will be awarded a prize identical in character with that tied for.

STAN LAUREL and OLIVER HARDY in "Leave 'Em Laughing" and "The Battle of the Century" established themselves as screendom's newest fun-makers.

CHARLEY CHASE has won thousands of laugh-loving followers. See "The Family Group!"

ALL of the
BEST theatres
ARE now showing
COMPLETE M-G-M
QUALITY programs—
M-G-M short films
AS well as M-G-M's
BIG feature films—
DEMAND the best!
THAT'S M-G-M!

MAX DAVIDSON never permits a dull moment when he is on the screen in his uproarious 'dialect comedies.

M-G-M NEWS within a year has become the most popular of all news-reels. *Issued twice each week.*

The Czarina's Secret—
M-G-M GREAT EVENTS (entirely in Technicolor) are something new in films. Ask your theatre manager about them.

Battle of Octopus and Lobster—
M-G-M ODDITIES are thrilling moments from Life. Are you seeing these wonder films at your theatre?

"OUR GANG" chases the blues away. Never pass up a chance to see these rascals at work. If your favorite theatre doesn't show "Our Gang" comedies ask the manager to book them right away!

METRO-GOLDWYN-MAYER
"MORE STARS THAN THERE ARE IN HEAVEN"

MGM began distributing Hal Roach's short comedies in September 1927, and released all of the studio's output through August 1938.

Left: Hal Roach was a successful producer all through the 1920s, but the Depression of the early '30s brought some challenges to his studio.
Right: The 1933 feature film *The Devil's Brother* was Laurel and Hardy's first excursion into operetta, and was a smash success all over the world.

they never looked cheap, Roach's films acquired an even more impressive presentation thanks to the bigger budgets afforded by Metro.

By the time Laurel and Hardy made their last silent film in mid-March 1929, they had become internationally famous, and since Charlie Chaplin, Buster Keaton and Harold Lloyd had graduated from shorts to feature films, Stan and Ollie were now the most popular comedians in two-reelers. The coming of sound films didn't bother them a bit, and actually deepened and enriched their characters. Now, audiences could hear Ollie's plaintive tones with "Why don't you do something to help me?," and "Well, here's another nice mess you've gotten me into." Stan's north-country English accent may have surprised some moviegoers, but they soon enjoyed his catch-phrases of "That's a good idea" and "It certainly is."

The team would make 40 starring sound shorts for Roach from 1929 through 1935, including such gems as *Perfect Day* (1929), in which their attempts to go on a picnic are foiled by problems with their Model T; *Hog Wild* (1930), where the boys attempt to put up a radio antenna on the roof of Mr. Hardy's home; *Helpmates* (1931), with Stan trying to clean Ollie's house after a wild party but causing it to go up in flames; and *The Music Box* (1932), in which the boys struggle to carry a piano to a home atop a long, long flight of steps. This last short won an Academy Award for the Best Short Subject (Comedy) of 1931-32, proving that Laurel and Hardy were appreciated and enjoyed by professionals in the film industry, as well as by theater managers and the worldwide public.

In the 1920s, Roach had moved Harold Lloyd from short films into features, and in 1930 he began doing the same with Laurel and Hardy, alternating the occasional full-length film with the shorts through 1935. *Pardon Us*, released in 1931, cast the boys as a couple of would be "beer barons" in those days of Prohibition, and being thrown into prison as a result. The next year brought *Pack Up Your Troubles*, with Stan and Ollie trying to find the grandparents of their deceased war buddy's child. With *The Devil's Brother* (1933), Roach produced (and co-directed) a worldwide smash, putting Laurel and Hardy into the unusual milieu of Italy circa 1800. Based on an operetta written in 1830 by Daniel-François-Esprit Auber, the film seemed unlikely to succeed even to the comedians, but the singing of Dennis King, the high-spirited performance of lovely Thelma Todd, and the inimitable comedy of Stan and Ollie made this Hal Roach's biggest financial success to date with his starring team.

In late November 1933, as Laurel and Hardy's next feature, *Sons of the Desert*, was being prepared for release, Hal Roach was traveling to New York to purchase the film rights to *Babes in Toyland*. Making this elaborate fantasy film would be one of the biggest challenges Roach had faced as a producer.

It would bring more challenges than anyone could have anticipated.

Chapter 5

The Boss Shoots the Works

Babes in Toyland was a popular and successful film upon its release in late November 1934, and it remains a cherished favorite many decades later – but for Hal Roach it was a bitter and persistent memory. I interviewed him at his Bel-Air home in January and February 1981, and on both occasions, before I could ask my first question, the normally affable 89-year-old producer launched into a diatribe about the film, and his disappointment with it.

"Why I let Laurel and Hardy go was because of *Babes in Toyland*," he said. "I knew that after *Babes in Toyland*, I was through making Laurel and Hardy pictures. At that time it got to the point where it was no longer any fun, or anything else to me. When I let Laurel and Hardy go, it had nothing to do with money. I said I didn't want to make any more pictures with them." Roach in fact continued to make films with the team through late 1939, but the fact that he remembered *Babes in Toyland* as the end of their association was significant.

Fantasy films were in the news in Hollywood in September 1933. On the 16th, Charlotte Henry, a 19-year-old model and actress who had been on Broadway at 14 in a dramatic play, *Courage*, and in a few films, was signed as the title character for Paramount's all-star film *Alice in Wonderland*. It had already been filming for a week, and featured an impressive cast including Gary Cooper, W.C. Fields, Cary Grant, Richard Arlen, Edna May Oliver, Jack Oakie and many others.

On September 21, *The Hollywood Reporter* stated, "Owing to the influence of Paramount's *Alice in Wonderland*, MGM has revived its interest in the Frank Baum story, *Wizard of Oz*, and is considering it as a starring vehicle for Laurel and Hardy." Two other studios were bidding for the rights; Samuel Goldwyn won by paying the author's son, Fred Baum, $75,000 for the property. However, by June 25, 1934 Goldwyn dropped his plans to produce it. He had purchased it as a potential starring vehicle for Eddie Cantor, but the comedian rejected it, saying that the story was just not his type.

Paramount had *Alice in Wonderland* and Goldwyn owned *The Wizard of Oz*, but RKO didn't seem to be doing anything with *Babes in Toyland*. That studio's proposed film had been aggressively promoted in the movie trade publications before being put on the shelf. The Technicolor spectacle that RKO had envisioned in 1930 was now too expensive to make, and Roach figured that the studio would be happy to recoup its outlay for the filming rights.

Late in November 1933, Roach went to New York and met with executives at the beautiful new 31-story RKO Building at 1270 Sixth Avenue. Likely at the table was Merlin H. Aylesworth, who succeeded Hiram Brown as president of RKO in July 1932. They reached an agreement for Roach to purchase the option on film rights for *Babes in Toyland*, which RKO had bought from Ella Herbert Bartlett and Clifford Herbert on April 9, 1930. The deal was finalized on December 28, but by that time Roach had already made the plans for his new feature known to the trade press. Roach also made a ten-year distribution license with the Herbert heirs, but beyond that the terms of the RKO contract remained intact.

What Roach did need was a new story, as the original 1903 plot was too disorganized, and much too violent, for 1933 audiences – especially with the Catholic Church and women's groups clamoring for censorship of movies, which in the last couple of years had become much more provocative.

When a new story was needed for a Laurel and Hardy short, Roach was often the man who came up with the initial idea. He explained, "The way we worked was this. We had about six or eight writers with Laurel and Hardy.

Hal Roach's polo-playing buddy, Walt Disney, told him about RKO and the film rights. Roach had just bought the option and told his story to Stan and the gag men when the studio's 20th anniversary party was held on December 7, 1933.

Now, they might not all stay with Laurel and Hardy; but when Laurel and Hardy were shooting a picture, I would bring the writers in and I would have an idea of what the next picture should be like. I'd say, 'All right, they're gonna be a couple of sailors,' or whatever the hell it was. We would discuss it – and certain guys would be way off the track. You know what I mean, they weren't associated with that comedy idea at all. Others would begin to grasp it. Some others went off on a tangent that had nothing to do with what I had in mind. Then, after two or three hours, I would say that a couple of these writers knew what kind of a thing we're talking about. So I would say to these two writers, 'All right, you guys pick it up. Give me a treatment as soon as you can.'

"Now, they would write a treatment, not trying to put gags in or be funny, but writing the storyline to see where it would go. If they were on the right line, then great. If they were on the wrong line, I would try to straighten them out, or maybe decide to try somebody else, or change the idea completely. But as a rule, they would go ahead. Then we would have another meeting with all the writers to see if anybody had a gag that would go into that story. So by the time that Laurel and Hardy were through with the picture they were working on, this story would be ready to submit to the director, to Laurel – Hardy never paid any attention – and as a rule, to a couple of gag men who worked on the set. They would try it out, and if it didn't work, if there were drastic changes

needed, we'd have another conference, and might even go into an absolutely different story."

It's important to emphasize that, especially during the very prolific period of 1928-29, story ideas were being fashioned by other hands for Laurel and Hardy while they were busy filming on a studio stage or out on location. Hal Roach contributed many of these story outlines.

Stan Laurel often functioned as a story editor, working with the writers and using the ideas which most appealed to him. He had been hired as a writer in 1925 and continued to develop the scripts after he'd made a return to acting.

In the days of the Laurel and Hardy silent shorts, Mauri Grashin and future director Hal Yates were the two writers always on the payroll with the Laurel and Hardy company. Starting around 1928, a very valuable addition to the writing staff was an Englishman, who like Stan Laurel had many years' experience in English music halls and American vaudeville. His name was Charlie Rogers. Hal Roach recalled, "I don't think Charlie ever originated a damn thing, but he had a good memory. He remembered what they had done in pantomimes in England. He was a gag man; he never was a writer. I don't ever remember him being in a conference when we were starting out to write a new story, but he was always on the set when they were working. When they'd get into something that didn't work, he was the guy that helped them out of it. If Laurel wanted to discuss an idea, he usually did it with Charlie. And Laurel most always figured a part in the picture for Charlie, you know, something to keep him on the set anyway."

Stan's daughter Lois recalled always seeing pads of paper in practically every room in the family home, so that Stan would be able to write down an idea as soon as inspiration struck. She also remembered that her father would joke

> The N.B.C. network broadcasts a half-hour portion of the Hal Roach anniversary banquet from Culver City at 9 p.m. through facilities of KECA with Charley Chase, comedian, acting as master of ceremonies. The occasion marks the twentieth anniversary of Hal Roach as a producer and he will be honored as the youngest "veteran" producer of all time.
> Laurel and Hardy, Thelma Todd and Patsy Kelly are scheduled to speak, and music will be provided by Harry Jackson's orchestra.

Bottom: The music for Roach's anniversary party, and a radio broadcast over NBC, was provided by Harry Jackson. This would lead to his becoming the musical director for *Babes in Toyland*. *Top Left*: Paramount's expensive all-star feature of *Alice in Wonderland* was a career boost for Charlotte Henry, one of the few performers whose face was visible in the film. *Top Right*: Charlotte's performance as Alice definitely gave Hal Roach the idea to cast her in *Babes in Toyland*. *Courtesy Rick Greene*.

Many people contributed to the Laurel and Hardy stories. Leo McCarey was an important writer-director for Laurel and Hardy from mid-1927 through December 1928.

around and play with her a lot – until the writers came over to the house to work on the script. Then she would be sent out to play, because working with the writers was a more serious kind of fun.

During the silent era, supervising director Leo McCarey was sometimes the source for the stories. He vividly remembered contributing the story for the 1929 silent classic *Wrong Again*. McCarey recalled, "One day we were stuck for the next Laurel and Hardy. I'm sitting in the living room with a highball – somebody said it would be good for my tonsils (I think it was my own idea) – and the phone rang, and it was the studio. They said, 'The gang is sitting around here, and they've come up with nothing and Stan suggested we call you and see if you've got anything.' And I started ad-libbing.

"We had a large facsimile of Gainsborough's *Blue Boy* hanging in our living room, so I said, 'Yes, I've got an idea. It opens on a millionaire who owns this painting, Gainsborough's *Blue Boy*. It is stolen, and he offers a handsome reward, and there's a big article in the paper. Then we cut to the racetrack, where Laurel and Hardy are two race touts reading this article. They remark about the sizable reward and say how they can use it. Just then a horse goes by, and on its blanket, it says *Blue Boy*, and –' That's the way we did it. We just winged it."

Similarly, in an interview conducted by Jordan R. Young, director George Marshall remembered providing the idea for the team's two-reeler *Towed in a Hole*. "We'd been stuck for four or five days or a week maybe," he said. "We hadn't come up with any particular story outline that seemed to progress or have any base to it. So I drove to the studio one morning, and in Culver City I passed one of these little fish wagons; and this fellow was touting his wares with a long horn as he drove down the street. So I thought, 'Well, maybe that could be the answer, with the boys selling the fish, but to make more money, catching their own fish.

"I had about that much when I got to the studio. Stan was sitting in his room. I told him about the idea and he said, 'Yeah, that just might work.' We went to work on it there in the room; we started kicking it around, just the two of us that morning, making some notes. Charlie Rogers, he was making notes and possibly interjecting a gag of some kind as we talked, and out of it came the idea that if you're going to catch fish you have to have a boat, naturally. The boat they get is pretty dilapidated and has to be fixed up before it'll even float, and that's the way it went.

"That's how those films were built. You'd think of many things beforehand in story construction, but then you got on the actual set, and the props would often lead into better things than we had written."

Marvin Hatley, musical director of the Roach lot from 1929 through 1939, was often also on the payroll as a gag man early in the '30s. He remembered the writing sessions as gleefully chaotic: "Stan had three or four guys hanging around, you know, but he was the main one who did everything. He always had these other people to offer suggestions, and he'd twist them around. Then they'd get up in the projection room and they'd act out their ideas. If somebody had a gag where a character was choking, he'd demonstrate it; he'd put his hands to his neck and say, 'He's choking!' They wanted to show the other guys what they meant."

In his authorized biography of the team, *Mr. Laurel and Mr. Hardy*, John McCabe wrote, "The idea men on the Roach lot were classified literally as gag men, and story conferences were really bull sessions in which the gag men would sit with Stan and the director to weave out the semblance of a plot for Laurel and Hardy... Sometimes

Director George Marshall (right), later to make *Destry Rides Again* and many comedies with Bob Hope and Jerry Lewis, was an important collaborator with Stan in 1932-33. On the Roach backlot during the filming of *Pack Up Your Troubles*, they're joined by co-director Ray McCarey (left), who was later chosen to direct *Babes in Toyland*.

the idea for a film would come from an object. One gag man happened to be passing a partially constructed house on his way to work. He brought a few thoughts to the gag session and a general working script [for *The Finishing Touch*] was fashioned out of the discussion that followed...

"Another Roach gag man found a starting point for a picture by watching a group of musicians playing in a nearby band shell. From this came *You're Darn Tootin'* (1928), directed by Edgar Kennedy of slow-burn fame."

McCabe quoted Stan Laurel as saying, "I don't by any means take credit for most of the comedy ideas since gags and routines were suggested by many of the gag men. I would take the one that appealed to me, and with their help, work it out to fit our characters." Charlie Rogers, also quoted by McCabe, added, "We were all friends, thank God, and that helped a lot. But whenever Stan suggested something in conference or during shooting, it almost always proved to be the right thing. He, perhaps more than anybody else, knew by instinct the kind of gags needed. He watched closely over the pictures, but it was like kind of a beneficent father, not a bossy one who always wanted his own way at any cost. You see, by nature he is a polite man and a gentle fellow, and those two qualities always came over, in front of the camera and behind it."

On August 14, 1957 – exactly one week after Babe Hardy's death – Stan was being interviewed in his Santa Monica apartment by UCLA professor

Arthur Friedman. When Friedman asked Laurel if he had generated the stories, he replied, "Oh, well, I wouldn't take credit for – no one man can make a picture, that's silly. No, I had some very fine boys who worked with me, and we all were like a happy family. We'd all have ideas, and no one thought one was any better than the other. We just – we'd work out a script and get to shooting as quick as we could. I don't believe in sitting for weeks and months on a comedy picture, comedy especially... We did a lot of what we call 'off the cuff.' Sometimes we'd start on the script and something would come up, and we'd forget the script and keep on going."

Hal Roach maintained that Stan Laurel was a brilliant gag man, but deficient when it came to writing stories. In 1981, he said, "Stan Laurel, next to Charlie Chaplin, was the best gag man in the business. That's for gags, or individual pieces of business. As for writing a story, Laurel wasn't worth a nickel. Somebody else had to do that, not him. The things that he thought would be funny as a picture, you'd think a little kid had written.

"Laurel was equally good as Chaplin in remembering many of the sight gags from English music halls. In writing visual comedy, approximately 50 percent of what you write, which sounds very funny on paper, does not work. When you get on the set and start to rehearse the thing, you realize that it doesn't come off. That was where Laurel's ability came in great. He would remember something that had been done; not necessarily by himself, but in one of the hundreds of different pantomime theaters all over England."

Conversely, George Marshall felt that Stan's ability in story construction was superior to Roach's. In a 1974 interview, he said, ""When we saw Hal, he'd have a gag, and nobody could understand what he meant — because he would say, 'You know, they come in here, they go out there, you know what I mean.' And that would be the end of the gag! We picked it up from there, but that was sort of a standing joke on the lot; we'd all say, 'You know what I mean?'

"Hal would go through the script at first," Marshall recounted, "but then once the script was set up, I don't think I saw Hal two or three times during the shooting. After he'd look at his dailies, Hal was usually gone. There was never any producer interference. I know he and Stan often talked things over — that was probably business — but I had nothing to do with that.

"Stan was a pleasure to work with. He was so bright in story — we often worked on our story material together. That mind of his was always working, to piece things together; Stan was so creative. I learned a lot from him, rather than he learning anything from me."

The first two Laurel and Hardy features – *Pardon Us* and *Pack Up Your Troubles* – had been criticized for being very episodic. As a result, Roach decided to hire outside writers to construct the stories for future L&H full-length films, starting with *Fra Diavolo* (or *The Devil's Brother*) in 1933. He hired Jeanie Macpherson, who had written more than 30 films for producer-director Cecil B. DeMille; she turned in a mammoth script, the size of a large telephone book, describing 378 scenes. For the team's next feature, *Sons of the Desert*, Roach hired comedy specialist Frank Craven and all-around journeyman writer Byron Morgan to construct a story that was strong enough to sustain the length of a feature. For *Babes in Toyland*, Roach was so passionate about the project that he decided to write the story himself.

Roach was enthusiastic about aviation – he'd had his own plane, *The Spirit of Fun*, which he had loaned in November 1932 to MGM executive Arthur Loew and Loew's attorney, Joseph Rosthal, for a trip to visit MGM

A working lunch in October 1934 with gag men Frank Terry (*left*) and Charlie Rogers (*right*), flanking Stan, Babe and Ruth Laurel.

Left: Stan at work with gag men and co-writers James Parrott, Charlie Rogers, and Felix Adler. *Right*: Charlie Rogers, who also had a background in English music halls and American vaudeville, joined the Roach studio by 1928 and became Stan Laurel's closest associate, writing scripts, working as a gag man on the set, occasionally playing supporting roles and eventually directing.

distributors in Africa. It had crashed in Victoria Falls, Rhodesia, leaving Loew and Rosthal with minor injuries, but killing pilot James Dickson, just a few days before his 32nd birthday. Undaunted, Roach had already placed an order for a new, even faster plane, with which he hoped to achieve more aviation records.

After his meeting in late November 1933 with the RKO executives in New York, Roach normally would have flown back to the studio, but this time he decided to take the train back to Los Angeles, as the four-day trip would give him time to develop a much-needed story for *Babes in Toyland*.

"I worked like a sucker on that thing," Roach declared when I interviewed him in February 1981. "In the first place, it was a great musical – but it had no story. When it was produced on Broadway, they had just started with color spotlights. And they were so intrigued with them, that the show was vignettes from different fairy tales, but it had no storyline. So after I bought the property in New York, I came back on the train, so I would have the time in order to write a story for it.

"I stayed alone in my room and wrote all the way, and I had what I thought was a hell of a story. Hardy was supposed to be the Pieman, and Stan Laurel was Simple Simon. You remember, 'Simple Simon met the Pieman going to the fair.' The Pieman says, 'Where's your penny?,' and Simple Simon says, 'I haven't any.' Well, now it's with Laurel and Hardy. Stan gets a pie and he eats it, and Babe says, 'Where's your penny?' Stan says, 'I don't have a penny.' Babe says, 'All right, then you push the cart until you *earn* the penny.' So now, they're teamed together. And the song, 'Put Down Six and Carry Two,' would have been a perfect thing for them to sing.

"The finish was that the heavy, who was a spider turned into a man, wants to destroy Toyland and puts hate into the wooden soldiers. The wooden soldiers come out to destroy Toyland, but Laurel and Hardy find out that they're put together with glue, and water kills glue, and by putting water on the wooden soldiers they save Toyland at the end.

"One of the gags I thought of was, to get the hate to put into the soldiers, the heavy has to get great big drums full of love and happiness. He puts them through a machine, and out comes a little bit of hate. When he gets the hate, the heavy says, 'Destroy love and happiness with this,' to the soldiers. The soldiers go out, each one with a big container of hate on his back, and if anybody argues with them they give them a shot of hate. Laurel can't resist, so he puts his finger in the hate, and tastes it – and right away he punches Hardy in the nose. Now Laurel and Hardy give everybody a shot of love and happiness, but they screw it up, and finally they fall in love with each other."

In Glen MacDonough's 1903 script, the Toymaker wants to put souls into the toys so that they will murder the children on Christmas Day. He does this by spraying them with a mysterious mist. This element of the script is dispensed with quickly, but Hal Roach greatly expanded it in his story, adding all of the business about the barrels of liquid love and happiness and extracting a little vial of hate. He probably got the idea of turning the wooden soldiers into villains from this scene as well. The spider in the original stage show existed only to have a specialty number, a fight with a brown bear, so the idea of Barnaby being "a spider turned into a man" was Roach's invention.

"That was my conception of *Babes in Toyland*," Roach continued. "I thought Stan was going to go nuts over it. I gave Stan the story when I got home, and he said, 'Oh, we can't do this.' I said, 'Why?' He said, 'We can't work without the derby hats. They are our trademark.' I said, 'In the first place, the derby was Chaplin's trademark. You can put a bandana handkerchief on your head and you'll still be Laurel and Hardy.'

"We argued for about two weeks. *Babes in Toyland* was a big property, and I was paying real dough for it. I had worked so hard on this thing, and I was so disgusted in light of this opposition, that I just said, 'Enough. I'm out of the thing completely. Go make the picture.' I never paid a bloody bit of attention to what they did, and it was a flop. It didn't even get the cost back. And I know that the story that I had written would've gone very well. Could've been one of the biggest pictures in the business."

Roach's recollection warrants some scrutiny. If Stan rejected the story simply because he and Babe needed to wear the derby hats, he must have been grasping at straws to avoid simply telling his boss, "I don't like this." Laurel and Hardy had already appeared in several films in different costumes without the derbies, among them Stan's kilt in *Putting Pants on Philip*, sailor suits in *Two Tars* and *Men o' War*, pajamas in *They Go Boom!*, and exotic garb of 18th century Italy in *The Devil's Brother*. The missing derbies should have caused no problem at all.

We can often believe something which has no basis in fact, simply because we've heard it so many times. Roach told his account of Stan's script rejection many times, and in almost the same words.

In 1967, Roach told a reporter, "It was the Chaplin complex. Chaplin has wrecked more comedy careers than booze. No matter who they are – Stan Laurel, Buster Keaton, Fatty Arbuckle, Jacques Tati, yes, and Jerry Lewis – they all begin thinking they can't realize their potential unless they direct themselves, as Chaplin did. But the difference is that Charlie had a backlog of comedy that the others didn't have. The pantomime tradition had started in France, then moved to England where there were hundreds of companies that dealt in pantomime comedy. Fred Karno had a stable of 40 different acts, out of which came Chaplin and Laurel. Chaplin borrowed from all those old pantomime routines and he was great – until he ran out of them. His later films showed none of that early brilliance." Roach further told the reporter that after Laurel rejected his story and substituted his own, the producer told him, "Your contract is expiring, and I do not intend to renew it – at any price."

In 1986, he told an audience at the London Hilton on Park Lane, "The reason I let Laurel and Hardy go was that Laurel's great ambition was to be another Chaplin. He wanted to do the whole thing. Unfortunately, the kind of pictures he wanted to make were almost childish and I had to be the guy to say 'This is the kind of picture you're going to make.' This all started when I bought a musical, *Babes in Toyland*. And after I bought it I came back on the train, although there were planes flying at the time, in order to write the story, because there was no story for *Babes in Toyland*.

"All of Stan's friends, no matter what they were doing, Stan claimed that he had written it. We came back and the mistake I made was calling the writers in and telling them this was what they were going to make next. They always had the idea that I talked to Stan, then he gave me the ideas and I told the writers what to do. Then, because I wrote this on the train and brought the writers in, even Stan didn't know what I was going to talk about.

"I thought I'd bought a great thing and a great thing for them. And Stan was so mad. He said he couldn't do it, because they wouldn't wear the derbies. Anyway, we fought for about a couple of weeks and finally I said 'All right, you go and make it yourself"... so I turned it over to them and they made a very bad picture. It was a bad finish; it made the Parent Teachers Association condemn the picture because of these goons coming out of the woods, and so on. I mean, everything was wrong. I had enough dough that I could say I didn't want to make any more Laurel and Hardy pictures."

These are controversial statements, and should be addressed. Chaplin and Laurel, as Roach himself noted, had much the same background and training thanks to both being born into theatrical families, and working together in the Fred Karno company.

Many would dispute Roach's opinion that Keaton was not the equal of Chaplin as a director. Arbuckle, Tati and Lewis also have their passionate advocates.

Roach's statement that he dropped Laurel and Hardy after *Babes in Toyland* is clearly untrue, as they made another four shorts and eight starring feature-length films together, collaborating for another five years.

Another puzzler is Mr. Roach's comment that "They always had the idea that I talked to Stan, then he gave me the ideas and I told the writers what to do." Likewise, Roach told historian Anthony Slide in 1970 and author Craig Calman in the late 1980s that, specifically regarding *Babes in Toyland*, "Laurel couldn't take it that somebody else was writing the picture." However, we have Leo McCarey, George Marshall, Charlie Rogers, Marvin Hatley, Stan Laurel, and Hal Roach himself stating that the process of creating the stories was always a collaboration. Since the writers and gag men invariably worked with Roach on story ideas right from the initial spark – by Roach's own admission – it seems highly unlikely that Stan would have tried to hoodwink the other writers into thinking that he came up with all of the story ideas.

It's surprising that Roach didn't remember his own oft-stated credo that "50 percent of the script will not play," which was a very wise rule of thumb; when one reads the Laurel and Hardy scripts, again and again it becomes clear what a perceptive principle this was, as half of the script will seem familiar, but half will seem entirely new. About half of that new material can prompt a reaction of "what on earth were they thinking?" If Mr. Roach had reminded himself that 50 percent of his own script might not play, perhaps he wouldn't have been so stung by Laurel's rejection of the story.

Stan had plenty of experience with fantasy stories tailored for children, like *Babes in Toyland*. His first professional engagement, in 1907, was as a member of the Levy and Cardwell troupe, in a production of *Sleeping Beauty*. Stan, age 17, played a Golliwog, or a large stuffed doll. Christmas pantomimes, which were comedy interpretations of famous children's stories, were a tradition in the English theater, and Stan undoubtedly saw many of them.

Without question, Hal Roach contributed many of the story ideas for the Laurel and Hardy pictures. He rarely took credit for this. Nor did Stan Laurel receive credit in the film titles for his writing contributions. The only writing credit in the short subjects was given to H. M. Walker for either titles or dialogue. While most of Mr. Roach's stories were first-rate, we should examine his ideas for *Babes in Toyland* to determine if there were other reasons why Stan couldn't accept it.

Two documents of Hal Roach's original story for *Babes in Toyland* survive. They are undated but both are very probably from November or December 1933. One is a synopsis, running 13 standard 8 ½ by 11 pages. The other is a longer treatment, which runs to 23 legal-sized 8 ½ by 14 inch pages. The issue of whether Hal Roach's plot would have made a better film than the one created by other hands has been an item of speculation for decades. Although it will remain a matter of personal opinion, the best way to compare them would be to present Mr. Roach's original synopsis, complete and unaltered. And so....

Chapter 6

Mr. Roach's Story

The following is the original 13-page document of Hal Roach's original story, very likely what he wrote on the train coming back to Los Angeles from his New York meeting with the RKO executives:

SYNOPSIS OF
B A B E S I N T O Y L A N D"
-o-

THE PROLOGUE

A New York street, toward the East Side, on Christmas Eve.

Two ragged waifs, Spanky and his sister, Jean, eight, are gazing longingly into a toy shop window. Spanky is bitter because they have no Christmas; Jean tries to bring him hope of Santa Claus, but Spanky is dubious.

Nearby, LAUREL & HARDY, two piemen, are trying to make some sales, but without success; Laurel works in reverse whenever a sale is imminent. (Comedy sequence to be worked out by their unit.)

A drunk, sorry for a dray horse he feels is hungry, suddenly appears before the gloomy pair and buys all their pies, and their basket, too, paying them twenty dollars.

Voicing plans for a merry Christmas, they start jubilantly down the street, but hear Spanky saying he hates Santa Claus, and learn from overhearing the argument between the two children that they will have no Christmas cheer at all.It is a wrench, but Laurel and Hardy return and are accepted by the waifs as the real Pieman and Simple Simon from Toyland, agents of Santa Claus.

We next find Laurel, in a shabby bedroom, entertaining the children with misquoted nursery tales and verses, while Hardy buys toys and a tree. Then both men put the children to bed, with the kids' heads full of Mother Goose and Toyland. There is comedy in the other room where the men prepare to decorate the tree. They are to sleep together on a narrow old spring couch, as they gave up their bed to the children.

The children sleep, and dream that Mother Goose comes through the window and tells them a story of how Hate once brought trouble to Toyland.

-o-

THE FANTASY

Toyland's workers have come to Toyland to join the townspeople in celebrating the day after Christmas... next day they must start preparing toys for the following year. Toytown's street is gay with dancing folk, and we see Little Red Riding Hood, Little Miss Muffet, Boy Blue, Tommy Tucker, and many other characters.

The Town Cryer heralds the arrival of the Master Toymaker, who, from the top of a sugar barrel, gives the people a "pep" talk.

He announces that conventional toys will no longer satisfy the modern child. A new conception of toy making must be evolved or the entire organization may be discredited among the children of the world. The Toymaker admits, in answer to a question by Boy Blue, that he himself has an idea – or rather a hop – that may

```
              SYNOPSIS OF

           "B A B E S  I N  T O Y L A N D"

                     -o-

               THE PROLOGUE

     A New York street, toward the East Side, on Christmas
Eve.
     Two ragged waifs, Spanky and his sister, Jean, eight,
are gazing longingly into a toy shop window.  Spanky is
bitter because they have no Christmas;  Jean tries to bring
him hope of Santa Claus, but Spanky is dubious.
     Nearby, LAUREL & HARDY, two piemen, are trying to make
some sales, but without success;  Laurel works in reverse
whenever a sale is imminent.  (Comedy sequence to be worked
out by their unit.)
     A drunk, sorry for a dray horse he feels is hungry,
suddenly appears before the gloomy pair and buys all their
pies, and their basket, too, paying them twenty dollars.
     Voicing plans for a merry Christmas, they start
jubilantly down the street, but hear Spanky saying he hates
Santa Claus, and learn from overhearing the argument between
the two children that they will have no Christmas cheer at all.
     It is a wrench, but Laurel and Hardy return and are
accepted by the waifs as the real Pieman and Simple Simon
from Toyland, agents of Santa Claus.
```

```
                       -2-

     We next find Laurel, in a shabby bedroom, entertaining
the children with misquoted nursery tales and verses, while
Hardy buys toys and a tree.  Then both men put the children
to bed, with the kids' heads full of Mother Goose and Toyland.
There is comedy in the other room where the men prepare to
decorate the tree.  They are to sleep together on a narrow
old spring couch, as they gave up their bed to the children.
     The children sleep, and dream that Mother Goose comes
through the window and tells them a story of how Hate once
brought trouble to Toyland.

                     - o -
```

The first two pages of Mr. Roach's 13-page original story.

revolutionize toy making: It is to give toys a soul. Then, the benign old man explains, the children will love their toys and keep them forever. But how can he find the method?

Boy Blue speaks of a man named Barnaby .. and here the townspeople hiss, and cries of "Miser!" and "Skinflint!" are heard. But Boy Blue goes on to say that nevertheless, Barnaby is an alchemist, and it is understood he has developed in his laboratory the essence of Life. If toys can first be given Life, then they can be given a soul.

Overjoyed, the Toymaker sets out to visit Barnaby.

As he goes, we hear the clanging of a bell, and Laurel as Simple Simon, comes in ringing it, followed by Hardy, the Pieman.

(NOTE: Here an introductory comedy sequence to be devised by Laurel & Hardy unit)

Little Bo-Peep is discovered weeping, because she can't find her sheep, and there follows the...

"BO-PEEP NUMBER"

Barnaby has skulked around the crowd, carrying a bouquet, snarling at the children, now on their way to school, who scoff at him. He presents the flowers to Miss Muffet, Mother Hubbard's daughter. She accepts them reluctantly, and, when Barnaby tries to make love to her, dismisses him stormily and throws his bouquet aside without reading a note he has placed in it.

But it is this note which separates her and Tom-Tom, the Piper's son. He finds the bouquet and wonders. He finds the lovingly-worded note, signed "Your future husband," and is violently jealous. Hurt, Miss Muffet becomes almost as unreasonable as Tom-Tom, and they part in wild quarrel.

Barnaby knows the identity of his rival, and plants a pig in Tom-Tom's room. There are only Three Little Pigs in Toyland, and the theft of even one is punishable by life imprisonment.

Laurel and Hardy, selling their pies, reach the school house, and from within hear the empty-headed children recite in chorus: "Six and six make ten," and the teacher shriek, "No! You're wrong again!" Working with the children as a chorus... Laurel and Hardy do the

"I CAN'T DO THAT SUM" NUMBER

(Perhaps followed by comedy sequence to be worked out by them in which they have to take teacher's place)

Carrying out his plot, Barnaby complains to the police, and the pig is found in Tom-Tom's room. A mob forms, and Tom-Tom hears them and knows he is being sought by the police. He starts to hide, but meets Barnaby, who hypocritically pretends sympathy and advises Tom-Tom to escape through the Enchanted Forest. Through Boy Blue, Miss Muffet learns where Tom-Tom is going. She knows that the Forest is full of deadly monster spiders, but despite her fear of them, she hurries to find Tom-Tom there.

Returning to his house, Barnaby finds the Toymaker waiting. The innocent and lovable old man is no match for the alchemist, who reveals that he has all but found the secret of Life, and promises to be in the Armory at Toyland early next morning to bring several hundred wooden toy soldiers to life. The Toymaker leaves, overjoyed... and then we learn that Barnaby has distilled something diabolical to use with his Life Essence.

But Barnaby needs aid in carrying out his plans, and encountering Laurel and Hardy, he finds business dull with them, and engages them to be at his laboratory before daylight next morning.

Miss Muffet finds Tom-Tom in the Forest, and together they wander past terrifying danger, escaping monster spiders and grasping tree branches that reach out to strangle them. Tired, they sing the verse of the

"SLUMBER SONG" NUMBER

and then discover a moth-girl caught in a giant spider web. Tom-Tom rescues her and she flutters away.

The spider stops to repair the broken web, and Tom-Tom carries Miss Muffet away, singing the chorus of

"SLUMBER SONG" NUMBER

So they arrive at the entrance to the Moth Queen's Palace, where Tom-Tom puts Miss Muffet down and she sleeps, while he watches the

"FLORAL BALLET"

in the set built of mirrors. At the end, they are carried on a magic carpet of fluttering moths to the Christmas Tree Grove, where Grumio, the assistant Toymaker, agrees to conceal them beneath some Christmas Trees he is carting back to Toyland. Then he will ship them safely out of the country in packing cases of toys.

Laurel and Hardy are outlined in silhouette against the glow of early morning as they approach Barnaby's house. Hardy is leading the way and carrying a lantern. Laurel is perceptibly frightened at approaching the alchemist's house in the dark. Hardy goes back and urges Laurel along, impatient at the latter's fright.

They are now in front of the forbidding looking house, around which bats are flying. Just as Hardy finishes a talk intended to shame Laurel, a bat swoops around his head and he drops the lantern and wildly swings around, unnerved for the moment. The two pull themselves together and go up to the front door, where there is a knocker composed of a realistic-looking bronze spider. Pretending nonchalance, one tells the other to knock, but neither one has generated the courage to do so, when suddenly the knocker starts knocking by itself; the huge door swings slowly open and from the inner darkness a grotesque dwarf appears and silently beckons them to enter. After a couple of false starts, they go inside.

Barnaby's laboratory is an awe-inspiring mass of test tubes and boiling cauldrons. Around the walls are various esoteric symbols associated with alchemy and Devil Worship, including the signs of

Roach's idea of casting Stan as Simple Simon and Babe as the Pieman was used by Walt Disney for his 1938 cartoon *Mother Goose Goes Hollywood*, as this preliminary art shows. Copyright © *The Walt Disney Company*

the Zodiac, spiders and goats' heads.

Barnaby, tense and evilly triumphant, is standing over a small test tube beneath which is flaming a Bunsen burner, which outlines his face. The liquid in the test tube bubbles faster and faster with a perceptible sound. Barnaby watches it with increasing intensity of interest until suddenly it gives off a puff of smoke, and tossing his arms wildly into the air, Barnaby gives a yell of triumph. He cries that he has found it .. the secret of Life is his!!

Now from the other end of the laboratory we hear Laurel and Hardy stumbling in. The dwarf attendant closes the sliding panel through which they enter. Barnaby hastens to them, while they gaze bewilderedly around. He cautions them immediately that they are not to touch anything unless ordered to. Triumphant after his long experimentation, he can not forebear explaining to the two men what he has accomplished. Hardy follows close to him, and Laurel lags along open-mouthed as he follows them to enormous glass retorts, one filled with an amber and the other a pinkish liquid. One is labelled "HAPPINESS" and the other "LOVE," and he explains that from enormous quantities of these he has distilled a small vial of "HATE." In all Love and Happiness there is a certain percentage of such qualities as jealousy and envy, and it is from these baser elements that the Hate comes. A tiny bit of Hate will be used with each spark of Life.

Beneath each of the retorts is a flame. Laurel loiters first at the Happiness retort. The liquid within it is dancing with thousands of brightly-colored bubbles and from it we hear a faint sound of happy laughter. Laurel hears this and leans closer until his ear is almost against the retort. The sound of laughter becomes louder and louder as he does so. Then while he listens with his ear up close, we hear the different varieties of laughter that are bubbling in the retort ... baby chuckles, the silvery laughter of young girls, hearty male laughter, and punctuating it, a goat-like bleat.

Laurel now hastens to the retort labeled Love, where Barnaby is continuing his explanation to Hardy. This retort is also bubbling merrily and within the huge glass globe we see mist arising, which takes on various symbolical forms. The rising mist first forms the heads of a young man and girl and they kiss; then the mist dissolves and passes on upward toward the neck of the retort. Next we see the forms of two little children, arms around each other, as they skip across the retort and then break up and pass on upward in the mist. Then a mother holding her baby to her breast.

Laurel now goes on to where Hardy is intently listening to Barnaby explain about the distillation of Hate as the dregs of Love and Happiness. The necks of the two retorts converge above a small funnel and beneath the funnel is a tiny vial a little more than half full of a black liquid. The vial is labeled "HATE."

Laurel and Hardy get a shock of surprise as they see the distillation process. At the top of the neck of each retort the vapor forms into a tiny snake which wriggles and hisses its way down to the outlet where slowly a drop of the black liquid of Hate is formed and it drops into the vial. Laurel is particularly fascinated by the vial of Hate. He puts his ear down close to it and as he does so, we hear it hissing. He goes to touch the vial, but Hardy slaps his hands and whispers fiercely, "Don't touch that .. there's no telling what effect it might have!" Laurel seems to fear the liquid of Hate and yet he is drawn to it as a bird is to a snake.

Barnaby starts to explain the Life Essence in the test tube to Hardy and Laurel starts toward them but again is drawn back by the fascination of Hate. Hardy grabs him firmly by the arm and holds him while Barnaby tells the two that he has completed the distillation of sufficient Hate and he is now going to draw off all the Love and Happiness in the retorts, and put them in compression tanks and have Laurel and Hardy release them in some deserted spot so that humanity will not have the use of them anymore. While this is being explained, Laurel's head is drawn back toward the little vial of Hate.

They draw off all the Happiness into one compression tank and all the Love into another. Laurel still casts a fascinated glance toward the vial of Hate, but lets it alone when Hardy scowls at him. Barnaby hurries Hardy to the door and throws it open, exiting up a stairway to his rooms. The dwarf appears to usher the pair out.

Laurel, lagging behind again, cannot resist the vial of Hate. He sticks one finger into the vial, getting it wet with the liquid and then licks it off his finger. He puts the vial back hastily. Immediately he starts to do a "Mr. Hyde" transformation. He seems to shrink, his hair falls across his forehead, a look of malevolence and hatred appears on his face.

When Hardy calls him, Laurel does a grotesque movement and rushing down, kicks his surprised companion in the pants and dashes out the door. The front door opens and the dwarf is astonished as Laurel, still looking like "Mr. Hyde," dashes past him... and then bewilderedly comes out of it.

Instead of throwing away the Happiness and Love they carry, Laurel and Hardy are led to use it on various quarrelling people and perhaps even animals, in a comedy sequence to be devised by their unit.

Tom-Tom and Miss Muffet arrive at the gates of Toyland and concealed in the cart beneath the Christmas trees, they are conveyed by Grumio to the Packing Department. He asks where they wish to go, and Tom-Tom's answer leads to the

"CASTLE IN SPAIN" NUMBER

Grumio sings this, and in trick effects toy soldiers hold a bull fight, while Miss Muffet and Tom-Tom, in miniature size, appear on a balcony and watch.

Then the two young people get into packing cases to be shipped away.

In the Armory, Barnaby brings the toy soldiers to life, endowed secretly with Hate, and they grow to full man-size, overpowering the Toymaker and leaving him almost dead. Then they storm out into the Shipping Department, knocking aside and breaking the case in which Tom-Tom is concealed, and continue on through the gates, taking with them their wooden cannon shooting huge corks. They descend on Toytown.

Barnaby comes out of hiding, and to save himself, seizes Tom-Tom and cries that he stole the vial of hate from him and gave it to the soldiers. He conceals the empty vial on Tom-Tom, who is led away to the dungeons.

Toytown is being sacked and wrecked by the ferocious soldiers, who, marching to

"THE MARCH OF THE WOODEN SOLDIERS"

are maiming and terrorizing the people.

Laurel and Hardy sequences follow, to be worked out by their unit, in which they first find themselves cornered by the soldiers, escape, then discover by accident that water causes the soldiers to come apart, because they are put together with mucilage. This leads to their first using a bucket and dipper, and after that supply runs out and they are in terrible danger, using the town fire apparatus. With various characters pumping, Laurel and Hardy hose the army off the face of the earth and find themselves heroes. They are carried on the shoulders of the populace to Santa Claus, King of Toyland, and to their dismay, made the Royal Executioners, with orders first of all to cut off Tom-Tom's head.

As they cannot bear the sight of blood, or even to swat a fly, their position is a desperate one. But they go ahead with arrangements, and Hardy gets down to measure the neck place in the block, while Laurel is practicing swings with the axe. The results is that the axe is brought down, and sticks in the block, holding Hardy's head there.

After he is released, the two propose to Tom-Tom, who is in stocks awaiting his execution, that he save their feelings by ending his own life in some way. He has learned that Miss Muffet has married Barnaby, without learning she did so on Barnaby's word he would save Tom-Tom's life. So Tom-Tom is anxious to die, and agrees to drink poisoned wine. Immensely relieved, Laurel and Hardy hasten off to get it.

Barnaby and his bride, Miss Muffet arrive, and there she learns that Barnaby does not intend to save Tom-Tom. When Laurel and Hardy bring the glass of poisoned wine, Barnaby mocks Tom-Tom by drinking to his health .. and falls dead.

The old Toymaker has recovered and told the King about Barnaby, so Tom-Tom is released, and Laurel and Hardy are being Knighted as we

DISSOLVE BACK TO:-

THE EPILOGUE

The sleeping waifs awaken .. and it is Christmas morning! They rush into the other room, where the Christmas tree is decorated and waiting, and toys are in profusion around it.

Laurel and Hardy are sleeping on the narrow old spring couch they had to occupy when they gave up their double bed to the kids. And in a comedy scene bring the picture to ..

THE END
-o-

Chapter 7

Rewrite

Hal Roach wrote a longer treatment of his story, 23 legal-sized pages, which made a few changes from the synopsis and expanded some sections.

The opening scene had Spanky and his unnamed older sister gazing longingly at the toys in the window of a shop. Spanky has grown embittered and says that there is no Santa Claus. This prompts the longest and most detailed Laurel and Hardy sequence in the treatment:

Among the street noises, we have heard indistinctly the voices of Laurel and Hardy offering pies for sale. Now the CAMERA discloses them at their stand farther down the street. They have a sort of covered push cart with a heater for keeping their mince and pumpkin pies warm. They have a comedy routine in trying to sell the pies but owing to Laurel's mistakes, Hardy can make no sales. He says, "It's tough enough facing Christmas Eve busted without having a partner who tries to ruin the business."

Arthur Houseman [sic], drunk, dressed in evening clothes and silk hat, comes along sidewalk and notices with sympathy a cab horse standing in the gutter up to its fetlocks in slush. The cab driver is muffled up and asleep on the seat of his vehicle. Houseman feels that here it is Christmas Eve and the horse is getting chilblains and hasn't any Christmas dinner. He spies the pie wagon, goes over and buys all the mince pies, throwing down a greenback. Laurel and Hardy pick up the bill and register with joy that it is a large one.

Houseman returns to feed the horse and the horse stamps, splashing him. Angry, Houseman aims a pie at the horse, which ducks or stumbles and the pie hits the cab driver. Enraged, the cab driver stumbles down to the sidewalk wiping off the pie and Hardy, who has noticed the occurrence, steps over to him and says sympathetically, "You know what I'd do? I'd buy all the pumpkin pies over at that stand and get even with him." The angry cab driver accepts the suggestion, stamps over to the stand, throws down a greenback and Hardy, who has sidled over to serve him asks, "What is it you want, sir?" The cab driver takes all the pumpkin pies and starts a pie throwing contest with Houseman who, handicapped by having the wrong kind of pies, is getting the worst of it.

Laurel and Hardy register that the cab driver's bill is another large one. They pay no attention to the pie battle, but elated at the unexpected sell-out, close their stand, talking excitedly over what they are going to buy for themselves to celebrate Christmas Eve. They intend going to the Hotel Metropole where they will get a fine turkey dinner with two bottles of wine, two big expensive cigars, a liqueur at the end of the meal and then a taxi ride home. By this time, arm in arm, they are passing the two waifs at the toy shop window. Hardy says jubilantly, "Who says there is no Santa Claus?"

As if in answer, Spanky says heatedly, "I say there <u>ain't</u> no Santa Claus!"

Surprised at this retort, the two men stop, turn and see that Spanky is arguing with his sister and is paying no attention to them. The girl continues her efforts to convince the embittered Spanky. For a moment the two men listen to the argument then they look at each other, shrug and resuming their eager manner, start toward the Metropole.

After two or three steps Laurel stops Hardy and

asks, "I wonder if we locked our stand up tight?"

He and Hardy return as far as the toy shop widow where they gaze toward their stand. Laurel nods and says, "Yep, she's locked all right." Both turn and look uncertainly toward the two children for a moment. Spanky is developing a new line of argument to show there can't be any Santa Claus – a real Santa Claus would be able to find any kids any where. Laurel and Hardy look at each other, either willing to admit that he is weakening. Hardy says gruffly, "Well, let's get that dinner."

They start off more briskly than ever but suddenly stop. Hardy says angrily to Laurel, "All right, you talked me into it!"

They turn back toward the children again and in passing a refuse can Hardy takes out some excelsior and arranges Santa Claus whiskers on himself.

Hardy steps up behind Spanky, taps him on the shoulder and in a hearty Santa Claus voice says, "Well, who do you think I am?" Spanky looks up sourly and says, "Aw, you can't fool me; you're the pie man." Hardy gives a hollow laugh and throws the whiskers away. He admits he is the pie man. The little girl wants to know who Laurel is and, still sore at him, Hardy says, "That's Simple Simon." The little girl is overjoyed. Of course she has read about both of them. She says to Spanky, "Remember Spanky—it was in that book we picked up; about the pie man and Simple Simon and Santa Claus – remember?" Hardy seizes on this opportunity to say that, "Of course they are in the same book with Santa Claus – they're pals – in fact Santa Claus sent them to represent him in taking care of Spanky and his sister that Christmas." The girl, overjoyed, accepts them at once.

Spanky is a little dubious until Hardy proves their supernatural power by picking a couple of coins out of Spanky's ear and the little girl's shoe. Spanky is convinced and looking up at the two men with an anticipatory smile asks, "Well then, what are you going to do about it?" Hardy tells him, "You'll be surprised."

Soon we see that Stan and Ollie have brought the two waifs to their shabby apartment and have bought them lots of toys. They tell the kids that they know all about Toyland, because they live there a good deal of the time. Finally, the children go to sleep, only to encounter Mother Goose, who shows them the magic city of Toyland.

The first page of Hal Roach's 23-page treatment.

Santa Claus figures more prominently in this treatment; he is King of Toyland and he, not the Toymaker, wants to find a new kind of toy which will captivate the kids who have grown tired of traditional playthings.

The idea of Barnaby holding a mortgage on Mother Hubbard's home is introduced, but never really developed.

The longest sequence in the treatment is a very dark, humorless sequence in which Barnaby makes his evil elixir of Hate, pulling a fast one on the gentle Toymaker, who only wants to put a soul into his toys. The treatment notes, "The Toymaker...describes to Barnaby the happiness of little children who will have living toys to play with; toys to cherish and love. Barnaby smirkingly agrees but when the door closes on the Toymaker, his demeanor changes to malicious triumph and he shrieks, 'Yes! The dear little children will have my toys but not to give them happiness – to give them DEATH and INJURY and TORMENT!'"

Barnaby's laboratory would likely have given pause to the censors at the Production Code Administration office, as the treatment describes it as "an awe-inspiring mass of test tubes and boiling cauldrons. Around the walls are various esoteric symbols associated with alchemy and

Devil Worship, including the signs of the Zodiac, spiders and goats' heads."

After Stan puts his finger in the vial of Hate and tastes it, the treatment offers a much more detailed account of his deviltry:

> Immediately he starts to do a "Mr. Hyde" transformation. He seems to shrink, his hair falls across his forehead, a look of malevolence and hatred appears on his face.
> When Hardy calls him, Laurel does a grotesque movement and rushing down, kicks his surprised companion in the pants and dashes out of the door. The front door opens and the dwarf is astonished as Laurel, still looking like Mr. Hyde, dashes through and on down the street.
> Hardy, completely astonished, follows carrying the two compression tanks.
> Laurel now goes through a routine of villainy – Laurel style. Peering around a corner like a predatory animal, he spies a child with a stick of candy. Rushing out with fiendish howls, he grabs the candy and rushes around another corner where he eats it, cackling evilly. A fat, prosperous but gouty man is limping along with a crutch. Laurel kicks the crutch out from under him. He sees a little girl putting down a saucer of milk for a tiny kitten; snatches it up and drinks the milk and throws the saucer away laughing fiendishly while the kitten swells up and spits at him. He takes a hoop away from a child and breaks it.
> Meantime Hardy has been pursuing Laurel, at first bewildered but now realizing what has happened. Laurel comes rushing around a corner and bumps into Hardy. Both fall down and before Laurel can escape, Hardy grabs him by one leg. They have a wrestling match in which Hardy finally gets on top. Laurel applies all the fiendish tricks he can, including poling Hardy in the eye with his finger. Getting hold of the Love tank, Hardy sprays Laurel liberally and we witness the transformation back from the fiendish Mr. Hyde to the usual Laurel but evidently Hardy has applied the Love too liberally, for Laurel gets very affectionate and tries to kiss him. Finally, in exasperation, Hardy hits him over the head with the now empty compression tank and this restores Laurel to normal.

Stan's inappropriate affection for Ollie would certainly have caused some concern with the Production Code Administration folks. In this story, Laurel and Hardy are not always the good guys we assume they'll always be, because they become henchmen for the evil Barnaby, echoing the roles of Gonzorgo and Roderigo from the 1903 story. Further, instead of saving Toyland, the wooden soldiers appear in this treatment only as instruments of evil:

> The wounded and apparently dying Toymaker raises his head and denounces the alchemist for his deception but Barnaby only sneers at him...
> The main body of soldiers march down the street... In the menace of their even stride and force of their heavy marching, is the suggestion of violence, murder and rape to the inhabitants of Toytown.

Rape? Really? The soldiers then entirely disrupt a banquet which Santa Claus is holding: "The soldiers wreck everything in the room, and pull Santa Claus' chair out so that he sits on the floor. He crawls under the table as one soldier kicks him in the pants."

Another development in the treatment is that Santa Claus not only orders the execution of Tom-Tom for pignapping, he rewards Laurel and Hardy for vanquishing the soldiers by making them the Royal Executioners. This results in another detailed – and grisly – Laurel and Hardy routine:

> Tom-Tom has been placed in a stock. Laurel and Hardy are diffidently standing near him trying to appear at ease. Now they are startled by the tramp of feet and they turn to see attendants marching in with the grooved block, a huge axe, a bucket and a basket. They inspect the block and axe, then ask what the bucket is for. One of the attendants stops whistling long enough to say, "You catch the blood in that." When they recover from this announcement, they ask the meaning of the basket and the attendant again stops whistling to explain, "That's what the head rolls in to." The attendants withdraw, leaving Tom-Tom guarded by the Constabulary.
> Laurel and Hardy eye each other speculatively. Hardy whispers to Laurel, "I've never killed anything in my life – maybe you'd better do it." Laurel whispers back, "I can't even bear to swat a fly – you know that." They sigh unhappily and then Hardy says, "Well, I guess we better get going." He starts moving the block, bucket and basket around so that each will be in its proper place.
> Laurel takes off his coat, spits on his hands and picks up the axe, examining it.

Hardy asks Tom-Tom what size collar he wears and learns that it is a size 15. "Let's see," hardy says, "I wear a 17. If mine fits, yours ought to." He gets down and lays his neck in the groove of the chopping block; meantime, Laurel has made a few preliminary swings with the axe and, not seeing Hardy's position, he now swings the axe behind him where the razor-sharp blade cuts his suspenders. He then brings the axe forward with such effort that his hat falls down over his eyes and he buries the axe blade in the block, luckily missing the groove, but pinning Hardy's neck in it. Now, his pants start to fall down and when he lets go of them to lift his hat up they start down again so Hardy has a tough time of it until finally Laurel gets around to releasing the axe. During Hardy's struggles, he breaks off his front suspender buttons and thereafter, like Laurel, he has to do everything while handicapped with the necessity for holding up his trousers. When Hardy gets to his feet he says disgustedly, "Here we've been trying to get some place all of our lives and just when we get a couple of fat political jobs, you have to take all the dignity out of it."

The treatment ends with a denouement straight from the 1903 play, with Barnaby drinking poisoned wine, which leaves Miss Muffit, now a widow, free to marry Tom-Tom. As Barnaby drinks the wine, his true identity as a "huge, loathsome spider" is revealed, and the Toyland townspeople stone it to death.

There are long stretches in this treatment where Laurel and Hardy disappear, not to mention Victor Herbert's music. The dark, grim scene of Barnaby extracting the Hate from barrels of Love and Happiness goes on and on, without offering anything in the way of entertainment, much less comedy. Laurel and Hardy become Barnaby's evil if unenthusiastic henchmen, and Stan goes on a rampage of violent misbehavior. Santa Claus is far from the benevolent character we expect, ordering the decapitation of Tom-Tom. (The last lines of the treatment have Spanky and his sister awakening from their dream. "The children are babbling about Toyland and Santa Claus and how glad they are that Laurel and Hardy didn't cut off Tom-Tom's head.")

Roach's idea of Stan and Ollie being Simple Simon and the Pieman was not a bad one; in fact, Walt Disney would cast them in these roles in cartoon form for *Mother Goose Goes Hollywood* in 1938. As Roach noted, the song "I Can't Do the Sum" would indeed have been a charming number for them to sing. However, once the characters are thus established, how does this help resolve the story?

This might have turned out like some of Laurel and Hardy's weaker films, made in the early '40s after they'd left Roach and had signed with 20th Century-Fox and MGM. In *Air Raid Wardens*, the boys run a bicycle shop. In *Jitterbugs*, they are the proprietors of a mechanical swing orchestra. In *The Dancing Masters*, they are instructors in terpsichore. None of these occupations provide anything except an opening scene; they're then forgotten and have nothing whatsoever to do with furthering the story. It was far better to instead cast Laurel and Hardy as assistant toymakers, where Stan's mistake of creating 100 soldiers at six-feet-high turns out to be the blessing in disguise that saves Toyland and provides the finale.

Roach's idea of having the villain being "a spider turned into a man" was no doubt inspired by the spider in the original 1903 stage production. Again, what purpose did this serve, especially since it's introduced only at the very end of the story? Surely the Roach optical effects team of Kenneth Peach and Roy Seawright could have accomplished the transformation, but why?

Regarding the idea of the wooden soldiers obeying the orders to destroy love and happiness by spraying everyone in Toyland with their big containers of liquid hate, this turns the soldiers into villains, when they should be – as they are in the finished film – the heroes who save Toyland. The idea of Stan and Ollie saving Toyland by spraying the soldiers with water doesn't seem like a particularly funny or exciting sequence, and the protracted scene where they're about to decapitate Tom-Tom is unfunny and tasteless.

All these years later, it is still perplexing that Hal Roach, who understood comedy better than any other producer, whose judgment was almost always right on the money, and who created so many great stories for Laurel and Hardy and other comedians at his studio, should be so attached to this one – which frankly seems to be deficient as a musical, as a comedy, and as a story intended for children. We have Hal Roach to thank for hundreds of wonderful comedy films with Harold Lloyd, Snub Pollard, Will Rogers, *Our Gang*, Charley Chase, Thelma Todd and of course Laurel and Hardy, who wouldn't have existed as a team if Hal Roach hadn't provided a creative oasis where they could develop their comic gifts and gradually form a team. Roach's script for *Babes in Toyland*, however, was not his finest hour.

Whether Stan Laurel declined to use Hal Roach's script because he and Hardy weren't funny without the derby hats, or perhaps for other reasons, a complete overhaul of the story was needed if Roach was going to recoup the $50,000 he'd paid for the filming rights.

Chapter 8

Production Starts

Far from telling Stan, "I'm out of the thing completely," and then never paying "a bloody bit of attention to what they did," Hal Roach was intensely involved in all phases of the film's production, as we'll see. As Mr. Roach's close associate Richard W. Bann explains, "He didn't really ever wash his hands of the film. The things he said later on were just his way of expressing lingering resentment for all the trouble Stan was causing the studio and everyone who worked there at a time when Roach was trying to keep the doors open – so everyone could feed their families during the Depression, while other studios all over town were falling into receivership and bankruptcy."

Although he was clearly very disappointed in Stan's rejection of his story idea, Roach had good reason to placate his star. Laurel and Hardy were vitally important to the continuation of the studio. With the deepening of the Depression, more and more theater managers were dropping short subjects in favor of "duals," or double feature bills, in which the cartoon, newsreel and short comedy were replaced by another feature-length film. These second features were usually called "B-Pictures" in the film industry, because they were produced on small budgets and often were populated by actors and actresses who had not yet attained full prominence (many never would), or by performers whose popularity had withered. These films were usually less entertaining than the cartoon, newsreel and short would have been, but many of the paying customers thought they were getting a better value for their precious dimes and quarters.

Short subjects were not necessarily dying out. In fact, in 1933 Columbia was just starting to make two-reel comedies and musical shorts under the supervision of Jules White. The next year, The Three Stooges would begin a series that would run through 1959. RKO was just beginning its long-running series starring Edgar Kennedy and another with Leon Errol. MGM recently had begun making shorts with Pete Smith as narrator, and would soon start producing comedy shorts starring Robert Benchley, and a dramatic series, *Crime Does Not Pay*. The difference was that all these series were produced in-house by the major studios, not by independent producers like Hal Roach, Al

If Stan Laurel and Hal Roach were arguing about the *Babes in Toyland* story, it certainly didn't show at the studio's 20th anniversary party on December 7, 1933.

Babe and Stan, and former Roach studio star Will Rogers, greet Hal's wife, Marguerite.

Christie, or Mack Sennett, who lost his studio at the end of 1933.

Hal Roach was the only independent producer whose films were distributed by MGM. Since the MGM money men at the New York parent company, Loews Incorporated, were providing most of his funding, and since the market for short subjects was dwindling, Roach had to prove to the Loews executives that he could make feature films of the same caliber as MGM's own product.

Roach found himself in the dilemma of having to serve two masters. MGM was not a studio known for slapstick comedy. The studio had acquired Buster Keaton in 1928, but instead of allowing him to write, produce and direct his pictures as he'd done since 1920, his producers gave him stories and directors so unsuitable that Keaton turned to alcohol; his life was spiraling out of control in 1933, to the point where MGM fired him. MGM wanted glamour, romance, drama, all produced with sheen and luster. Stan Laurel, on the other hand, wanted comedy, and especially didn't want stories where he and Babe were just "sandwiched in between" a dramatic plot. *The Devil's Brother* had worked because it was a saucy, sexy comedy even when Laurel and Hardy weren't onscreen; it also had ample music provided by singer Dennis King. Finding another property that would satisfy Roach's primary creditors and his most important stars would be difficult. Roach was sure he had found it with *Babes in Toyland*, so he was doubly disappointed when Stan rejected his story.

But *Babes in Toyland* now had to be made. Roach had paid $50,000 for the rights to RKO, a sum which he couldn't afford to simply write off. Another story would be written, and Hal Roach would still be involved in all phases of the production.

In late November, Roach had been communicating with the money men at Loews Incorporated in New York about the film. Evidently, they had wondered if the film could be made in color. A November 29 letter to Roach states, "You ask us if it will be satisfactory to make your next Laurel & Hardy feature, 'Babes in Toyland,' in black and white only, and request us to increase our advance for this picture up to $250,000 [from $150,000]."

On December 7, 1933, the Roach studio held a lavish party marking its 20th anniversary. A half-hour radio broadcast was carried nationwide by NBC to mark the occasion, with Charley Chase and Laurel and Hardy among the performers. Will Rogers, Jean Harlow and other alumni of the studio attended this soiree, along with Hal Roach's polo buddy Walt Disney. Harry Jackson's orchestra, popular on Los Angeles radio programs and at many local society events, provided the music. If Hal Roach and Stan Laurel were having any sort of disagreement, it certainly didn't show in the many photographs taken of Stan, Babe and their boss, who were all wearing enthusiastic smiles.

On December 9, Edwin Schallert of the *Los Angeles Times* recounted the event and made the first official announcement of Roach's new project. His account of the advance from Loews was double the actual amount:

ROACH SLATES "BABES IN TOYLAND"

The twentieth anniversary of the Hal Roach studio, duly celebrated Thursday evening, has turned out to be the signal for several steps forward in the activities of this organization. For one thing, there is "Babes in Toyland," which will be produced by the studio with $500,000 financing aid by the heads of MGM, with which the Roach interests are allied, which assures a big production.

In this picture Stan Laurel and Oliver Hardy will be seen as Simple Simon and the Pieman, and it is understood that various MGM players may be included in the cast. It appears that one of the things that brought this all about was the success of "The Devil's Brother" abroad, where it was presented under the more natural title of "Fra Diavolo."

In addition to projecting this picture, Roach has appointed Frank Butler head of the story department, who may possibly plan some other special productions.

Butler was no stranger to the Hal Roach lot. He was born in December 1890 in Oxford, England and thus was yet another of the many English expatriates who found favor with Roach. He started his American film career in 1920, playing very British types such as "Sir Aubrey Mayo" in the Rudolph Valentino feature *The Shiek* (1921). In the summer of 1923, he starred in the first of 24 two-reel comedies for Roach as "J. Tewksbury Spat," paterfamilias of *The Spat Family*. After the series ended in June 1925, he continued to write for Roach for a couple of years. With the coming of talkies, he moved to MGM, and then to Paramount; just before joining Roach on *Babes in Toyland*, he had co-written the notoriously "Pre-Code" Paramount feature *Search for Beauty*, which had Robert Armstrong and James Gleason supposedly publishing a health magazine which was in fact filled with salacious photos.

Butler and Laurel had gotten along very well during Butler's earlier tenure at the Roach lot. Not long before his death in June 1967, he told biographer John McCabe that "Stan had the deepest creative feelings of any of our actors on the lot... the fact that he was invaluable in the gag sessions made him someone rather special."

Top: Harry Jackson was a popular bandleader on Los Angeles radio and at society functions such as Roach's anniversary party. Although Jackson hadn't worked for movies before, Roach hired him as musical director on *Babes in Toyland*. *Bottom*: We've no idea was the "radio concentration" method was, as mentioned in the January 21, 1934 edition of the *Los Angeles Times*, but John Swallow had been an announcer at radio station KFVD when it was located inside the Roach studio from 1929 through 1931.

As soon as Roach's plan to make *Babes in Toyland* became public, he began receiving letters from many people, no doubt cash-strapped by the Depression, who hoped to attain some employment on the production. Helen Marr Bartlett wrote to tell Roach that her late husband John had managed the original *Babes in Toyland* stage company for five years, and that her daughter, Hope, would be a natural for an ingenue part, as she had "the divine spark." The 70-year-old Louis F. Gottschalk, who had composed scores for the silent features *Orphans of the Storm* and *The Three Musketeers* among many others, hoped to "be of service to you either with the music or in some capacity."

Dance director Jack Laughlin exhorted, "Put me out there and let me work night and day to give you some really different and brilliant numbers." Another choreographer, Bud Murray, proposed to create the dance numbers and had "more than 100 exceptionally talented singers, dancers and actors of ability, ages 2 ½ years to 11 yrs of age," ready to be interviewed and tested. Still another dance director, William R. Holbrook, sent a telegram declaring that "I have something new and just what you need for *Babes in Toyland* including ballets and new camera angles."

Writer Cosmo Morgan, Jr., offered to provide "new ideas, gags, twists to dialogue," and fervently wished "to be a member of the N.R.A. (New Roach Achievement) during its construction and production." A 23-year-old would-be actor, Charles H. Weeter, Jr., wrote that he "had the training of high school and

Roach Tests Unknowns
Hal Roach yesterday tested William Felix Knight, Atwater Kent audition winner in 1931 and now appearing in Grauman's prologue, and Doris Paxton of the Pasadena Community Playhouse for featured spots in "Babes in Toyland." Studio hopes to find unknowns for the featured roles.

Top: Frank Butler had been an actor in Roach's *Spat Family* series, and returned as head of the scenario department. *Bottom*: Felix Knight was appearing in a live musical prologue before the movie at Grauman's Chinese Theatre when Hal Roach tested him, as noted in the January 16, 1934 issue of *The Hollywood Reporter*.

Among the many singers considered for the film were (*top left*) silent film star (and now concert singer) Ramon Novarro, (*top right*) radio and recording favorite Rudy Vallee, (*lower left*) up-and-coming crooner Donald Novis, and yet unknown but talented Felix Knight.

college and feel quite confident I could handle a youthful role."

Alas, none of these hopefuls were destined to work on *Babes in Toyland*, but Roach was starting to make plans for the casting and production. By December 23, studio business manager Henry Ginsberg was negotiating for the 34-year-old former silent film star Ramon Navarro, who in fact had a fine singing voice, to play the part of "the romantic singing lead." However, Navarro was planning a European concert tour and wasn't available, so Roach began to haggle with popular radio crooner Rudy Vallee.

Along with Laurel and Hardy, principal roles would be given to Charley Chase, Patsy Kelly, Spanky McFarland and other Roach contract stars. Roach was planning to use amateurs around sixteen years old in the parts of Alan and Contrary Mary, and was considering using a girl as the male juvenile character if he couldn't find a suitable boy. The script was still on hold, Roach announcing that work would begin on it after the cast was set.

Meanwhile, miniatures and sets were already being prepared. Kenneth Peach, noted for his work in trick and "process" photography, was overseeing stop-motion animation sequences. Peach was born in Oklahoma – or what was then El Reno, Indian Territory – on March 6, 1903. He got into the picture business at the age of 20 and was a cameraman three years later. He was particularly interested in special effects, working with matte shots and miniatures at Tiffany Pictures, Warner Bros., and RKO. When a 1933 strike caused Art Lloyd and the usual Hal Roach cameramen to temporarily leave the Roach studio, Peach came in and received his first credit as cinematographer on the 1933 Roach All-Stars short *Crook's Tour*.

By December 30, *The Hollywood Reporter* noted:

HAL ROACH SHOOTS WORKS ON "TOYLAND"
Planning it as the most spectacular production ever made on the lot, Hal Roach will personally supervise "Babes in Toyland" and will sign four directors to handle the subject. One director will handle the dramatic and straight plot of the story, another will direct the comedy sequences, a third will be in charge of dance and musical numbers, while another will be in charge of technical and trick material.

Picture will definitely get into work by February 1 in order to make a nationwide release Easter week. Stan Laurel has been assigned the role of Simple Simon, and Oliver Hardy will be the pieman in the screen version of The Victor Herbert operetta.

At the same time, Roach was shooting the works domestically, moving his wife Marguerite, daughter Margaret and son Hal, Jr. from their longtime home at 22 Berkeley Square in the West Adams district of Los Angeles to a lavish Colonial-style home at 610 North Beverly Drive in Beverly Hills. It had been built in 1922 by silent screen star Priscilla Dean, who had worked with Laurel and Hardy in 1927's *Slipping Wives*. She sold it to silent screen star Pola Negri, who sold it to philanthropist Max Strauss, who sold it to Roach. It would be Roach's home for the next couple of decades.

With the start of 1934, Henry Ginsberg signed writer Ray Harris to work on the screenplay for *Babes in Toyland*. A working screenwriter since 1924, Harris had 30 film credits and had worked for Paramount and RKO. Meanwhile, the studio was in the middle of a two-week layoff for the holidays. The current Laurel and Hardy short, *Oliver the Eighth*, had already been interrupted in the middle of filming, owing to the sudden death of Stan Laurel's 32-year-old brother, Edward Everitt "Teddy" Jefferson, who had suffered a fatal heart attack while having a tooth pulled. In happier news, Laurel and Hardy's just-released feature film, *Sons of the Desert*, was garnering excellent reviews and rapidly pulling in the customers.

On January 9, *Film Daily* published a full-page display advertisement promoting MGM's lineup for the coming season of 1934-35. Included was "STAN LAUREL, OLIVER HARDY in Victor Herbert's comic operetta BABES IN TOYLAND," the first official mention of the production by Roach's distributor.

Roach continued quickly signing talent for his lavish project, on both sides of the camera. John Swallow, who had been an announcer at radio station KFVD when it was headquartered at the Roach lot from 1929 to 1932, and who was now producing the NBC show *Hollywood on the Air*, was hired to be technical director for all of the music. Harry Jackson's orchestra, which was featured on that program, had played at Roach's big anniversary party,

Patricia Ellis was auditioned for the part of the female lead. She would later work with Laurel and Hardy in their 1938 feature *Block-Heads*.

Left: Thanks to her starring role in *Alice in Wonderland*, Charlotte Henry was attracting publicity in fan magazines, such as the January 1934 issue of *Movie Classic*. *Right*: She was getting more favorable attention than the movie, thanks to the makeup and costumes which obscured most of the big stars, as shown in the February 1934 *Picture Play*.

and was a natural to provide the orchestral music. The film required a larger group than the modest dance band which had played the cues used for Roach's short subjects. Jackson, a violinist, had been popular on Los Angeles radio station KFWB going back to 1925, and would remain a mainstay of the region's programming well into the 1940s. Later in that decade, he operated a recording studio on West 48th Street in New York.

Some of the arrangements and the music for the "ducking" scene were written by 25-year-old Myrl Alderman, who composed and arranged music for films and television well into the '60s but is best remembered for being shot in 1938 by gangster Moe "the Gimp" Snyder, ex-husband of famed singer Ruth Etting, who evidently did not approve of Ruth's new boyfriend. Myrl recovered, he and Ruth married, and they were a very happy couple until Myrl's death at their Colorado Springs home in September 1966.

Since Roach envisioned *Babes in Toyland* as a singing and dancing film, he signed 32-year-old dance director Eddie Prinz to stage the musical numbers. Prinz had designed the choreography for three films, the most recent being MGM's *Dancing Lady*, starring Clark Gable, Joan Crawford, and someone making his debut in movies – Fred Astaire. Meanwhile, with Ramon Navarro and Rudy Vallee both proving unavailable, Roach was trying to obtain the services of 27-year-old singer Donald Novis to play the romantic lead. Novis had been a featured crooner at the Cocoanut Grove at Los Angeles's Ambassador Hotel, with the dance band of Jimmie Grier. The young crooner had appeared in 20 movies, eight of them shorts, including three for Mack Sennett. Novis had also appeared in minor roles for Hal Roach in 1931, in the Zasu Pitts-Thelma Todd shorts *Let's Do Things* and *The Pajama Party*. For smaller roles, Roach was beginning to audition winners of the annual singing contest sponsored by Arthur Atwater Kent, an inventor and manufacturer of high-quality radios. Novis had won this contest in 1928.

On January 16, Stan and Babe finished filming their latest three-reel short, *Oliver the Eighth*. *The Hollywood Reporter* mentioned that "Hal Roach yesterday tested William Felix Knight, Atwater Kent audition winner in 1931 and now appearing in Grauman's prologue, and Doris Paxton of the Pasadena Community Playhouse for featured spots in 'Babes in Toyland.' Studio hopes to find unknowns for the featured roles." Knight was appearing at Grauman's Chinese Theatre in a live prologue before the daily screenings of the Katharine Hepburn film of *Little Women*. (Doris Paxton went on to appear in 16 Broadway shows through 1956, but doesn't appear to have made any movies.)

Felix Knight was born in Macon, Georgia on November 1, 1908. He came to Los Angeles as a young man, studied with vocal teacher Mebane Beasley, and alternated concert and radio work with occasional film appearances. In 1981, he recalled, "In the early '30s and the middle '30s, Atwater Kent, before he sold out to Philco Radio, used to have a national audition of young singers from the ages of 18 to 24, who would audition in districts. I won the local contest in Los Angeles, then I won the Western states, then I came to New York and came in at the top here in New York on the Atwater Kent auditions. That was the first national publicity I received – but I primarily got the role in *Babes in Toyland* because I was the best young singer they auditioned and tested at that time, and I looked like the part that they wanted to cast. My agent knew that MGM was looking for somebody who could sing, and also look young enough to do the part. And I went through a series of screen tests, and that was it. Before that I had done *Down to Their Last Yacht* at RKO, which was a movie that was, uh, a bomb; I played a native South Sea Islander in that."

Knight elaborated on being cast for *Babes in Toyland* in a later interview with writer Laura Wagner. "I made four or five screen tests," he recalled. "One director said no, I was too pretty and [the audience] wouldn't believe I was a young man, which I thought was the stupidest observation of all! Stan Laurel finally said, 'Look, I like this boy. Not only is he good looking, but he's the best singer we've heard.' Then someone said, 'But he doesn't have any acting experience,' and [Stan] said, 'How much acting does he have to do?' So, it was Stan who got me in, and we became very good friends. He was a very, very nice human being."

News about this exciting new Hal Roach project continued to fill the trade papers, and Los Angeles newspapers, on a daily basis. On January 20, the *Los Angeles Times* reported:

FANTASY PLANS TO BE ELABORATE
With production of Victor Herbert's immortal extravaganza, "Babes in Toyland," set to start February 15, elaborate preparations for its filming are under way. Thousands of feet of stop motion and trick shots have been photographed under the direction of Kenneth Peach. Scores of vocalists have been given auditions by John Swallow, in charge of the musical division of the fantasy, and casting of the principal parts will start next week.

Roach continued to test young performers for the leading roles. Patricia Ellis, an ingenue under contract at Warner Bros. (who in 1938 would appear in Laurel and Hardy's *Block-Heads*), and MGM stock player Earl Oxford were under consideration. Oxford had sung on Broadway in the 1930 revue *Three's a Crowd*, and in the MGM feature *Should Ladies Behave* (1933). Charlotte Henry had starred in Paramount's *Alice in Wonderland*, which had been released during Christmas week of 1933. She was also being tested by Roach, and Los Angeles newspapers noted that she "had the inside track" for the leading female role, which at this point appeared to be Little Miss Muffet. Wrote Edwin Schallert in the *Los Angeles Times*, "'Alice in Wonderland' has been such an interesting-attracting production that this young girl's personality – which as a personality completely overshadowed the masked figures in the film – has caused her to become a bright name on account of this one feature." Indeed, the primary complaint lodged at Paramount's fantasy film was that the all-star cast was all but invisible, thanks to the overly elaborate masks and costumes. (The critic for *The New Movie* wrote, "You don't appreciate how important a thing facial expression is until there isn't any.") Roach noted this; it was a mistake he would not make.

Babes in Toyland was well on schedule for its planned start date of February 15. Then, suddenly, it looked as though *Babes in Toyland* would never be made – nor any other Laurel and Hardy film.

On January 24, Stan notified the studio that he has been unable to work because of the condition of his health, and therefore did not wish to be paid for any work since January 16. Henry Ginsberg wrote back to Laurel, agreeing to suspend Stan's contract as of the 16th and stating, "We are desirous that you resume the rendition of the services provided for and specified in such agreement in existence

Left: Stan, wife Lois and daughter Lois Junior had a happy vacation in Hawaii in April 1931. *Right*: Myrtle and Babe Hardy enjoyed a hectic but exciting trip to England in July 1932.

between us [Stan's contract, dated January 7, 1930] at the earliest possible moment, and of which resumption we shall be glad to receive notice from you. We, indeed, regret the incapacity so occasioned by the condition of your health."

Ginsberg, Stan and Roach all knew that the "incapacity" was really a plot to reduce the amount of alimony that Stan was paying to his soon-to-be-ex-wife Lois. Married on August 13, 1926 and producing daughter "Little Lois" in December 1927, Stan and Lois's union had soured by 1932. Despite several attempts to reconcile, Lois obtained a divorce in the court of Los Angeles Superior Judge Walter S. Gates on October 11, 1933. She had been receiving a full 50 percent of Stan's earnings since July 22.

On January 31, the powerful Hollywood gossip columnist Louella O. Parsons, a close friend of Hal Roach and his wife, wrote this story, which was published in the many newspapers all over the country which were owned by William Randolph Hearst:

> The sad-faced Stan Laurel is growing sadder by the minute. He is taking a suspension on his Hal Roach contract and at the moment is not receiving one cent in salary. The rotund Oliver Hardy is sad, too, because he is out of a partner and unless Stan has a change of heart, Wallace Beery and Raymond Hatton will replace the famous comedy team in *Babes in Toyland*.
>
> The Laurel peeve isn't aimed at Oliver, nor is it aimed at his boss, Hal Roach. It's leveled, as we hear, against his ex-wife. At the time of the divorce, Laurel practically turned everything he owned over to his wife and, in return for his freedom, also agreed to give her a large part of his salary.
>
> Realizing that he wasn't working for himself, Stan asked for an alimony compromise, which was refused him. So he has decided his health isn't robust enough for him to continue working in strenuous comedies.

Hal Roach evidently felt that this crisis could be smoothed over, as he continued to test more performers for *Babes in Toyland* at the start of February. By February

8, Anita Louise had been tested for the role of Little Miss Muffet, the part for which Charlotte Henry was testing. Charlie Rogers was being tested for the role of Grumio, the assistant to the Toymaker. So was English comedian Duggie Wakefield, who was concurrently starring in some Roach shorts with fellow Brits Billy Nelson and Jack Barty.

On February 12, production of the film hit a further snag, as chronicled by *The Hollywood Reporter*:

ALIMONY HEADACHE CHASES LAUREL AWAY

> Hal Roach has the biggest headache in town today, with Stan Laurel definitely making plans to leave the country the end of the month, due to alimony trouble, and splitting the comedy team of Laurel and Hardy, which has been a big box-office winner for the producer for some time.
>
> Laurel has offers to make personal appearances in London and other European cities, which he plans to accept.
>
> Roach, it is reported, will try to build up a new comedy team with Babe Hardy and Patsy Kelly.

Also on this day, Louella O. Parsons wrote another column for the Hearst papers:

> Stan Laurel is still among the missing. He just cannot make up his mind whether to return to England, to stop payments on his alimony, stage a reconciliation with his wife or make a settlement with her. That's all right for him, but it's tough for Hal Roach, who finds the plump Oliver Hardy without his screen partner.
>
> Hal is optimist enough to believe Stan will come to his senses and return to the Roach studios. If he doesn't, Hardy will go it alone, with Patsy Kelly as his leading lady. But there won't be any attempt to team Hardy, for the present at least.

Hal Roach said in 1981, "The tragedy in Laurel's life was that his first wife, Lois, got a divorce. She was the one who handled him beautifully. Stan didn't handle his liquor very well. After he had two or three drinks, he'd begin to do things that weren't quite proper. She knew his capacity, when he should quit. Stan would take a couple of drinks at home in the evening, or at a party, and she'd say, 'That's it.' And he minded her. She was also his agent. When I made a financial deal with Laurel, I made it with her, I didn't make it with him. If there was anything at the studio that was wrong, she was the one who came to me.

"I think his career was terrifically affected. I was after Stan all the time. He couldn't have been more stupid about the whole thing. He was very much in love with Lois, and he never dreamed she would get the divorce. But he kept nudging her, going all the time, and all of a sudden he thought he was John Barrymore. Girls were nuts about him, and how were you going to tell the guy, 'Hell, these dames are only after you for your dough. They're not interested in anything you've got physically.'

"So, he decided to divorce Lois. He agreed to give her two trust funds and the house. Ben Shipman was his attorney. He went to Shipman and got the property settlement papers made out, and she signed them, and he signed them, and now when they only have to go to court, Stan says, 'Lois, I was only kidding.' She said, 'Stanley, I wasn't.'

"And, oh, he was going to commit suicide, and then he was going to go to the South Sea Islands. I tried to talk to her, but she said, 'Hal, it's not worth it.' She said, 'I'm like his keeper, and if I go back to him, I've got to take care of him every day when he comes home. I don't know if he's going to get drunk, or what he's going to do. He's not very pleasant to live with anyway, and besides, I've got enough to last me.' And she took the money – and made a lot of dough out of it, incidentally. But she said, 'I've had it. I just don't want to go back into that rat race again, and I'm not going to.' I couldn't talk her out of it. So that was that."

In 1989, Hal Roach's longtime friend Richard W. Bann showed the producer the Louella Parsons column. Roach's comment after reading it was, "Stan could not believe it when Lois called his bluff and left him. He only threatened to walk out of the studio and go home to England in hopes Lois would make up with him and take him back. She would not. I wish she had."

For decades, Stan's daughter Lois retained letters that her father had written at this time, "pleading to go back with my mother."

Sadly, Babe Hardy's marital situation was not much better. He had married Myrtle Lee Reeves in November 1921. She was an Atlanta girl, and although she had been a film actress in the 1910s, she felt out of place in the Hollywood community and had taken to the bottle in loneliness. She and Babe had almost divorced in 1929 and again in 1932, but each time she promised to reform and stop drinking. By early 1934, she was spending more time at the Rosemead Sanitarium trying to dry out than she was at the Hardy home on Alta Drive in Beverly Hills. Babe sent her copious amounts of flowers with cards expressing love to her from "Daddy," but he was also seeing another woman, Viola Morse.

As for the future of Laurel and Hardy, on February 16, the Associated Press ran a story which offered a glimmer of hope, in which Stan denied that the team would be split. "I wouldn't think of negotiating a contract on my own hook," Stan said. "I realize my value as a comedian lies in the fact that I am teamed with Hardy." Babe also told the press that there was no impending split.

With the future of *Babes in Toyland* in doubt, Charlotte Henry – who was still under contract to Paramount – was loaned to 20th Century to co-star with famed actor George Arliss in *Head of the Family*.

On February 26, Roach reluctantly suspended production on his film. As noted in *The Hollywood Reporter*, "The picture was originally intended as a co-starring vehicle for Oliver Hardy and Stan Laurel, and with the latter out of the picture for the time being, Roach is waiting until Laurel can be brought back into the fold. No writers are working on the script at present."

With actors being tested, animation filmed, music arranged and a script started, *Babes in Toyland* had been well on schedule – but now it looked as though the film might not be made at all, which would be a personal setback for Hal Roach, and possibly a lethal blow to his studio.

Roach Suspends on 'Babes in Toyland'

Hal Roach has suspended production on the musical fantasy "Babes in Toyland" which he planned to put into work the first part of March.

The picture was originally intended as a co-starring vehicle for Oliver Hardy and Stan Laurel, and with the latter out of the picture for the time being, Roach is waiting until Laurel can be brought back to the fold. No writers are working on the script at present.

Top Left: Unfortunately, the Laurels' marriage did not last. Lois obtained a divorce on October 12, 1933. *Bottom*: Stan's agreement to give Lois fully half of his earnings had a drastic impact on his career, and on *Babes in Toyland* specifically, as noted in the February 26, 1934 issue of *The Hollywood Reporter*. *Top Right*: By May 7, 1934, Stan had decided that half a salary was better than none, and went back to work at the Roach lot.

Chapter 9

Adrift

If he hadn't already invested so much time and money in *Babes in Toyland*, Hal Roach might well have reconsidered making an elaborate fantasy film, judging from the tepid reviews that Paramount's *Alice in Wonderland*, starring Charlotte Henry, was garnering as March 1934 began. Frederic F. Van de Water wrote in *The New Movie*, "Three quarters of the actors and actresses speak their parts from behind masks... [it] turns out to be more of a marionette show than a movie." *Picture Play* noted, "The chief interest of the spectator comes from the game he will play with his memory of familiar voices. Otherwise, *Alice in Wonderland* must take its place as a curiosity of the screen, a technical stunt more than a satisfying picture."

No doubt Roach read these reviews and took their message to heart. *Babes in Toyland* would convey a warmth and human appeal by keeping its characters as recognizable people, and not encasing them in fanciful masks. Now, with Stan's behavior clouding the future of the production, Roach had to concentrate on other films. At the start of March 1934, he had completed 29 of the 42 short comedies which were due before June 1, so he closed the studio for two weeks. Roach and his wife Marguerite took a ten-day vacation to see the polo matches at Del Monte, a coastal California community about 325 miles northwest of Culver City.

Meanwhile, Stan was receptive to appearing in front of the cameras again – but not at the Roach studio. Back in September 1933, he and Babe had worked for four days on a loan-out for MGM's *Hollywood Party*, an all-star musical comedy. This troubled project had been in production for over a year; it had already cost its studio an astounding $900,000, about five times the budget of a standard feature film. Jimmy Durante was the nominal star, but the studio had decided that Laurel and Hardy's scenes were particularly good – and since *Sons of the Desert* had recently been doing excellent business, more footage with them would bolster the picture.

On March 8, Stan wrote to the Roach studio for permission to work with Babe in the MGM film. "I feel it my obligation and duty to do my best to appear therein and finish this work, and have so stated to Metro-Goldwyn-Mayer Studios, and in view of the fact that it involves only the completion of some work to the extent of a day to two of my services, I would not wish to receive any compensation therefor."

With permission granted by Henry Ginsberg, Stan and Babe made new scenes on March 11 and 12 for MGM's *Party*. Their longest sequence, a tit-for-tat egg-breaking skirmish with the hot-tempered Lupe Velez, received by far the most enthusiastic reviews, as exemplified by *The Hollywood Reporter*: "That sequence is worth the price of admission, and is the highlight in an otherwise dull musical... The picture hardly rates the time and money that MGM has expended."

On March 19, the Roach studio reopened, welcoming back sound recording engineer Elmer Raguse, who had built and installed the lot's audio equipment in late 1928, and who had been fired by Henry Ginsberg in December 1931. This was one of Ginsberg's cost-cutting moves that had proven too costly. A new arrival to the studio was four-year-old Scotty Beckett, joining the *Our Gang* series as a new sidekick for Spanky McFarland.

Stan Laurel, however, did not return. He was in the four-bedroom house at 303 South Palm Drive in Beverly Hills where he'd moved five months earlier after the split with Lois. He was not alone, having as housemates his assistant Pete Gordon – a former vaudeville and silent-film comic – and a cook, a black lady named Tomasina. However, Stan was feeling very much alone. Despite his statements to the press, there had been no offers from England for

Cost-cutting executive Henry Ginsberg, despite his friendly appearance, was a very important and much-feared man around the Roach lot. However, his methods kept the studio running when others faltered.

him to make personal appearances. There was no work on the horizon at all, unless Stan decided that receiving 50 percent of his salary was better than none. Having worked for only two days since mid-January, and with Lois unwilling to either reconcile with him or to reduce her alimony demands, Stan felt that his career – and life – might be beyond repair.

In despair, on March 26 he wrote to an old friend, Ethel Stanley, a former vaudeville singer who lived in New York:

> Dear Friend Ethel –
> Please excuse pencil.
> Thanks so much dear for your kind letter. It was awfully sweet of you & I appreciate your kind thoughts. I know exactly the foolishness of my doings – but my spirit & ambition have been broken & I just don't care anymore – I have tried to keep going & its too much for me – it is impossible to be funny with a broken heart & rather than make pictures that wouldn't be good I prefer to finish at the Peak.
> I have no one to blame but myself – I just made a mess of my life & career & hate myself for it – someday I'll probably get over it & make a fresh start – if it isn't too late – but it seems like I never will – However I'm not going to dwell on the subject, as I brood & fret over it so much – at times I think I'll go crazy – again

many thanks Ethel for your kindly interest. Trust alls well & happy with you. I will still be coming East – if I do will let you know.
      Kindest regards always!
      Stan Laurel.

 PS – Please destroy this Ethel – This is in confidence. Thanks!
 SL

Babes in Toyland was still in limbo, but Hal Roach was making plans for another elaborate feature film, one that would be very different from his usual family-oriented fare. He assigned several of his staff writers to create a treatment for a proposed screen version of *Lysistrata*, a Greek comedy written by Aristophanes and first performed in Athens in 411 B.C. The title character of the story is a woman who calls for a meeting of all the women of Greece; they devise a plan to end the Peloponnesian War by denying sex to their husbands until they sign a peace treaty.

Thanks to the ever-present Depression, movie producers for the past couple of years had lured customers into the theaters by presenting feature films with controversial themes such as prostitution, adultery and drug abuse; even cartoons had included an occasional "hell" or "damn" in their dialogue. With the Catholic church and much of the public clamoring for cleaner films, Roach instead seemed to be trying for a saucy, sexy comedy before censorship clamped down on the freedom of the screen. One can only wonder what Roach's distributors and financiers at MGM would have thought of his plans to produce what *The Motion Picture Herald* called a "torrid sex play, penned by Aristophanes, the ancient Greek philosopher, in a weak moment. Hollywood is conjecturing whether Hal will film his feature as was written, modernize it, or burlesque it."

MGM might have looked askance at such a film; however, Roach's short comedies were receiving the company's full support. Henry Ginsberg announced to the trade press on March 29 that MGM had 1,000 more accounts with exhibitors for the Roach studio's entire output than it had had a year before. Ginsberg further stated that the studio had spent $100,000 more on the current schedule's films than it had in 1933, and that "returns have justified the expenditure."

Ginsberg may have been whistling in the dark, however. *Film Daily* noted on April 7, "At this particular time nearly everybody is bearish on shorts. Not since Charlie Chaplin abandoned two-reelers for the feature field has there been so much general gloom among short subject producers over the prospects for their output.

"As for double-feature competition, there is only one way to combat it, and that is the very simple and very obvious expedient of making shorts that have more box office appeal and therefore are more desirable bookings for the exhibitor than a second feature…

"[Hal Roach's] Laurel and Hardy comedies top the field in their class because they are painstakingly constructed by craftsmen, instead of being just a hodge podge of stale and unrelated slapstick… At the same time there have been too many inane affairs, outmoded in idea, handled without the least ingenuity, apparently thrown together solely to fulfill schedules, pictures that never should have been made at all. These occasional clucks are enough to make both exhibitors and the public sour on short comedies in general."

On this same day, April 7, Stan Laurel was in the headlines – but not because he had returned to making films at the Roach studio with Babe. Stan had acquired a new partner. On April 3, at the Agua Caliente Hotel in Ensenada, Mexico, Stan had married Virginia Ruth Hansberger Rogers, a 35-year-old "society widow" who designed dresses and sold them at her own shop and in other retail stores in and around Los Angeles. She and Stan had met during the Labor Day weekend of 1933, when Laurel and director William Seiter had taken a working vacation on Catalina Island to discuss plans for *Sons of the Desert*.

Stan was already separated from Lois at that time, and Ruth became a frequent visitor to the Roach studio during that film's production in October. Intelligent and lively, she exuded refinement but still had a vivacious sense of humor. She was with the *Sons of the Desert* company during a night when they filmed a sequence in which the boys would be soaked by rain. She later recalled, "I was waiting off camera with [Stan's] double, Ham Kinsey, and threw a blanket around him, then we rushed him into his dressing room and I grabbed a bottle of whiskey and put some lemon and sugar in it. You know, a hot toddy. And we had the shower running, and Stan took the hot toddy and started to cry. Then he said, 'Baby Ruth, as long as I was married to Lois, she never took an interest in my work. She didn't care what I did. She never treated me this way.'"

Stan's October 1933 divorce from Lois had not yet become final, because the mandatory one year "interlocutory" waiting period was not yet over and wouldn't be for another six- and one-half months. Stan told reporters that he and Ruth would not live together. Ruth wouldn't hear of their cohabitating. She was a true lady – and besides, she told Stan, "It would kill mother." They would remarry in California when the final divorce papers were handed down. However, their marriage was

Left: Kentucky humor writer Irvin S. Cobb embarked on a series of shorts for Roach in the spring of 1934, clearly meant to emulate the huge success of Will Rogers. Audience apathy caused only four of the intended seven shorts to be made. *Right*: With Stan Laurel away indefinitely, Roach had to rely on his other stars to keep the studio running.

recognized as legal in all states but California.

With a new bride, Stan needed to generate income again, even if Lois was going to gain half of it, and on April 12, he signed a new contract with the studio. *The Hollywood Filmograph* announced, "Studio Doors Wide Open – for the lost Stan Laurel, now that he has recovered from his latest honeymoon, and the firm of Laurel and Hardy will once more grace the mikes and cameras for Hal Roach, who seemed glad to see Stan." That same day, Roach closed the studio for a month, which was a customary vacation for everybody on the lot. He still needed to complete two shorts starring Thelma Todd and Patsy Kelly, three Laurel and Hardy two-reelers, and the L&H feature that had been on the back burner for two months.

Roach took his private plane to Pyramid Lake, Nevada, with Laurel and Hardy's frequent writer-director James Parrott and comedian-director-writer Gus Shy "to fish and perhaps work on stories." Roach returned on April 24 and hosted a party for a new personality who was going to star in a series of seven two-reelers. Irvin S. Cobb, from Paducah, Kentucky, was a noted author and humorist whom Roach hoped to turn into the next Will Rogers. Roach and Rogers had collaborated on several silent shorts in 1923-24 with only modest success; by 1934 Rogers was starring in features for Fox and had become one of the top box-office attractions in America.

The party, for men only, was held at the Bel Air Country Club. As each guest arrived, he was escorted by guards through an iron door. There, he was fingerprinted and given a prison number and a striped suit to wear. Then he

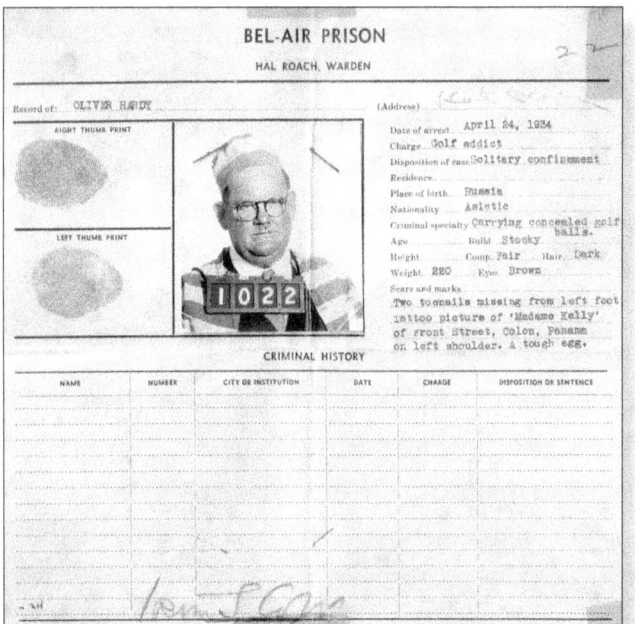

Irvin S. Cobb introduced himself to the Hal Roach Studio employees at a "prison party" hosted by Roach at the Bel-Air Country Club on April 24. Cobb noted Babe's passion for golf.

was photographed and taken through another iron-barred door into the dining room. Its windows were barred; an orchestra was playing while attired in prison stripes, and the plain wooden tables were set with tin plates and cheap cutlery.

One of Roach's financiers, A.P. "Doc" Giannini of the Bank of America, was dubious about being photographed in prison garb. So was another famous producer, who angrily said, "I'll go home before I'll put on those stripes," and did. However, Walt Disney, Irving Thalberg and other guests enjoyed the elaborate joke, especially the "rap sheet" which Irvin S. Cobb typed up for each of the attendees.

Babe Hardy kept his personal rap sheet, typed up and signed by Cobb, in his own collection of photographs. The heading reads, BEL-AIR PRISON – HAL ROACH, WARDEN. A photo of Babe in a striped convict's uniform (and glasses, which he wore offscreen) is accompanied by Cobb's description of him: "Charge: Golf addict. Place of birth: Russia. Nationality: Asiatic. Criminal Specialty: Carrying concealed golf balls. Scars and marks: Two toenails missing from left foot; Tattoo picture of "Madame Kelly" of Front Street, Colon, Panama, on left shoulder. A tough egg." The evening's hilarity was a welcome tonic for Babe, as *The Hollywood Reporter* that day had published a gossipy note about his alcoholic wife, Myrtle, who was "in a sanitarium for the steenth time at the moment with 'pink elephant' trouble."

The studio finally reopened on Monday, May 7, with Irvin S. Cobb starting the first film of his new series, and Thelma Todd and Patsy Kelly embarking on a new two-reeler, *I'll Be Suing You*. One would think that Hal Roach would want to oversee this new activity, but the next day, he flew in his personal airplane to Seattle, where he joined the *Hussar* – the yacht of his friend, financier E.F. Hutton. Roach's wife Marguerite was not so enthusiastic about flying in small planes and took the train.

A party including Hutton's wife and daughter, investment manager Ernest H. Rice and his wife Miriam, and aviator David McCullough cruised on Hutton's yacht along the coastal waters of Alaska to hunt for bear, mostly in islands near Juneau. (Roach had lived in Alaska as a young man for the better part of two years, driving a stage from Valdez to Fairbanks.) The celebrants played a lot of bridge, saw 76 black bear and 59 brown bear, and brought a friendly cub aboard, which they named Barney. Roach and the other men did a fair share of hunting on the trip. However, the excursion was cut short on June 3, after David McCullough was wounded in a shooting accident by one of the guides.

During Roach's almost month-long absence, Laurel and Hardy finally got back to making movies, but not *Babes in Toyland*. On May 15, Stan, Charlie Rogers and another gag man named Frank Terry began work on a script tentatively titled *Public Enemies*, which was inspired by the concurrent misadventures of John Dillinger and other gangsters. It was the first new L&H short since *Oliver the Eighth* in January.

Terry was yet another Englishman at the Roach lot, born in Worcester in 1871. He had toured Europe and Asia as an acrobat and comedian from his early youth (and engaged in a fair amount of gambling and possibly bigamy during his travels). He was working for Roach by 1918 as a writer, director, and sometime actor; he directed and co-starred in one of Stan's very first films for Roach, the 1919 one-reeler *Hustling for Health*. That year, Terry had the misfortune of handing Harold Lloyd a prop bomb at a photo session which turned out not to be a prop and blew off the thumb and index finger of his right hand. Terry was still so valuable – and Roach and Lloyd were so sympathetic – that he remained employed as a gag man at the studio into the mid-'30s. With Laurel and Hardy in 1933, he played Ollie's butler in *Me and My Pal* and a wily safecracker in *The Midnight Patrol*.

Charlie Rogers had co-directed *The Devil's Brother* with Hal Roach in early 1933 and made a return to the director's chair with the new L&H short, which ultimately gained the title *Going Bye-Bye!* The picture, which co-starred Walter Long as escaped criminal "Butch Long" and Mae Busch as his moll, was filmed from May 21 to 26. Just

before this, in Hal Roach's absence, Henry Ginsberg made a new contract with director Gus Meins, who was alternating between shorts starring Thelma Todd and Patsy Kelly and entries in the *Our Gang* series.

On May 19, Ginsberg spoke to the movie industry press, and confidently predicted that short subjects would return to more theaters, and double-feature programs would be "a thing of the past within six months." (Carl Laemmle, the head of Universal, had a different opinion, stating, "I shall sell double features 'till the cows come home.") Despite Ginsberg's optimism, the planned Roach studio program for the forthcoming 1934-35 season included only four two-reel shorts with Laurel and Hardy, down from the usual eight. The shorts would be accompanied by two features – one of which would be *Babes in Toyland*.

After a long period of relative inactivity at the Roach lot, production suddenly revved into high gear. Immediately after finishing the filming of *Going Bye-Bye!*, Stan, Rogers and Terry began working on the script for another new short, eventually titled *Them Thar Hills*. Gus Meins began directing a new *Our Gang* short, *Mike Fright*, which *The Hollywood Reporter* of May 25 noted, "It will be the Gang's first 'musical,' calling for instrumental and vocal performances by Spanky, Scotty and Stymie." Hal Roach returned from his Alaskan vacation on June 4, and proudly told a reporter from *Variety* that he had bagged two grizzlies and four black bears.

On June 7, Roach signed Ray McCarey, Leo's younger brother. He had directed Laurel and Hardy in *Scram!* and *Pack Up Your Troubles* in 1932 and had spent 1933 in New York making shorts for Vitaphone. *The Hollywood Reporter* noted that this contract was expressly for feature films, and that McCarey "will pilot the next Laurel and Hardy production."

On June 9, Mae Busch, Charlie Hall and Billy Gilbert were signed by Roach for the new Laurel and Hardy short. Billy had just finished a long-term contract with Roach, during which he was a gag man and frequent supporting player in Laurel and Hardy and *Our Gang* shorts. He'd graduated to co-starring roles in Roach's series *The Taxi Boys* and a series of musical comedies teaming Gilbert with little Billy Bletcher as the German beer garden proprietors "The Schmaltz Brothers." Now freelancing, Gilbert likely received a better salary as a "per

Top Left: Stan and his new bride, Virginia Ruth Rogers Laurel, greet the Los Angeles press on April 7, 1934. *Top Right*: While work continued on the *Babes in Toyland* script, Stan and Babe quickly made two new short subjects. *Going Bye-Bye!* had them trying to escape the wrath of an escaped convict.... *Bottom*: ... while *Them Thar Hills* sent them into the mountains for Ollie's health, and accidentally getting drunk on "good old mountain water," actually booze left behind by some moonshiners.

Left: Cobb began work on his first film for Roach on May 7. The next day, Roach and his close friend, financier E.F. Hutton (*right*) left for an almost month-long hunting trip to Alaska. *Right*: On June 13, 1934, Roach announced that *Babes in Toyland* was back on the schedule, and Stan's suspended contract was extended.

diem" player for his turn as Ollie's physician in *Them Thar Hills* than he would have received under contract.

On June 12, Roach renewed contracts with Thelma Todd and Patsy Kelly for a new series of eight shorts. However, the most important development of that day was that Roach put *Babes in Toyland* back into work. On June 13, *Daily Variety* reported:

> "BABES IN TOYLAND" UP AGAIN FOR LAUREL AND HARDY
> Hal Roach's proposed "Babes in Toyland" starring Laurel and Hardy is on the fire again. It is now planned to start production the middle of July. Yesterday Raymond McCarey was engaged at the Culver City plant to direct it.
> Earlier, idea to make this picture was shelved with Roach and Metro execs declaring the time not then propitious.

The Hollywood Reporter also noted that the team was still planned to portray Simple Simon and the Pieman, with the *Los Angeles Times* adding that "it begins to look as if Thelma Todd and Patsy Kelly will be in the cast." The time for making the film was now propitious indeed.

Six months after buying the option to the film rights for *Babes in Toyland*, Roach had very little to show for his investment. But finally, Stan's alimony and marital situation seemed to have calmed down; he and Babe had finished one short and were in the middle of filming another. As soon as they finished *Them Thar Hills* on June 20, they could at last begin to focus on the studio's ambitious new musical feature, one which, if made carefully, would please the Loews executives, Stan and Babe, Hal Roach, and audiences everywhere.

Chapter 10

"Babes" Back in Business

The big news in Hollywood in June 1934 was the establishment of the Production Code Administration, inaugurated on June 13 and headed by Joseph Ignatius Breen, a tough Irish Catholic and former newspaper reporter.

The PCA was a division of the Motion Picture Producers and Distributors of America, which had been formed in 1922 to ensure that movies had a clean moral tone, and that the performers in them behaved properly offscreen. The MPPDA was headed by former Postmaster General Will H. Hays, who was an enthusiastic spokesman for the movie industry, but not very effective as a censor.

As we've noted, with the coming of the Depression, studio heads were desperate to keep people coming to movie theaters, and in 1930 they began making films that were provocative, and sometimes downright salacious. Even today, films such as *Safe in Hell* (1931) with Dorothy Mackaill, *Red-Headed Woman* (1932) starring Jean Harlow, *Three on a Match* (1932) with Ann Dvorak, and *Baby Face* (1933) starring Barbara Stanwyck are surprisingly frank and even shocking in their depictions of sexual situations and substance abuse.

Will Hays had given studios a list of "Don'ts and Be Carefuls" in 1927, but they were largely ignored, with studios submitting only about 20 percent of their scripts to the MPPDA before they were filmed. The onslaught of suggestive and controversial films in 1933 triggered the formation of the Production Code Administration – and unlike previous attempts to censor movies, the rules of the PCA were binding. Starting July 1, 1934, no film could be exhibited in the United States without the MPPDA seal of approval; any attempt to do so would result in a fine to the studio of $25,000. The Code would have a major impact on American movies until 1968.

Studio chiefs were very nervous about this new development, wondering if dozens of stories they'd bought would now be unusable.

The Code would have little effect on most of the output of the Hal Roach Studios, but it did mean that its scripts had to be submitted to "the Breen office" before they could be produced. It likely meant the end of Roach's plan to produce *Lysistrata*, at least with Aristophanes' story. However, the Code would probably not bring about any changes to *Babes in Toyland*. There was already no way that anyone could create a suitable picture from the 1903 libretto, littered as it was with attempted murders on children, and adults being dispatched by poison and volcano.

Left: Joseph I. Breen, chief censor of the new, and immediately very powerful, Production Code Administration.

Left: Handsome Henry Kleinbach transformed himself into evil Squire Cribbs each night when he performed in *The Drunkard*. *Right*: The Theatre Mart, at 605 North Juanita in Los Angeles, presented *The Drunkard* from 1933 through 1959.

Roach was now so enthusiastic about *Babes in Toyland* that he told Edwin Schallert of the *Los Angeles Times* that he wanted to do one big musical each year. He was planning to make musical films of *Robin Hood*, and of the 1843 Michael Balfe operetta *The Bohemian Girl*. Frank Butler was exercising his new power as head of the scenario department by assigning Nick Grindé (pronounced Grin-DAY) to work on preparing the *Babes in Toyland* script with director Ray McCarey, with plans to start filming around July 15.

Grindé's full name was Harry Andrew Grindé, and he was born in Madison, Wisconsin on January 12, 1893. A graduate of the University of Wisconsin at Madison, Nick was working on a North Dakota farm in 1917, but by 1920 he was in Hollywood, working as an assistant director on films such as *Riders of the Dawn* for Zane Grey Pictures. Within a year, he'd worked for the Triangle, Universal and Selznick studios.

He landed at MGM in 1925, where he was an assistant director on big pictures such as *Excuse Me* starring Norma Shearer, and a director on more modest efforts like the Tim McCoy Westerns *Riders of the Dark* and *Beyond the Sierras* (both 1928). From mid-1928 through early 1931, he directed MGM musical shorts and a feature, *The Bishop Murder Case* (1929), starring Basil Rathbone. Early in 1934 he had directed an MGM Pete Smith short, *Vital Victuals*, and an RKO two-reeler starring Bert Lahr, *No More West*. That year, Grindé had also been a second unit director for MGM's *Tarzan and His Mate*. Frank Butler must have had some prior association with him, since he wasn't known prominently as a writer. His lone previous credit in that field was on the 1930 MGM Norma Shearer feature *The Divorcée* – a film which, coincidentally, would never have been approved by the Production Code Administration.

If certain vices could no longer be depicted in movies, alcohol, or at least some form of it, had become available again in the United States. This would eventually have a significant effect on *Babes in Toyland*. Two theater producers, Preston Shobe and Galt Bell, took advantage of the new freedom and reopened the defunct Theatre Mart in 1933 at 605 North Juanita in Los Angeles, turning it into a dinner theater, serving beer. It had been built by wealthy artist and theater patron Alice Pike Barney in 1928, using it as a forum for her own plays and those of other nascent playwrights. The building was declared unusable as a theater by the Los Angeles Fire Department in 1931; Shobe and Bell remodeled the venue and intended to open with a season of classic plays. Their initial offering, a revival of *The Drunkard* or *The Fallen Saved*, a melodrama written in 1844 by William Henry Smith, proved to be so popular that it continued to run, and run, and run – until October 17, 1959.

In its 1844 engagement, the play had been so successful that it brought about a reinvigoration of the temperance movement. However, at Shobe and Bell's Theatre Mart, one could imbibe, thanks to the Beer and Wine Revenue Act, signed by President Roosevelt on March 22, 1933. This allowed the manufacture, sale and consumption of beer and wine with a mere 3.2 percent alcohol content, not thought to be intoxicating.

The villain of *The Drunkard*, evil lawyer Squire Cribbs,

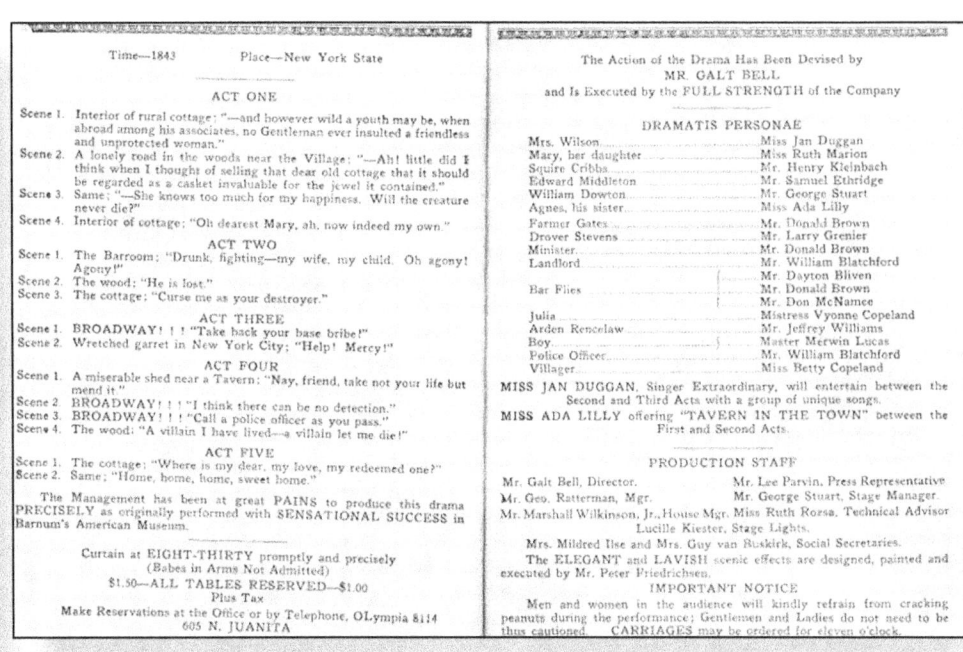

Left: This program is from the time when Henry Kleinbach, later Brandon, played Cribbs. *Right*: Of this cast, Jan Duggan, Samuel Ethridge, Ruth Marion, Larry Grenier, William Blatchford, Jeffrey Williams and Donald Brown appeared in W.C. Fields' 1934 Paramount feature *The Old-Fashioned Way*.

who sets the handsome hero on the road to ruin with alcohol, was played with gusto and a fair amount of scenery-chewing by a 21-year-old actor born in Berlin on June 8, 1912 as Heinrich von Kleinbach. Young Heinrich's family – Hugo R. Kleinbach, wife Hildagard, and older siblings Hugo O. and Maria – emigrated to the United States and arrived at Ellis Island on October 22, 1912; soon after, they had settled in Los Angeles. Heinrich was immediately Anglicized to Henry. His name was further altered in 1936 when he changed his surname to Brandon, a shorter version of his mother's maiden name, Brandonburg. Henry became active in school plays in elementary school and at Benjamin Franklin High School in Glendale. Attending Stanford University from 1928 to 1931, he continued in the school's dramatic productions.

By January 1932 Henry was performing at the Pasadena Playhouse in a production of *Berkeley Square*. By July, he was in *Peer Gynt*, doubling in the roles of "A Buttonmoulder" and "A Voice in the Darkness" in a cast that included future notables Lee J. Cobb, Douglass Montgomery (in the leading role), and Gloria Stuart. One year later, he was much more prominent in *The Drunkard* when it opened at the Theatre Mart on July 6, 1933.

In January 1981, Brandon recalled, "We didn't know when we opened *The Drunkard* that it would become a legend in the theater. It ran 26 and a half years. It was mainly because we very luckily opened just with the repeal of Prohibition. We were the first show where you could sit and have a glass of beer and hiss and boo and cheer, and make a fool of yourself, and have a good time. And the place became the place to go. All the movie stars used to come – it was quite a wonderful experience."

Within a couple of years, the program given to patrons included testimonials from famous performers. Mary Pickford wrote, "One of the gayest evenings I ever remember." Irvin S. Cobb commented, "The most fun I've had in 40 years." Billie Burke said, "I go again and again," while W.C. Fields enthused, "The greatest show on earth." In fact, Fields thought so highly of the show that he built a 1934 film, *The Old-Fashioned Way*, around it and included many of the Theatre Mart troupe in its cast. Since Fields himself took the part of Squire Cribbs, Henry did not appear in the movie, but he was paid to be a consultant to Fields.

In 1981, Brandon fondly recalled the many celebrities that came to see the show, and a few that were hoped for. "We'd peek through the hole in the curtain every night and say, 'My God, Cecil B. DeMille's out front,'" he said. "That became a running gag. But anyway, one night, somebody said, 'Hal Roach is out front.' And sure enough, he was."

On June 16, John Scott wrote in the *Los Angeles Times*, "One of the marvels of 'The Drunkard,' still running at the Theatre Mart, is the make-up of Squire Cribbs, villain of the piece. Henry Kleinbach is the gentleman who receives the hisses of the audience and he is a young man. Visitors who wander backstage usually ask to see the 'old meanie' and usually receive a shock when Kleinbach, minus make-up, greets them." Right around this time, Hal Roach came to see the show and would have exactly that reaction.

"He didn't see me backstage at all," Brandon continued,

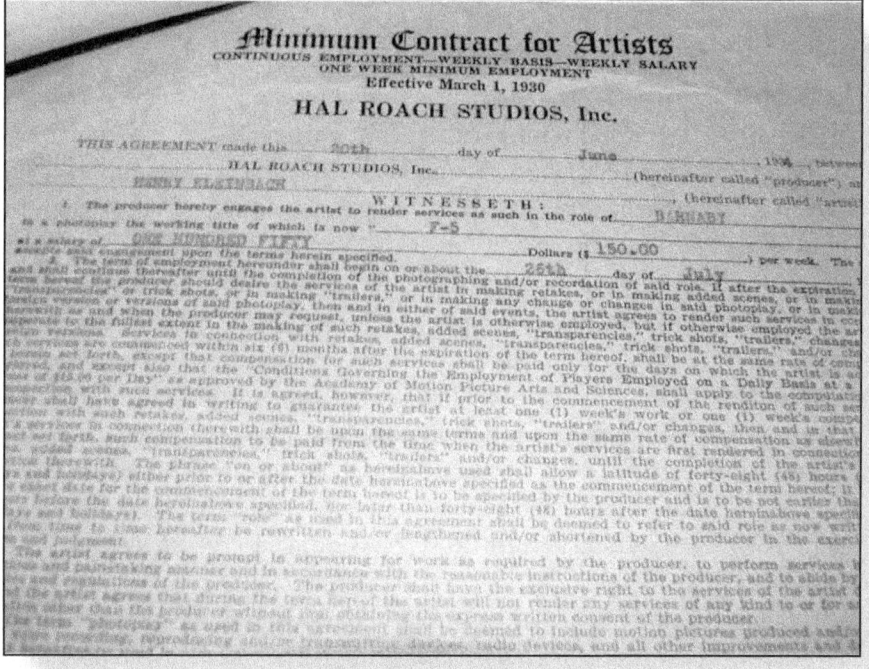

Top Left: Rudy Vallée, a fan of the show, recorded the song sung between acts. The sheet music provided a nice picture of the Theatre Mart's interior and stage; Henry is at extreme right. *Top Right:* Henry Kleinbach did not appear in *The Old Fashioned Way*, because Fields was playing his part of Squire Cribbs. Henry was, however, paid as a consultant. *Bottom Right*: On June 20, 1934, the just-turned-22-year-old actor signed a contract to perform in *Babes in Toyland* for $150 per week. *Bottom Left*: Henry's friend from the Pasadena Playhouse, Corliss McGee, designed Barnaby's costume. Sadly, he died at 27 on June 7, 1935.

"he just thought I was an old man. Most of the people who used to come to our dressing rooms used to come in and say, 'Look, I've got work for you!' And they were all a little drunk; we very soon found out that didn't mean a damn thing. They were just indulging themselves. But Mr. Roach did that nice thing – he called up the theater, and asked me to come in and see him. I played this old man in the play, Squire Cribbs, the villain. And I walked into his office, and I'll never forget the look on his face. He said, 'You're not that old son of a bitch I saw in the play last night!' I said, 'Yes I am, Mr. Roach.' And he said, 'How are we gonna make you up to look like an old man?'"

Hal Roach never shied away from a challenge, and knew he would find a way to make the young actor look convincing as an old one. (Studio publicity articles would describe the Barnaby character as "a 68-year-old man.") Brandon recalled, "Makeup was a little primitive in those days. Jack Casey was the head of makeup at Roach's. He didn't do the makeup – he couldn't do it! But he was the head of the department, and he knew a wonderful old guy who had been head of makeup at Paramount, Jim Collins. Jim used all sorts of primitive methods, but he turned my young face into an old face. He did things like putting glasses on me, and putting on a little chin piece – you know, to age me.

"They made several tests, and finally after about the third test, it worked out so that they could photograph me. Mr. Roach liked what I was doing in *The Drunkard*, and he wanted that same kind of overacting. 'Cause, you know, this is for the kids, and it had to be larger than life. Roach said, 'I want exactly what you're doing on that stage. I want that same old man.' And that's the way it worked out. I never went to see rushes during the picture – I don't think there was time – but I saw my tests, that I can remember. It was a scene from the script. This wasn't really my first film; I'd had a one-day job in DeMille's *The Sign of the Cross* a couple of years before, but that was nothing much. So this was really my debut."

On June 20, Hal Roach Studios, Inc. made an agreement with Henry Kleinbach. It was a "Minimum Contract for Artists... Weekly Salary – One Week Minimum Employment." He was to play the role of Barnaby at a salary of $150.00 per week, to start on July 26. The checks were payable on Wednesdays for services rendered up to and including the preceding Sunday. (The payroll clerk at

Henry continued to please audiences and bedevil the other characters (here, the lovely daughter of the title character, played by Ruth Marion).

Top: The early makeup for Barnaby did not include his wire-rimmed glasses or his chin whiskers. *Bottom*: The Roach studio used this before-and-after photo to emphasize the extreme change wrought by the makeup.

Top Left: Frank Butler was chosen by Hal Roach to collaborate on the new script. *Bottom*: Nick Grindé, normally a director, worked with Frank Butler to fashion the new story. *Top Right*: Roach makeup department head Jack Casey, with the considerable help of Jim Collins at Paramount, transformed 22-year-old Kleinbach into a "68-year-old" villain. Here, Jack congratulates Henry on the creation of the final makeup.

the Roach lot was conveniently named Grace Cash.)

Henry took an active hand in creating his costuming. "They just had a wardrobe man at Roach," he said. "We knew that my wardrobe would have to be pretty eccentric, so I went over to the Pasadena Playhouse, and the scenic artist and costume designer there, Corliss McGee, drew up the sketches for my costumes just out of friendship. And those were the costumes that I used; they made those up at Western Costume, from those sketches. They were based on what I wore as Squire Cribbs in *The Drunkard*, except for Barnaby the hat was much taller. The costume only changed a little bit – with the lace on the cuffs."

Born in Denver, Colorado in 1908, Corliss McGee worked as a scenic designer for the Pasadena Playhouse and the Music Box theater in Hollywood, starting in 1930. For the latter theater, he created the sets for a 1930 staging of Moliere's *The Imaginary Invalid* and a 1933 production of four Grand Guinol playlets. Married to Ione McCallum in 1929, they had a son, Fritz, before divorcing on June 18, 1934. Corliss was working at the Harman-Ising cartoon studio at the time of his premature death at 27 in Los Angeles on June 7, 1935. McGee might well have been a good choice to design the scenery for *Babes in Toyland*; in October 1930, he had designed the sets for *The Poor Little Rich Girl* at the Pasadena Playhouse, taking his inspiration from children's storybooks.

Director Gus Meins, Stan, Charlotte Henry and Charlie Rogers. Charlie directed the Laurel and Hardy scenes, while Meins handled the rest.

"Because children love color, the settings are a riot of color," he said. "The backgrounds are hazy and fade off into nothingness while the foregrounds are elaborate and fanciful."

Henry Brandon had turned 22 twelve days before signing his Roach contract. For decades, he admired Roach's boldness in casting such a young actor in this important role. "It was very courageous of him to give me the part," he said. "But several of the old character men told me they were all mad because he gave the part to a young man – and I didn't have the courage to tell them that the part would have killed them. Because they ran me ragged! An old man couldn't have played it! Because they chased me for two weeks through those catacombs, and threw everything on the lot at me!"

One advantage of Brandon's youth was that he could continue to act in *The Drunkard* at night while filming during the day. "I lived in North Glendale, and it was a sleeper jump to Culver City," he recalled. "So I probably got up at five o'clock or six o'clock, and then got down there at seven, and the makeup took over an hour, and I had to be on the set at eight-thirty or nine. And then at the end of the day I was always praying they'd let me go, so I could get to the theater in time to do the show. And then home, and then four or five hours' sleep. But when you're young, you can do that." Playing the part of Barnaby would be very similar to the role of Squire Cribbs, since in *The Drunkard* the evil lawyer is seeking to evict an elderly widow and her charming daughter, as Barnaby attempts in *Babes in Toyland*.

Also signing a Roach studio contract for the film on June 20 was Virginia

Thelma Todd's niece, Shirley Todd, came for a visit, and Thelma took her on a tour of the set. Mother Peep's giant shoe was one of the most impressive structures. *Courtesy of Richard Finegan.*

Karns, who at this point was intended to play the Widow Piper for $125.00 per week. Born in Dayton, Ohio on May 30, 1907, Virginia studied music at the Cincinnati Conservatory and voice at Chicago Musical College. She began her professional career playing Shubert theaters in a stock company presenting *The Student Prince*, and toured with musical comedy troupes from 1925 to 1932. She occasionally sang on radio in New York City and in Cincinnati. Coming to Los Angeles in 1932, she found regular work on local radio stations and also made stage appearances.

In the early '30s, Virginia provided the singing voice in films for actresses who couldn't, among them Norma Shearer. She's onscreen in four films, all made at the Roach studio and released in 1934: *Four Parts* with Charley Chase as a Nurse; *Soup and Fish* with Thelma Todd and Patsy Kelly as "daughter;" the musical short *Music in Your Hair*, singing "Lover, Come Back to Me;" and of course singing "Toyland" in *Babes in Toyland*.

On June 22, Hal Roach was in Chicago, for a convention of MGM salesmen and distributors. Fred Quimby, who oversaw the sales of short subjects distributed by MGM, brought to Chicago a print of the first Irvin S. Cobb short. Newly completed, this would provide the sales force's first viewing of what was intended to be a series of seven shorts. With any luck, Cobb would achieve something like the popularity of Will Rogers, who was one of the top box-office attractions in the country in features for Fox.

Roach was certainly pinning his hopes on the success of this new series. He paid Cobb $5,000 per week – more than anyone else was earning at the studio, far surpassing Stan Laurel's salary, which was $3,500 per week, and more than the $2,000 he paid weekly to Babe Hardy and to himself.

Rogers was from Claremore, Oklahoma; Cobb was from Paducah, Kentucky. But while Rogers' humor was universal and based on relatable observations, Cobb's humor was strictly rooted in the south, and his personality was more like W.C. Fields. Furthermore, Cobb was anything but photogenic, being portly, balding and jowly, with thick lips and bushy eyebrows, while Rogers had a rugged handsomeness. The reaction by the salesmen and distributors to the Cobb short isn't precisely known, but an onslaught of publicity articles by and about Cobb began to appear in fan magazines, intended to whet the public's appetite for his forthcoming film appearances.

Roach immediately followed the Chicago convention with a meeting in New York with the Loews Incorporated executives, including Felix F. Feist, a former lyricist for popular songs, now an executive overseeing the sales of MGM-distributed shorts. Roach emerged with an agreement to make 32 two-reel comedies for the 1934-35 program and four feature films. He had already completed the first Irvin S. Cobb short, as well as one *Our Gang* and one Charley Chase comedy. Two of the features would star Laurel and Hardy (*Babes in Toyland* being one of them), and the other two would have "all-star casts with players from other studios as well as the MGM roster," according to *Film Daily*.

Roach was still trying to find a way to produce the bawdy *Lysistrata*; this would be much tamer than it would have been before the implementation of the Production Code, which was about to go into effect on July 1. *When Greek Meets Greek* was planned to start production on September 1, featuring Charley Chase, Thelma Todd, Patsy Kelly, Irvin S. Cobb, Benny Baker and the *Our Gang* kids as well as one non-contract player: Buster Keaton. Reporters were skeptical about the propriety of the racy original story, but Roach told them, "We will stick to our policy of making clean comedies for family trade." (Laurel and Hardy's latest short, *Them Thar Hills*, received approval from the PCA on July 13 despite having a lengthy scene of riotous drunkenness. It was given certificate number 32.)

Another major role for *Babes in Toyland* was cast on June 25, when the Roach studio sent a letter to Edwin Lester at the Behymer Artist Bureau in Los Angeles, confirming the engagement of "William Felix Knight for the part of Tom-Tom in our production tentatively titled F-5, for a period

Shirley Todd sits on a saucer.

of three weeks, his services to commence on or about July 25th, 1934."

Knight had been tested by the Roach studio back in January, so it was likely a relief to finally be signed for the picture in July. Although this would be the movie role of a lifetime for the young tenor, it was not a terribly remunerative one. The Roach letter continued, "For such services to be rendered by William Felix Knight, we agree to pay the sum of One Thousand Dollars ($1,000.00), Five Hundred Dollars ($500.00) of which amount shall be deducted by us for the training to be received by the artist."

Casting for *Babes in Toyland* continued into early July. On the 7th, Edwin Schallert wrote in the *Los Angeles Times*, "Months ago it was forecast that Charlotte Henry might appear in 'Babes in Toyland.' Now it's a fact. And the little girl, who appeared in 'Alice in Wonderland,' will be seen when the film is released as Bo-Peep. The contract was closed yesterday... The story is being prepared by Frank Butler and his staff. Laurel has also turned to writing, and is preparing in particular the material for Hardy and himself."

On July 9, Hal Roach closed a deal with Technicolor, Inc., to make a series of *Our Gang* shorts in the two-color process. This early version of Technicolor strongly emphasized green and orange hues; it wasn't a natural-looking color, but in its way it was pleasing. It was also obsolete, because Warner Bros. in April and May had produced a couple of two-reel comedies starring Leon Errol in the new and vastly improved three-strip process. *Service with a Smile* and *Good Morning, Eve* displayed the full range of color in vibrant hues and were a revelation to 1934 audiences. Another short in the new process, *La Cucuracha*, was produced by financier John Hay "Jock" Whitney and released by RKO in August 1934. (It would win the Academy Award for the Best Short Subject, Comedy for that year.) Since the two-color system's days were numbered, Roach might have gotten a bargain; the studio always had to be cost-conscious.

John Swallow was still overseeing the technical direction of the music for *Babes in Toyland*, ensuring that proper arrangements of Victor Herbert's music were being written and recorded by the large orchestra directed by Harry Jackson. However, as of July 9, someone else was not going to be directing, as detailed by *The Hollywood Reporter*: "Ray McCarey, who was set to direct *Babes in Toyland* for Roach studios, walked out yesterday, being unable to agree on story. McCarey, who has been directing shorts for the majors, was to have had this as his first feature directorial assignment, and wanted the story framed to suit him." Henry Brandon confided the reason for McCarey's departure in 1981:

"He and I had had a lot of conferences together. We worked quite a bit on how we wanted to do it, how he wanted me to do it. And then suddenly one day I went over and they said Ray was no longer on the lot. Then he phoned me and invited me to a football game, and while we were watching the football game – with his alma mater, Loyola – he told me what happened.

"He said he was in Roach's office, and Stan was there, and Ray was explaining something. He had his hand up in the air, and he noticed that the door had opened; Charlie Rogers walked in behind him, and Rogers was holding his nose and going 'Nyeeehhh...' Ray said his hand just described an arc and hit Rogers in the face! He said Mr. Roach wasn't watching – he had his head down, he was sort of thinking, and he looked up and said, 'What's going on here?' Nobody said anything. Then, the next day, he was told that Charlie Rogers would co-direct with him. So, he lost his temper and walked out on the job. He said, 'If I weren't a crazy Irishman, I could've just held out and they would've had to pay me off. I lost $12,000 by walking out!' I hated to see him go; he was a wonderful guy. But they brought in a wonderful guy named Gus Meins to take his place."

McCarey very soon got a job directing comedy shorts at Columbia. One of his first for the studio was *Men in Black* starring the Three Stooges as energetic but highly incompetent doctors running amok in a hospital; it was nominated for an Academy Award.

The announcement of McCarey's departure and Meins' replacement hit the trade papers on July 12. Meins had directed 113 shorts since 1922, but *Babes in Toyland* would be his first credit on a feature film. Roach moved the starting date of filming to August 2. Accordingly, several of the supporting players who had been scheduled to start their work on the film on July 25 were notified that their new first day would be August 6. The script was also being rewritten significantly, as Edwin Schallert noted in the *Los Angeles Times*:

"BABES IN TOYLAND" CHARACTERS SWITCHED
We now know just about what everybody of importance will play in "Babes in Toyland." Instead of impersonating Simple Simon and the Pieman, Stan Laurel and Oliver (Babe) Hardy will appear as Tweedle-dum and Tweedle-dee, two characters incidentally borrowed from "Alice in Wonderland." Felix Knight will play "Tom-Tom," Charlotte Henry "Bo-Peep," Henry Kleinbach, "Barnaby," and Virginia Karns, interestingly enough, "Mother Goose."

Despite the setback of McCarey's departure, Hal Roach continued to be actively involved in the film, and had a brilliant idea. The nursery rhyme for Tom-Tom went, "Tom-Tom, the Piper's son, stole a pig and away he run." Being the handsome hero in the reworked story, Tom-Tom couldn't actually steal the pig, but he could be accused of it – and Roach had a particular pig in mind. His polo-playing buddy, Walt Disney, had produced a Silly Symphony cartoon of the children's story *Three Little Pigs*. Upon its release on May 27, 1933, it had become a nationwide sensation.

"Who's Afraid of the Big Bad Wolf" was a song written for the cartoon by composer Frank Churchill and lyricist Ann Ronell. (Her other big hit was about as different as could be – the moody ballad "Willow Weep for Me.") The song had become a smash in records by the bands of Ben Bernie, Harry Reser, Don Bestor, and Victor Young. Depression audiences found it to be a happy gesture of defiance against economic hardship; they, too, were trying

Alice Moore as the Queen of Hearts strolls by her domicile, prominently adorned with a windmill.

to keep the wolf from the door. Roach wanted to use the song, along with Disney's porcine threesome. Employing the song in *Babes in Toyland* would be a departure from a score otherwise composed entirely by Victor Herbert, but Roach knew that the tune, along with Disney's trio of swine, would be recognized and appreciated by audiences, children and adults alike. On July 17, Roach wrote to Disney at his studio, at 2719 Hyperion Avenue in Los Angeles.

> Dear Walt:
> On the idea of using the Three Little Pigs in "BABES IN TOYLAND," that I talked to you about the other day, the only thing we would like from you is the right to use the theme music and possibly get the girls who sang the music or a sound track of their voices.
>
> We would use but a very small part of the music – just enough to introduce them. If the make-up on the children that I mentioned, does not work out satisfactorily, we will use three real little pigs, instead.
>
> Please let me know what you would like me to do about this. Kindest regards.
> Sincerely,
> Hal Roach

Disney responded ten days later, on July 27:

> Dear Hal:
>
> Answering your letter of July 17, you have our permission to use the characters and music from THE THREE LITTLE PIGS in your Laurel and Hardy feature, BABES IN TOYLAND, in the manner which you outlined to me, recently.
>
> However, our contract with Irving Berlin, Inc. is such that you will have to pay Berlin music royalties for the use of any music from the THREE LITTLE PIGS. I am sure you will have no trouble in making arrangements with them but if you should, please get in touch with us and we will see that you are taken care of properly.
>
> Please be assured that we are more than willing to cooperate with you on this and anything that might come up in the future, and this letter is more or less a form which is made necessary because of the many licensee contracts we have already entered into for the use of these characters.
>
> If you would like to use the original girls who did the voices, I would be glad to get them together for you or you may use any piece of the sound track, as well as any models of the characters. In other words, with my best regards, I am,
>
> Sincerely yours,
> Walt Disney

In these days of corporations being fiercely litigious and extremely protective of their copyrights and trademarks, Disney's easygoing cooperation – probably extending far beyond what Roach himself expected – is proof that Roach's gift

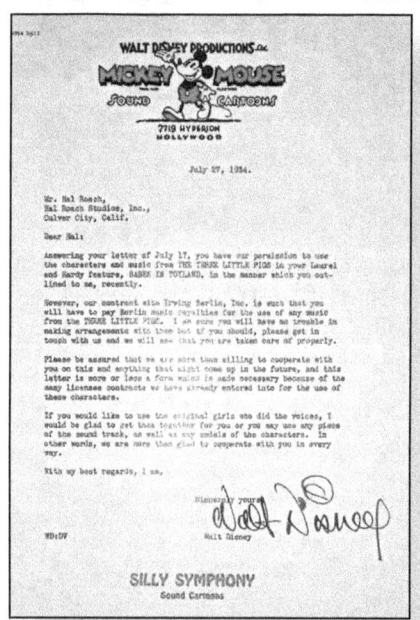

Bottom: Walt Disney very generously gave Hal Roach everything he wanted for *Babes in Toyland* and offered even more. *Top*: Stan and Babe each received a beautiful Disney drawing which featured three porcine co-stars in the film. © *The Walt Disney Company*.

Babe got his own drawing; perhaps he and Walt golfed or went to Santa Anita together. ©*The Walt Disney Company.*

for socializing paid off in many ways. As his longtime associate Richard W. Bann put it, "Hal Roach belonged to more country clubs, lodges, chapters, social brotherhoods, and professional organizations than most people could list together working as a group all day. Roach was an outgoing and affable person; he was hard-charging, active and enjoyed himself."

While other producers of shorts, notably Mack Sennett, complained that Disney's cartoons had run them out of business, Roach had no such objection. Knowing that kids were fond of Mickey Mouse and the Three Little Pigs, Roach did not see them as competition but instead incorporated them into *Babes in Toyland* even though they were not part of the Mother Goose stories. This was also proof of Roach's continuing involvement with the film. Far from being "out of the thing completely," he was, as usual, paying close attention.

During the time when Roach was waiting for Disney's reply, production continued. Edwin Schallert noted in the *Los Angeles Times* on July 19 that "Set construction has started for 'Babes in Toyland,' which will probably start filming before the first of the month." Even in an era when movie credits acknowledged only the department heads and none of the hundreds of people who worked under them, the Roach films' opening credits were especially skimpy. One would think that the set designers who created the amazing Toyland sets, among the most lavish that the studio ever built, would get some form of credit in the film, but this was not the case. Given their limited budgets, the people who created the sets for the Roach films, even going back to the mid-1920s, worked minor miracles, with beautiful settings that belied their modest budgets.

For a small studio, the Roach lot was remarkably well-equipped, its 19 acres filled with a costume department, a separate wardrobe building, dressing and makeup rooms, an art department, a huge planing mill, shops for plasterers, painters and prop makers, a property storage room, two scenery docks, and more.

Evidently a chief designer for the sets was Chris E. Christensen, born in Denmark on September 4, 1895. He had been working for Roach since 1920 and possibly earlier; his job classification was variously given as "technical chief," "technical director" and "technical support." Later, his position was refined to being the head of the construction department. Another designer who was on the lot at the time was John DuCasse Schulze. Born in Nokomis, Illinois on April 23, 1876, Schulze was 58 at the time *Babes* was filmed, and had been in pictures since 1918, first as a technical director, then as an art director since 1921. He'd worked on Mary Pickford's *Little Annie Rooney* (1925) and *My Best Girl* (1927), followed by a stint at Fox in 1930 and '31. Sometimes credited as Jack Schulze, in the early '30s he was a freelancer working for a variety of small studios; his recent credits included *Hearts of Humanity* for Majestic Pictures, *Tomorrow's Children* for Bryan Foy Productions, and *The Count of Monte Cristo* for Reliance Pictures.

The Old Woman's shoe may well have been inspired by a popular restaurant on Colorado Boulevard in Pasadena, the Mother Goose Pantry. Built in 1927, the restaurant resembled a giant shoe; it had two levels of dining, and was augmented by a painted sign showing Mother astride her goose; this rotated on a track around the top of the building. Robert Fennally "Slim" Gragg, who had been at the Roach lot since 1926 as a carpenter and assistant with special effects, oversaw the construction of the *Babes in Toyland* shoe; many years later, as a hobby he carved wooden miniature recreations of the set, including a remarkably detailed replica of the shoe.

Three draftsmen put the ideas for the sets on blueprints for the construction crew. Building the sets were, according to the payrolls, six laborers, 15 carpenters, 15 "carpenter laborers," and 26 "laborer carpenters." What the precise difference was we don't know, but in any event it was a large crew for the Roach lot. Working under paint foreman Jim Follett and his assistant L. R. Woods was a crew of 30 painters. Other sections of the sets were made by plasterers George McGonigle and B.G. Allen and "cement man" C. Angel. They were further dressed by drapers Al Aronson and Ralph Campbell and upholsterers Arthur Anderson and W. F. Hoffman. Any needed changes to the sets or their furnishings during filming were handled by a 16-man "swing gang."

Five mechanics were also on hand. Whatever props needed to be bought were purchased by property agents W. L. Stevens and James Harris, but most of them were made at the lot by a six-man prop crew, headed by longtime Roach employees Bob Sanders and Charlie Oelze; Charlie was renowned for the many unusual props and vehicles he'd made for the *Our Gang* series. On July 28, *Film Daily* noted, "Four six-hour shifts of carpenters and other artisans are being used at the Hal Roach studios to complete the 'Babes in Toyland' set. Two hundred extra mechanics have been added to the regular staff. Production of the Laurel and Hardy feature is scheduled to start Aug. 2."

The director of publicity at the Roach lot in 1934 was Samuel Washington Bert Cohn, who had previously been a newspaper reporter in Seattle and Portland. He opened an advertising and publicity agency in Spokane and wrote the first column publicizing movies and their stars in 1909 for the *Seattle Times*. Like other publicity men of his time, he was prone to some wild exaggerations for public consumption, but for what it's worth, here's what he wrote for the *Babes in Toyland* "Campaign Book," which was filled with behind-the-scenes articles and prefabricated rave reviews that theater managers could submit to their local newspapers:

> Statistical hounds and movie fans alike may be interested in learning some astounding facts relative to the building materials and electrical energy that goes into the making of a feature production. Some authentic figures on this subject were recently compiled by the producer of "Babes in Toyland," the Hal Roach-MGM picturizaton of the Victor Herbert operetta, which is now showing at the ------------Theatre.
>
> Following are the statistics:
>
> The weight of the nails used in constructing the sets and properties for this elaborate spectacle totaled 7,000 lbs. Also used were:
>
> Slightly more than 1700 gallons of various kinds of paint and varnishes with a total weight of 20,400 lbs.
>
> 196,000 square feet of lumber weighing 588,000 lbs.
>
> 240,000 square feet of wall board
>
> 192,000 pounds of plaster
>
> 80,000 square feet of chicken wire
>
> 80,000 square feet of burlap

Philip K. Scheuer of the *Los Angeles Times* toured the Toyland set during the filming and wrote about it enthusiastically:

> Hal Roach has caused a dream to come true. The dream is any child's, the coming-true a vast and enchanting nursery-rhyme town which covers two full stages, a space 250x440 ft., in Culver City...
>
> The artisans who work movie magic have really outdone themselves.
>
> Some thirty dwellings line the little street, each a magnified representation from some fairy tale: An ark, a toy factory, a shoe lived in by the Widow Peep, with a window in the toe; a doll's house with walls that swing open, a collapsible house of blocks, a jack-in-the-box, a police station inside a drum, a school with giant pencils for pillars, inkstands beside the entrance and walls like slates.

The only run-down dwelling in Toyland is, of course, Barnaby's lair. Jean Darling and Johnny Downs as Curly Locks and Boy Blue will probably want to vacate the premises soon.

There were also the dwellings of the Three Little Pigs, faithfully built of straw, sticks and bricks, not to mention several walkways with steps and paving stones. A giant teacup, saucer and plates were behind the pigs' houses. A balloon man lived, appropriately, in a giant, shiny round house, and another dwelling shaped like a ball had a mysterious face panted on its front, with the mouth as the doorway. The Toyland streetlights were statues of candles, which were aflame during the nighttime sequences. The entire town square was adorned with lots of white picket fences, gardens with tall sunflowers and little sculptures of gnomes and mushrooms. A large circular pond was in the center of the town square, with a maypole behind it. Along with the massive set showing the exteriors of these fanciful Toyland buildings, there were the interior sets of Mother Peep's shoe, and the Toy Factory workshop, storage area and warehouse.

The only dark building in a town that otherwise radiated light was Barnaby's house, a crooked house with a shingled roof, a misshapen front door, a dead tree in front, and an unkempt patch of grass. (Walking in a stooped manner and brandishing a gnarled tree limb for a cane, Barnaby seems to be the embodiment of "The Crooked Little Man" in the Mother Goose rhyme.) The interior of "Barnaby Hall" was likewise spare, with a fireplace that looked more like a pit, strange animal heads mounted on the wall, and plain wooden tables and chairs. There were also the massive Bogeyland sets, starting with the stream that carried unfortunate miscreants on a raft from the gates of Toyland to this land of exiles.

The interior sets of the Bogeyland caves were huge – one was either about 30 feet tall or partially a matte painting – with cliffs, steps, and stalactites growing ominously from the cave ceiling.

All of the sets were filled with inventive props. Mother Peep's shoe had a small kitchen stocked with utensils; a grandfather clock with a painted smiling face was next to the front door. The toy factory warehouse had a half-dozen long shelves filled with little circus train cars, building blocks, a fire engine, tambourines, soldiers carrying tubas, little horses drawing milk wagons and a toy ocean liner.

The sets were painted in color, perhaps with the hope that Roach would film them in the two-color Technicolor process for which he had recently closed a deal. Henry Brandon recalled, "That set was an enormous thing, and it was in beautiful colors that they use in children's books; you know, the bright blues and bright scarlets. It was such a shame that color filming wasn't in yet, because it was so exciting just to walk on and see all these colors. They were beautifully done."

Stan Laurel felt the same, as he expressed to fans in letters in the early '60s: "I've always felt that 'Babes In Toyland' should have been made in Color, the sets to actually see were really beautiful. [They] had colors of the rainbow like a story book picture effect. The matter was discussed at the time, but due to expensive cost of color photography then, it was decided [to film it in] Black & White. Being shot on black & white film, it lost a lot of glamour & turned out very disappointing. 'Fra Diavolo' too should have been in color, also 'Bohemian Girl' & 'Bonnie Scotland.'"

There are several reasons why the film was made in black and white. Entire features made in the two-color process had not proven popular enough to justify the extra cost. The last one had been Warners' *Mystery of the Wax Museum*, released a year and a half earlier, in February 1933. The color film stock was very slow and required extra light. It was already difficult to properly illuminate the massive Toyland set. The figures given in Roach publicity releases are no doubt inflated, but the official studio line was this:

"Despite the fact that the Culver City plant of the Roach studios is conceded to be one of the best equipped in all filmland, it was found necessary to rent and purchase hundreds of extra sun arcs and other electrical lamps and to lease additional generator trucks in order to supply the vast amount of illumination required to light up the mammoth sets used in this feature picture. A total of 2,952,000 watts per hour were generated to illuminate the sets of 'Babes in Toyland.' This energy was consumed in burning 912 gigantic lamps ranging in size from massive sun arcs to baby spots. Thousands of cities and towns in the United States use less wattage and possess fewer illuminating devices than this."

Ultimately, Roach didn't make any *Our Gang* comedies in color, and didn't experiment with color film until 1937, when he produced a short in Cinecolor, *Constance Bennett Presents Her Daily Beauty Rituals*. He tried making some Cinecolor films again in 1947-48 (*Curley, Who Killed Doc Robbin?, The Fabulous Joe*), but as he said to me in 1981, "It was a lousy color!" Because the film was shot by two separate units, cameraman Francis Corby, filming the "plot" scenes with director Gus Meins, had to ensure that his lighting matched that of Art Lloyd, who was shooting the Laurel and Hardy scenes under Charlie Rogers' direction. Stan preferred a bright, even light all over the set, which engendered a happy, sunny look conducive to laughter. This also ensured that whenever the boys began ad-libbing, they would be properly lit no matter where they moved around the set.

Stan had another reason for wanting bright, hot light. At age 44, the rigors of a tough career in vaudeville, and being a four-pack-a-day smoker, were showing in his face. Lines in the face were not in keeping with his childlike character. As Art Lloyd's widow, Venice, recalled in 1980, "Art would be dying to do something artistic, but it was very seldom that he got the chance. Stan wouldn't let Art put any contours into his face; he made Art photograph him so that he looked absolutely white — and you don't get any awards for photography that way. Stan would say, 'Now, wash me out, Artie. No shadows. I want to be flat-faced, and as long as you do that, you're my cameraman.'

"Art would take all kinds of time lighting the girls, and sometimes they'd go out on location and he could get some good photography. But as far as putting a shadow into the face on Stan and Babe, I'll tell you, they wouldn't have it. Still, Art was very fond of Stan. He'd say, 'Well, I'll never win an Academy Award, but I'll sure please Stan Laurel.'"

Around July 21, the Roach studio prepared a list of actors cast in the film and their salaries:

• Barnaby – Henry Kleinbach - $150.00 per week for 3 weeks

• Widow Piper – Margaret Seddon - $350.00 per week – Two week guarantee

• Bo-Peep – Charlotte Henry - $875.00 for picture

• Tom-Tom – Felix Knight - $500.00 for picture – Five week guarantee - $100.00 per week thereafter

• Toy-Maker – Wm Burress - $100 per day for three or four days

• King Cole – Kewpie Morgan - $50.00 per day – 1 week approximately

• Santa Claus – Ferdinand Munier - $75.00 per day – 4

days to 1 week
- Chief of Police – Billy Bletcher -- $125.00 per week – 3 weeks
- Mother Goose – Virginia Karns - $125.00 per week – 3 weeks approximately
- Candle Snuffer – Gus Leonard - $75.00 per week for picture.
- 3 Little Pigs – [No names listed] - $7.50 per day for picture – each
- Jack and Jill - $75.00 per week for picture – each 3 Characters in Doll House - $66.00 per week for picture – each
- Queen of Hearts – Alice Moore - $75.00 per week for picture
- Little Red Riding Hood – Sarah Dudley - $66.00 per week for picture
- Little Boy Blue – Johnny Downs - $100.00 per week for picture
- Contrary Mary – Marie Wilson - $68.00 per week for picture
- Jack Horner – Sumner Getchel - $75.00 per week for picture
- Barnaby's Henchman – John George - $100.00 per week for picture
- Cat & the Fiddle – Pete Gordon - $75.00 per week for picture
- 3 Policemen – 1 – Richard Powell - $100.00 per week for picture;
    2 – Baldy Cooke - $75.00 per week for picture
    3 – Arthur Lovejoy - $66.00 per week for picture

Also cast and receiving basic salaries, generally "$66.00 per week for picture" were Charles Rogers as Simple Simon, Buster Brody as a Jack in the Box, Scott Mattraw as a Town Cryer, Ann Brown as Sally Waters, Alice Dahl as Miss Muffet, Jean Darling as Curly Locks, Russell Coles as Tom Tucker, and Robert Hoover as Bobby Shaftoe.

The preparation of *Babes in Toyland* was running so smoothly that Hal Roach embarked on a four-day fishing vacation at Catalina Island.

Frank Butler and Nick Grindé, likely aided by Charlie Rogers, turned in an early, undated script and then a "Final Script" on July 28, although several key comedy scenes for Laurel and Hardy had yet to be written.

The scripts offer quite a few differences from the finished film. There was no storybook prologue in the script, which begins with a tour of the various fanciful buildings in Toyland. A cute running gag had Jack and Jill frequently tumbling down a hill and being soaked with their bucket of water. The widow who lives in the shoe is referred to in the earlier script as "Mrs. Piper," when she should be "Mrs.

As their stand-ins endure the lights while a shot in front of Barnaby's house is set up, Babe reads the paper and Stan chats with Charlie Hall – normally a supporting actor or carpenter but here probably a dialogue coach – and an unknown visitor.

Peep." This was corrected in the July 28 script.

We never see Laurel and Hardy's upstairs room in the film, except for their bed in the prologue. Notes the script, "The room is neat and trim – the odd thing about it being that there are two of everything. Side by side stand two old-fashioned wash-hand-stands with basins and jugs to match – one, however, much LARGER than the other. Over the large one there is a sign: DEE. Over the small one a sign: DUM." A deleted gag in the earlier script had L&H in bed, a beam of sunlight streaming through a window and burning Ollie's nose. He awakens and sees that Stan has a football player's nose guard protecting him.

Stan has very little dialogue in the scripts, and Ollie's is a bit too formal and flowery. When Stan brings up the fact that they owe the widow ten years' worth of room and board, Ollie says, "A thousand apologies, my dear Mrs. Peep, and a gentleman's word." The early script has no mention whatsoever of the "pee-wee," but the July 28 script mentions that "a Pee-Wee Stick routine," as yet unwritten, and the boys' entry into the Toymaker's workshop, will precede the scene with Barnaby proposing marriage. That scene was moved earlier into the proceedings, before Stan and Ollie awaken.

During the time when the "final" script was being written, on May 28, 1934, the Dionne Quintuplets were born and became a sensational news story. This was reflected in the July 28 script, when the Toymaker welcomes Santa

Claus into the shop. "Business is picking up, my boy!," Santa exults. "What with the depression being over and people going in for such large families... quintuplets, sextuplets and heaven knows what else!" The Toymaker responds, "Yes, I saw the other day where a woman had oct – octi – well, anyway, she had four pairs of twins, all at once!" This was probably decided to be a bit too topical and was deleted.

The Toymaker is much nicer in the script than the grouchy old codger in the movie. After the oversized soldiers are revealed, much to Santa Claus's consternation and causing significant damage to the workshop, the Toymaker says to Dum and Dee, sadly, "I'd hoped for better things of you boys – really I had." Stan, almost crying, says, "I suppose we're fired." The Toymaker responds, "No, Dum – I'm not going to fire you – but I am afraid I shall be forced to withhold the bonus I promised you. It will just about cover the damage. So if that's agreeable – I'm sorry, boys."

After Tom-Tom proposes to Bo-Peep, she's so excited that she runs home to Mother Peep and breathlessly rattles out all of her plans: "Everybody in Toyland's coming and there ought to be six bridesmaids and two little girls to scatter flowers and oh it's going to be the most marvelous wedding you ever saw, Tom-Tom's and mine, and oh I love him so and he said for me to tell you that he'd be over himself to ask you if it'll be all right and we're going to live in the little house his father left him although I don't like the drapes I can put up new ones that'll look perfectly adorable and he'll never let me lose my sheep again and maybe Ollie would give me away and Stan could be best man."

The boys' attempt to steal the mortgage papers by wheeling a very early Christmas present into Barnaby's house – actually Ollie in an oversized crate – is slightly different. Ollie explains the plan: "As soon as you get me inside, you leave, see! Then wait outside until he goes back to bed and the light goes out, see! Then count fifteen and give me the signal. Then I'll get out of the box and open the door for you, and we'll get the mortgage! Got that?" This is complicated by Stan's repeated inability to count to fifteen – he keeps running out of fingers. Both boys spoil the plan when Stan passes the crate as he leaves and cheerfully says, "Good-night, Ollie!" From the crate, Ollie says, "Good-ni..." and checks himself hastily. (In the film, he lifts up the lid and responds, "Good-night, Stannie!," before realizing his error and ducking back inside.)

The script offers a longer finish for this sequence. Through a knothole in the crate, Barnaby sees a small tuft of Ollie's hair and begins plucking hairs "as one would pluck a petal from a daisy," intoning, "She loves me – she loves me not –" and then running off to the police station, past Stan, who is still counting on his fingers. With Barnaby gone, Ollie brings Stan inside and they decide that the mortgage papers are probably hidden inside the chimney. Stan climbs inside and indeed finds the precious papers, coming back down with a shower of soot just as Barnaby and two policemen arrive. Caught red-handed, Stan and Ollie are sentenced to "be taken hence to the place appointed by Law and forthwith be ducked," according to a royal proclamation.

The ducking scene does not have the beginning and ending gag about Ollie's precious watch. Instead, Stan wears a large, heavy overcoat. After Ollie is ducked, Bo-Peep in an effort to free Stan and Ollie agrees to marry Barnaby, who withdraws the charges. Since Stan isn't going to be ducked, he smiles in relief and removes the overcoat. "Then I won't need this anymore," he says, revealing a life-preserver strapped around his chest.

The greatest change in a Laurel and Hardy scene is in the scripted version of the wedding. The wedding is to be performed by Old King Cole. When Bo-Peep is about to be unhappily wed to Barnaby, Ollie proposes that Stan take her place, dressed in her wedding gown. Stan vigorously objects, but Ollie knocks him out by hitting him on the head with his shoe. Ollie dresses the unconscious Stan in Bo-Peep's wedding gown, then takes him before the king. When the king asks if this is Little Bo-Peep, Ollie yanks Stan's head vigorously as if he's nodding in the affirmative. After the wedding is pronounced, Ollie tears up the mortgage paper, and Barnaby "with an oily smile," says, "And now to sip the honey from my little peach blossom." He lifts the veil, sees the still semi-conscious Stan, "looking particularly dumb and unattractive, still half out from the blow on the head," and has a "terrific reaction," described in the script as "His eyes nearly pop out of his head – and he goes nuts!"

As written, this scene has no real punch line and the idea of Stan substituting for Bo-Peep is given away right at the outset. In the film, we get instead the surprise reveal of Stan in the wedding dress – usually the biggest laugh-getter in the entire movie – and Ollie's mocking repetition of "Big bait catches big rat!" Since the wedding is performed in the film by a parson and not the king, Barnaby now has an exit line – "The king shall hear of this!"

This is followed by a scene in which Barnaby, humiliated, walks by the Toyland schoolhouse just as class is letting out. The children, with Herbert's "I Can't Do That Sum" underscoring the scene, poke fun at him and yell, "Did you ever get left at the altar?" When the idiotic Simple Simon approaches Barnaby and giggles, "You got left at

In a deleted scene, Barnaby is taunted by Simple Simon (Charlie Rogers) and children including Curly Locks (Jean Darling) after being left at the altar. *Photo courtesy Matthew Lydick; restoration by Jorge Finkielman.*

the altar, didn't you?," Barnaby grabs him by the lapels and hisses, "You idiot! Barnaby hasn't even started yet! Those two brats will feel the crush of my fingers before I'm through!" The Three Little Pigs then exit the schoolhouse, which gives Barnaby the idea to kidnap one of them. This was replaced by a scene in Barnaby's house where he calls his diminutive servant an "idiot, dolt, imbecile, pig," getting the inspiration for the pignapping, and placing incriminating evidence in Tom-Tom's house.

That house is the location for another deleted scene, a feast celebrating the triumph over Barnaby. "Enter, my friends," Tom-Tom exults, "and a feast fit for a king will be served you in less time than you can say 'Jack Robinson!' Stan takes him at his word, and very slowly says, "J-a-c-k-R-o-b-i-n-s-o-n!" He then turns and looks around to see if the feast is ready.

Just as a bulletin is being hammered to a wall of the Police Station, offering "one hundred golden crowns" for information leading to the person who pignapped Elmer, Stan and Ollie are discovering Elmer's hat and flute, and the sausages, without understanding their importance. Tom-Tom says, "I guess one of the little pigs has been here and forgotten them," and then plays "Country Dance" on the flute. This prompts a musical number in which Ollie wraps a Spanish shawl around his middle, with Stan doing the same with a tablecloth. Notes the script, "The two then go into a barn dance sort of cake-walk... they dance forward and back, swinging each other around by the fingertips." Ollie places the string of sausages around Tom-Tom's neck like a Hawaiian lei, inadvertently incriminating him just as Barnaby and two policemen burst into the room.

Barnaby gleefully accuses Tom: "Just as I anticipated! But I little thought he would be so brazen as to flaunt the gruesome souvenirs of his unspeakable crime before the eyes of decent folk!" Bo-Peep proclaims Tom's innocence to the Chief of Police, with the same speech that she gives to Old King Cole in the film.

The climactic battle between the Bogeymen seems much longer in the script. It is accompanied by "March of the Boogies" – possibly a newly-written melody. (In the film, it's scored by Herbert's "The Spider's Den" as well as "March of the Toys.") Stan and Ollie have another weapon – a keg of itch powder which they load into a cannon. It sprays the "Boogies," causing them to scratch feverishly as the wooden soldiers, referred to here as "the robots," advance upon them.

Barnaby's demise was depicted more definitively in the script. (In the film, he escapes into a house made of building blocks. It collapses on him, the blocks then spelling out A RAT.) The script proposes that Barnaby have Tom-Tom strapped to a giant rocket, but this plan is foiled. "Mechanically, implacably, the robots drive the hordes of Bogieland towards the water's edge. They turn – but the wall of steel presses on and, struggling and screaming, they are thrust into the crocodile-infested river.

"Barnaby is now bound to the rocket. Ollie and Stan apply one of the Boogies' torches. The rocket steaks out of the scene heavenwards. (Whistling scream of giant rocket.) All eyes turn upwards – following the fiery flight of the rocket – it flashes towards the stars. CAMERA MOVES in a semi-circle to show all the characters of our story as they stare upwards. Bo-Peep is safe in Tom-Tom's arms. As they watch intently – the rocket bursts in a shower of brilliant flaming stars. In letters of fire across the sky we read: AND THEY LIVED HAPPILY EVER AFTERWARDS. As the letters dim – FADE OUT."

Butler and Grindé's script was a vast improvement over Hal Roach's 1933 treatment and the 1903 Glen MacDonough original. The storyline was much more straightforward. (It omitted Jane and Alan, the Babes, but this also eliminated a lot of confusion.) The songs now had a more logical and meaningful placement, so that they furthered the story. This plot presented a more direct threat, the eviction of Mother Peep – to be prevented only by the unwanted marriage of Barnaby to her daughter, Bo-Peep. It eliminated the attempts to drown or otherwise do away with children and omitted the fiery death of the Toymaker. Barnaby no longer drank poison. There were no more toys with demonic souls being sprayed into them by a mysterious potion. Tom-Tom no longer faced the chopping block.

The new story introduced Santa Claus; it presented Christmas as a joyous holiday, not a day of fatalities for children, and made it much more prominent in the story. The new script introduced the invading Bogeymen, made the soldiers heroes, and gave the entire story an exciting and uplifting finish – with Herbert's "March of the Toys," the most exhilarating number in the score, properly placed as the finale.

Most importantly, Laurel and Hardy were now cast as good guys consistently, no longer henchmen to Barnaby. Their jobs in the toy factory provided a better occupation and setting for their comedy than they would have had as Simple Simon and the Pieman, especially since Stan's confusion over Santa's order turns out to be a blessing in disguise and resolves the story.

As now required, the script was submitted to the Association of Motion Picture Producers, the parent company of the Production Code Administration. Some inter-office correspondence survives regarding *Babes in Toyland*, much of it from board member Douglas Mackinnon, who had formerly helped to produce two-reel comedies for Educational Pictures. It reveals that as early as January 23, 1934, Mackinnon had conferred with Roach about the film. On August 2, Roach studios executive William Terhune sent the script to Mackinnon with a hopeful cover letter. It read in part:

> The remaining unfinished portion of this script is now being prepared and will be forwarded to you immediately upon its completion.
> Will you kindly go over this material and advise us by letter, after you have received the full and complete script, through the regular channels, as to whether or not it conflicts in any way with the tenets of the censorship code.

That same day, an otherwise unidentified "EEB" read the script and reported to Mackinnon:

> Doug,
> This starts off grand and would be a delightful thing, especially for children.
> However, I worry about the gruesome, frightening effect of Bogieland. They would

Gus Meins, atop the crane (in white) with cameraman Francis Corby, gives instructions to Felix Knight, Charlotte Henry and others for the "Don't Cry, Bo-Peep" number.

just scare an impressionable kid to death and make him have nightmares. I think the studio should give careful thought to that.

There is a shot of Stan in a wedding gown (he is impersonating Bo-Peep). The wedding gown is torn off and he stands in a pair of long, lacy underpants. What about this?

D-52-24. There is a yell of "Lynch him" (a despicable character).

There are other shouts and perhaps "Lynch him" is not needed – I think it would be better cut.

In several instances the characters of the THREE LITTLE PIGS and THE BIG BAD WOLF appear. Can they use those characters without Disney's permission?

EEB

Mackinnon went over the script, and quickly sent a letter to Henry Ginsberg at the Roach lot (who was higher on the executive totem pole than William Terhune), stating that the script "complies with the tenets of the Production Code and should encounter no reasonable censorship difficulties."

Mr. EEB need not have worried about Disney's permission, because as we've seen, Walt was more than happy to help his polo buddy Hal.

The cry of "Lynch him" was in fact deleted, replaced by "Let's get him!"

In the finished film, the Bogeymen scenes remain intact, as does Stan's wedding gown. It's surprising that the PCA raised no objection to Stan being married to Barnaby – possibly thanks to his cry of "I don't love him!"

By August 4, more of the script had been completed. Terhune sent Mackinnon "blue revision sheets (2) covering sequence numbers A-28-A, A-38-B, A-38-C for insertion at page 24," as well as a new portion, "pages 17 to 30 inclusive of Sequence E." Mackinnon replied on August 7 – once again, to Ginsberg – that all was well with the new material.

Although filming was supposed to begin on August 2, it appears that the "plot" scenes, directed by Gus Meins with Gordon Douglas as his assistant, started a couple of days later. Laurel and Hardy commenced their work on August 6, directed by Charlie Rogers with Chet Brandenburg assisting. *The Hollywood Reporter* noted on August 7, "More than 100 players and extras were at work yesterday, and an equal number are expected to be busy there for another week on the picture." *Daily Variety* on that same day noted that Laurel and Hardy had "started their end of the picture," and that two-year old Ricardo Cezon, usually a stand-in for Baby LeRoy at Paramount, had been signed to play the "Baby in the Tree-Top."

Young Henry Brandon was getting an education – really, a baptism of fire – learning how to adapt to the very unusual situation of working in two units with two different directors, and contending with Laurel and Hardy's departures from the script. "Charlie Rogers did all the Laurel and Hardy scenes, and Gus Meins did all the rest of it. Gus ended up directing all the scenes that the boys weren't in, and Charlie Rogers directed all the scenes that the boys were in, so it was a 50-50 directorial thing. Gus worked beautifully with the kids. We grew very fond of each other. He was a wonderful guy. Marvelous. Very sensitive and quiet. Charlie Rogers took his orders from Stan.

"My first day on the set, I was 22 years old, playing that old man. And I was pretty scared. But we had a very long scene to do – I don't remember which one it was. But they all sat down, and there was quite an entourage – mostly Stan's. Babe had no entourage at all, but Stannie had a lot of friends, a lot of co-workers, and they sat around and told jokes for about a half an hour. It was hilarious. And then they said, 'All right, let's look at the script.'

"So, they got out the script, which was, I thought, very well written – and they said, 'Well, let's throw that out, let's throw that out. Now you say that, and you say that, and Henry, you say that, and then I'll do that, and then Babe'll do that, and we'll do this, and you do that, and then, you will do that, and I will say this, and you'll do that.' Then Stannie got up and said, 'Okay, let's shoot it!' And I said, 'Aren't we going to rehearse?' And Stannie turned to me, and he said, 'Do you want to *spoil* it?' I never made that mistake again.

"The only things they rehearsed were the physical things. They never rehearsed the dialogue. With comedians it's that magic of the first time they want to capture. Very often, I guess they've proved themselves right, or they wouldn't do it – because if you rehearse comedy, you can rehearse it to death. And they had their whole set of reactions that they used, and they knew exactly what they would do."

Brandon said that this film provided the ideal transition for him from stage acting to film acting. "It was easy, because my characterization was based on my performance in *The Drunkard*. So it was very easy for me – if I was overacting, it was all right. Later on in pictures, I had to learn to cut it way down. But my overacting in *Babes in Toyland* was exactly what they wanted for the purposes of the story. So, it was really a very easy introduction to films for me."

As filming continued, the importance of *Babes in Toyland* to the survival of the Roach studio was made plain by the continued decrease in the market for short subjects. Henry Ginsberg joined other producers at a meeting of the Los Angeles clearance and zoning board, calling for the complete abolishment of dual-feature bills. Back in March, Ginsberg had rosily told the film trade press that MGM had opened 1,000 new accounts for the Roach studio's short comedies, and that the studio had spent $100,000 more on the 1933-34 product than on the previous season's output. But things had changed for the worse. Now, in August, he maintained that the Roach studio in its 1934-35 program showed a decrease of over $100,000 on the general payroll "compared to what was paid out during the heyday period of single [bills]. In the current year, Roach has reduced its short subject output to 32 [down from 40], all brought about by the dual bill system."

The board ruled to ban double-feature programs in Los Angeles, which for the Roach studio was a stay of execution. It was imperative that Roach show his financiers and distributors at MGM that he could make feature films at his little studio with the same quality and polish for which Leo's domain was renowned.

For now, Roach was confident enough to speculate that there would be "similar rulings in all parts of the country," which would revive the market for short subjects. He announced that he would soon begin an expansion of the studio, costing more than $100,000, and requiring seven new writers and "more than a score of skilled artisans."

He was also indulging his other interests, welcoming

as a guest to the studio Tommy Hitchcock, renowned as the world's greatest polo player. They both paid a visit to Arcadia and the site of the Santa Anita racetrack, which was nearing completion. This was another of Roach's pet projects, for which the producer had enlisted several investors. They paid $5,000 each for a cooperative ownership-membership privilege in the new Southern California Turf Club; among them were Babe Hardy, Harold Lloyd, Chico Marx, Robert Montgomery, director Frank Borzage, Fox executives Darryl Zanuck and Joseph Schenck, and Roach's close associate Arthur Loew.

Stan was settling in to his not-quite-yet marriage to Ruth. He had bought a house at 10353 Glenbarr Street in Cheviot Hills, two miles northwest of the Roach studio. Built in 1925, it had 4,650 square feet in two stories. Stan also set about furnishing it, writing a check on August 7 to Barker Bros., an upscale furniture store, for $4,127.15.

The next day, Hal Roach accepted delivery of a new airplane with a cruising speed of 210 miles an hour. He wanted to leave on a nonstop flight to New York for a meeting with Loews executives, accompanied by his polo star friend Eric Pedley. Unfortunately, his physician, Dr. Harry H. Wilson, advised him that he needed to go to a hospital and have his appendix removed immediately. Roach's pilot, Don Marshall, said that a propellor needed some repair, so he underwent the surgery.

August 9 saw the completion of the deal in which Walt Disney allowed the Three Little Pigs to be used in the film. If Roach had not been such a close friend of Walt's, he could have used the pigs anyway, as their story was not a Disney original. It dated to 1886, when it was published in "The Nursery Rhymes of England" by James Halliwell-Phillipps. *The Hollywood Reporter* stated, "Three children, dressed in pig disguise, will play the pigs, but Disney will furnish the same voices that were heard in his cartoon." Those voices were Pinto Colvig as "Practical Pig," Dorothy Compton as "Fifer Pig" and Mary Moder as "Fiddler Pig," but in *Babes in Toyland* they had no voices at all, save for a couple of squeals when Barnaby attempts to kidnap one of them.

In Roach's film, the porcine characters would be played by four-year-old Payne Johnson as Jiggs, the pig who built his house with bricks; 36-year-old little person Angelo Rossitto as Willie, with the house of sticks; and four-and-one-half-year-old Edward Earle Marsh as Elmer, creator of the house of straw. They were disguised in full-body costumes – overalls and long-sleeved shirts – with large rubber masks encasing their entire heads and false hands covering their own. They had already been manufactured when the studio held a casting call for these roles on

Four-year-old Payne Johnson didn't complain about the hot, heavy costume for "Jiggs" in an audition, and thus won the part. *Courtesy of Payne Johnson.*

August 10. It's likely that casting director Lawrence Tarver and his assistants, Ben Chapman and Louise Campbell, were auditioning the army of 30 to 40 kids.

Sam W.B. Cohn outdid himself when he wrote this outrageous press release for the film's Campaign Book:

"Various strange characters in 'Babes in Toyland' gain additional weirdness from masks, which when placed on the human head, not only change the features of the wearer but in addition lend to perfect animation in coordination with the facial muscles.

"These masks, used for the first time in the Hal Roach-MGM picturization of Victor Herbert's operetta, were developed by Bob Cowan, make-up expert. They are manufactured of a specially processed latex rubber composition, which is highly elastic and as thin as a sheet of paper.

"They fit tightly over the head, and have openings for the eyes, nostrils and mouth. As the masks are only five-thousandths of an inch thick where they cover the face, every expression and grimace made by the wearer is transmitted through the rubber and easily photographed.

Margaret Seddon played Mother Peep in the footage shot before Stan's accident.

"Any human face or animal head, grotesque or beautiful can be duplicated by these masks. In addition, their surface will retain make-up and paint, which permits further weird effects and expressions….

"Several hundred masks, most of this new type, were manufactured. Besides the masks, grotesque feet and hands were thus made, as well as heads and feet for 'Three Little Pigs,' 'Mickey Mouse' and other animal characters of the film. In some cases the masks were worn for hours with very little discomfort."

Well, it's true that Bob Cowan designed the masks and that they were made of latex rubber, but they certainly were not "five-thousands of an inch thick," and as anyone can see in watching the film, they did not coordinate with the facial expressions of their wearers. There were two sets of masks made for the pigs – a smiling one, and a grieving one, worn by Elmer when he's trapped in Barnaby's cellar, and by Willie and Jiggs when they sadly hang a wreath on the front door of the straw house in honor of their presumably deceased brother.

Payne Johnson was already a film veteran at age four; he had six siblings, and all seven kids were acting in the movies. *Babes in Toyland* was Payne's eleventh movie, in a career that had begun with an appearance as a baby in the 1930 MGM Joan Crawford feature *Paid*. At only one-and-one-half years old, he had an important role in the 1932 Barbara Stanwyck feature *So Big*. As her baby, he would respond to her question, "How big is the baby?" by opening his arms wide on cue, prompting her to say "Soooo big," and thus justifying the movie's title.

In 2011, he recalled how he won the part. "Hal Roach had a big casting call for young kids, and my mother took me to it," he said. "You'll see from the movie that the Three Little Pigs wore these big, very hot, rubber faces, about an inch thick, that fully enclosed your head in sweat – and some rubber hooves. We were supposed to look fat, so we had padding all around us under our costumes. My mother told me that there were 30 or 40 kids who put on the costumes, and of all these kids, I was the only one who didn't cry and make a fuss about it. Now, if you're the youngest of seven kids, you're used to getting knocked around – you survive. I was always just a happy kid, and I got the part."

The character of Mickey Mouse would be played mostly by a capuchin monkey supplied by Tony Campanaro, who lived with his wife Irma on Hal Roach's "Arnaz Ranch" property about a mile from the studio. Tony supplied the animals for the *Our Gang* shorts and other comedies, and prior to working in films had been an organ grinder with a trained monkey, Josephine. She attained immortality through her remarkable performance in Buster Keaton's 1928 feature film for MGM, *The Cameraman*. Josephine may have passed on by the time of *Babes in Toyland*; another capuchin monkey is prominent in the 1931 *Our Gang* short *Bargain Day*, and it's likely that this is the animal who was dressed in the Mickey Mouse costume.

Although the picture had just begun filming, Sam W. B. Cohn was already busy securing publicity for it. He wrote to Loews Incorporated in New York, and specifically to MGM publicist Howard Dietz – who is better remembered today for his concurrent career as the lyricist, with composer Arthur Schwartz, of such great standards as "Dancing in the Dark." Cohn was sending a batch of stills to Dietz, including several precious close-up portraits of Stan and Babe in costume – precious because "you probably realize how extremely difficult it is for us to get them in the gallery or to pose for special stills." Cohn also remarked that "After we 'shot' the portraits of Henry Kleinbach as 'Barnaby,' it was decided to change his make-up a trifle through the addition of a tiny whisp of beard and some odd-shaped spectacles." Also in the package were some stills of Laurel and Hardy with the "pee-wee" and stick, "in the hope that we might secure a commercial tie-up in connection with a toy novelty manufacturer."

The Hollywood Filmograph of August 11 noted that production was well underway, with Margaret Seddon featured as the Widow Piper (actually the Widow Peep). Born in Washington, D.C. on November 18, 1872 and 61 at the time of filming, she had been on Broadway in 1911 and began working in films in 1915, ultimately making more than 100. Her debut came with the Mary Pickford feature *The Dawn of a Tomorrow*. Other notable performances were in *Headin' Home* (1920) as Babe Ruth's mother; *Little Johnny Jones* (1923), starring comedian Johnny Hines, as Johnny's mother; and *Gentlemen Prefer Blondes* (1928), as the mother of Lorelei Lee, who was played by Ruth Taylor. Obviously, she specialized in "mother" roles. Her only other film at the Roach studio was *The Nickel-Hopper* (1926), starring Mabel Normand with Oliver Hardy in a supporting role.

The same issue of *Hollywood Filmograph* reported that "Alberta Dubin, a sweet little cutie who is very talented on screen, radio and stage, just finished a nice bit in 'Babes in Toyland,' at the Hal Roach Studios." Alberta later went by Roberta Linn, and on early TV was Lawrence Welk's first "champagne lady." In 2005 she wrote a memoir, *Not Now, Lord, I've Got Too Much to Do*. Of her days as a child actress, she wrote, "Eventually, at Hal Roach studios, I did *Babes in Toyland* with Laurel and Hardy. I was in the school scenes, with the kids, and I did the second series of the *Our Gang* comedies, plus several other movies." Rumors persist that there was a schoolroom sequence, in which several kids sang "I Can't Do the Sum," the song which Hal Roach remembered as "Put down six and carry two," and had planned for Laurel and Hardy to perform as Simple Simon and the Pieman. If this was filmed, it didn't survive the final cut, as proven by the cutting continuity which was prepared after the film had finished production.

Two other supporting players were former *Our Gang* kids Johnny Downs and Jean Darling, now 20 and 13 respectively, who played Little Boy Blue and Curly Locks. Their scenes in the film were very brief but generated a great deal of publicity in newspapers and fan magazines. *The Los Angeles Times* wrote, "They cried when they parted eight years ago. And Jean Darling and Johnny Downs, juvenile film players, almost cried when they were reunited yesterday." In truth, they were only cast in three pictures together in 1927; Johnny was leaving the gang as Jean was making her debut. They shared one notable movie, *Chicken Feed*, in which Johnny played a magician, "Professor Presto Misterioso," and Jean played his assistant. But – anything for publicity.

As Hal Roach recovered from his appendicitis surgery, his star comedian Charley Chase was having surgery on August 10 at the Hollywood Presbyterian Hospital. Because of ulcers caused by Chase's alcoholism, he'd had part of his stomach removed in early November 1929 at the Mayo Clinic, and now had more of it taken out, with his doctor cautioning him that he had to stop drinking or die; there wouldn't be enough stomach left to perform the

Johnny Downs and Jean Darling had only appeared in three silent *Our Gang* comedies together, but the publicity department made much of their "reunion."

surgery again.

The accidents continued. Hal Roach's wife Marguerite and daughter Margaret drove to visit him at the Good Samaritan hospital on the night of August 12, and on their return home, they suffered minor injuries in an auto collision. But another, much more costly, accident happened on Tuesday, August 14. *Daily Variety* told the full story:

STAN LAUREL OUT TWO WEEKS WITH BUSTED LEG

Stan Laurel tripped and fell off a raised platform while making a scene for 'Babes in Toyland' at Hal Roach Studios yesterday afternoon, sustaining torn muscles in his right leg that will lay him up for two weeks. Laurel was working in a scene with Babe Hardy and Henry Kleinbach.

Player was rushed to the Culver City

Felix Knight as Tom-Tom announces his engagement to Bo-Peep (Charlotte Henry). The news is celebrated by Scott Mattraw (Town Crier), Fred C. Holmes (Balloon Man), Hank Mann (Pieman), Jackie Lynn Taylor and Jerry Tucker (kids), Charlie Rogers (Simple Simon), Virginia Karns (Mother Goose), Jack Hill (Townsman), Johnny Downs (Little Boy Blue), Alice Moore (Queen of Hearts), Alice Dahl (Little Miss Muffet), Billy Bletcher (Chief of Police), Charlie Hall (Policeman), Maurice Murphy (Jack), Baldwin Cooke (Policeman), Tommy Bupp and Dickie Jones (Boys) – among others.

Emergency Hospital after the accident, and his leg was put in plaster cast by Dr. E. G. Replogle. He was later removed to his home.

Production will resume today, with company shooting around Laurel until Saturday, at which time the unit will stand by pending the return of the comedian. In the meantime, Roach will rush the next Irvin Cobb two-reeler into production ahead of original schedule.

Interruptions in the production of *Babes in Toyland* were becoming routine. First, there was the conflict between Laurel and Roach over Roach's proposed story. Then Stan had his "health problem" and withdrew from work because of Lois's excessive alimony. Next was a further delay thanks to Ray McCarey walking out and being replaced by Gus Meins. And now, Stan Laurel's torn ligaments would suspend the filming for two weeks.

This film seemed to be cursed.

Chapter 11

Limping Along

Because *Babes in Toyland* was being shot by two units, some filming could continue after Stan injured his leg. Gus Meins shot a few of the scenes that didn't need Stan and Babe, but even he could only work for a couple of days. Production ceased at midnight on Thursday, August 16, and would be resumed on Monday, August 27, by which time Stan was expected to be fully fit again.

As if Stan Laurel's torn ligaments in his right leg weren't enough to hobble the production, assistant director Gordon Douglas made his own contribution to the injured list. He was attending to something atop the Old Woman's Shoe, which was fifteen feet high. Suddenly he slid off, and tore a ligament in his *left* leg. *Daily Variety* wryly commented, "Lightning does strike twice in the same spot, picking the *Babes in Toyland* set at Roach for the dualling."

The pause in production was a relief for Henry Kleinbach, since he was still appearing in *The Drunkard* at the Theatre Mart every night after working on the movie all day. In 1981, he recalled, "We were told that the picture would stop production that night, and would be picked up in about ten days. They invoked the Act of God clause, which means that you're off salary. That's God's fault, not Hal Roach's or Stannie's or anyone else's. But that night, after *The Drunkard*, I thought I'd go out and celebrate, because I knew I had a week off or something.

"So, I went off with Larry Grenier, the second heavy in *The Drunkard*, who outweighed me by about 40 pounds, and George Ratterman, the bouncer-manager, who was a football player for Georgia Tech, and a guy named Burt Morris, who the following year became Wayne Morris and starred in *Kid Galahad* at Warners. Well, I was the baby; I was the little one of the group. And we went to a bar on Hollywood Boulevard called The Brass Rail, which was owned by an old fighter named Jim Jeffries. And we got a little drunker and a little drunker, and we got a little more obstreperous and a little more boisterous, and suddenly the four of us were in a fight with about twelve waiters, and a little bouncer named Tiny Eagan.

"Somewhere during the fight, I'd hit one of the waiters rather badly, and I was standing back, and he threw a sugar bowl with perfect aim and hit me right on the nose. And I felt something snap. Suddenly the police cars came up, and they trundled us all off to the Lincoln Heights jail.

"*The Drunkard* had become sort of a cult place, where everybody in Hollywood went to it. Every night there were movie stars. And so, I became a local celebrity. Well, the papers took it up, and they had pictures of me as the old villain, and a straight picture, and they said, 'Everyone

> **Comedian Hurt in Unrehearsed Fall on Stage**
>
> Stan Laurel, sober-faced comedian, stubbed his toe yesterday—and he will be laid up in the hospital in a plaster cast for two weeks.
>
> His accident will be costly, for within a few days suspension of production on his feature length comedy, in which he is co-starred with Oliver Hardy, will be necessary.
>
> The accident occurred yesterday on the set at the Hal Roach studio where the two are filming "Babes In Toyland." Laurel was supposed to run into a scene. His toe caught on an obstruction and felled him, tearing the ligaments in his leg.

On August 15, 1934, the *Los Angeles Times* ran a story about the injury to Stan Laurel's leg.

wanted to beat up on this old bastard and finally last night they did.' This went on for days, and the papers had a lot of fun with it."

One paper that had a measure of fun with the skirmish was the *Los Angeles Times*, which ran this story on August 18:

PLAY VILLAIN ARRESTED

Henry Kleinbach of "The Drunkard" Fame Seized With Three Others in Street Fight

For fifty-nine weeks that stirring melodrama, "The Drunkard," has played before capacity audiences in the little auditorium of the Theater Mart, and for fifty-nine weeks the audiences roundly hissed the villain, who in real life is Henry Kleinbach, 22 years of age, of 746 Cavanaugh Road.

Maybe this constant hissing finally got the better of Kleinbach, or maybe he was rehearsing a part for a new play, or maybe he wasn't doing anything at all, but in any event he and three others were arrested yesterday on charges of drunkenness following a battle which police reported started in a restaurant at 6321 Hollywood Boulevard and ended in the street in front of the place.

"FIGHTERS" LISTED

Those said to have been in the fight with Kleinbach are George R. Ratterman, 35, a theater manager, of 875 Sanborn avenue; Bert Morris, 20, actor, of 1718 Oakdale avenue, Pasadena, and Lawrence D. Grenier, 28, actor, of 605 North Juanita street. All except Ratterman appeared before Municipal Judge Aggeler in Sunrise Court and pleaded not guilty.

Their trial was set for 2 p.m. next Thursday. Ratterman was treated for bruises at the Hollywood Receiving Hospital.

FOUR ARRESTED

The four were arrested by Officer Bates, who said he found them with their clothing torn to shreds, but still battling vigorously.

Unable to quiet them alone, Bates called for assistance and Lloyd Eagar, an employee of the cafe, aided him.

Predictably, the laugh makers at the Hal Roach lot had a few at Henry's expense. He recalled, "About ten days later, when I came back, I had an old Chrysler, which had a cracked exhaust manifold, and we used to park around in back of the main buildings on the Roach lot. Everyone knew my old, old car because it had this cracked manifold, and it had a rather flatulent sound as I came in. Well, they were all waiting when I came back from jail. They all came out of their bungalows and applauded me, and made siren sounds; that was my welcome back to work. Everybody on the lot was tremendously amused – except Hal Roach. He came over and said, 'Not funny. No more barroom brawls.'

"I had a very straight nose at the beginning of filming. But suddenly that sugar bowl hit me and somewhere in the middle of the picture, my nose was way over here. See, it isn't straight now! The doctor couldn't get it quite straight. Fortunately, I wasn't playing Felix Knight's part, and I wasn't having to look beautiful, so they could cover the whole thing with makeup, and I got away with it."

Fortunately for Henry's reputation, the day after the *Los Angeles Times* ran the article about the Brass Rail fracas, the paper ran a complimentary article about his formula for not going stale in his long-running role in *The Drunkard*. He was quoted as saying, "When the part seems to become ridiculous, as nearly any part is apt to do after you've played it for months, I merely say to myself as I go on the stage, 'this audience has never seen this before.' If one can remember that what he is doing is new to his audience, it doesn't seem too hopelessly stale to him."

The trade papers provided a thorough documentation of Stan's recovery.

Daily Variety, August 21: "Stan Laurel, whose injury held up the picture, was at the studio yesterday with indications he will be through hobbling this week."

The Hollywood Reporter, August 28: "Laurel is unable to go to work in *Babes in Toyland* for a few days yet, but work on the picture resumed yesterday.

The Hollywood Reporter, August 30: "Stan Laurel will get back to work Monday in 'Babes in Toyland' at the Hal Roach lot."

Daily Variety, September 5: "Production on 'Babes in Toyland' was resumed at Hal Roach Studios yesterday, but stopped after a few scenes until next Monday [the 10th] at which time it's expected Stan Laurel will be able to work. Comedian was due back today, but suffered a setback over the weekend when he tried to navigate unsuccessfully on his bum leg."

Motion Picture Daily, September 5: "Unable to continue 'Babes in Toyland' without his services, the Hal Roach plant has closed to await the complete recovery of Stan Laurel, who recently injured his leg. All but contract players and necessary operating employees have been laid off."

The Hollywood Reporter, September 11: "Studio watchmen will furnish the only activity on the 'Babes in Toyland' sets again this week at Hal Roach's studio. Stan Laurel's leg is not yet well enough for work."

The Hollywood Reporter, September 13: "Stan Laurel threw away his crutches yesterday and appeared at the Roach studio, limping and using a cane. 'Babes in Toyland' is still on the shelf, awaiting his complete recovery."

Daily Variety, September 15: "'Babes in Toyland' is held up again for another week, with Stan Laurel's injured leg still talking back. Was to resume Monday, but now goes over until September 24th."

By September 18, Stan's lengthy recovery was causing serious problems at the Roach lot, not only on *Babes in Toyland*, but on the shorts which remained to be

On September 1, 1934, with Stan Laurel's injury yet to hold up production for another three weeks, either the Roach studio or MGM placed this hopeful full-page advertisement in the *Motion Picture Herald*.

completed. The Laurel and Hardy feature was becoming a giant headache for Roach. The producer was struggling to keep his studio doors open. His friend and fellow comedy producer Mack Sennett had lost his studio in 1933. The big studios were not immune to financial peril; Paramount and RKO were in receivership. The Fox studio was also suffering money problems, which would soon result in its merger with another studio, Twentith Century. Roach was fortunate to be distributing his movies through MGM, which would still make a profit in 1934, but far smaller than in previous years. With the depression in its fourth year, fewer and fewer people had money for a luxury such as going to the movies. Theaters had closed by the thousands, particularly in small towns which were such a vitally important part of Roach's audience. Things were tough enough without having the studio's star comedian on the injured list.

Roach was directly responsible for the livelihood of close to 500 people – actors, writers, film developers and cutters, projectionists, sound engineers, electricians, painters, bus drivers, mechanics, carpenters, watchmen, firemen, gardeners, janitors, the cooks and waitresses who ran the Our Gang Café, the *Our Gang* teacher Fern Carter, the gang maintaining Roach's ranch, and even the four studio gatemen. It was imperative that some films remained in production while Laurel recovered.

The Toyland set was so massive that it took up two of the studio's four stages. It couldn't be dismantled, so those stages were unused for over a month. Roach still needed to finish two-reelers with *Our Gang*, Thelma Todd and Patsy Kelly, Charley Chase, and Irvin S. Cobb. On September 18, *Motion Picture Daily* noted, "Roach's short subject schedule will be upset and Laurel's late return may force him to rent space at another studio." Fortunately, some good news arrived the next day.

Daily Variety, September 19: "Hal Roach schedule, which was knocked from pillar to post recently, resumes normal Monday [the 24th] and will progress without a halt until Christmas. The many times-postponed *Babes in Toyland* resumes on that day, with Stan Laurel's leg now reported Okay by doctors. 'Our Gang,' in hiatus for several months, gets going October 1st, and a second two-reeler from the same unit begins October 22nd. Another Todd-Kelly goes in October 8th, and another Charles Chase the week following."

Hal Roach should have celebrated the return to full production, but on September 21 he was resting at the Long Island home of his friend, executive Arthur Loew, having taken ill after a business meeting in New York.

Except for some animation being overseen by Kenneth Peach, filming on *Babes in Toyland* had been halted from August 17 to September 24, a total of 38 days. With Roach and MGM planning for a Christmas season release of the film, production now had to go into high gear.

Chapter 12

Rushing to Conclusion

As *Babes in Toyland* went back into production on September 24, a new cast member joined the company. Margaret Seddon had filmed some scenes with Stan and Babe early in August, but now she was replaced in the role of Mother Peep by Florence Roberts, a stage and film veteran who specialized in playing mothers – or grandmothers.

Late in 1933, she had appeared in Charley Chase's short *The Cracked Ice Man*, and she returned early in '34 to play the mother of identical Charley Chase quadruplets in *Four Parts*. No doubt her work was appreciated by Roach, and he may well have made the casting change. (Margaret Seddon next appeared in MGM's *David Copperfield*, and continued to work in talkies and radio dramas in the 1930s and '40s, making a notable contribution to Frank Capra's *Mr. Deeds Goes to Town* (1936), as one of the "pixilated" sisters with Margaret McWade. She is the matron in the fancy automobile that W.C. Fields attempts to repair in *The Bank Dick* (1940). Her last known credit was a television episode of *The Loretta Young Show* from September 1953, in which she worked when she was 80.)

Florence was in familiar surroundings with *Babes in Toyland*, because around the turn of the century, she had played Bo-Peep in a stage production, *The Moth and the Flame*, at the Fourpaugh Theatre in Philadelphia, where she was the leading lady of its repertory company for a decade.

She contributed some magnificent work to *Babes in Toyland*. In the scene where she begs Barnaby to reconsider marrying Bo-Peep, her performance is so earnest and heartfelt that she transforms a fantasy film into something utterly believable.

After all of the delays and setbacks, most of *Babes in Toyland* was filmed very quickly and efficiently – from September 24 to October 17, 1934, with Sundays off, meaning only 21 filming days. Shooting in two units no doubt expedited the production. The approval of the Production Code Administration was vitally important, and on October 5 Douglas Mackinnon wrote an inter-office memo that he had "attended story conference with Bill Terhune of Hal Roach studio about BABES IN TOYLAND."

Even though Henry Brandon would again be losing some precious hours of sleep, he enjoyed his return to the Roach studio and playing what studio publicity described as "68-year-old Barnaby, ugly and sinister villain."

Brandon recalled, "Gus Meins ended up directing all the scenes that the boys weren't in, and Charlie Rogers directed all the scenes that the boys were in, so it was a 50-50 directorial thing. I don't remember Stan telling Charlie Rogers how to set up a shot, but Charlie was completely subservient to him, so you know the inspiration all came from Stannie.

"I was a little nervous about working with them at first, but you get over that. It was very easy to get along with them. Hardy was very – you know, as fat people often are, very easygoing. Very easy to get along with. He just came and did his job, and let Stan do all the yelling and barking, and fighting with Hal Roach. Stan had a much larger salary, did you know that? But that didn't bother Hardy at all. He was very easygoing. Such a sweetheart. But Laurel was never disagreeable to me. He always treated me very well. Stan would direct me, to the extent of where to be positioned in a scene. And you wouldn't mind, because you knew damn well he knew what he was doing.

Brandon continued, "The script was not very strictly adhered to in their scenes. On the scenes without the boys, we stuck completely to the script. I wish I still had the script. It was a collaboration between Mr. Roach and a wonderful British guy named Frank Butler. Hugo Butler,

With Florence Roberts now playing Mother Peep, Gus Meins visits the set.

his son, is a very big screenwriter now. Frank Butler was always very elegant – always in beautifully tailored sport jackets. It was a beautiful script! It was really a fairy-tale script. But Stan and Babe did it their way, and who's to say they were wrong? It's a beautiful movie!

"They knew their craft so well they didn't have to rehearse it. It made it a little difficult on the other actors, but if somebody flubbed a line, somebody else would say it. They'd just improvise around it. You got into the routine of how they worked, and you learned your lines, and if you didn't get a cue, you'd say something else. They rarely shot a scene twice. If something went wrong with the camera or the sound, they could do it over again – but they wanted to do it once. They wanted to capture the magic of the first time.

Brandon had fond memories of his fellow cast members. "Felix Knight had a fantastic tenor voice," he said. "He got the part mainly on his voice. They tested several others; there was one young actor from Pasadena named Alec Courtney, who was a much better actor, but he didn't have one hundredth the voice. Years later, when I was working in New York, my mother went to the Metropolitan Opera; it was an opera called *The Abduction from the Seraglio*, and Felix was a lead in that. This young singer-actor, who sang these easy songs for an opera singer, later was a Metropolitan Opera star, which I think is kind of wonderful.

"Charlotte Henry had done *Alice in Wonderland* at Paramount, and that's

Gag man Frank Terry (*center*) had been a notorious gambler in his youth; Henry Kleinbach seems to have discovered something unusual in Frank's cards.

the reason she got this part. Roach had liked her in that. Oh, she was a lovely girl. She used to throw tea parties on Sunday afternoons – cocktail parties. I met a lot of Hollywood people there. Florence Roberts, who played Mother Peep – she was always at Charlotte's parties. She was a wonderful old actress, a lovely lady.

"And then there was Stannie's entourage. They were the original gofers. They didn't have that term in those days. But they ran and fetched, and they laughed and scratched, and made suggestions – most of which he threw out! They were old vaudevillians, most of 'em. Frank Terry, he was a little Cockney guy – very funny little guy.

"In the cast there was Alice Moore – she was the daughter of Olive Moore, a silent picture star. Lovely girl. She and Felix Knight got married about a year after we did the film. Gordon Douglas was the assistant director on *Babes in Toyland*. He later became a big director; he was under contract to Warners for years. I remember Chet Brandenburg, the other assistant director. He was a stunt man, too. He was a very nervous guy, because he and his brother used to do dynamite stunts. And they had it all timed – when they felt the rumble, they would jump in the air. But one day, they mistimed it. And he was a little bit shaky, like this, for the rest of his life."

Brandon noticed the off-screen harmony between Stan and Babe. "Laurel and Hardy got along wonderfully, because Babe never made waves," he said.

Left: The Mickey Mouse lookalike was a capuchin monkey owned by Roach studios animal trainer Tony Campanaro. The cat was played by Pete Gordon, a close friend of Stan Laurel's, who lived with him for a time after the divorce from Lois. *Right*: As Charlie Rogers and Felix Knight chat in the background, Charlotte Henry and Henry Kleinbach prove to be more cordial off-screen than on.

"Just got up and did it and went home. He knew exactly how to get along with Stan. Never made any trouble. He was a sweetheart.

"Mrs. Laurel was a fixture. I guess she enjoyed the camaraderie, you know. She was on the set every day. I can't remember a moment when she wasn't there – just there, being very pleasant.

"Everything was for laughs on the set. They horsed around a great deal. I think comics need that to keep up their energy; they need to be kept in that kind of a mood, so there was enormous laughter all the time on the set. I worked quite a bit with Bob Hope; Hope was a million laughs. Martin and Lewis – I worked in about three of their films. It was always fun working with them. Danny Kaye, though, was no fun at all; he's the only one. But Laurel and Hardy had that fun atmosphere – they were having a good time, and that transmitted itself to the screen."

Occasionally, the fun atmosphere got a little extreme, as Brandon remembered: "Stannie had a lot of fun pushing people in the pool. The only one he didn't push in was me, because it took an hour to make me up. He was a pretty shrewd businessman, and he knew it would hold up production if he pushed me in, because they had to put all that makeup on. I'd made up my mind that if he pushed me in, I'd grab him and pull him in with me.

"Stan was sued by one of the bit players. I've seen him in one scene in the movie, sitting there. A great big lummox. One day, this big dumb kid walked by, and Stan pushed him in. Well, he hurt his back or something, and a lawyer got hold of him. The doctor came and said this kid had a bad back. Well, you can't prove anything about backs, as they found out in the army. If you wanted to get out of a detail, you'd say that your back hurt. But he was kept on the picture, on a fairly decent salary for the whole run of it. So he just sat around. I'm sure they got off pretty cheap with him. I don't think he had a very good lawyer."

"You know, all this talk about all the democracy in Hollywood is, and always was, a bunch of bull. It's a completely stratified society. Usually according to your salary, unfortunately. But there was no caste system between those people. They were all old shoes. The Roach studio was the friendliest lot in Hollywood – well, that and Republic. They were small lots, and everybody got to know each other. Everybody said hello, and good morning – by name. It was never the same on the big lots, where it's impersonal, and all these units are shooting, and so forth. But they had the Our Gang Café, where everybody ate, just right there on Washington Boulevard.

"It was lovely – you'd drive on the lot, and the parking area was in back of this whole string of executive buildings. Everybody parked there, and they'd come out of their offices, the writers and so on, and pass the time of day. The other actors would come and visit on the set. Thelma Todd and Patsy Kelly – they were wonderful girls. Charley Chase was always coming in – and, you know, everything would stop. They'd watch the shooting and they'd comment on it. A lot of gags and funny stuff would go on and then we'd go back to work maybe in half an hour. And the assistant

Left: A goat-drawn milk wagon transports Charlotte around the set... *Right*: ... and takes her to the "New York Street" of the Roach studio's back lot.

director would be going crazy.

"The *Our Gang* kids were a lot of fun. Later, they wrote a bogeyman into an *Our Gang* comedy [*Our Gang Follies of 1938*], and I did it. Then of course, I worked with Spanky in *Trail of the Lonesome Pine*. He's the one I blew up in the steam shovel. Gordon Douglas, as I mentioned, was the assistant director on *Babes in Toyland*. He also directed that *Our Gang* episode. In fact, I think he suggested my doing that film.

"I think the most heartbreaking thing of all was when I came back from Europe in the early '60s, and I drove down to look at the lot – and found a big, empty space there. I just – I pulled up the car, and sat there and cried. Because they'd taken all those memories away."

Virginia Karns opens the film by stepping out of that massive storybook and singing "Toyland" (at least in complete prints with the prologue). Otherwise, she's seen mainly in crowd sequences, often carrying her goose. She spent more time on the film, and with Stan and Babe, than her modest role would indicate. Her friend Jim Kerkhoff, a longtime Laurel and Hardy devotee and scholar, knew Virginia for years, and he elaborates:

"Virginia told me that she made more in salary – $2,500 – than any of the other actors in the cast, except for Laurel and Hardy; that was due to her being on the picture longer than anyone else. Originally her contract called for her to play the old lady in the shoe, but when she reported to the set she was informed there had been a change and that she would sing the opening song as Mother Goose. (After working in stock companies and on radio, Virginia had sung 'Lover, Come Back to Me' in Hal Roach's musical short *Music in Your Hair*.) She was brought in when principal photography began in order to film the sequence, but it's not the opening scene everyone is familiar with in the film.

"The original opening featured Virginia sitting side-saddle on a large papier-maché goose that was hung from the rafters with wires. This was to be the extent of her involvement in the film. But Gus Meins and everyone took a look at the rushes and the wires holding Virginia and the fake goose were far too noticeable onscreen, which spoiled the shot. There was no way to fix the problem optically and no time remaining to figure out something else, since filming was scheduled to begin. So, Virginia was kept on during production, with the plan being to re-shoot the opening after all other scenes were completed."

Kerkhoff continued, "Gus Meins told her that since she would be on salary anyway, he'd use her in some scenes. One of these features her singing in the lost sheep number. She also did walk-ons with other cast members in large crowd scenes, and Virginia is one of the women in nightshirts, carrying a candle holder, at the conclusion of the film. (She held on to the candle holder as a keepsake, and it's still in the family.) They had devised the storybook idea when it came time to re-shoot the opening. However, you'll notice the goose walks out with her from the pages rather than her carrying it. The reason? Virginia said the plan was for her to hold the goose, but the goose didn't like that idea and kept biting her.

"Virginia said that her lifelong friendship with Stan and

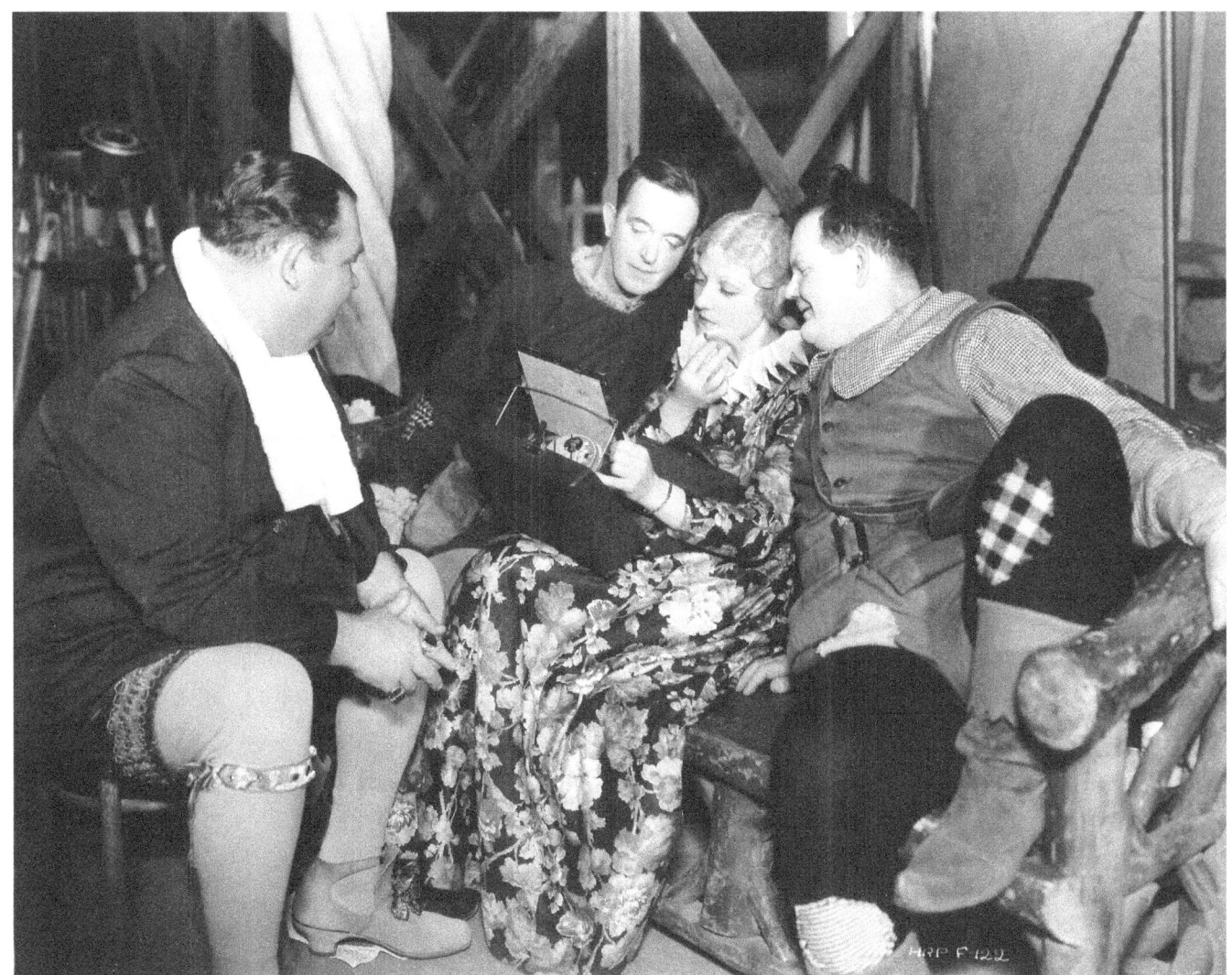

Kewpie Morgan, Stan and Babe watch Virginia Karns adjust her make-up.

Babe grew out of one of Stan's practical jokes. Stan's buddy Baldwin Cooke was a master at double-talk. He'd strike up a conversation and say things that sounded like they should make sense but didn't. They were taking a lunch break and Stan put Baldy up to sitting next to Virginia, to pull the double-talk routine on her. The anticipated outcome was that she would look totally confused, ask what he said, and then he'd go at it again. What they didn't know was that Virginia was a master of double-talk herself. She had learned it from comedian Joe Frisco when she toured in a musical stock company. So, Cooke sat down and struck up a conversation with her, making no sense whatsoever, but she caught on quickly to what was happening. When he stopped talking, Virginia responded by double-talking to him. She said that everyone was on the floor laughing, especially Babe and Stan. That completely endeared her to both of them."

Kerkhoff relates that Stan and Babe continued their friendship with Virginia and her husband Bill Patterson, even though they had worked on only one film together. "When they appeared in Dayton, Ohio during their 1942 stage tour, she invited them to her home for a reception and also invited friends over to meet them. Everyone stayed and her small house was full of people. Stan kept taking people to the nursery to see Virginia's newly born twin sons and gushing over how cute they were. Virginia stayed in touch with L&H over the years, exchanging Christmas cards and that type of thing."

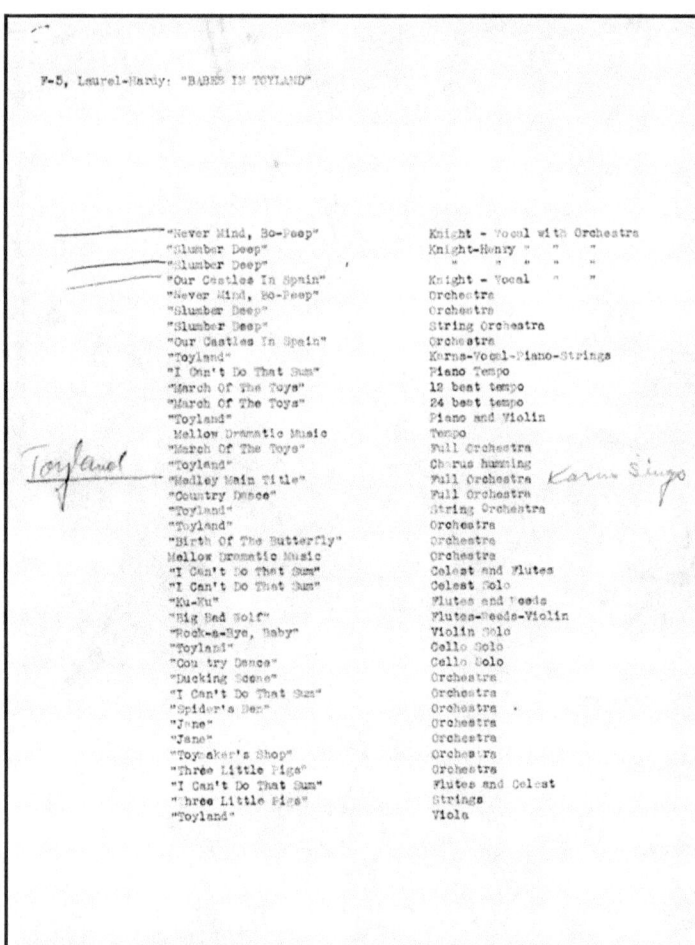

Left: While the film had only five major musical numbers, much of Victor Herbert's music was used in the underscoring. "Karns sings" was a notation to the opening "Toyland" number. *Right*: As always, many visitors to the studio were photographed with Stan and Babe, among them this unknown gentleman.

One letter from Stan to Bill and Virginia Patterson survives, from February 9, 1942, when Laurel and Hardy were on tour at the Palace Theater in Cleveland:

> Dear Bill:
> We did swell in Cincinnati & doing same here - Again want you to know I deeply appreciated your extreme kindness & hope to have the pleasure of reciprocating in the near future, Virginia & yourself are swell persons - I will never forget you.
> Kind thoughts always,
> Sincerely,
> Stan

Felix Knight also shared memories, in 1981, of working on the film.

"My first day on the set, I didn't meet Stan and Babe. The first day, we did the soundtrack. The first time that I saw them and worked with them was doing the scenes that preceded Bogeyland. We did all of that together. At that time, Stan was having marital problems, so we had to shoot around him a lot!

"It was fortunate that I had very little dialogue with them. I appeared in scenes with them, but if you'll notice, most of the scenes I appeared in with them, they were doing most of the dialogue, and Charlotte Henry and I were running around after them. Especially in Bogeyland. So there wasn't any problem. Their only ad-libbing 'problem' was between themselves, but they'd worked together so long that it didn't seem to be a problem for them at all."

Left: Stan and Babe's friendship with Virginia Karns Patterson continued long after the film's production. The boys visited her family while on tour in Dayton, Ohio in 1942. *Right*: A visitor from Burma – F. DeMonte, "Chief Engineer of the Indian Postal Telegraph," according to this photo's original caption.

Knight worked with both of the film's directors, as he related: "Gus Meins was a wonderful, fatherly kind of man, and very calm, and very easy to work with. No temperament, no high pressure, and he always got what he wanted in the end, without any big fuss.

"Charlie Rogers was a friend of Stan's who had come over, as I recall, from London. He came up with most of the on-the-spot lines, because he understood them both so well, that he could see them play one scene, and see what would carry over and make a funny situation in the following scene. He played Simple Simon, who I think was the guy who was fishing in the pond – the kids are chasing him, and he fished the boot out.

"Hal Roach would come onto the set almost every day. I would stop and talk to him. As I recall, he had a lot of suggestions for the comedy part of it. He didn't interfere too much with the musical sequences, but I would see him huddling quite often with Stan and Ollie, and with Charlie Rogers. But I just spoke to him, passed the time of day."

Knight felt that Stan contributed to the film, but unobtrusively. "Pretty much in his own quiet way, he would make suggestions," he recalled. "He would come up with very, very intelligent suggestions. And I don't know just what Ollie contributed. I don't remember that he did too much. He would have ideas about things that he could do. His looking into the camera, for instance, was his own invention, and certain little things that became characteristics of his. But I always felt that Stan was the brains."

In contrast to Henry Brandon's memories, Felix Knight did not recall a lot of hilarity on the set. "They were very serious; not much horseplay at all," he said. Knight also had a very different relationship with Babe Hardy: "I didn't get along too well with Ollie – I came from Georgia, and Oliver came from Georgia, and I don't know why but he didn't seem to care too much for me, and I returned the compliment by keeping away from him. I remember we had a still photographer by the name of Stax. S-T-A-X. [Clarence "Stax" Graves, who was head of the stills department for decades.] And of course, we'd do a scene; sometimes the scenes would get a little bit hairy, and people would be tired, and it was Stax's job to make photographs – and the director would say, 'Okay, fellas, take your places, we want to get a still of that.' And Stax was using an old 8x10 camera with the cloth over his head – that's what they had in those days. And if he took more than a few seconds, Ollie would start yelling at him, and abusing him, calling him names. And nobody ever seemed to come to Stax's defense. I didn't, because I was the new boy in town, and I didn't want to stick my neck out. But I found that happened several times, and I've always been for the underdog, so I didn't have too much of an affinity with Ollie.

"As for the singing scenes, we did a soundtrack film first, and then the scenes were shot silent. The film that was being shot in the camera would be matched with the soundtrack in the laboratory – you know, they have to synchronize that. And I sang out; I couldn't fake, I actually sang. And that's why, even though I was new at the business, it's a pretty good synch job. Fortunately, we didn't have to do too many takes, so that I could use the voice quite a lot during the shooting schedule without getting too tired.

Left: Although many visitors came to the set, none was more special than Stan's daughter Lois. *Right*: Dorothy Hope, a writer for *Film Pictorial,* came from England to visit.

Knight didn't have much of an opportunity to see his work as the film was being made. "I saw the rushes very, very seldom," he said. "They always seemed to come at a time when I was busy on the set. Stan and Ollie would see the rushes, usually the next morning, and if they were looking at the rushes, we were busy shooting our stuff, so I didn't get a chance to see too many of the rushes."

Felix also enjoyed the company of his fellow performers. "Charlotte Henry was a darling young girl, very frightened of having to sing, because she'd never sung professionally before. She'd never studied music either, but she was very musical – and she was very sweet, very kind, a lovely human being. Everybody liked Charlotte; after we did the movie, though, our careers went in different directions, and I only saw her once in person after we finished that particular movie.

"Henry Brandon was a hell of a nice guy! He was one of the most amazing young actors – doing heavies and characters – that I had ever run across. He was a very nice guy; very easy to work with, very pleasant, very professional. I only saw Henry once or twice after we finished the movie, but I liked Henry very much.

"Florence Roberts had appeared as Bo-Peep on Broadway, if I remember correctly. She was a charming lady – all pro, very charming; everybody liked her. She was just a doll."

The sneak preview was an important part of the post-production for any Hal Roach film, and, as Knight recalled, this applied to *Babes in Toyland*. "I went to one preview, you know, the sudden things, when they call you and say, 'There's gonna be a preview tonight, over in Highland Park,' or something like that. As for my reaction to the film when I first saw it, well, I have always been very critical of myself. Even though my career later went on to opera and concerts and radio and recordings, I never really did a job that completely pleased me. I always felt that if I'd used my head a little more, I could've done a better job.

But I was very impressed, because I had never done a lead before, or anything as important as that. As I recall, I was quite pleased with what I had done. However, I saw things I could have done better, and with experience, I did do them better."

Someone who felt he could have done better was Stan Laurel, who was surprisingly blunt in a letter dated March 29, 1957 to fan Earl Shank, Jr. (The punctuation is Stan's; all of his surviving letters have apostrophes before "nt" instead of between the letters.) "I do'nt know what became of Felix Knight," Stan wrote, "he certainly had a wonderful voice but unfortunately he was a very poor actor, could'nt read lines & was very awkward in appearance. He sang a number in another picture with us, 'Bohemian Girl', no part, just one of the gypsies; after that I never heard of [or] saw him again. The 'Soldiers' was his very first film, someone found him working in a garage, Roach gave him an audition with some others for the part & was carried away with his voice & did'nt stop to think about the guy's acting experience, so we had quite a time trying to teach him to troupe."

Felix Knight actually did work in a garage, or more accurately as a mechanic at an aviation field in Pensacola when he was 17. Here he met a music teacher, Mebane Beasley, who gave him his first vocal training. Generations of fans have found his performance as Tom-Tom utterly beguiling, striking just the right tone for a fantasy film. With his dark hair and expressive eyes, sharply defined features and a prominent cleft in the middle of his chin, he looks like the hero in a storybook illustration. His acting is not exaggerated, but one might say that it's magnified. If Felix had to endure the Roach studio deducting half of his $1,000 salary "for the training to be received by the artist," at least he was trained well.

Early in the filming, Stan had torn ligaments in his right leg, assistant director Gordon Douglas had torn ligaments in his left leg, and Hal Roach had undergone an appendectomy. Another member of the cast was about to suffer some physical discomfort. Kewpie Morgan had been prominent in Mack Sennett silent comedies; in fact, he was prominent everywhere, since he weighed more than 300 pounds. He was cast as Old King Cole, that merry old soul. In order to properly convey his merriness, Kewpie was called upon to laugh almost continuously, especially during the lengthy scene in which Ollie is repeatedly submerged in the ducking pond. (Barnaby and the King are just about the only Toyland residents who find this funny; everyone else feels sorry for Ollie.) An account in the film's Campaign Book takes up the story:

"As the scene had to be retaken many times, it was

Top: Ollie is subjected to the "ducking pond," quite a feat for the Roach studio set designers and prop men. *Our Gang* kid Jerry Tucker, probably one of the children at the bottom of this photo, had vivid memories of watching this being filmed. *Bottom*: Mr. Hardy certainly earned his salary on this day.

This scene underwent the greatest change from script to screen. It originally had Stan unwilling to substitute for Bo-Peep. In the revised version, the revelation provides the movie's biggest laugh.

evening before the final retake was filmed. Although Morgan complained about feeling 'a little tired' as a result of his day's work, it was not until he arrived home that he realized he had injured himself through his raucous laughter. When his personal physician was called in, 'Kewpie' was ordered to bed for three days suffering from a painful internal strain. He had actually 'laughed himself sick.'"

Most of the movies produced by the Roach studio took place in the here and now of Culver City in the 1930s. Actress Dorothy Granger enjoyed a starring role in Roach's series *The Boy Friends* and had supporting roles in *Hog Wild* and *The Laurel-Hardy Murder Case* with Stan and Babe. She described the usual procedure for makeup and costuming on an average Hal Roach short. "We didn't have any 6:30 or 7:00 make-up call; we'd start shooting at 9:00. You'd arrive at the studio a little before then for make-up — which you did yourself! You did your own hair, too. They did have a wardrobe department at Roach's; in those days, you had to have two or three dresses alike, because there was no telling when you'd have to go into the drink — or they'd wreck your dress, and you had to have a standby. And you needed another for your double."

The fanciful costumes needed for *Babes in Toyland* were unlike anything previously used in a Hal Roach film. Many of them appear to be modified from pre-existing costumes used for movies about the Pilgrims or the Revolutionary War. Several of the men wear tall "stovepipe" hats with buckles in the middle,

Silas Barnaby prepares to commit a pignapping.

or three-cornered hats; the women frequently wear bonnets, blouses, skirts and aprons that seem to be from the 1700s. These were probably rented from the Western Costume company, which had a long association with Hal Roach. The Roach studio had constructed what looked like steel girders (actually made of wood) on top of the Western Costume building, at 939 South Broadway in Los Angeles, for "high and dizzy" thrill sequences in the *Our Gang* comedy *The Old Wallop* (1927) and Laurel and Hardy's *Liberty* (filmed in October and November 1928). Western Costume had supplied the 18th century wardrobe for *The Devil's Brother*, and the firm definitely provided some of the attire for *Babes in Toyland*. In 2019, a light brown woolen tunic, augmented with brass studs and leather lacing in the front, came up for auction; inside was a label reading "Felix Knight" and another with the Western Costume logo.

Payroll ledgers for the Roach studio in 1934 list as costumers Harry Black, Grace Hayes, Clara Gale, and Mary Bernard. Presumably they would have designed the unique costumes for Stan and Ollie, the Three Little Pigs, the Wooden Soldiers, and the Bogeymen. Their sketches would have then gone to seamstresses Katy McDonald, Dorothy Callahan, Nellie Fahringer, Irene Callahan, Helen Finch and Mary Bragg. The Roach studio had a separate building for the costume department, where new garments were created, and a second-story area in another building for wardrobe, where they stored clothing likely to be used repeatedly.

Remembering that the studio publicity written by Sam W.B. Cohn was likely to be exaggerated, we find this in the film's "Campaign Book":

"Every independent costumer in Los Angeles was called upon to help supply the necessary wardrobe for the production after this department at the studio became swamped. For the bogeymen alone, two hundred furry and grotesque costumes were required while the dressing of the colorful Toyland villagers necessitated the making of one hundred period costumes. Each of the principals of the cast had to be fitted with custom made outfits which were fashioned in triplicate to avoid production delays in the event their wardrobe was soiled or otherwise rendered useless."

The most uncomfortable costumes were worn by the

Left: Jiggs is unwilling to be Barnaby's victim. *Right*: Little Elmer worries as Barnaby and his minion (John George) admire the sausage which is supposed to be proof of Elmer's demise.

most vulnerable performers – the one-inch-thick rubber heads and padded costumes worn by the Three Little Pigs: four-year-old Payne Johnson, four-and-one-half-year-old Edward Earle Marsh, and 36-year-old Angelo Rossitto, who had attained his full height of two feet, eleven inches. Payne Johnson – who had won his role back on August 10 and was now filming in late September and early October – recalled that the heavy, one-inch-thick rubber masks "fully enclosed your head with sweat." The only ventilation was provided by holes for eyes and nostrils. Furthermore, the Pigs were in costumes with heavy padding underneath to give them a portly physique. All of this under the especially hot lights needed for the mammoth set should have made for a grueling ordeal, but Johnson happily recalled, "It was a wonderful experience; I can remember sitting on Hardy's lap. The whole cast was really friendly, and because I was so young, at the end of the film, they gave me a big book of Mother Goose rhymes, and a miniature fire engine, the kind that you sit in and pedal, about four feet long with little ladders and things. That was my gift for playing the part."

Bob Cowan, who designed and manufactured the heads and claws for the pigs, also created the masks for the Bogeymen, which were likewise made of latex rubber. Henry Brandon took one home and used it for years as a Hallowe'en decoration until it disintegrated. One full costume lasted through the middle of May 1938, when it was used in a haunted house sequence for *Our Gang's* last Hal Roach short, *Hide and Shriek*.

Just about everyone in the film was fitted with a wig; these may have been chosen by Peggy Zardo, the chief hairdresser on the Roach lot. Stan's usual "fright wig" was augmented by a wig which gave him longer hair, especially on the sides. Ollie was fitted with a pageboy. These were exactly like the hair styles they'd had in *The Devil's Brother* and were probably the same wigs. Again we quote from Sam W.B. Cohn: "Wig makers enjoyed unusual prosperity as a result of the picturization of the elaborate fantasy. Three hundred wigs ranging in quality from the beautiful blonde tresses used by Bo-Peep to the tawny mane-like hair of Barnaby, the villain, were supplied by outside specialists and were cared for during production by a staff of twelve hair dressers." Kewpie Morgan as Old King Cole was fitted with a white wig that had curls on the side; Toymaker William Burress had a scraggly white wig underneath his skullcap hat. Ferdinand Munier was supplied with a magnificent flowing white beard which covered most of the top of his Santa Claus suit.

Jack Casey was head of the makeup department and furnished many of the men with elaborate mustaches; he also likely applied the cosmetics for two white-faced clowns and the "living" wooden soldiers, who had red cheeks and lips. Sam Cohn found a novel way of using the makeup department to promote one of the film's starlets:

"Owner of the world's longest and most luxurious eyelashes, that's what John Casey, Hal Roach studio make-up expert claims for Marie Wilson, eighteen-year-old screen actress who portrays 'Contrary Mary' in 'Babes in Toyland,' Hal Roach-MGM feature production.

"Miss Wilson's eyelashes measure fifteen-sixteenths of

Poor Tom-Tom is unfairly banished to Bogeyland.

an inch, according to Casey, who discovered that fact while making up the petite blonde actress for her part in the film.

"'During my fifteen years' experience as a make-up specialist I have never encountered a woman with such long and beautiful lashes,' Casey asserted. 'It is necessary for Miss Wilson to constantly trim and curl them to keep the eyelashes from interfering with her vision.'"

Marie's eyelashes, happily, were not the extent of her talents, as she came to prominence a few years later in Warner Bros. films such as *Colleen* with Dick Powell and Ruby Keeler, and *Boy Meets Girl* starring James Cagney and Pat O'Brien. She was a protégé of *Babes* screenwriter Nick Grindé; for a time, they were engaged, but never married. In 1942, she was featured in *Ken Murray's Blackouts* at the El Capitan Theater on Vine Street in Hollywood. She continued with this show for the rest of its southern California run, through 1949. Concurrently, in April 1947, she began starring on radio as the endearingly daffy title character of *My Friend Irma*, which was broadcast through 1954; the series spawned two feature films and a television version that ran for two seasons. Her vocal talents are scarcely used in *Babes in Toyland*; she has one line when Tom-Tom and Bo-Peep are trying to locate the lost sheep. Marie as Contrary Mary says angrily, "No, I haven't seen them!" Although her one big moment in the film lasts for perhaps five seconds, by 1950 she had attained

This scene never quite happens in the film; Tom-Tom encounters a few crocodiles, but not the Bogeymen.

such fame that the posters for the *March of the Wooden Soldiers* reissue listed as the only supporting players Charlotte Henry, Felix Knight and Marie Wilson.

One of the bit players had a direct connection with Babe Hardy. Margot Sage from Atlanta was Babe's niece, daughter of his half-sister Elizabeth. Margot's paternal grandfather was Ira Yale Sage, wealthy railroad magnate. Sage had willed Margot's parents an inheritance of more than a million dollars, but it had been lost to bad investments, and now Margot was working as an "atmosphere" extra and earning between $5.00 to $7.50 a day. "I'm not a wealthy girl out here trying to rob some more deserving person of a job," she said. "I need the money as bad as anybody in Hollywood." Margot and her twin sister Mary would work as extras in Hal Roach films for the next couple of years.

The Toyland set was decorated with several live plants, including a tall tree for the "Rockabye Baby" and his cradle. While the many sunflowers appeared to be artificial, there were many real plants, and the huge amount of light required to adequately illuminate the Toyland set caused some problems. Again, we quote from publicist Cohn:

"Even plants in Hollywood have their doubles.

"Strong Klieg lights used in picture making, and other studio conditions, are so hard on flora of most varieties that plants can remain on the set only

Left: Longtime Laurel and Hardy associate Bobby Burns (the "Spider" of the 1903 stage production) in costume as the Sandman. *Right*: A prop man (possibly Don Sandstrom) holds two of the kids who played gnomes in the "Go to Sleep" sequence.

four or five days at a time --- and then must be removed for rejuvenation in the sunbathed enclosure of the nursery.

"On a picture like the Hal Roach-MGM production of Victor Herbert's operetta, 'Babes in Toyland,' where the filming often runs through weeks and sometimes months, the scenic effects must remain the same for the duration of the production. As a result, exact duplicates of the more important and noticeable plants must be kept on hand.

"According to Dan Mauerhan, Los Angeles horticulturist, who 'dressed' the floral portion of the 'Babes in Toyland' sets, the lack of ultra-violet rays – not supplied by the Kliegs or other studio lights – is responsible for the most deteriorating effect on the plants used. In fact the actual cost of deterioration of the plants on the 'Babes in Toyland' set amount to about $200 a week. This despite the fact that two men were on the set every day, caring for the flora. The maintenance cost for the plants and fernery amounted to an additional $350 a week.

"The value of some of these plants can be realized when it is known that 40 of the ferns used in the 'Toyland' set alone were valued at an average price of $100 apiece. The strong rays from the Kliegs burns some of these ferns so badly that they could not be used again. In other cases, they had to be taken back to the nursery, trimmed almost to their roots, and sent on a 'vacation' of almost a year, before they could be again put in service.

"Obtaining appropriate flora also proved a problem in the 'Babes in Toyland' film. For an especially weird cave scene only a special type of Spanish moss would give the desired effect. It was finally found in Sherwood Forest, near Ventura, California – but the forestry department refused to allow any of it to be taken away. As a result, Mauerhan was forced to make a tour of outlying ranches of this district and pick up the moss in small quantities until the required amount was gathered.

"Mauerhan traveled more than 3,500 miles in filling the floral needs of the 'Babes in Toyland' picture. The Klieg

Barnaby leads the Bogeymen in an invasion of Toyland.

lights destroyed so many of the plants that the three largest wholesale nurseries in Los Angeles were denuded because of the purchases necessary to replace the flowers destroyed. Orders had to then be placed with nurseries in Santa Barbara, San Diego and San Bernardino. In one case a lamp fell on one of the more valuable ferns. It was completely destroyed. Another, much larger, had to be obtained immediately, and then trimmed to look identically like the one destroyed. A suitable fern was finally located in a nursery outside of San Bernardino."

Adding to the discomfort of plants and people under the brutally hot lights was the Culver City weather. A heat wave baked the city from September 28 to 30 – hitting 96 degrees on the 29th. Another heat wave followed from October 8 to 11. Typical of southern California weather, this was followed by a cold snap from October 13 through 18.

Toward the end of the filming, the Meins company shot the scenes with the crocodile-infested stream, with Tom-Tom being carried on a raft to his exile in Bogeyland, and Barnaby and the Bogeymen crossing the other way to invade Toyland.

Henry Brandon recalled, "I was doing *The Drunkard* at night, while I was doing the picture. And one night they gave me something like two days' warning, and said I'd have to do some night shots – out at the studio pool, with the Bogeymen. I had no understudy, so I got a friend of mine, who was

The Bogeyman outfits (*center*) were probably designed by makeup department head Jack Casey, mask designer Bob Cowan, and costumers Harry Black, Grace Hayes, Clara Gale, and Mary Bernard. They were possibly inspired by Wally Westmore's creations for the 1932 Paramount feature *Island of Lost Souls* (*left and right*). That's Bela Lugosi glaring at us at the left.

an incredibly quick study, and I got him up in the part overnight. He played my part for one night. And the director said to me later, 'Well, it was smart of you to get a dull actor to substitute for you, so we wouldn't get interested in him.' I said, 'Dull actor? He's a damn good actor! You're lucky he said the words, what're you talking about? All you needed was somebody to get on there and say the words, and he said 'em!'"

The scene where the wooden soldiers force the Bogeymen back through the gates of Toyland, and into the pond, where presumably some of them become food for the crocodiles, prompted Sam W. B. Cohn to once again engage in some fanciful exaggeration with his publicity: "A Los Angeles crocodile 'farm' [no doubt the California Alligator Farm in Lincoln Heights] supplied the school of reptiles which is used in the Hal Roach-MGM production, 'Babes in Toyland'.... The lizard-like amphibians ranged in size from six to nine feet and were so ferocious that it was necessary to have armed guards stand by while expert swimmers, playing the role of bogeymen, were in the water with them. According to experts, it is impossible to tame one of this specie of the reptile family and the only way to ensure absolute safety for a person working in the water with them, is to securely tie up the massive jaws of the crocodile. As this would spoil the desired effect in the picture, guards were employed instead." While there are some frightening shots of the swimming crocodiles opening their jaws, they are never visible in the shots where the Bogeymen fall into the stream. Skillful editing gives the impression that the Bogeymen and the reptiles were together in the same shots.

Probably as a nod to the team's many fans in England, these creatures are almost always referred to as "the Bogey men," the British way of referring to these monsters, instead of the American "Boogie men," as one can hear Spanky McFarland say in the 1933 *Our Gang* short *Bedtime Worries*. In 1932, the British dance band of Henry Hall had made a popular record, "Hush, Hush, Hush, Here Comes the Bogey Man." (Ollie slips at one point and says, "And Stannie and me chased Barnaby and the Boogiemen so far, they'll never come back!")

The Bogeymen, with their furry bodies, shocks of unruly black hair, and faces with snouts and long fangs, have more than a passing resemblance to the "half man, half animal" monsters in *Island of Lost Souls*, released by Paramount at the end of 1932. Those were designed by Wally Westmore, of the legendary Westmore family of makeup artists. Charles Laughton, who starred in that film, decried the fur that was always being flung all over the sets, and one wonders if similar hairy messes were being made on the sets of *Babes in Toyland*. John George, who plays Barnaby's minion, was one of the creatures in *Island of Lost Souls*, and perhaps he did double duty on *Babes in Toyland*, but the full encasing of the costumes and masks prevents us from knowing who is inside them.

While some reviewers would comment that they thought the Bogeymen sequences were too frightening for children to view, the kids who participated in their filming apparently had a great time. Gene Reynolds, who would later become the renowned producer of the television series *M*A*S*H*, was 11 years old in 1934; his family had just moved to Los Angeles from Detroit, and to bring in extra money, young Gene began working as an extra in films. His first film was *Babes in Toyland*. "I was an extra, one of the kids running around in Toyland," he recalled. "We were in a whole bunch of scenes running through the film. The boogie men would come and grab me and I would scream and holler. I was the kid whose mouth was wider open than anybody's. I had a lot of enthusiasm, a lot of energy."

This shot of kids being frightened in their bed by the Bogeymen probably bothered Hal Roach (and other censors) more than any other. However, filming it didn't worry Jerry Tucker, Jean Darling or Dickie Jones, all of whom had long, happy and successful lives.

In a composite still, we see the toy soldiers (actually one foot tall) being saluted by Stan and Ollie, as well as the impressive interior of the toy warehouse.

Another kid, easily visible in the scene when a Bogeyman invades the bedroom of the kids in the shoe, was Jerry Schatz, who as "Jerry Tucker" was appearing in *Our Gang* shorts, notably as the rich kid in *Hi'-Neighbor!* In 1993, he recalled to historian Steve Randisi, "It was a great experience seeing Laurel and Hardy on that Toyland set. I won't comment on their prowess as comedians because I think people already know that; their work certainly speaks for them. But I will say this, in person they were just as warm and gentle as you see in the film.

"As to what kind of people they really were — they were very hard workers. When you see a scene in Toyland, such as when Ollie is dunked in that pool, it's funny and everyone laughs. But that poor fellow was dunked not once, not twice, but I'd say about fifteen times before they got the scene the way they wanted it."

Another young actor is in a memorable shot, holding on to the leg of one of the soldiers as he marches and rids Toyland of the Bogeymen. This was Dickie Jones, who a few years later would gain immortality as the voice of Walt Disney's

The soldiers advance on the Bogeymen and send them into the crocodile-infested waters beyond Toyland's gates.

Pinocchio. Born in Texas in 1927, Jones at the age of four was billed as "The World's Youngest Trick Rider and Trick Roper." By the age of seven he was appearing in films, and would primarily work in Western movies and TV shows, notably with Gene Autry.

The wooden soldiers who save Toyland from the Bogeymen were played by about 50 actors in heavy costumes, topped with tall black hats like those worn by the British Royal Guard. In other scenes, the soldiers marched in stop-motion animation achieved by Kenneth Peach and Roy Seawright. Ironically, the soldiers used for the animation were really one foot high, but the studio didn't make 600 of them. They were made of lead, and their sharply creased "trousers" were painted a light yellow with a black stripe down the middle. Their tunics were made of black leather, and their faces were painted white with red dots on the cheeks. Most of them carried rifles, but some were buglers and drummers. The stop-motion animation was outstanding, with the soldiers marching in time with Victor Herbert's stirring "March of the Toys."

Stop-motion animation – moving real objects in very small increments and photographing them frame by frame – had existed in movies since J. Stuart Blackton and Albert E. Smith had made *The Humpty-Dumpty Circus* for Vitagraph in 1897. George Méliès had employed the technique in several films early in the 1900s. Willis O'Brien used his finely crafted miniature figures to film T*he Dinosaur and the Missing Link* in 1915, and expanded on this with the feature film *The Lost World* in 1925. He took stop-motion animation to a new level in 1933, however, with the stunning sequences for *King Kong*. Roy Seawright and Kenneth Peach had nothing like the budget or time available for that film, but created some very impressive animation nevertheless. Like O'Brien, Seawright found a way to combine the animated footage with live action – in this instance, some shots of Laurel and Hardy outside the factory watching the soldiers march by.

In 1981, Roy Seawright recalled his work on the animated sequences. "When Stan and Babe opened up the toy factory, you look up and you see all of the toy soldiers lined up. It was my job to make a traveling matte. They opened the door onto a brick wall; we replaced that in the shot with a miniature set which we had concocted on an old handball court – we used to play squash and handball, but we converted it for stop motion and trick work. The soldiers were all made of ball and socket; there must have been 80 of them. Every one of them had big lead feet, flat shoes with each one being a half-circle. They had to be moved about a quarter of an inch to the frame. It took us two weeks to shoot the one scene from different camera angles – low shot looking up, cross angles, long shots – they came out the door and marched right past the camera. Back in the '20s and '30s, we were working with spit and baling wire and cotton and tape. This was really a big challenge, because we didn't have the stop-motion technique or really the knowledge." Nevertheless, the animation is impressive, particularly the split-screen shot where Stan and Ollie at the right of the frame watch the toy soldiers smoothly marching out of the toy factory.

Equally impressive is the sequence in the underground lair of the Bogeymen. Creepy stalactites grow from the ceiling of the cave, which has a little island surrounded by a stream that's populated by snapping crocodiles. One interior shot shows sharp stalactites that appear to be about 30 feet high; this may well be a matte painting. Small triangular trees adorn the ground, and bats fly around for further chilling atmosphere. Not all the denizens of this place are evil, however: after Tom-Tom sings "Go to Sleep, Slumber Deep," an elderly sandman with a long white beard flies in and begins to sprinkle sleep-inducing sand on Tom-Tom and Bo-Peep. He is accompanied by several little gnomes (mostly played by children, although Angelo Rossitto is visible). The gnomes and the sandman are shown in a double-exposure shot combined with another partial shot; they seem to be transparent while Tom-Tom and Bo-Peep retain their full corporeal form. The sandman (flying in on a harness) is played by Bobby Burns, who had played the giant spider in the original stage production of *Babes in Toyland*. In 1915, Burns starred as "Pokes" to Walter Stull's "Jabbs" in a series of one-reel comedies made for the Vim company, first in Bayonne, New Jersey and then in Jacksonville, Florida. Babe Hardy was a supporting actor in 11 of these shorts. Now, 19 years later, Burns was playing small supporting roles in Laurel and Hardy comedies.

It took quite a bit of time for the writers to create a suitable conclusion for the film. Felix Knight remembered, "They kept changing the script – that was one of the things that took so much time. As a matter of fact, we shot three or four different endings to the movie, because they couldn't come up with one that they thought would be conclusive, and make the boys the heroes, and still make it funny at the same time. They finally used the one where they load up the cannon with the darts, and the cannon switches over and the darts hit Ollie in the rear end."

Henry Brandon recalled, "The end of the picture originally was a little macabre. They put me into the cannon and shot me into the sky. And the bits and pieces of my body spelled out, 'And they lived happily ever after.' Well, someone nixed that one, but that was in the original script. That was the fade out."

Principal photography on the film finished on October 17. Other work, probably special-effects photography, continued from October 21 to 27. As a fitting finale to a production so plagued by medical emergencies, on October 19 Babe Hardy checked into St. Vincent's Hospital to have his tonsils removed by Dr. George R. Diven. *The Hollywood Reporter* noted wittily, "The picture also goes to the cutting room today."

There were two cutting rooms busily working on *Babes in Toyland*. William Terhune, who had been editing Hal Roach comedies since 1926, had cut the "plot" or non-Laurel and Hardy footage on *The Devil's Brother* and was now performing the same function on the footage directed by Gus Meins. Stan's favorite editor, Bert Jordan, worked closely with Stan on cutting the L&H scenes, as the two had for several years.

"I was officially named the Laurel and Hardy film editor," Jordan stated in 1980. "I was the only one that Stan would have to cut his pictures, unless I wasn't available. He used to crab if he had anybody else cutting them – so I was flattered by that." Jordan would sit on the sidelines during the filming as often as he could to get a sense of how the film should be edited, and he would also begin the day watching the previous day's footage – an essential part of the filmmaking process, to determine if anything needed to be filmed again, or in a different way. "I used to see all the rushes; Babe didn't care whether he saw them or not, but Stan would always look at them," Jordan said. Gus Meins and Charlie Rogers would be there to see the results of the previous day's work and try to ensure a unified look to the film despite its being shot by two separate units. Also watching the dailies every morning would be Hal Roach, who preferred to exercise his judgment in the projection room rather than on the set.

After each day's filming was finished, cameraman Art Lloyd or his assistant Edward L. White would deliver the magazines of exposed film to the laboratory on the Roach lot. Every night, a crew of 14 men would take care of developing the day's precious footage and making work prints that could be projected and edited without disturbing the original camera negative. This crew was headed by Charlie Levin, who had performed the same service for Chaplin when he was making his landmark series of shorts for Mutual in 1916-17. The crew included Levin's brothers Harry and Marshall, and film editor Louis McManus's brother Robert.

The Roach studio had a separate building for its projection room, which was run by Ham Bennett, Bruce Denny, Clive Churchill and Wesley Burke. Each morning's viewing of the previous day's work was usually a happy way to start the day. Seeing the scenes for the first time, Stan would fly into hysterics. Bert Jordan said, "He used to just laugh like the dickens when he saw the gags." Roy Seawright, who also frequently sat in on the morning's screenings, agreed. "Stan was his own greatest audience. You'd go into the projection room, and at the dailies, he'd sit there and scream! He'd beat the goddamn table; he'd go nuts! But it wasn't ego.

"Stan lived in two personalities. When Stan performed in front of the camera, he performed just the way he felt it. He did not know how it would look, coming through the camera and onto the screen. In our projection room, he'd look at it, and he actually had no relationship to the guy in the dailies. He was not that guy on the screen, but he sincerely reacted to what he saw on that screen. Stan was like a painter who would sit back with his canvas in front of him – maybe two days later, he'd look at his work and say, 'Hey, that's good!' He was a true artist."

Bolstering the idea that Stan's laughter was not a

Stan Laurel Defendant in Damage Suit

Stan Laurel, screen comedian, doesn't do all his comic antics before the camera, according to his double, John D. Wood.

In a suit for $40,500 damages filed yesterday in Superior Court, Wood declares Laurel and Hamilton McKenzie tossed him into a pool at the Hal Roach studio last October 20 and that he suffered serious injuries. The suit, filed by Attorneys Charles R. McCarty and Cyril Moss, names the comedian and McKenzie as defendants.

The bit player who sued Stan for throwing him in the ducking pond had a better lawyer than Henry Brandon recalled, as detailed in this article from the November 23, 1934 *Los Angeles Times*.

PACT CLOSES LAUREL SUIT

Ducking Episode Charges Placed Off Calendar by Agreement

With a compromise settlement yesterday ended the $40,000 damage suit filed against Stan Laurel, film comedian, and Hamilton McKenzie, an actor, by John D. Wood, also a film player, who complained he was thrown into a pool of water in an ill-conceived prank.

Wood, whose action was called for trial by Superior Judge Edmonds but placed off calendar when the compromise was announced, complained that in October of 1934 Laurel and McKenzie tossed him into the pool at the Hal Roach studios for a ducking episode which they had previously arranged to have filmed.

"Stan Laurel was just writhing in laughter," Wood testified in a deposition which was to have been used at the trial. "I struck my head and my back on the edge of the pool."

What amount, if any, figured in the compromise, was not disclosed.

The case wasn't settled until June 10, 1936, as also reported by the *Times*.

– 123 –

Left: Henry Kleinbach (now Brandon) returned to the Roach studio from November 11 through 15, 1937 to play a villain – called "Barnaby" in the script but not on screen – for a dream sequence in *Our Gang Follies of 1938*. Before Alfalfa's dream, Henry is a vocal coach; Alfalfa asks for advice, to the consternation of singer Gino Corrado. *Right*: Barnaby has Alfalfa under a lifetime contract to sing opera, which the youngster soon regrets signing.

function of his ego, George Stevens, the team's cameraman from 1927 through 1931, remembered, "I walked into the projection room once, when a film was being run for one man, and there's a fellow sitting on the edge of his seat, holding onto it to keep from falling down, and it was Stan Laurel watching Babe Hardy on the screen."

After everyone had looked at the footage, an assistant would cut the individual takes and pin them on racks in the editing room. Laurel and Hardy liked to shoot their films in sequence as much as possible. This was not standard procedure at other studios, where each day's filming schedule was determined by available sets, locations or actors regardless of where that footage belonged in the story. Stan and Babe would often improvise or deviate from the script, and their changes would have to be reflected in future scenes, so it made sense to shoot the film according to the progression of the story. As a result, editing could be accomplished while later scenes were being filmed, and this greatly reduced the time needed for post-production.

Bert Jordan would work with the film after each morning's screening of the rushes. He said, "After Stan looked at them, I'd put the film together the way I thought it should be. Now, after I put together my version, the director and Stan would look at it, and they had the privilege of making changes – but the first cut was for me to decide.

"The editing was just between Stan and myself. Sometimes, they didn't make many changes. Stan may have said, 'Well, I tell you, Bert, I think that would look better if you played it in the long shot.' But I always knew what they wanted.

"Mr. Roach would sometimes look at what Laurel did as far as the cutting was concerned, and he'd suggest some changes – but if Stan didn't agree with them, they weren't changed. Roach thought a lot of Stan Laurel, I think; he pretty near always agreed with what Stan said."

The sneak preview was a standard procedure, and an important one, for Hal Roach's films. These would take places in communities away from the movie colony, often in Pomona, 40 miles east of Culver City. Usually about 20 people from the studio would sit in various areas of the theater. Art Lloyd and his wife Venice were often among them. "Artie would come home and he'd say, 'Well, Friday night there's going to be a preview out in Alhambra,'" Venice recalled. "They tried to preview the pictures in little outlying areas, to start with. Later on, with the longer pictures, they'd preview them in quite prominent theaters. It was really great fun, because it was all supposed to be very, very secret."

"A Laurel and Hardy picture was usually previewed at least three times before we ever let it out," said Hal Roach. "We'd preview it first, then re-cut it, maybe make some retakes, then look at it again. If the dialogue was furthering the story, then if the audience laughed over it and didn't hear the line, it didn't mean anything. Sometimes you'd see the picture and the audience would be laughing so hard that you didn't want to come in with more dialogue — you'd have to put in another shot of Laurel to slow them down, so that your next line could be heard."

The preview was primarily used to gauge the audiences' reactions to the comedy. This was accomplished with the aid of a little device that turned one number every time

On October 22, 1934, four days after filming on the set wrapped, the *Our Gang* kids play host to some local orphans. "Gorilla Man" par exellence Charles Gemora is at extreme left in the suit he wore for Laurel and Hardy's *The Chimp* (1932). He's toting a shotgun, in case any Bogeymen should appear.

you pressed a button. The Roach people called these "clickers." Roy Seawright recalled, "At the previews, the cutter, the producer, and Stan and Babe all carried clickers, and they sat at different spots in the theater. Whenever they thought they had a legitimate laugh, they'd click the clicker." Since nobody had the same number of laughs, they were totaled up and averaged.

Venice Lloyd remembered, "After the preview, we'd wait in the lobby, and there's where the yakking started. Then we'd go out for a sandwich, and we'd all yak again. That would go on until 11:00 or 12:00. And Roach would generally lead the discussion; he was the Godfather."

Bert Jordan added, "Stan and I would notice which gags didn't get very big laughs. And maybe the show ran over its usual length; something would have to come out. So we'd just make notes in there, and Stan would decide what to cut. Nobody interfered with what he wanted."

In 1981, Hal Roach reflected upon the importance of previewing and re-cutting the films. "The comedies made for television today are not so good; whatever they make, that's it. But in those days, we could afford to do retakes. On most every picture that we made with Laurel and Hardy, we previewed the picture and then re-did the picture afterwards.

"If I went to a preview and it went great, I was on top of the world," Roach said. "If it went badly, I was as low as a snake. And never in my life was it, 'Oh, my God, the money I'm going to lose on this,' or 'The money I'm going to make on that.' The whole basis was either how good or how bad the picture was. That applies to everything I made. I never in my whole career paid any particular attention to the finances."

However, Roach was forced to pay attention to the cost of *Babes in Toyland*. The money men at Loews Incorporated had first advanced him $150,000 for the film, and then a total of $250,000. But nobody could have anticipated Stan's fabricated illness (the alimony blues) from the start of February through the middle of June, and then his real injury which caused a layoff from mid-August through late September. Roach had already invested significant money and labor before the first interruption, and had to keep many people related solely to *Babes in Toyland* on the payroll all through these months of idleness caused by Stan. As a result, the cost of the film ballooned to $421,810.68, which was $54,000 more than the cost of producing *The Devil's Brother* and *Sons of the Desert* combined.

All of this had been happening while trade papers were predicting the demise of the short subject, and other studios large and small were closing or being forced into bankruptcy. Roach had 500 employees and their families depending on him for their survival. He had no choice but to accommodate his difficult star comedian, because the Laurel and Hardy pictures, and to a lesser degree, the *Our Gang* films, were the only dependably successful product he had. MGM had agreed to a unique distribution arrangement of Roach's feature-length L&H films, something the company did for no other independent producer, only because Laurel and Hardy were big at the box-office.

On October 22, with the Toyland sets still standing, the *Our Gang* kids played host to about 100 local orphans, who got to tour the set, watch some of the gang's comedies, and devour many gallons of ice cream. On the 25th, Stan and the writers began working on the story for a new short, *The Live Ghost*, which featured Stan and Ollie as workers in a fish market who are shanghaied into being part of the crew of Captain Walter Long's "ghost ship." The film would be shot in a fast six days and entrusted to Louis McManus for editing, since Bert Jordan was still working on *Babes in Toyland*.

On October 26, Hal Roach announced to reporters that soon he would try to establish a west-to-east speed record in his upcoming flight to New York to show Loews executives the first print of *Babes in Toyland*, which would also be the name of his new airplane.

It was vitally important that *Babes in Toyland* be a success. Roach's much-publicized series starring writer Irvin S. Cobb had not been well received. Seven shorts were planned, but thanks to exhibitor and audience apathy, only four were completed. Furthermore, aside from the *Our Gang* and Laurel and Hardy comedies, Roach's other product was thought to be slipping in quality. *The Motion Picture Herald* published a section in every issue, "What the Picture Did for Me," in which exhibitors from all over the country wrote in to share their opinions of new films, and describe how well they had done at the

The July 20, 1939 issue of the *Munster, Indiana Times* reports that being strongly identified with roles as children hindered Charlotte Henry's later film career.

box office. Reviewing the Todd-Kelly short *Back to Nature*, exhibitor Paul McBride of the Avalon Theatre in Fillmore, Utah wrote, "This is only a fair comedy. Patsy Kelly is a very poor substitute for Zasu Pitts. Hal Roach comedies have fallen below par in comparison with other company's shorts." Assessing Charley Chase's short *It Happened One Day*, J.A. Verchot of the Opera House in Abbeville, South Carolina wrote, "Only a few laughs in this one. All comedies have been sorry lately." As for Irvin S. Cobb's *You Bring the Ducks*, Harriett A. LeRicheux of the Arcade Theatre in Camden, New York, wrote, "Not much to these comedies. Cobb had better stick to his writing."

It was also vitally important that *Babes in Toyland* receive the blessings of the Production Code Administration. The Bogeymen had been causing concern for months. On November 9, Douglas Mackinnon and two other executives of the PCA, Geoffrey Shurlock and Karl Lischka, viewed the film and rendered their verdict. Mackinnon wrote to Henry Ginsberg with a qualified approval:

> Congratulations on your production, BABES IN TOYLAND. It is a thoroughly enjoyable picture.
> However, because of children's reaction, we very seriously suggest that you cut down as much as possible the grotesqueness of the close-ups of the bogey-men.
> Attached is Certificate of Approval No. 401 for this production.

Hal Roach may well have been surprised when *The Hollywood Reporter*, usually friendly to his productions, gave a curiously mixed pre-release review to *Babes in Toyland* in its issue of November 10: "So far as concerns the discriminating elders who will accompany their young hopefuls (and their young hopefuls should see it), the picture will be a curious jumble of good, bad and indifferent from both the technical and artistic sides. The script is so loose and spotty, and the grown-up humor dragged in so painfully, that they will wish the picture had been approximately cut in two….

"Laurel & Hardy have a few scenes that are really funny, but mostly it must have been a tough job to fit them in all the way through the picture. Charlotte Henry is pretty deadly as Bo-Peep, and Felix Knight as Tom-Tom has at least got a voice, although the synchronization is not at all times perfect. Henry Kleinbach plays the villain Barnaby like Douglas Fairbanks Jr. in a fright wig doing the 'Cabinet of Dr. Caligari.'…

"The direction is a little slow, and the timing of comedy, and for the benefit of those for whom this picture is solely designed, it might be just as well to cut the "Bogeyland" sequences to a minimum, because they upset children's nerves and are unimaginative enough to look just like the tunnels in Coney Island. Corby and Lloyd in their photography do both swell and poor work. As a small feature, this might have been A-1 audience entertainment. As it stands, it's a kiddie festival that should have an annual holiday release."

Variety's verdict, published the same day, was more reassuring: "Hal Roach has succeeded with 'Babes in Toyland' in bringing fantasy to the screen, something that Paramount muffed in 'Alice in Wonderland.' While 'Babes' is nearly perfect Christmas entertainment for the kids, it is not without a great deal of adult value. Picture should be a moneymaker, particularly if Metro gets it into the British fields during the Yuletide. In this country, it will undoubtedly be a more than satisfactory draw…

"Story as developed by Frank Butler and Nick Grindé is perfect for kids. Though playing to the junior minds, the writers have injected sufficient adult comedy to take care of the grown-ups. Smacking of English pantos, Butler's work is very evident. Dialoging is a neat job with laughs garnered without aid of meaningless gags…

"Individual performances are all okay. Laurel and Hardy do their usual stuff without their usual effort. Laughs gotten by the pair are all legitimate. Though the story is not woven around them, sufficient of the comedians is seen to make the picture theirs. Charlotte Henry shows a great deal of improvement since 'Alice.' Felix Knight is okay as Tom. Pip of a performance is given by Henry Kleinbach as the heavy, Barnaby."

Late in November 1934, after previews and refinement in the cutting, *Babes in Toyland* was at last ready for release. It had been exactly a year since Hal Roach had purchased the filming rights from RKO. This was certainly one of the most hectic years of Roach's life. This movie had caused a major clash between Roach and Stan Laurel, and had struggled to be completed despite illnesses, injuries and delay, but it was now about to be put on display. With luck, it would be a great success – but *Babes in Toyland* so far had not been a lucky production.

"I Went to Toyland with Laurel and Hardy"

British journalist Dorothy Hope wrote a charming article about the filming of *Babes in Toyland* for the December 29, 1934 issue of *Film Pictorial*. It also sheds some light on Stan and Ruth Laurel's life away from the studio. Their home, which still stands, was at 10353 Glenbarr Avenue in Cheviot Hills, a little over two miles northwest of the Roach studio at 8822 Washington Boulevard in Culver City. Alice Brady's movie premiere was probably for *The Gay Divorcée*, the first film to star Fred Astaire and Ginger Rogers, which was released to the public on October 19, 1934.

"I Went to Toyland with Laurel and Hardy"
With an Intimate Close-up of the Inimitable Stan at Home
By Dorothy Hope for *Film Pictorial*, December 29, 1934

Arriving in Hollywood on a visit from London, the first person I got in touch with was Stan Laurel, of the famous laughter-firm of Laurel and Hardy. I hadn't seen him since he and Oliver Hardy paid a visit to England about two years ago. I was promptly invited over. Dinner with the Laurels at their delightful house "The Laurels" (which is surrounded by a high wall) is an adventure. It's all so spirited and jolly; there is no ceremony, no splurging, if you know what I mean.

When the door of "The Laurels" opened, Hospitality (with a capital H) greeted me. There was a reunion with an old friend, an introduction to his charmingly pretty wife, Ruth, followed later by an introduction to the bar. There were attractive glasses with "England" printed on the outside of them, and a delectably iced gin fizz on the inside.

Stan and I had so much to talk about that we almost forgot to be polite to the real master of the house, Chico, an ancient and learned parrot. This parrot has an amazing

– 128 –

vocabulary; he can talk as gently as a clergyman, or swear like a trooper – it all depends on the way he takes you. He swore at me! But when the talented Alice Brady arrived, after dinner, fresh from the successful preview of her latest picture, Chico sang with her. They sang very long and very loudly for nearly an hour.

"Quite operatic," said Stan. Maybe it was, but a *very* off-key opera.

Chico was so pleased with his performance that he refused to "pipe down." So he was put to bed. After all, every bird has his day, and Chico had had a very full one. He had even dined with us. He was let out of the cage and stood on the table by Ruth, helping himself to nuts, and keeping a watchful eye for an unsuspecting nose to bite!

The bird having regretfully retired, we asked Stan to sing for us. He did – entrancingly. "Is it that you really have a good voice, Mr. Laurel? Or is it because Alice Brady and the bird were a bit of a discord?" someone asked.

Anyway it was all right to me. Stan also played the guitar – all the old sentimental songs – "Daisy, Daisy, Give Me Your Answer, Do," "The Old Kent Road," "All the Nice Girls Love a Sailor," and many other old favourites. We all joined in the choruses. Then he sang one or two pleasantly naughty little ones. We couldn't join in the choruses of these because unfortunately we didn't know them. But the faces of his friends smiled down from their places on the knotty pine wood of the bar as if they did. Pictures of all your old favourites are there, including Charles Chaplin, Dan Leno, George Robey, and a host of others.

After the songs came the high spot of the evening.

It was 1 a.m. The music was over. Led by Stan Laurel, we all tiptoed out of the house and across the garden, under the deep starlight sky, to where a greenhouse lay gleaming whitely in the mysterious light. In we crept. We stood in a row, breathing in the warm, deep smell of earth that only a greenhouse exudes. Stan produced a flashlight. What were we to see? We were all puzzled. For before us stood only a row of pots, containing soil and small sprouting leaves.

Then, in reverent whisper, Stan explained. "I have grafted an onion with a tomato so that your salads of the future will be delicately flavoured. In that pot lies a tomato grafted with mint, so that your lamb will need no sauce, though the taste will still be there."

"Oh, what a genius!" we murmured, as we reverently withdrew. Yes, Stan's look of pride was a beautiful thing to observe.

A few days later I was invited over to the Hal Roach Studios to see the big set for *Babes in Toyland*, which is one of the Yuletide holiday films. I'm sending a photograph of Stan and Oliver (I should have explained that everybody calls Oliver "Babe") taken with me on the set. Yes, I look a bit peculiar because I had just eaten a huge lunch. Stan and Babe, discovering I was hungry, had ordered chicken and salad for me. It was brought onto the stage accompanied by a large pot of tea.

Stan and Babe sat on either side of me and my tray, dressed just as they are in the pictures you can see on this page; being perfect hosts they watched me eat with obvious enjoyment, while six hundred "extras," going through their paces as inmates of Toyland, also watched me eat – enviously, I thought.

Then Victor Herbert's son strolled along (his father's music is a tremendous asset to the picture). He gazed at Babe and then in tones of great astonishment remarked, "I never knew you took tea."

Babe gave him such a look of disgust and passed on another to me for daring to have a teapot there at all. Then he vanished behind the model boot of which I have also secured a picture.

Most Americans, I should point out, think it is rather girlish and silly to drink tea. All studio workers over here are certain that everyone in our studios stop filming for at least an hour every afternoon, whatever they may be doing – even if it is in the middle of a most important scene. If you believe that story you had better ask my husband, John Stafford, if they do. He is a producer; he knows. True, tea is taken to him, but he swallows it in a second when it's half-cooled. That's all any of the studio workers do.

Anyway, my beloved American friends, you consume more coffee beans to the minute than we do tea leaves to the hour, so what? But Babe, dear, if you'll come over to England again and "Come up and see me sometime," I'll give a tea party just for you!

Meanwhile, I would advise you readers of *Film Pictorial* to watch for *Babes in Toyland* – a different Laurel and Hardy full of ingenious ideas and crammed with holiday fun.

Portrait Gallery

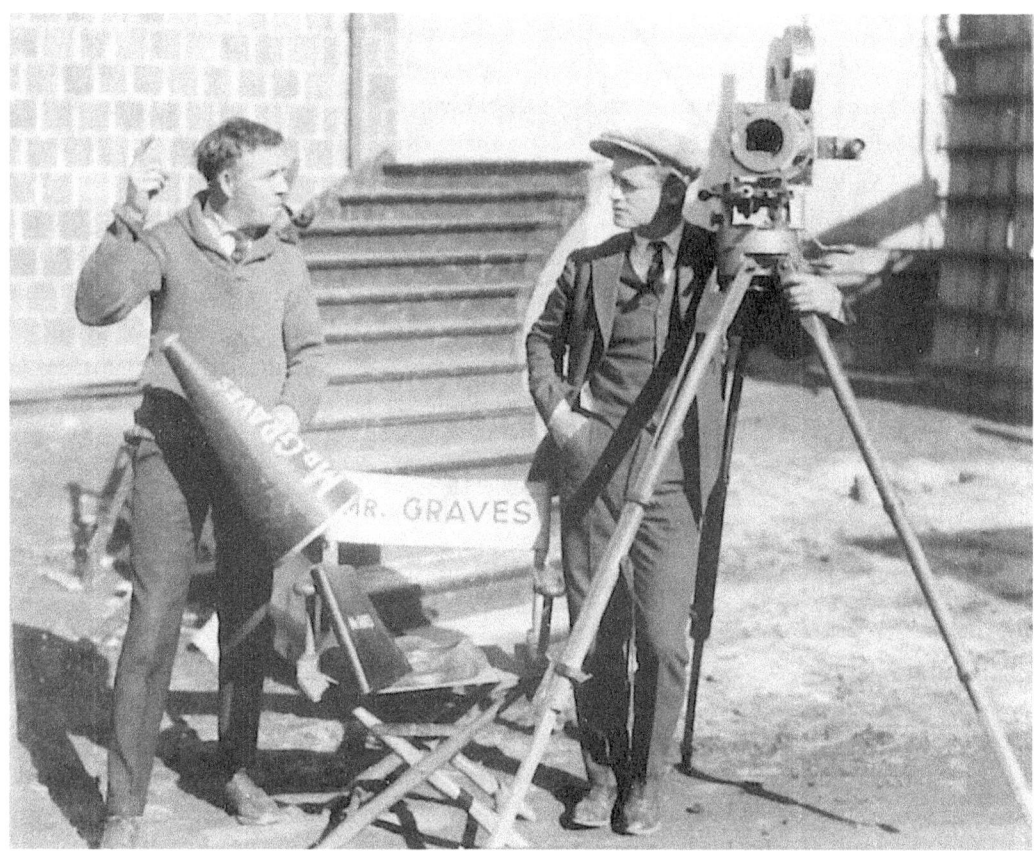

The thousands of photographs or "stills" produced at the Hal Roach Studios were primarily taken by Clarence "Stax" Graves, born in Falmouth Kentucky on October 1, 1885. He was the head of the stills department at the Roach lot from 1923 through 1940; his Russian-born wife, Anna J. Graves (known as "Googie"), did the retouching. Stax remained active in photography at least through 1949 and died on June 15, 1972 at 86 in Indio, California. Here, he aspires to the director's chair as cinematographer Art Lloyd looks on with incredulity.

According to surviving Roach studio documents (and the memory of Felix Knight), Laurel and Hardy weren't crazy about posing for stills, either on the set or in Stax's studio, but were the subject of hundreds of photos which were distributed to newspapers, magazines and theaters.

- 131 -

Pete Gordon dons the cat costume and proves to be a dangerous feline.

Charlotte Henry will recover her sheep by hook or by crook.

Felix Knight cuts a dashing figure as Tom-Tom.

Florence Roberts was a most endearing Mother Peep. Henry Brandon as Barnaby is a menace to Mother Peep.

These were taken before Barnaby received his glasses and chin whiskers.   Henry Kleinbach made quite a transformation to Silas Barnaby.

Virginia Karns as Mother Goose provided a beautiful musical prelude to the film.

Co-director and writer Charlie Rogers played Simple Simon, the role that Hal Roach had intended for Stan Laurel.

Kewpie Morgan had a lot of laughs as that merry old soul, King Cole – perhaps too many for his own good.

Ferdinand Munier proved that there is a Santa Claus.

Billy Bletcher (who provided the voice of the Big Bad Wolf in Disney's *Three Little Pigs* cartoon), as the Police Chief, looks askance at one of his men.

Future star Marie Wilson as Mary Quite Contrary was publicized as having extremely long eyelashes – proven in the closeup portrait.

Jean Darling, formerly of *Our Gang*, returns to the studio as Curly Locks.

Alice Dahl as Little Miss Muffet is scared off her tuffet by a spider – despite Hal Roach's intentions, the only one in the movie.

Chapter 13

Ballyhoo, Release and Reception

When Hal Roach had first announced his intention to make *Babes in Toyland* in December 1933, he planned it as a release for the following Easter. Because of the many delays, the film was now going to be an attraction for Christmas 1934. This was probably the only benefit created by the setbacks, as the film is wonderfully appropriate for the Yuletide season, especially since Santa Claus is a prominent part of the story. However, the movie does not take place around Christmas – Santa Claus visits to inspect his order with the Toymaker in advance of the holiday. When Laurel and Hardy try to break into Barnaby's home under the ruse of delivering a Christmas present (a large crate with Ollie inside), Barnaby's reaction is, "Christmas present – in the middle of July?" This was Henry Brandon's favorite line in the picture, and he often repeated it with great relish at Sons of the Desert functions in the 1980s.

Hal Roach was pleased with Felix Knight's performance in the film, to the extent of signing him to a long-term contract on November 12. Also being retained through the month of November was the massive Toyland set, which was so gorgeous that Roach wanted to donate it to the city of Los Angeles as a playground for kids. On November 30, the Los Angeles Park Commission declined Roach's offer "with thanks." The *Los Angeles Times* noted, "A report by Park Construction Superintendent Gibson avers that if the 'village' is placed outdoors it would not be able to withstand rapid deterioration. Another drawback, he reported, is that it would cost $500 to remove it to the park."

Originally, Roach had planned to put the Toyland set on exhibit at the Chicago "Century of Progress" World's Fair, which ran from May 26 through October 31, 1934, but the delay in filming caused by Laurel's injury prevented it.

If Roach wasn't permitted to give Los Angeles this Christmas present, he gave one to himself and to horse-racing enthusiasts with the opening of Santa Anita Park in Arcadia on December 25. The races attracted 30,077 visitors on opening day, each paying 15 cents for admission. One of the visitors was Clark Gable, who posed for pictures with Roach. As noted earlier, Babe Hardy was one of several actors, directors and executives from the film industry whom Roach had recruited as investors in the project, each putting up $5,000 for an ownership-membership in the Southern California Turf Club. Babe's investment was not lucrative. "Hardy lost his shirt playing over there," Hal Roach recalled. "Finally, he sold his stock; he knew nothing about horses and he just – put up his money and lost it. But I was the president, and I put up my money and lost it too. I never won at the damn place."

When filming on *Babes in Toyland* began back in August, Roach publicity man Sam W.B. Cohn was already writing a plethora of articles for the movie's Campaign Book. This contained stories about the film's production, usually with more than a bit of exaggeration. It also contained a variety of display advertising artwork. These large books, also called pressbooks, measuring 19 ¾" by 14", were created by MGM for all of their releases and sent to theater managers for use in local newspapers. The book for the new L&H feature also contained some ready-made reviews, which of course were raves. One was titled "'Babes in Toyland' Will Delight the Whole Family," and noted:

> You may know that Laurel and Hardy again triumph in roles which call forth all of the whimsy and humor these lovable rogues possess. We cannot visualize any other comics playing the innocent Dum and Dee and securing the vast amount of wholesome fun and so many genuine laughs out of the dumb but sympathetic characters.

– 140 –

Left: MGM congratulated Hal Roach for *Babes in Toyland* by taking out this full-page advertisement in most of the film industry trade papers, such as this from the November 24, 1934 issue of *Motion Picture Herald*. *Right:* In the December issue of *Philadelphia Exhibitor*, MGM regional salesman Bob Lynch encouraged theater managers to book the picture.

You mustn't miss "Babes in Toyland"! We have been crying for clean and wholesome feature productions that are at the same time exciting, interesting and thoroughly enjoyable. Hal Roach's picturization of Victor Herbert's operetta is all of that – and more. And don't make the mistake of thinking that this is "a great picture for the kids but too elementary for us sophisticates." You'll be sorry if you do. For "Babes in Toyland" offers, besides the inimitable fun of Laurel and Hardy, a real romance, glorious music and a spectacle that you will long remember.

Happily, as the film was awaiting release, authentic preliminary reviews from film trade papers and general audience newspapers were just as enthusiastic.

Film Daily, November 12: Youngsters of all ages and sizes will have a swell time at this Hal Roach production…. The picture reaches a stirring climax when the Wooden Soldiers come to life and fight off Barnaby's ruffians. Direction by Gus Meins and Charles Rogers is excellent.

Motion Picture Daily, November 12: Hal Roach, with an expert showmanship eye, has produced a smashing box-office feature… It is highly entertaining and imaginative, assembling all the thrilling characters from the "Mother Goose Rhymes."… It's gorgeous fun and those two marvelous dopes Laurel and Hardy are just that…. The production is all that can be desired with the cast good throughout. Youngsters, no matter what age, will get a big boot out of this fantastic tomfoolery. In fact, it looks like a toss up as to who will take who, the children the parents or the parents the children…. Frank Butler and Nick Grindé did a swell job of writing the screenplay. "Babes in Toyland" seems set for a cleanup for the holidays or any other day.

Hollywood Filmograph, November 24: Hal Roach has a great picture in "Babes in Toyland"… Whoever created the sets is deserving of a medal, for the entire setting of the picture is the most unique and fantastic idea ever put on the screen… The kiddies will just love it. The grown-ups will marvel at the technical accomplishments… Directors Meins and Rogers certainly deserve all the credit possible for the patience and keen insight they had of this most difficult subject to command attention with, for it has its limitations, and they sure enough surmounted every obstacle to make this a truly great picture.

Motion Picture Herald, November 24: As a seasonal holiday feature this fairyland fantasy appears to possess one quality which most of its predecessors lacked in that while it is exceptional juvenile entertainment it is also a potential adult attraction…. For audiences, it's straightaway amusement every foot of the way; for exhibitors it's an exploitation gold mine, to be sold so that the maximum interest of both adults and children is aroused.

Philip K. Scheuer in the *Los Angeles Times*, November 25: Sheer delight awaits you in "Babes in Toyland," Hollywood's first successful venture into the realm of sound-film make-believe… At the finish a stunning new camera trick brings the Wooden Soldiers to the rescue of the besieged Toylanders, and the audience cheers. Months ago, visiting the Toyland set, I had a hunch the picture would be something. There I sensed an esprit, a teamwork, rare in a citadel of commercialized art; even the gentleman who disburses publicity appeared to believe in at least half of what he was saying. You will appreciate the distinction when you see 'Babes in Toyland.'"

MGM's publicity department created a three-and-one-half minute trailer, which audiences likely saw in mid-November, a couple of weeks before the film was released. It opened with a couple of shots not in the movie – the first being an overhead crane shot of the Toyland set with no residents in view, except for one citizen, looking a lot like Johnny Downs in his Little Boy Blue costume, running at the very left edge of the shot. This was followed with another unique shot of Scotty Mattraw as the Town Crier, ringing his bell in front of the Toyland School.

Accompanying this footage was the voice of Los Angeles-based announcer Ken Carpenter, later renowned for many years of bantering with Bing Crosby on radio, proclaiming, "Here they come! Call out the guard! Break out the colors! Summon the marines! Hasten the royal musicians! Thousands upon thousands of musicians! Strike up the band!" The baroque-style arrangement of Marvin Hatley's "Ku-Ku," created for *The Devil's Brother* the year before, introduced "Stanley Dum and Oliver Dee" as "the balmiest pair of toymakers that ever tuned a zither!" Close-ups introducing Charlotte Henry, Felix Knight, Henry Kleinbach, Florence Roberts and the Three Little Pigs were also unique to the trailer, as were a couple of lengthy shots depicting Ollie's distress in the ducking pond.

The trailer concluded with shots of the animated soldiers marching out of the warehouse, with a title promoting the film as "A royal romp through the land of make-believe," and advising, "Don't send the kiddies – BRING THEM!

The manager of the Loews Theater in Harrisburg, Pennsylvania created a lavish lobby display.

Another impressive bit of showmanship adorned a theater in Scranton.

YOU will enjoy it as much as they will!" Clearly there was some concern that the grown-ups would think the film too juvenile for their tastes. This would have a significant effect on the profits, since children's ticket prices were much lower than that for adults.

The trailer presented some slightly deceptive advertising when it promised "1 ½ hours of howling hilarity," since the film only ran 79 minutes, not 90. MGM can be forgiven for this, because the film was indeed divided into nine reels; it's likely that someone in the publicity department assumed that each reel had the usual running time of ten minutes. Had each of those reels run the full 900 feet, or 90 feet per minute at 24 frames per second of 35mm film, the movie would have run 90 minutes. However, several of the reels had less footage than this, particularly reel six, which measured only 675 feet, and reel nine, which ran 636 feet. The divisions were probably made for artistic reasons, so that a sequence would not be interrupted in the theaters with a projector change-over.

MGM assembled a special "Advertising Approach and Analysis" paper for exhibitors, which exhorted, "The Hal Roach production IS NOT an attempt to revive or imitate the stage-hit of 1904 [sic], grand as it was. IT IS the 1934 version of the most popular musical comedy ever written. Even in view of the fine precedent set, it outstrips the most lavish attraction of stage fame. As a motion picture it is bigger in every sense... more colorful... the music, with full-symphony quality, has the modern touch... the fantastic settings are a spectacle impossible to stagecraft. For comedy... LAUREL AND HARDY do it their way... an hour and a half of rib-cracking laughter... a full-length feature traveling the speed of their famous two-reelers."

MGM placed a full-page display advertisement in many of the trade papers, with a drawing of Leo the Lion using a tape measure on Hal Roach and proclaiming, WHEN A SHORT MAN GROWS LONG! Congratulations Hal Roach! "BABES IN TOYLAND" is sensational. Your biggest and most ambitious full-length feature is everything you dreamed it would be. Leo says, HOORAY FOR LAUREL-HARDY IN "BABES IN TOYLAND!"

MGM wanted to promote the film on radio but was hamstrung by the 1930 agreement between Victor Herbert's daughter, Ella Herbert Bartlett, and RKO, which now applied to MGM. On November 5, 1934, Thomas Gerety at MGM's offices in New York wrote to Sam Cohn at the Roach studio:

> Dear Sam:
> As you know our contract for "Babes in Toyland" limits our use of radio to three broadcasts and furthermore prohibits making of disc records for radio or other purposes. Our theatre department has been successful in arranging fifteen minute broadcasts in behalf of important feature pictures and they desire to do the same with "Babes in Toyland." I have already talked with Mrs. Bartlett and the Burken office and have an idea that I might be able to get Mrs. Bartlett to revise the contract sufficiently to permit us to make records of the fifteen minute program to be spotted on individual stations definitely tying up with the opening of the picture in those cities. Of course it is impossible to do this unless these programs can be put on disc records. Of course there is the possibility that we might

"Grotesque" masks supposed to be a clown and Mickey Mouse caught the attention of potential patrons in Davenport, Iowa.

The Astor Theater in New York re-opened with a marquee display that neighbors thought was too gaudy, but it packed in the customers.

take advantage of the opportunity which we have of arranging a national broadcast.

MGM produced a 15-minute transcribed radio show, *Leo Is on the Air*, which promoted forthcoming films. Thanks to its musical content, *Babes in Toyland* would have been a perfect property for radio exploitation. Back on October 2, Mrs. Bartlett's attorney, Charles Schwartz, had written to Ben Shipman, legal counsel for the Roach studio, and he indicated that a national, coast-to-coast broadcast would have been permissible:

> My dear Ben:
> Mrs. Bartlett has just been in to see me and has gone over with me the contents of your letter.
> As she construes the contract, you have a right to do the following:
> (a) To give not more than three broadcasts of a synopsis or story of your motion picture version;
> (b) A broadcast embraces any hook-up. In other words, if you give a broadcast over the National Broadcasting System, and the National Broadcasting System embraces a tie-up of twenty stations, that broadcast would be deemed in her opinion under the contract, one broadcast;
> (c) If in connection with the broadcast of the synopsis or story of the picture, you desire to use the numbers or some of the numbers of the operetta which are contained in the picture, that would be agreeable;
> (d) No disc records of any kind are permitted to be made.
> I trust the foregoing is clear.
> Mrs. Bartlett tells me that the separate broadcast of a synopsis or broadcast version of a play itself is a very valuable right and that she has been receiving for such broadcasts $400.00 per broadcast.
> If your people are interested in the broadcasting of tabloid versions of the operetta itself, you might communicate directly with Mrs. Bartlett, whose address is 116 East 68th Street, New York City.
> With kindest personal regards,
> Yours very sincerely,
> Charles Schwartz

Sadly, no such network program was ever broadcast – but Sam Cohn had other avenues for publicity. Although MGM executives concluded that it wasn't possible to use discs in any form to promote the story, there was no restriction on the music, as the copyrights were owned by the M. Witmark and Sons music publishers. As a result, "Toyland," "March of the Toys," "I Can't Do the Sum" – which was only in the film as underscoring – and a "Selection" of the tunes for piano were newly published, each with a bright red cover showing the massive Toyland set, the marching soldiers, and some of the townsfolk, with Chief of Police Billy Bletcher front and center. While Laurel and Hardy were mentioned on this cover art, their images, strangely, were nowhere to be seen.

The studio had the right to publish a "screen magazine fictionization" of the movie not exceeding five thousand words. Sam Cohn wrote about such a "fictionization" to Douglas Lurton, Managing Editor of Fawcett Publications, who suggested that this would work for the company's magazine *Romantic Movie Stories*; the article appeared in the March 1935 issue, when the film had come and gone in many cities, but was still yet to be screened in some parts of the country. Cohn did succeed in placing Laurel and Hardy, in their *Babes in Toyland* costumes, on the cover of the Winter 1934 edition of *1,000 New Jokes* from the Dell Publishing Company.

The official release date for the film in major cities was November 29, 1934, which was also Thanksgiving Day. The amazing sets, the Mother Goose characters, and the start of the holiday season all combined to make *Babes in Toyland* a wonderful subject for theater lobby displays. In these Depression days, theater managers who were real showmen created lavish exhibits which were sure to pull in the customers.

Loews Incorporated executive Milton Harris coordinated with Harry Long, manager of the Loews Stillman theater in Cleveland, to stage the biggest premiere in the city's history. On the night of Wednesday, November 28, the city was ablaze with klieg lights, as bands marched through the streets and state officials made speeches through a tie-up with radio station WGAR. Harris was able to get a long-distance call through to President Roosevelt, offering to turn over the entire receipts of the film's opening day (which started at midnight as November 29 began), as a donation to the Georgia Warm Springs Foundation. This was one of Roosevelt's favorite charities, as it maintained the resort which helped him and many others afflicted with polio. *Variety* noted, "Chief executive was quoted as saying that he heartily endorsed such theatre benefits, as he thought they would draw larger attendance than the infantile paralysis charity balls to be held on his Jan. 30

MGM's artists, among them Al Hirschfeld, created some wonderful promotional artwork, as in these window cards.

birthday, and expressed a hope that other theatres in country would follow precedent set in Cleveland."

The Quigley Publishing Company, which created and distributed the *Motion Picture Herald*, sponsored an annual award for showmanship. The Loews Incorporated people were so impressed with the Stillman display that they took out a full-page display advertisement in that publication nominating the theater's campaign for first prize.

Film Daily described the amazingly elaborate and thorough quest for publicity engaged by Harry Long and the staff of the Stillman theater:

> SPECTACULAR CAMPAIGN FOR "BABES IN TOYLAND"
>
> One of the most spectacular campaigns ever put over for a feature picture was launched in Cleveland in connection with Hal Roach's Laurel-Hardy special, "Babes in Toyland" at the Stillman theater.
>
> Front page publicity was derived for the show when President Roosevelt in person responded by telephone to an offer to give the proceeds of a midnight show to the Warm Springs fund.
>
> The first showing of the film, which was also a world premiere, was preceded by a colorful band parade, with red flares and banner, to the doors of the theater. Arc lights there made more of a display than anything Cleveland has seen since political convention days. A broadcast was conducted on the sidewalk outside the theater, with Mayor David, Governor-Elect Davey and other celebrities among the speakers. All invited guests received Jumbo telegrams, delivered by regular Postal Telegraph messengers.
>
> An attention-commanding "Babes in Toyland" float was sent

through the chief streets of the city as an advance ballyhoo. Two scenes from the picture were mounted on a large flat truck, with illumination at night. The truck later became an important unit in the monster Cleveland Press parade staged on Thanksgiving Day.

Ten thousand teaser heralds were distributed at the "Cleveland News" Skippies football game at League Park, while a similar number were used at the Western Reserve-Carroll game. A thousand stickers were pasted on newspapers delivered to guests at the Carter, Hollenden and Fenway Hall hotels. A thousand stickers were also sent to private homes on Mullaire cleaning bags.

An extensive tie-up with Old Gold resulted in placing of theater and play date stickers in all important cigar stores and counters in the city. Leading department stores in the city tied up for toyland window displays, using special easel signs.

Large posters were spotted on both sides of thirty-five Superior Transfer trucks, delivering local newspapers from plants to railroads and merchandise to principal stores.

Approximately eight thousand "Babes in Toyland" novel advertising toys were distributed to school pupils in cooperation with the theater and newspapers.

Among the additional accessories which were utilized to great advantage were bookmarks in 25 public libraries, one sheet novelty card posters exhibited in the lobbies of the Statler, Allerton and Cleveland hotels, Laurel and Hardy "reserved" cards for tables in the leading restaurants and hotels, and "Babes in Toyland" ice cream cones for children in 48 Marshall drug stores.

This, mind you, was a local campaign staged by one theater for one city. The Stillman played *Babes in Toyland* for seven days – this in a time when it was common to replace the program after two days – and grossed $6,000 for the week when their average take for that period was $4,000.

So spectacular was the ballyhoo produced by the Stillman theater that the national publicity suggested in the Campaign Book was almost puny by comparison, but it still warranted a feature article in the December 8 issue of *Film Daily*:

"BABES IN TOYLAND" FITS IN WITH XMAS

With its long list of famous Mother Goose characters, from Bo-Peep, Three Little Pigs, Tom the Piper's Son, Old King Cole, Simple Simon and Humpty Dumpty down to Little Boy Blue, Little Miss Muffet and Jack and Jill, the Hal Roach feature production of Victor Herbert's extravaganza, "Babes in Toyland," released by MGM, is an ideal attraction not only for holiday entertainment value but for exploitation around the Christmas season.

Press book suggestions for the exploitation of this picture include the following:

Juvenile costume matinee, with kids in toyland characters.

Christmas Happiness Parade for children.

Mother Goose recitation contest, which can be staged on a Saturday morning in the theater.

Holiday parties for orphans, inmates of homes for the aged, etc.

Toy making in store window.

Prizes for best parodies on nursery rhymes.

A "Christmas Proclamation of Happiness," by the theater, getting the mayor to sponsor the proclamation.

Display of Mother Goose characters in the theater lobby and store windows.

A good street stunt suggestion is for one or two men to impersonate Laurel and Hardy in the role of Santa Claus, passing out small, inexpensive gifts to kids, and taking orders for Christmas gifts.

National merchandise tie-ups on M-G-M's "Babes in Toyland" include:

Kolor-Toons, paint set with figures of Stan Laurel for sale in 5 & 10 cent stores, etc.; Laurel and Hardy sweat shirts; Laurel and Hardy Pee Wee Game, the popular boyhood game of "Cat"; colorful masks of Laurel and Hardy; Movie Moods Game, jig-saw games which might be obtained from stores in a contest tie-up; papier mâché heads of Laurel and Hardy made by R. Fiore, New York; Jack-in-the Box Hanger, with a combination Laurel and Hardy in the box, available from exchanges.

Manager Bill Miskel of the Orpheum theater in Omaha, Nebraska, created such a lavish display in his lobby that the film was held over for a second week, as *Variety* noted: "Display consisted of the spacious lobby of the theatre

The Campaign Book offered all sorts of inventive tie-in merchandise.

filled with replicas of the better known edifices of Mother Gooseland and Toyland, such as the shoe-home of the old lady with all the children, doll house, etc. Nothing miniature about these, wither; shoe, for example reaching up better than 10 feet.

"To add life to the display, the doorman was stuffed into a toy soldier's uniform, and three dancing brown boys performed for the customers at all breaks. Patron interest, along with appropriateness of the display… occasioned the hold-over."

Manger Sam Gillman and assistant Bob Etchberger of the Loew's Regent Theatre in Harrisburg, Pennsylvania, also mounted a lavish publicity campaign, as reported in Philadelphia Exhibitor: "Two ushers were dressed to represent Laurel and Hardy, wearing over their faces giant cardboard heads of the two comedians. A 'mechanical man,' dressed in the costume of a toy soldier was also on display.

"Steady, slow movements of the 'mechanical man' and his motionless face were remarkable. The Laurel and Hardy ushers tried to make him laugh. They made everyone but him roar with laughter. Guest tickets were offered to anyone able to make the 'mechanical soldier' laugh, which proved impossible.

"A miniature railroad engine, made by a Harrisburg fireman of the Pennsylvania Railroad, was used during the busy hours in the city streets. It was appropriately bannered… The trick auto was parked near schools and attracted a lot of attention. It helped get the kid trade for the show."

The Astor Theater in New York, which had been a showcase for MGM releases, had gone dormant for a time after failing to entice Depression-stricken audiences into paying a top price of $2.00 per ticket. It reopened with *Babes in Toyland*, and the boldly colorful design of the marquee made it clear that the house was back in business – too clear for many, as Epes W. Sargent of *Variety* noted on December 25:

> Some of the experts along Broadway are decrying the Astor marquee for 'Babes in Toyland.' It is a four section sign, each in a loud color and fighting the other three tints. They argue that it is inartistic.
>
> Maybe that's true, but the point is overlooked that 'Babes' is on a grind run in a two-a-day house and that extreme emphasis must be given the departure. The usual tasteful sign work used by Metro on its prior attractions would have no sales value here. It is necessary to make a loud noise, and it cannot better be done than with strenuous coloring. It would have been all wrong to have put over 'Merry Widow' with a similar layout, but this merely stresses the fact that a front display should be made to match the objective.
>
> Here the design is to grab the man who is passing by and to make it easy for mothers, unfamiliar to Broadway, who are bringing the kids to see this feature. With the hard coloring and big lettering, they can spot the house two blocks distant and hear it three.

The marquee may have been gaudy, but the Astor's strategy paid off. At a top price of 55 cents, *Babes in Toyland* was held over twice for a total run of 20 days and grossed $30,000 for the house.

A less conspicuous way of obtaining publicity arrived on the afternoon of Tuesday, December 18, when a special screening of *Babes in Toyland* was provided for the bedridden and disabled children of the Bellevue Hospital in New York City. Four days before the event, *Film Daily* called this "One of the really fine evidences of the Xmas Spirit" and noted, "We are looking forward eagerly to this special performance. It's a cinch that these Bellevue youngsters will be the most appreciative and responsive audience in town."

As the film continued to be released in major cities

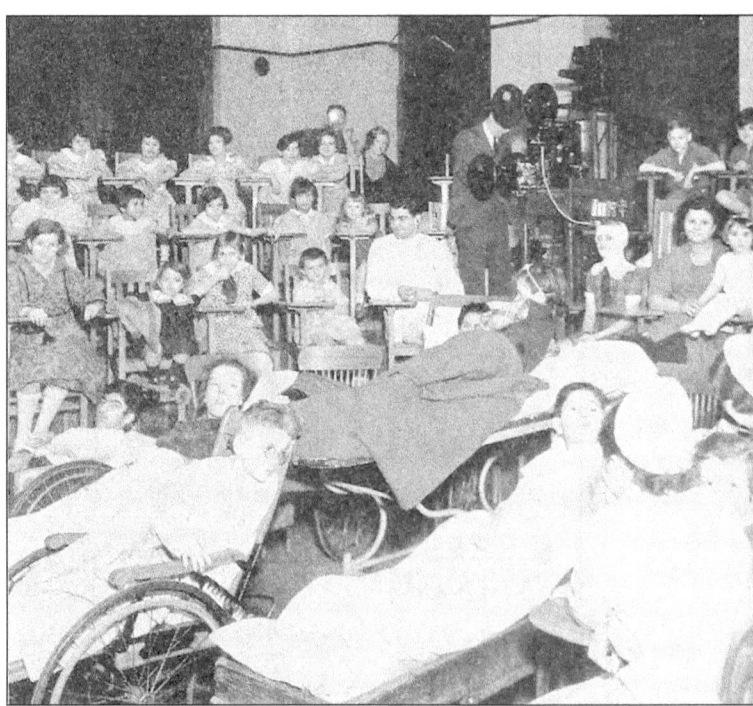

On December 18, 1934, a special screening of *Babes in Toyland* was held for children at the Bellevue Hospital in New York, as noted in the December 28 issue of *Motion Picture Herald*.

Hirschfeld may have provided this drawing for the MGM title lobby card.

through mid-December, reviews came pouring in. *Variety*, often highly critical of many Laurel and Hardy pictures, printed a glowing review from "Chic," the pen name of critic Epes W. Sargeant. Despite whatever misgivings he may have had about the movie, Hal Roach was properly applauded for producing it.

> If Hal Roach aimed at the production of a purely juvenile picture, to which children might conceivably drag their elders, he has succeeded in a measure beyond others who have sought to enter this realm. He has made a film par excellence for children. It's packed with laughs and thrills and is endowed with that glamour of mysticism which marks juvenile literature.
>
> 'Babes in Toyland' is as far away from the Victor Herbert original operetta as Admiral Byrd from his home port.... Of the original book there is no trace at all. This is not a musical brought to the screen. It is a fairy story in technique and treatment, but a gorgeous fairy tale which gives everything to Laurel and Hardy and to which, in return, they give their happiest best.... 'Babes' probably will get special holiday booking for four or five years to come....
>
> It will not bore those who have to accompany their children. It possesses a pictorial quality that will appeal. At the Astor there was a large sprinkling of men trickling into the house.... Children laughed freely when they were not thrilled by Bogeyland. Latter sequence is not so rough as to induce nightmares....
>
> This brings a smashing climax with the soldiers marching to the strains of 'March of the Toys.' It gives a full five minutes of smashing action that will lift children under 12 completely out of their seats, and yet it is not so terrifying as to alarm....
>
> All Mother Goose characters are woven into the plot, not to mention the Three Little Pigs, but it's Laurel and Hardy's picture. While they

Spanky McFarland proved to be just as skillful at the "Pee-Wee" game as Stan.

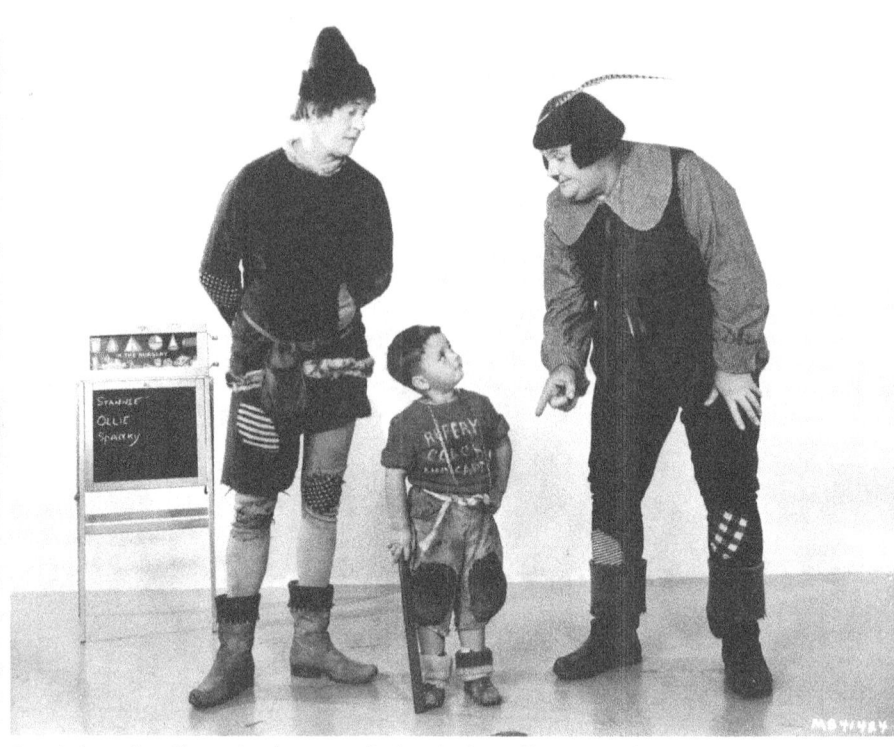

Spanky's outfit tells us that he was called away from filming *Washee Ironee* to appear in these photos.

are on the story zips along, but the mistake has not been made of asking them to fill the stage continuously. It is their absences which make their reappearances so effective. The same Laurel and Hardy of shorts, but in fancy dress and apt to endear themselves to parents because of this effort....

This picture may not be consistently big boxoffice, but it is the best juvenile product to date and deserves the long life it will have.

The New York Times, also not always enthusiastic about Laurel and Hardy, gave its endorsement in a review by Andre Sennwald. Again, it accorded full credit to the producer:

> Hal Roach, lord high master of the slapstick, ventures among the gargoyles of never-never land in his delightful 'Babes in Toyland,' which seems destined to cause a vast whooping and stamping of feet among the youngsters during the approaching holiday season. The film is an authentic children's entertainment and quite the merriest of its kind that Hollywood has turned loose on the nation's screens in a long time. Borrowing Victor Herbert's title and his music, as well as Walt Disney's dream-world secrets, the custodian of the royal custard has enriched the Christmas holidays with an original flesh-and-blood fantasy. Since the comic team of Laurel and Hardy has wandered into it, the elders, as well as their young charges, are advised to check their dignity at the door.... They are a marvelous pair of varlets, and in the course of 'Babes in Toyland' they succeed in doing many things the wrong way.
>
> If Mr. Roach had provided more room for Messrs. Dum and Dee his fantasy would prove as continuously hilarious for the adults as

Ollie is determined to score at least once.

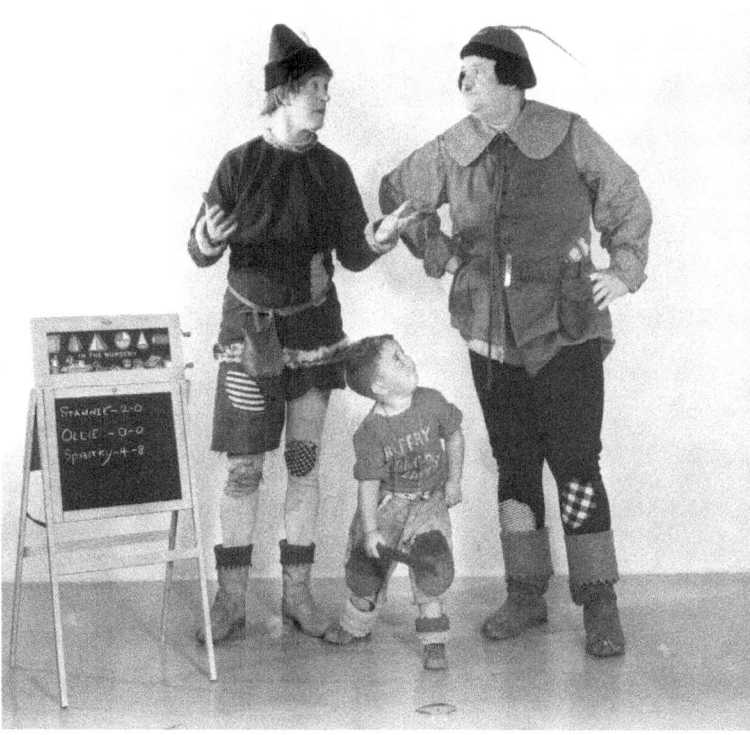

Spanky is even better at the game than Stan.

it is sure to be for the youngsters. But this is a juvenile picnic and Mr. Roach has preserved the faith with his audience. Still the two clowns, in their tattered doublet and hose, are remarkably funny in their limited repertoire. This midnight correspondent is most grateful for the episode in which the obese and prissy Mr. Hardy is dunked in the ducking stool. Also the scene in which Mr. Laurel smuggles his partner in a trunk into Barnaby's house to steal the mortgage....

Every youngster in New York ought to find a ticket for 'Babes in Toyland' in his Christmas stocking. If he is a good boy he should be permitted to see it twice.

Reviews from other New York newspapers ran the gamut.

Journal: "Babes in Toyland," devised as holiday fare for children, emerges as a delightful fantasy peopled with characters from Mother Goose rhymes and the Walt Disney cartoons. Youthful audiences should gurgle with glee, and their elders will find plenty to divert them as well.

Post: A bright, decorative and fancifully conceived version of the Victor Herbert operetta, built on the Mother Goose stories and sprinkled with some of the composer's better melodies. As a further recommendation, it has Laurel and Hardy in some of their rousing antics. It should appeal to grownups as well as children.

Mirror: Though modern children have developed a perverse preference for the robust realism of Mae West, this delightful "Babes in Toyland" should enchant them. It is a charming children's picture, refreshing, hilarious, imaginative.

Sun: "Babes in Toyland" is a children's picture every inch and note of it. Packed into its rollicking background are characters from Mother Goose, from Walt Disney, maybe even from Victor Herbert. It seems like a sure bet for any youngster's enchantment.

News: There is not much point relating the details of the plot, for the photoplay deals in fantasy, which gaily shatters the confines of credibility. It will thrill every boy and girl who sees it.

Herald Tribune: A quaintly nonsensical tale, sufficiently melodramatic to hold its small, or big attendants breathless during the frenzied suspense at the end.

Norbert Lusk reported from New York for the *Los Angeles Times*:

> The Hal Roach production is a knockout from every standpoint and a perfect holiday attraction. A clever adaptation of the original, it is more than a mere transference of a stage operetta to the screen. It qualifies as a robust Laurel and Hardy vehicle, at the same time coming through as a fantasy with a degree of childlike appeal that will make it a gold mine for exhibitors. Even the temptation to let

The boys are enjoying the "Movie Moods" puzzle that was promoted in the Campaign Book.

the tunefulness of Victor Herbert's music run away with editorial judgment has been resisted. In consequence, music never interferes with fun and surprises. Best of all elements which make the venture more than usually successful is the quality of childlike wonder that invests the whole, yet the picture is never childish, this being one of the reasons why it appeals to grown-ups and is more than a juvenile attraction.

In Los Angeles, the film received the unusual treatment of having its premiere at two theaters – the lavish United Artists theater at 933 South Broadway, and six miles west, the Four Star Theatre at 5112 Wilshire Boulevard. Philip K. Scheuer wrote a more local review for the *Times*:

> It is a gay and melodious holiday package for all. Particularly it is something for the children – not the very young ones, perhaps, for it has its share of creepy things, the inhabitants of Bogeyland. But over and above this, the production boasts a quality which until now has belonged exclusively to the cartoons, and those of Walt Disney especially. It never "plays down" to its audience....
> The climax [is] a brilliantly executed tour de force in which the battalions go clump-clumping out of the warehouse to the rescue

Artwork made by MGM for newspaper advertisements was creative and varied.

of the besieged Toylanders, Victor Herbert's inspiriting march to set the beat. It makes as pretty and martial a sight as the movies have given us since they grew voice-conscious; and yesterday, man and boy, we cheered them on.... I salute Mr. Roach and his aides for what they have accomplished.

May Tinée pseudonymously (matinee, get it?) praised the film in the *Chicago Tribune*:

It's been many a long day since I've had so much pure (and I MEAN pure!) fun as I had watching this picture....

Mr. Barnaby is all the Dickens and Dixiana showboat villains rolled into one.... Laurel and Hardy are awfully funny this trip... That march of the wooden soldiers...! Honestly – you want to stand up and cheer!...

Young Felix Knight, who plays Tom-Tom, made a hit with me. Never saw him before that I know of. He has a warmly magnetic personality and a splendid voice. His scenes with Charlotte Henry are charming.

"Babes in Toyland" is rich with humor and whimsy. It has been directed with perfect sympathy and good taste. Though preceded by no fanfare, it has "Alice in Wonderland" backed off the boards as entertainment.

However, not all of the reviews were raves. Again, from New York newspapers:

American: Putting aside the Christmas spirit, and regarding the film as a piece of cinematic craftsmanship, it shows up as a two-reel idea stretched tenuously to feature length. It doesn't always skip along with the gaiety intended, and not until the Bogieman sequences does any element of excitement enter.

World-Telegram: For about ¾ of its running time, "Babes in Toyland" is delightful whimsical musical extravaganza that should be a joy to holiday audiences both young and

Top: Local theater managers created their own inventive advertising artwork, as did someone at the Century Theatre in Minneapolis. *Bottom*: Stan's long absences postponed the planned Easter release. Christmas turned out to be a much more appropriate time for the film.

"BABES IN TOYLAND" FITS IN WITH XMAS

Saturday, Dec. 8, 1934 — The Film Daily

Exploiting the Christmas Bills

With its long list of famous Mother Goose characters, from Bo-Peep, Three Little Pigs, Tom the Piper's Son, Old King Cole, Simple Simon and Humpty Dumpty down to Little Boy Blue, Little Miss Muffett and Jack and Jill, the Hal Roach feature production of Victor Herbert's extravaganza, "Babes in Toyland," released by M-G-M, is an ideal attraction not only for holiday entertainment value but for exploitation around the Christmas season.

Press book suggestions for the exploitation of this picture include the following:

Juvenile costume matinee, with kids in toyland characters.

Christmas Happiness Parade for children.

Mother Goose recitation contest, which can be staged on a Saturday morning in the theater.

Holiday parties for orphans, inmates of homes for the aged, etc.

Toy making in store window.

Prizes for best parodies on nursery rhymes.

A "Christmas Proclamation of Hapiness," by the theater, getting the mayor to sponsor the proclamation.

Display of Mother Goose characters in the theater lobby and store windows.

A good street stunt suggestion is for one or two men to impersonate Laurel and Hardy in the role of Santa Claus, passing out small, inexpensive gifts to kids, and taking orders for Christmas gifts.

Film Daily noted how well the film fit the holiday season for exhibitors.

old. The rest, which involves a trip to Bogieland, is rather complicated, ponderous and, I imagine, a bit too terrifying for the minors for whom it was primarily intended."

The one controversial aspect of the film was the invasion of the Bogeymen. Some of the adults reviewing the film thought that these scenes were far too frightening for children to witness. The most critical review came from *Motion Picture Reviews*, written and published by members of the Women's University Club, the Los Angeles branch of the American Association of University Women.

"It is a lovely realm of unreality," wrote the reviewer, "until the crass touch of materialism is introduced in picturing a bogey land with writhing crocodiles and hairy, grinning apes to frighten little Bo Peep and her friends as well as children in the audience. The pursuit of these monsters, the crash of the gates of Toyland and the prolonged fight cannot be easily dispelled even by the final triumph of the wooden soldiers. It is stupid to have had adult interpretation ruin the suitability of a film whose appeal otherwise is chiefly for children's audiences." She felt that the film would be "possibly amusing" to adolescents ages 12 to 16, but was not to be seen by anyone under ten.

A subscriber to the British magazine *Picturegoer Weekly* also voiced her objection to the Bogeymen, without having seen the film: "May I put in an urgent plea for children's films without bogeys? That excellent Disney offering, *Lullaby Land*, was ruined for at least one child by the terrifying goblin shapes, which actually sent him in desperation to hide under his seat. Now I hear the same of *Babes in Toyland*. Would it not be possible to have humour, and even oddity, without ugliness?"

Picturegoer Weekly's reviewer didn't care for the film but ironically enjoyed the Bogeymen sequence most: "While it is spectacular in setting, it is not ingenious in presentation. One incident there is which stands out – a troop of toy soldiers attack the Bogeymen who have invaded Toy Town – but with that exception it is singularly lacking in inspiration. Stan Laurel and Oliver Hardy, in the leads, are starved of material and fall back on very conventional slapstick."

In England, *Babes in Toyland* had the unhappy distinction of being the only Laurel and Hardy film to not receive a "U" rating (acceptable for universal audiences) from the British Board of Film Censors. Instead, it was given a "PG" rating (for parental guidance) because of the Bogeymen

The perennial favorites from Herbert's score were published with a new cover to promote the movie.

MGM was impressed with the lavish publicity given by the Stillman Theater in Cleveland.

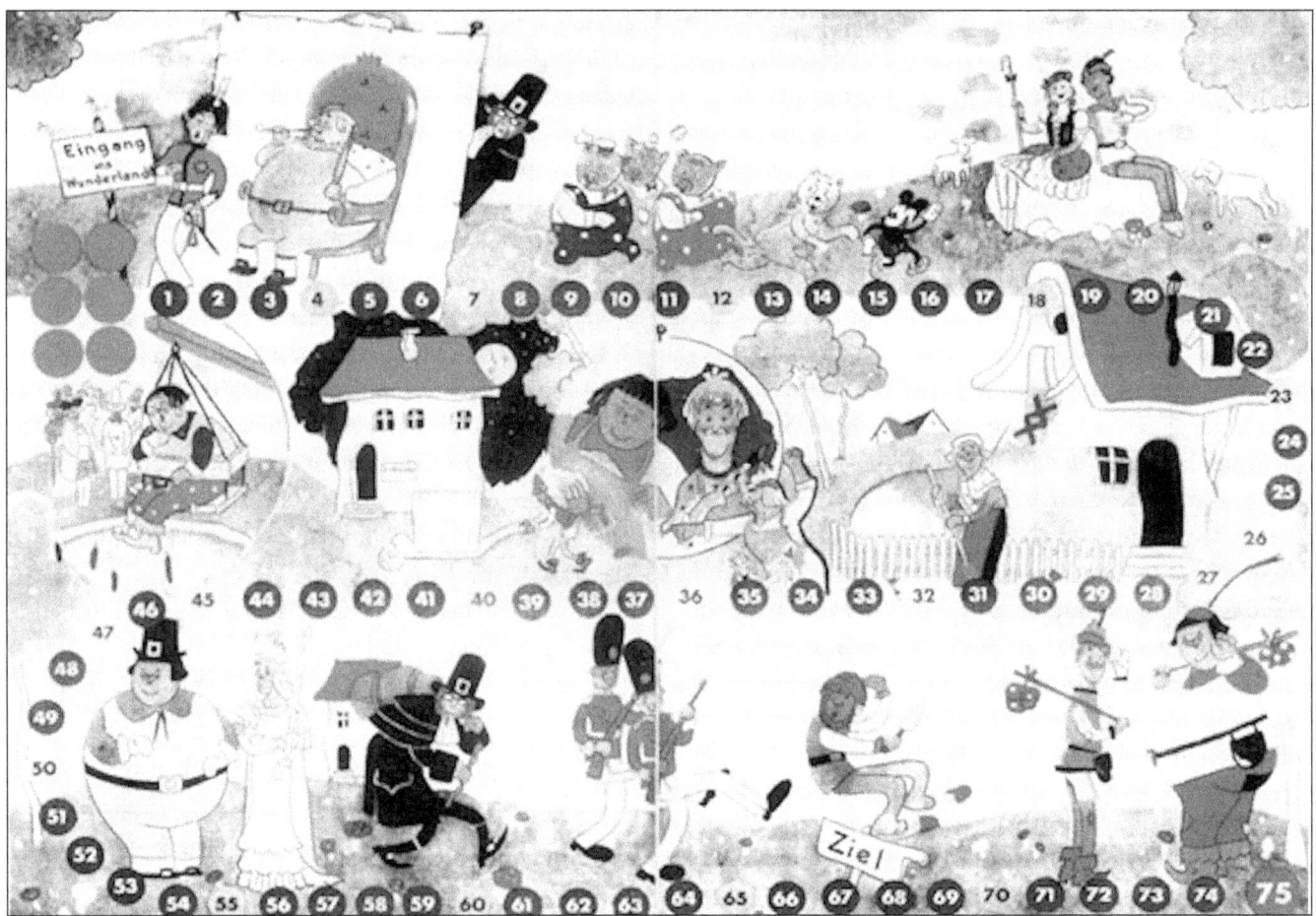

In Germany, kids could play a special board game depicting characters from the movie.

scenes which the BBFC found disturbing. A "PG" rating is described as being for "general viewing, but some scenes may be unsuitable for young children. A PG film should not unsettle a child aged around eight or older."

Back in the States, any film not only had to meet with the approval of the Production Code Administration, it also had to pass muster with State censor boards. In mid-to-late December 1934, these boards reported to Joseph I. Breen. The censors of Ohio, Massachusetts, Kansas, New York and Pennsylvania all approved *Babes in Toyland* without eliminations. However, on December 26, the board for the Canadian province of British Columbia requested the elimination of "four shots bogey men" from reel eight, and nine similar shots from reel nine.

Some European countries didn't receive the film until 1936. On January 28 of that year, the board for Austria sent Breen this notice: "Reel 9 – Eliminate scenes of bogeymen stealing children." Sweden was much stricter in its request of February 6: "Reels 8 & 9 – Delete all scenes in which bogeymen appear." This would effectively rob the movie of its climax.

The board for Latvia was the most severe of all, according to a note sent to Breen: "It is not possible to define with any degree of certainty what local censors will take exception to. Explanations are not given by the censors. The word 'Worthless' is usually applied by the censors and when used is sufficient for banning a picture. 'Babes in Toyland' was banned sometime back for juveniles despite Metro's protest. Other pictures that were summarily banned although passed without cuts in almost all other countries were 'Society Doctor,' "Evelyn Prentice,' 'Penthouse' and 'The Thin Man.' Even a number of Laurel and Hardy shorts were refused exhibition."

In his later years, Hal Roach counted among his many criticisms of the film the Bogeymen scenes, as he related to historian Anthony Slide in 1970: "They brought these goons in from the forest to destroy Toyland, and the Parent Teachers Association of America condemned the picture because that would scare children. Instead of being a picture for children, it was condemned!" Perhaps Mr. Roach was forgetting the violence of his original treatment, which had Barnaby exclaiming that he would bring "DEATH and INJURY and TORMENT" to children, not to mention the wooden soldiers bringing "violence, murder and rape" to Toyland, and a final scene of near decapitation for Tom-Tom.

Left: Unique line art promoted the film in the Netherlands. *Right*: A cute cartoon of the boys adorned posters in Denmark.

Most children, however, seemed to be more mature than the grown-ups realized, as the reviewer had noted about their having "a perverse preference for Mae West." Instead of being terrified, they seemed to revel in the Bogeymen sequences, as reported by Mrs. F. R. Warner, a Minneapolis mother and housewife in a letter to the editors of *The New Movie* magazine:

> Hats off and three cheers for Laurel and Hardy! At last little Bill, age seven, was allowed to see a picture. In fact, we all went to see "Babes in Toyland."
>
> And if you think children don't respond to suitable and well made pictures, you should have been in the audience watching this picture. Mouths open, eyes wide, and many wide grins, all attested a most appreciative audience. Each and every fantastic character was greeted with delight and recognition. The children lived, for a time, with Tom Thumb, the bogeyman, and the villainous landlord.
>
> Laurel and Hardy gave my child a fanciful but convincing afternoon. Furthermore, I know mothers appreciate a picture like this that is suitable and enjoyable for their children.

The film furnished excellent business during the week before Christmas, usually a notoriously bad time for theaters, as people were too busy making plans for the holidays or shopping for gifts to go to the movies. *Variety* reported in its December 25 issue that the picture was doing great business in Lincoln, Nebraska: "The smash of the layout this week is 'Babes in Toyland' at the

More charming caricatures on posters in Sweden (left) in Italy (right), where the promotion was especially enthusiastic.

Lincoln, which ran to excellent reception all through the opening day. A big play is made for the kids, and as a consequence the sidewalk is piled high with bicycles, and the usual squawking of mothers, PTA's and church groups about bad Xmas billing is allayed."

Another very exclusive audience in Lincoln did not care for the film, as *Film Daily* reported: "Because 'Babes in Toyland' and 'Peck's Bad Boy' were shown on two successive nights at the Nebraska state penitentiary, the inmates won't attend shows now unless the warden gives his personal guarantee that the films suit their taste."

The Century theater in Minneapolis did well with the picture: "Ideal Christmas week attraction. Kiddies are coming strong and bringing parents. Despite slovenly start, should finish with fair $4,000." The Fulton in Pittsburgh also had a success: "Last week 'Babes in Toyland' brought the kids in droves and enabled house to collect around $5,800 for its first profit in some time."

Many exhibitors around the United States couldn't screen the film until well into 1935. *The Motion Picture Herald's* feature, "What the Picture Did for Me," provided a venue for small-town theater managers to give their opinions of the films they ran and relate how their audiences responded:

- Wonderful. Laurel and Hardy do some fine work and the story is good. Production, cast, story, sound, sets and in fact everything is all that one could ask or expect. S.H. Rich, Rich Theatre, Montpelier, Idaho. Town and rural patronage.
- Very topical in Christmas season, but it was a washout playing it later. It is neither a kid's picture and neither was it an adult one.

It is elaborately mounted, good music, and strictly a holiday picture that should have been run either close to Christmas or soon thereafter. Laurel and Hardy are not popular with the adults, either. They were all right in two-reel comedies, but they are too much of a type to make stars to head a feature with. – A.E. Hancock, Columbia Theatre, Columbia City, Ind. General patronage.

• Great. The old fairy tales come to life and how! The parents could not drag the kiddies out after the first show, so they all stayed for the second show and some came back the second night. You cannot advertise this too highly for kiddies, and adults seemed to like it, too. Very clever impersonations. Exceptionally good. Played February 13-14. – Gladys E. McArdle, Owl Theatre, Lebanon, Kan. Small town patronage.

• Reporting this picture is rather hard. Personally I liked the picture but there were a lot of people who did not. It failed to draw. Did the poorest Sunday-Monday business in months. This too in face of the fact that it was sold through the schools. Played March 17-18. – H. M. Johnson, Avon Theatre, Avon Park, Fla. General patronage.

• This one pleased. Drew the grown-ups as well as the kids. Held up nicely for a three-day run. Laurel and Hardy always do good for us. Good business. Played March 18. – Esther Schaber, The Senator, Ashley, N.D. Small city and country patronage.

Babes in Toyland made its way around the world in the spring of 1935. *Variety* on March 13 reported that in Mexico City, retitled *Once Upon a Time There Were Two Heroes*, it was doing "whacko" business, that is to say excellent. In Berlin, "Dick und Doof" were packing them in at the Mozartsaal in *Boese Buben im Wunderland*.

In Paris, the newspaper critics had a divided reaction. The *Journal* stated, "Nothing as disagreeable as a farce which isn't funny, and this, laboriously composed to permit our friends Laurel and Hardy to amuse us, is lacking." Noted the *Jour*, "I do not think one finds the enthusiasm for the story of Tom and his shepherdess as for Mickey Mouse, Felix the Cat, Alice in Wonderland. Happily, however, Laurel and Hardy come with their foolery and gags." The reviewer for *Paris Midi* wrote, "This is a film for children and nothing but that. The comic quality is considerable, since Laurel and Hardy have been entrusted with the principle roles." The critic for *Intransigeant* sniffed, "For

Top: In Viagreggio, Italy, the Cinema Adua had a lavish lobby display. *Bottom*: So did this theater in Bologna, publicizing "In the World of Wonders."

A French artist created this beautiful poster for the release in that country.

children under twelve… as to older children and adults, there is not the grace of Alice in Wonderland." However, the film critic for *Comoedia* raved, "This is in every way successful. The humor of Laurel and Hardy is irresistible." Bad reviews did not dissuade the Parisian public from lining up to see the picture, as reported on May 25, 1935 by the *Hollywood Reporter*: "*Babes in Toyland* is breaking audience records for the Elysees Gaumont since the last Laurel and Hardy film, *Hollywood Party*."

Most of Europe first saw the film in April and May 1935. Finland and Denmark didn't get it in theaters until September and October. Norwegians had to wait until August 1936. Australians got their first chance to see the picture in June 1937, and Japan had the last premiere on July 22, 1939.

The title was translated into a cornucopia of colorful variations.

Austria – *Land des Lachens* (*Land of Laughter*)

Brazil – *Era uma Vez Dois Valentes* (*Once Upon a Time Two Braves*)

Denmark - *Bange for Bussemænd* (*Afraid of Bogeymen*)

Finland – *Surullisen Hahmon Ritarit* (*Knights of Sad Character*)

France – *Un Jour une Bergère* (*One Day a Shepherdess*)

Germany – *Böse Buben im Wunderland* (*Bad Boys in Wonderland*)

Greece – *Oi Kallikantzaroi* (*The Goblins*)

Hungary – *Egyszer Volt, Hol Nem Volt* (*Once Upon a Time*)

Italy – *Nel Paese delle Meraviglie* (*In Wonderland*)

Japan – 玩具の国 (*Country of Toys*)

Mexico – *Había una Vez Dos Héroes* (*Once Upon a Time There Were Two Heroes*)

Norway – *Helan og Halvans Store Eventyr* (*The Whole and the Half's Great Adventure*)

Poland – *Flip i Flap w Krainie Cudów* (*Flip and Flap in Wonderland*)

Portugal – *Era uma Vez… Dois Valentes* (*Once Upon a Time…Two Braves*)

Romania – *Marşul Soldăţeilor de Lemn* (*The March of the Wooden Soldiers*)

Soviet Union – Марш деревянных солдатиков (*March of the Wooden Soldiers*)

Spain – *Había una Vez Dos Héroes* (*Once Upon a Time There Were Two Heroes*)

Sweden – *Det Var Två Glada Gesäller* (*They Were Two Happy Companions*)

Ukraine – Малята в Країні іграшок (*Babies in the Land of Toys*)

By mid-1935, Laurel and Hardy were working on their next feature, *Bonnie Scotland*, which would cause an even more damaging rift over the story between Roach and Laurel, to the point that Stan walked out and Roach began promoting a new series, *The Hardy Family*, to star Babe with Patsy Kelly as his wife and Spanky McFarland as their son. Fortunately, Roach and Laurel were able to reconcile and continue working together through late 1939.

The "Negative Cost" of *Babes in Toyland*, the total cost of producing the film, came to $421,810.68, which was about $200,000 more than their formerly most expensive film, *Pardon Us*. Its gross earnings in the United States came to $376,467.20. The earnings from other countries totaled $567,178.06. Metro-Goldwyn-Mayer (the distributors) and RCA Victor (suppliers of the sound recording equipment) took their combined percentages of $122,096.18, which left a net profit to the Hal Roach Studio of $13,853.24, or just about one month's worth of Stan Laurel's $3,500

Italian artist Giacinto Galbiati drew the artwork for this puzzle (*left*) and for this book (*right*). *Courtesy of Andrea Ciaffaroni.*

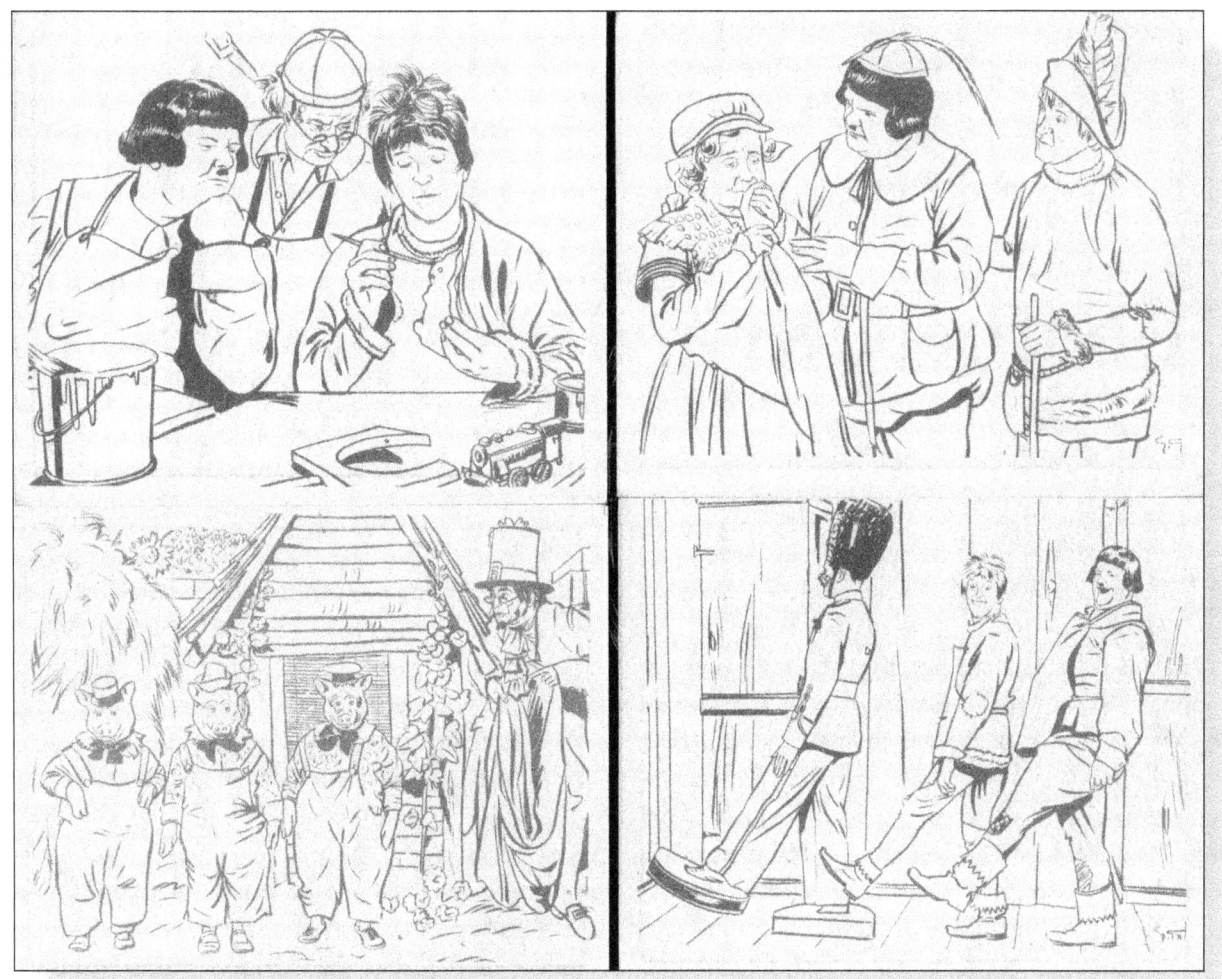

Another book from Italy had more realistic drawings.

a week salary.

If Stan hadn't caused the two lengthy delays – during which many people specific to this production remained on the payroll – *Babes in Toyland* very likely would have turned a healthier profit, even with the added expense of those massive sets, costumes, and dozens of extras. If it had been the box-office bonanza that *The Devil's Brother* had been, would Hal Roach have held the film in higher esteem in his later years? For many producers, directors and stars, a film that made lots of money was great, and a film that didn't was lousy, no matter what its artistic value might have been. Since Roach was so disappointed in Stan's rejection of his original story, he probably would have continued to think of the picture as a failure even if it had made a huge profit, given his later statement that "I never in my whole career paid any particular attention to the finances." MGM's full-page advertisements of congratulation, the thanks accorded to Roach by many film reviewers, and the special attention paid to the film by theater managers had little effect on him.

Roach's close associate Richard W. Bann has this viewpoint: "More than it just barely broke even, it tied up the entire studio to do what? To stand still for an entire year. And of course MGM was going to put the best face on the thing that they could, as they had an investment to recoup as well. They were never going to reveal to the public their displeasure with the cost overrun, missing the release date, having PTA groups complain that a film for kids was actually scaring kids. This was a terrible experience for Hal Roach, trying to keep the doors open at his studio with Stan causing so much trouble for him and the whole studio while so many other studios around him were shutting their doors. This was a frightening period in Hollywood."

Considering the year of frustration, the hard work, and the damage it caused to Hal Roach and Stan Laurel's working relationship, *Babes in Toyland* was very expensive in many ways. It would eventually be considered a triumph by generations of viewers, but before that, the film would languish in obscurity for many, many years.

Chapter 14

The Producer and the Counterspy

William LeBaron had almost produced *Babes in Toyland* for RKO in 1930. Following this, in mid-1932 he had become the head of production for Paramount, starting with *Hot Saturday* (Cary Grant's first film as a leading man), and ending 126 films later in 1941 with *Kiss the Boys Goodbye*, starring Mary Martin and Don Ameche. In between, he had produced films starring W.C. Fields, Mae West, Bing Crosby and Bob Hope, and supervised great comedies directed by Preston Sturges. Late in 1941 he moved to 20th Century-Fox and oversaw 13 features, including several of Betty Grable's best movies. In 1945 he left that studio to go into independent production; 15 years after his first failed attempt, he was again planning to make a new film from *Babes in Toyland*, in partnership with producer Boris Morros.

Born on January 1, 1891 in St. Petersburg, Russia, Morros was part of a privileged family. "My father was a teacher, my mother a singer," Morros wrote. "I, the oldest of their nine children, was a boy prodigy—a concert cellist at eight, an orchestra leader in my teens. My father saw that we all obtained the best education possible." From the age of eight, he spent his summers making concert tours. "I was presented as a Wunderkind where I played my quarter-sized cello, on bandstands in the public parks as well as in concert halls. Later I played before the Czar's court, where, like everyone else, I was both fascinated and frighted by the hypnotic eyes of Rasputin, the Mad Monk.... I left the country in 1922 because from everything I had heard of the Soviet leaders I had become convinced that they might not feel kindly toward a musician who had performed at the Winter Palace of Czar Nicholas."

He found a job accompanying silent movies on organ and piano in Boston, which led to a position as the traveling orchestra leader for the Paramount Publix theater chain. In 1929 he became regional music director of all Paramount theaters in the South. By the next year he was named music director for the 62 most prestigious of Paramount's movie palaces, and supervised the music and booked the talent for the stage shows which accompanied the films. "That meant," he wrote, "among other duties, auditioning scores of acts a week, from fire eaters, dog acts and acrobats to comics and coloratura sopranos, not to mention Wagnerian tenors."

In 1935, Adolph Zukor, president of Paramount, appointed Morros as general music director of the studio. Morros was credited on 148 Paramount pictures from 1936 (*The Trail of the Lonesome Pine*), to 1940 (*Texas Rangers Ride Again*). In 1939 he became an independent producer, making his debut with *The Flying Deuces*, starring Laurel and Hardy. This was a particularly significant film for Babe Hardy. Morros hired a freelance script clerk, Virginia Lucille Jones, who so impressed Hardy upon their meeting

Boris Morros and William LeBaron proudly announced the formation of their new company, Federal Films, in 1945.

When Morros had produced *The Flying Deuces* in 1939, he had gotten along well with Babe and with Stan, who seems to be making a point cordially but firmly.

that eight months later he married her. After years of sadness in his private life, this provided a wonderful happy ending which lasted for Babe's remaining 17 years.

Morros also produced *Second Chorus* (1940) starring Fred Astaire, Paulette Goddard and Artie Shaw, and the all-star anthology film *Tales of Manhattan* (1942). In the fall of 1943, he began negotiating for the film rights to *Babes in Toyland* with Victor Herbert's daughter and the executrix of his estate, Ella Herbert Bartlett.

It was a wonder that Morros was able to produce anything, since he was preoccupied with far weightier problems. In 1936, under the threat of "reprisal measures started against my family," his parents and siblings who were still in Russia, he was blackmailed into working as a spy for the Soviet government, which continued for the next eleven years. On July 14, 1947, racked with guilt, he went to the FBI office in Los Angeles and confessed everything. It took a full week of lengthy meetings for him to divulge all of it.

Instead of freeing himself from the espionage business, he got himself more deeply involved by agreeing to become a counterspy for the FBI. Morros put an FBI agent on the Federal Films payroll as his secretary at $50 a week. "He was so useful around the studio office that my partners complimented me on having acquired a gem of a secretary," Morros wrote. "He also earned his FBI salary by listening in on every phone call I made or received, by traveling with me everywhere I went – and by protecting my life, which suddenly the FBI considered important because of the strange and perilous position I had jammed myself into."

A short, bald, pudgy man, Morros was known for his thick Russian accent, his wildly colorful clothing and equally outlandish stories. "I am not a man to quarrel with the Broadway adage, 'A little embellishment never ruined a good story,'" he wrote. "Yet most of the tales I've told about my flamboyant early life are true."

Ella Herbert Bartlett was a tough negotiator. In 1944 she sued the record companies Columbia, Decca and RCA Victor for copyright infringement in selling more than a million copies of "March of the Toys." Her suit was settled out of court for a very substantial sum. She absolutely hated the Laurel and Hardy film, to the extent that when she entered into a contract with MGM in 1936 granting them the film rights to four other Herbert musicals, she expressly included the instruction that "No opera is to be 'burlesqued' or done by Roach with Laurel and Hardy, or a like team."

In 1945, Hal Roach was discharged from the Army Air Forces as a Lieutenant Colonel. His studio, which had been commandeered by the federal government to make training films, was returning to civilian production. Roach and his son, Hal Junior, were hoping to make a "streamliner" – a hybrid of short and feature running about 40 minutes – of *Babes in Toyland*, but the negotiations fell through. Given Mrs. Bartlett's opinion of Roach's earlier film, it's surprising that she even entertained a meeting with him.

The July 1945 issue of *Movieland* magazine contained the first information about the forthcoming Morros-LeBaron *Babes in Toyland* movie to be issued publicly. The producers had formed a new company, Federal Films. By announcing their film, they were acting prematurely, as a contract with Ella Bartlett had yet to be signed. Nevertheless, they maintained that was going to be "a big $3,000,000 production," with Claudette Colbert "under consideration for the lead role." George Pal, who had been making a series of stop-action animated "Puppetoons" for Paramount using hand-carved wooden puppets, would provide some sequences, combining the figurines with live action footage. This lavish production would be filmed in Technicolor. LeBaron and Morros added that they were also going to make *Carnegie Hall*, a history of the concert venue; *Carmen from Kenosha* ("a modern musical story based on the opera 'Carmen'"); and *My Immortal Beloved*, based on the life of Beethoven.

By February 26, 1946, Morros had closed a deal with United Artists to distribute the films. More news began to surface in July, with word that filming would begin in March or April of 1947, and the budget would be somewhere between $1,500,000 and $2,000,000. *Carnegie Hall* was being filmed in New York, and boasted appearances from many famed singers and musicians, among them Metropolitan Opera baritone Ezio Pinza, pianist Artur Rubinstein, and Vaughn Monroe's orchestra. However, *Babes in Toyland* and the other two pictures would be produced at the Hal Roach Studio, a logical move since Federal Films' office was on the Roach lot at 8822 Washington Boulevard in Culver City. A contract with Roach had been signed by July 27, 1946. This time around, Roach was providing only the studio facilities.

One wonders if he might have tried to convince Morros and LeBaron to use his unfilmed story from 1933.

On November 27, *Variety* noted, "With two years of negotiation with the Victor Herbert estate culminating last week in the inking of a contract, Boris Morros-William LeBaron unit, Federal Films, has put down 'Babes in Toyland' as next production on its schedule... Pact with the Herbert interests is for a flat sum, not a percentage. Herbert's son, John, of New Orleans, and daughter, Ella Bartlet of N.Y., signed on behalf of the estate... Operetta's libretto is being tossed out in favor of a story idea by Morros which will be developed by LeBaron when he finishes dubbing on the Coast on 'Carnegie Hall.' Latter is expected to be ready for previewing early in January and for release next Easter. 'Babes' goes before the cameras in May or June. It will use puppet sequences in at least two reels."

Morros and LeBaron bought the option to film *Babes in Toyland*, an agreement good for ten years, from the Herbert estate for $66,000.

By May 3, 1947, Edgar G. Ulmer, who had piloted *Carnegie Hall*, was announced as the director. Ulmer was noted for being able to make films very quickly and economically; for the ultra-cheap studio PRC he had made *Detour*, one of the greatest film noir pictures, in six days. He rarely had the luxury of time or a decent budget to match his undeniable talent, so this big-budget *Babes* would be a welcome change of pace.

Eleven days later, it looked as though the film would never made: the start of production was postponed indefinitely, thanks to a "lack of Technicolor facilities." But by June 9, *Film Daily* reported that LeBaron and Morros were "shopping around for as many internationally known artists as possible in their talent drive for 'Babes in Toyland.'" Morros was supposed to begin "preliminary work" on the film in Hollywood on June 19, but by the end of the month he and LeBaron were "currently huddling over the question of whether they will roll 'Babes in Toyland' or 'Carmen from Kenosha' next, depending on the availability of top players." With no further activity happening, Edgar Ulmer was loaned to the Eagle-Lion company to direct *Prelude to Night*, which was eventually released as *Ruthless*, starring Zachary Scott, Diana Lynn and Sydney Greenstreet.

By this time, a script had been prepared for the new *Babes in Toyland*, but it ran into problems with the censors at the Production Code Administration, over what they thought were "instances of implied bestiality and incest." Since a copy of this script doesn't seem to have survived, we can only wonder at how such elements could possibly have been thought appropriate. We can, however, infer that this created another obstacle for Morros and LeBaron to overcome if they were ever to make the film.

By August, *Babes* had been replaced on the Federal Films schedule by *The Woman of a Hundred Faces*, about a famous European model whose portrait was painted by 100 different artists. The company still planned to make a film of the Victor Herbert property, merely postponing it "until a Technicolor commitment is available." In mid-September, the film was planned as "probably for 1948 release."

It seemed less and less likely that the film would ever be made or released, yet a month later Boris Morros told a *Film Daily* reporter that Dennis Day, the Irish-American tenor who played a naive sidekick to Jack Benny on his radio show, had joined Ezio Pinza as a confirmed member of the cast. *Variety* noted on December 3, that Pinza "has a contract with Federal's Boris Morros to appear in a revised form of Victor Herbert's 'Babes in Toyland,' as the toymaker, for his first full-length feature role, and the 54-year-old singer has already received a $10,000 advance for signing. Pic was to start last June but was held up for lack of Technicolor equipment; it's due to roll next June."

Morros and LeBaron soon decided to forego Technicolor entirely in favor of another process, Cinecolor. Edgar Ulmer was replaced by Arthur Lubin, who had directed Universal's Technicolor remake of *Phantom of the Opera* starring Nelson Eddy, Susanna Foster and Claude Rains. He had recently completed another musical, *New Orleans*, although most of his pictures were comedies; he had directed Abbott and Costello's first five starring features for Universal, usually considered to be among their best.

Dennis Day was set to play "the leading part" in the new *Babes in Toyland* and quickly recorded his songs before the imminent strike by the American Federation of Musicians, which stopped all recording by their members from January 1, 1948 until December 14. By March 24, 1948, the project was again in jeopardy; Morros had had a commitment from the Irving Trust Company of New York for $1,200,000 in financing, but, according to *Variety*, "the bank has now backed out on putting up that much coin." He may have quickly found some new source of funds, because three days later, on March 27, Morros and LeBaron made a deal with Hal Roach – buying the Laurel and Hardy film. No doubt they wanted to keep the older movie out of release so that it wouldn't compete with their new picture. For a mere $3,000, Federal Films bought the film outright, including the 35mm negative and "all picture material, all copyrights of every nature, all literary material and assignments thereof." Federal's new film was still supposed to start shooting at the Roach studios in mid-May 1948 – yet not a frame was shot.

The alliance with Cinecolor caused a change in the plans for issuing the film. Cinecolor had recently bought Film Classics, a film distributor established in 1943. Originally the company concentrated on re-releasing older films (including Roach's Laurel and Hardy pictures) but began producing its own original films in 1947. The new owners were eager to promote Cinecolor in new Film Classics productions, so the distribution deal with United Artists was off, at least for *Babes in Toyland*.

October 1948 brought the news that Morros had returned to New York after a six-month stay in Europe, where he planned four more feature films (and no doubt conferred with the Soviet spies by whom he was still ensnared).

Although Morros and LeBaron announced several projects to the trade press, *Carnegie Hall* was the only film they produced.

Variety noted on October 20, "In addition to his European filmmaking plans, Morros will soon leave for the Coast to confer with William LeBaron, with whom he's partnered in Federal Films, regarding an early shooting of 'Babes in Toyland.' This yarn has been in the planning stage for a long time, but Morros feels that general releasing conditions are improving, hence his interest in getting it underway."

Nothing more was published about the project for a year and a half. On April 26, 1950, *Variety* noted that William LeBaron had a new partner, talent agent Noll Gurney, and had formed a new film company, Wellington Productions. *Babes in Toyland* would be the firm's first production. "Picture will be made in Technicolor this summer on a budget of $1,000,000," *Variety* noted. "Producers are angling for Jane Powell as femme star."

Ezio Pinza and Dennis Day, not to mention George Pal, were no longer affiliated with the project. Dennis continued to baffle Jack Benny on his radio show, while Mr. Pinza had begun rehearsals on February 2, 1949 for a little stage show called *South Pacific*, which opened April 7 at the Majestic Theatre on Broadway. Pinza stayed with the show through June 1, 1950 and won a Tony award for Best Male Performer.

Unfortunately, in 1950, Federal Films – or what was left of it – had to default on a $100,000 bank loan from Pacific Finance Loans, which thus acquired the story rights and the 1934 film. *Variety*'s issue of June 21, 1950 reported that rights to *Babes in Toyland* would become available on November 30.

This finally put an end to LeBaron's hopes of producing a new *Babes in Toyland*. Morros and LeBaron never made the movies they had announced; the sole release of Federal Films was *Carnegie Hall*, which turned out to be LeBaron's last film credit. In March 1952 he announced a new partnership with director Boris Petroff; they were going to produce a new half-hour television series, *Musicomedy Theatre*. Nothing came of these plans either. LeBaron died of a heart attack in Santa Monica on February 9, 1958, a week before his 75th birthday.

Boris Morros was able to produce a French film in 1950, *Le Tresor de Cantenac*, starring writer-director-actor Sacha Guitry, and was an uncredited co-producer of the international anthology *A Tale of Five Women* (1951). Morros was relieved to finally untangle himself from his precarious position in espionage in 1957, when with his help the FBI smashed a Soviet spy ring working in America. He wrote a memoir, *My Ten Years as a Counterspy*, which in 1960 was made into a film, *Man on a String*, starring Ernest Borgnine as "Boris Mitrov." He died of cancer in New York on January 8, 1963, a week *after* his 72nd birthday.

Although Morros and LeBaron's grand plans for a new Technicolor *Babes in Toyland* went unrealized, the property remained amazingly durable. It continued to be produced on stages all over the United States and would soon be introduced in a new medium, television. Laurel and Hardy's 1934 film would soon get a new lease on life – in fact, several of them.

Chapter 15

New Titles and a New Medium

In 1944, ten years after he'd produced *Babes in Toyland* with Laurel and Hardy, Hal Roach's agreement with the Victor Herbert estate, represented by Herbert's daughter, Ella Herbert Bartlett, expired. The rights to the film reverted to her – and soon created a web more tangled than the one spun by the spider in Barnaby's lair.

When Boris Morros and William LeBaron acquired the rights to film *Babes in Toyland* from Mrs. Bartlett, they also acquired her intellectual rights to the 1934 Laurel and Hardy film; they ensured that they completely owned every aspect of it through a further deal with Hal Roach. Knowing Mrs. Bartlett's distaste for the film, she was probably glad to be rid of it. We're lucky she didn't burn the negative. The copyright was reassigned from Metro-Goldwyn-Mayer Distributing Corporation to Federal Films.

While promoting *Carnegie Hall* around the world and trying to get their new *Babes in Toyland* movie into production, Morros and LeBaron needed some ready money. In October 1948, they sold some of the rights to the 1934 film to Chaim Josef Auerbach, a film producer and distributor originally from Austria-Hungary. Auerbach came to the Czech Republic in the 1920s and formed two film studios, Elekta Film and Slavia Film. Of the many movies he produced, the most notorious was *Scandalon* (1932), distributed in the USA as *Ecstasy*, which featured a largely unclothed performance by young model Hedwig Kiesler, who would become known at MGM as Hedy Lamaar. When the Nazis invaded Prague in March 1939, Auerbach fled to Paris, then England, then Brazil, then Argentina. He finally landed in the USA in January 1941. Based in Maryland, he Anglicized his first name to Joseph, formed a new company, "Copyright and Remake, Inc.," and soon created another distribution firm, Auerbach Film Enterprises Limited.

Morros and LeBaron withheld the 35mm distribution rights to the film for the United States and Canada, but granted the rights for the rest of the world – and 16mm distribution rights worldwide – to Auerbach, with the proviso that he could not promote his new acquisition as *Babes in Toyland*. Ella Herbert Bartlett did not want her father's masterwork to be further sullied by what she thought was a travesty from Laurel and Hardy, and Morros and LeBaron did not want an old *Babes in Toyland* competing with their new one. Auerbach came up with a title that had been used for at least six earlier films, including one made in 1903 by the great French film pioneer Georges Méliès. He took out a display advertisement in the *Motion Picture Herald*, which ran on November 13, 1948:

> **WE ARE PROUD TO ANNOUNCE**
>
> that we have acquired 35mm and 16mm re-issue Rights for the entire World (excepting 35mm for the United States and Canada) for the spectacular musical comedy—
>
> NOW TITLED
>
> **"REVENGE IS SWEET"**
>
> starring those two inimitable comedy actors
>
> **LAUREL and HARDY**
>
> in a full length feature
> 1½ hours of hilarious laughter
> BIGGEST AND FINEST
> MAJOR STUDIO RELEASE
>
> A Box-Office Leader Everywhere
> It Means BIG PROFITS for You!
>
> For Complete Information for Your Territory
> Cable: AUERBAFILM, NEW YORK
>
> or Write:
>
> **AUERBACH FILM ENTERPRISES, LTD.**
> 1501 Broadway
> New York 18, N. Y., U. S. A.

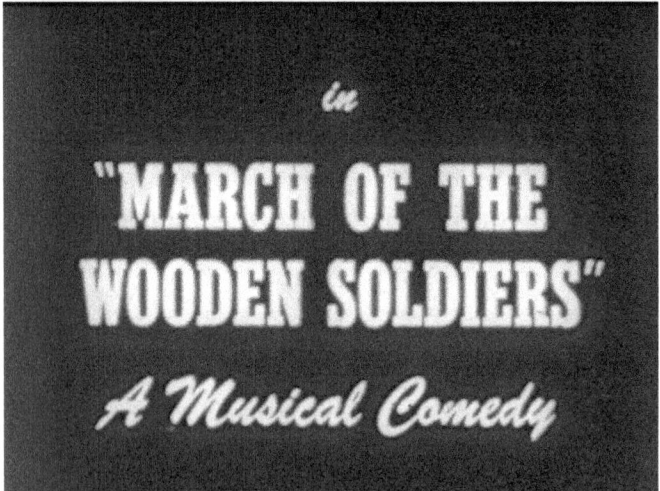
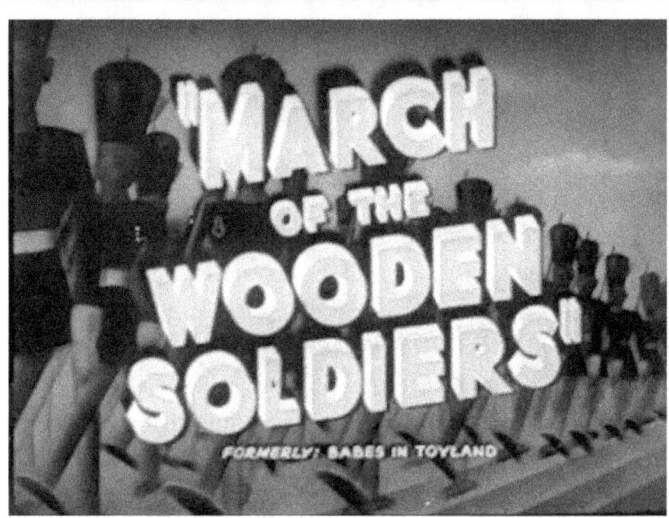

Babes in Toyland acquired new titles from various licensees. *Top*: Joseph Auerbach's 16mm USA version, Auerbach's 35mm and 16mm version for the U.K. *Bottom*: the ERKO main title in 16mm for purchase by schools, and the 35mm and 16mm Lippert reissue of 1950.

Meanwhile in 1948, another company, Erko, made the film available in 16mm for sale to schools, bearing the title *March of the Wooden Soldiers*. Their prints retained the storybook prologue, but deleted the close-ups of the Bogeymen, ensuring that the youngest viewers would not be too terrified. Erko's print ran 75 minutes and could be purchased for $350, a tidy sum for the time. Erko continued to make prints into the early 1960s. The distinction between Erko's rights and Auerbach's was that Erko made prints for schools only, while Auerbach had 16mm reissue rights for theaters.

In any event, Auerbach made quick use of his foreign distribution rights. A scant two months later, *Variety* noted in its issue of January 26, 1949 that the "oldie starring Laurel and Hardy has been dubbed in Italian and is very popular here." Auerbauch had other prints made for England, bearing the simple title *Toyland*. He soon acquired the American distribution rights for 35mm from Morros and LeBaron, and by July 8, 1950 had made a deal with Robert L. Lippert. Lippert had already made some sort of deal for the film, because in November 1949 he placed a double-page advertisement in *Showman's Trade Review* promoting a "Special Re-Release" of what he called *March of the Wooden Soldiers*. In any event, Lippert and Auerbach decided to coordinate. As of mid-1950, they also had to cooperate with Pacific Finance Loans, the company which now owned the 1934 film's negative and wanted to recoup the $100,000 loan on which Morros and LeBaron had defaulted. Plans for a major theatrical reissue through Lippert Productions were being made in July 1950.

Lippert was born in San Francisco on March 31, 1909. He loved movies from childhood and began to work in local theaters as a youngster, becoming a projectionist and an assistant manager. By 1942, he owned several theaters in northern California. They ran older films continuously – Lippert had a contract with Film Classics – and charged only 25 cents admission, which made his houses popular with servicemen on leave who wanted a cheap place to sleep.

In 1945, Lippert turned producer with a new company, Screen Guild Productions; its first release was a Bob Steele Western, *Wildfire*, produced in Cinecolor. By 1948, Screen Guild had been rebranded as Lippert Pictures and was creating a steady stream of low-budget but profitable films, often starring still-popular actors who had recently been released from their contracts with major studios. Cesar Romero, Zachary Scott, Veronica Lake and George Raft made films for Lippert, as did lesser lights Ralph Byrd, Tom Neal, Hugh Beaumont and Robert Lowery. His company would produce 130 films from 1948 through 1955; in addition, Lippert owned 61 theaters, mostly in northern California but also extending into southern Oregon, southern California and Arizona. Lippert bolstered his self-produced product with older films – he'd found success by re-releasing 32 *Hopalong Cassidy* Westerns – hence the deal for the Laurel and Hardy picture.

On July 17, 1950, the *Independent Exhibitors Film Bulletin* published an article highly critical of the new title. "'Babes in Toyland,' which Hal Roach

Nobody but Joseph Auerbach liked the *Revenge Is Sweet* title, yet it seems to have sneaked out in a reissue from sometime in the 1960s. The 1950 Lippert one-sheet poster was reprinted in 1972 and became a well-known decoration in the USA for years.

Left: Because Ella Herbert Bartlett detested the film and didn't want the name *Babes in Toyland* to be further besmirched by its association with Laurel and Hardy, the film was retitled and the opening prologue was either edited to omit this opening shot, or deleted entirely. *Right*: Censors found the shot of unmarried Tom-Tom and Bo-Peep sleeping in close proximity to be too salacious for young audiences, so the "Go to Sleep, Slumber Deep" number was cut entirely.

produced in 1934 as a Laurel and Hardy starrer, has been set for re-issue by Lippert, under the new title, 'Revenge is Sweet.' Joseph Auerbach, who now owns all releasing rights to the musical, set the deal with Lippert. It strikes this department that a grave error is being made by changing the title of the picture. Not only will many movie-goers be offended when they learn they are seeing a picture they viewed years before, but many who would actually like to see this truly outstanding picture again are apt to miss it. After all, a picture of the calibre of 'Babes' can stand up under its prestige on a re-issue."

The reissue was scheduled to come to theaters on October 1, 1950. *Film Bulletin* reported, "The film was to have been reissued last Christmas, but was held up until now to iron out difficulties with the Victor Herbert family which retains possession of the title and all remake rights." Evidently Lippert had some discussions with Auerbach, because the new posters and lobby cards heralding the 35mm theatrical reissue bore the name *March of the Wooden Soldiers*.

By the end of the year, Auerbach had made use of his rights for the 16mm home-rental market, and *March of the Wooden Soldiers* could be rented for $8.75 from the Peerless catalog, and for $7.50 from the Willoughby catalog.

Lippert's prints for the 16mm trade were complete (except for the new main titles); the 35mm theatrical prints, however, were missing six of the movie's original 79 minutes. Because of Ella Herbert Bartlett's adamant opposition to anything associating Laurel and Hardy with *Babes in Toyland*, the opening prologue, which featured Virginia Karns as Mother Goose singing "Toyland" while stepping out of a huge storybook with BABES IN TOYLAND emblazoned on the cover, was eliminated.

The movie was attacked on another front as well: the censors at the Production Code Administration insisted that the "Go to Sleep, Slumber Deep" number must be deleted, since at its end, Tom-Tom and Bo-Peep – an unmarried couple – were shown next to each other, asleep, on the floor of Barnaby's underground lair. (Oddly, this had not caused any concern back in 1934.) With the deletion of "Toyland" and "Go to Sleep," the film lost two of its five major musical numbers. This shortened, 73-minute version would be the most readily available and frequently seen edition for more than three decades.

The film suffered by the omission of this charming scene, which featured children and a few "little people" as gnomes, servants of the Sandman.

Beyond the theatrical reissue and the new availability for home, school and church group screenings, *March of the Wooden Soldiers* was about to find its largest audience in a new medium – television.

To match the tangle of theatrical and home-use rights held by Federal, Erko, Auerbach and Lippert, the television rights were first acquired by Quality Films, a distributor with offices at the General Service Studios (where Laurel and Hardy had filmed *The Flying Deuces* for Boris Morros) at 1040 North Las Palmas Avenue in Hollywood.

On August 13, 1951, *Broadcasting Magazine* reported that Charles Weintraub, president of Quality Films, had made a deal with Don Fedderson, general manager of Los Angeles television station KLAC-TV (soon to be renamed KCOP), to have exclusive television rights for one year to 52 feature films. The package included *The Moon and Sixpence* (1942) starring George Sanders, *And Then There Were None* (1945) with Walter Huston, *Angel on My Shoulder*

Top: Salt Lake City residents could enjoy the film on KSL-TV for Christmas 1952. *Bottom*: In 1952, the movie was offered as a Thanksgiving special on Detroit's WXYZ-TV.

(1946) with Paul Muni, and *Babes in Toyland* – oddly, not *Revenge Is Sweet* nor *March of the Wooden Soldiers*. The rights cost KLAC $302,500. Just how Weintraub acquired any rights to the film is a mystery – or *if* he acquired them. It's worth noting that in January 1959, he was ordered to pay $50,819 to United Artists for selling the television rights for four of that studio's films without having any authorization to do so.

A more legitimate distributor was Peerless Television Productions, created in 1951 by film producer Edward Small and syndication executive George T. Shupert; the firm's office was on the former Mary Pickford-Douglas Fairbanks studio lot, at 1041 North Formosa Avenue in Hollywood. Their initial offerings were 26 features which Small had produced, but gradually they acquired other titles.

On January 30, 1952, *Variety* reported that Peerless had acquired the TV rights to *March of the Wooden Soldiers* from Joseph Auerbach. By that October the company had sold broadcasting rights to stations in Atlanta, Boston, Chicago, Detroit, Dayton, Cincinnati, Louisville, Salt Lake City, San Francisco, Washington and Milwaukee. *Broadcasting* noted that these rights were sold on an "exclusive basis to one TV station in each market for Thanksgiving or Christmas period."

Through the next few years, *March of the Wooden Soldiers* continued to be sold to other television markets, and it was shown at all times of the year, not just at Thanksgiving or Christmas. Cincinnati's WKRC, Channel 12, ran it on September 6, 1954. WTMJ in Milwaukee ran it as a holiday special on December 19, 1954, while WPIX, Channel 11 in New York City, ran it at 12:30 in the afternoon on Saturday, April 9, 1955. Before long, however, executives at WPIX would see that the film had extra value when shown during the holidays.

Chapter 16

WPIX and a Thanksgiving Tradition

WPIX, the New York television station which described itself in publicity as "plenty gutsy" and "a scrappy little independent" first signed on the air in 1948, at a time when there were only 50,000 TV sets in New York City. It was the fifth station to debut in the metropolis and the second independent, not affiliated with a network, which it remained until 1995. Its gutsy, scrappy nature – shown by aggressive news coverage which included the first-ever documentation of a presidential nominating convention – emulated that of its parent company, the *New York Daily News*.

The station was founded by Joseph Medill Patterson, whose grandfather had founded the *Chicago Tribune*. During some time in London during his service in the World War, Patterson first saw the tabloid newspapers common in England, and decided to create a similar paper back home. On June 24, 1919, the first issue of *The Illustrated Daily News* was published, soon streamlining its name to *The Daily News*. The 16-page publication emphasized photographs, cartoons, and "brief, snappy stories," and sold for only two cents, while the *New York Times* and *Wall Street Journal* cost a nickel.

In 1939, Patterson became interested in television and made plans for a broadcast station to complement his newspaper, but World War II intervened, and Patterson died at 67 in 1946. On May 14, 1947, the Federal Communications Commission granted the *Daily News* a permit to build its television station; it would air on Channel 11 and have the temporary call letters of WLTV. The newspaper held a contest among its employees to create a better name. Vincent Krug, who worked in the circulation department, suggested WPIX since the *Daily News* was "New York's Picture Newspaper" and television dealt primarily in pictures. Krug won $100.

Reporter John Tillman – who would become the nation's first local television news anchorman – hosted the inaugural broadcast on June 15, 1948, a marathon debut lasting almost six hours and featuring celebrities such as Irene Dunne, Arthur Godfrey, Gloria Swanson, Basil Rathbone, Fred Allen and Ed Sullivan offering their congratulations. The station's studios and offices were located in the *Daily News* Building at 220 East 42nd Street, and from August 1951 maintained its transmitting towers atop the Empire State Building.

WPIX soon became a favorite with fans because of local news coverage and an outstanding sports division; it began broadcasting New York Giants games in 1948 and augmented this with Yankees games in 1951. The station boasted a very impressive library of movies, including major studio releases, lesser-known B-movies, prestige pictures produced by Samuel Goldwyn, and even some films made in Britain.

```
            (11)—Movie Quiz
    7:25-(2)—Weather Report
    7:30-(2)—News Reports
        (4)—Dinah Shore, Songs
        (5)—Death Valley Days
        (7)—Beulah—Louise Beavers
        (9)—Broadway TV Theatre: The
             Gold Diggers, With Gloria McGhee,
             John Newland
       (11)—First Show: March of the
             Wooden Soldiers, Laurel and Hardy
    7:45-(2)—Jane Froman's Canteen
        (4)—News Reports
    8:00-(2)—Ernie Kovacs Show (Premiere)
        (4)—Circus Hour—Joe F. Brown
        (5)—Bishop Fulton J. Sheen—Life
             Is Worth Living
        (7)—Short Story Theatre
       (13)—Film: Westland Case
```

A newspaper documents the first screening of *March of the Wooden Soldiers* on WPIX on December 30, 1952. *Courtesy of Jonathan DiDonato.*

For two or three generations of viewers, however, WPIX is most fondly remembered for its local hosts of programs designed for kids. News announcer and weatherman Joe Bolton, who was with WPIX on its first broadcast day and would remain through 1975, put on a policeman's uniform and became "Officer Joe Bolton," host of *The Clubhouse Gang* (which featured *Little Rascals* shorts). From September 1958 through May 1970, he hosted *The Three Stooges Funhouse* weekdays at 5:30 p.m. He became so associated with the Stooges that he was asked to make appearances in the team's feature films *Stop! Look! and Laugh* (1960) and *The Outlaws Is Coming* (1965).

In 1960, staff announcer Jack McCarthy – who would be commentator for the broadcast of the annual St. Patrick's Day Parade for 41 years – donned a skipper's cap, and as "Captain Jack" hosted *Popeye* and *Dick Tracy* cartoons and other shorts through 1972. Bill Britten, a former tummler at Jewish resorts and later a circus clown, high school teacher and stage producer, became the local version of Bozo the Clown for WPIX in September 1959 and remained through August 1964. Jazz singer Joya Sherill, formerly with Duke Ellington's orchestra, ran *Joya's Fun School* from January 1972 to November 1982. Along with puppeteer Paul Ashley, lifelong Laurel and Hardy admirer Chuck McCann created wild and wacky live comedy on

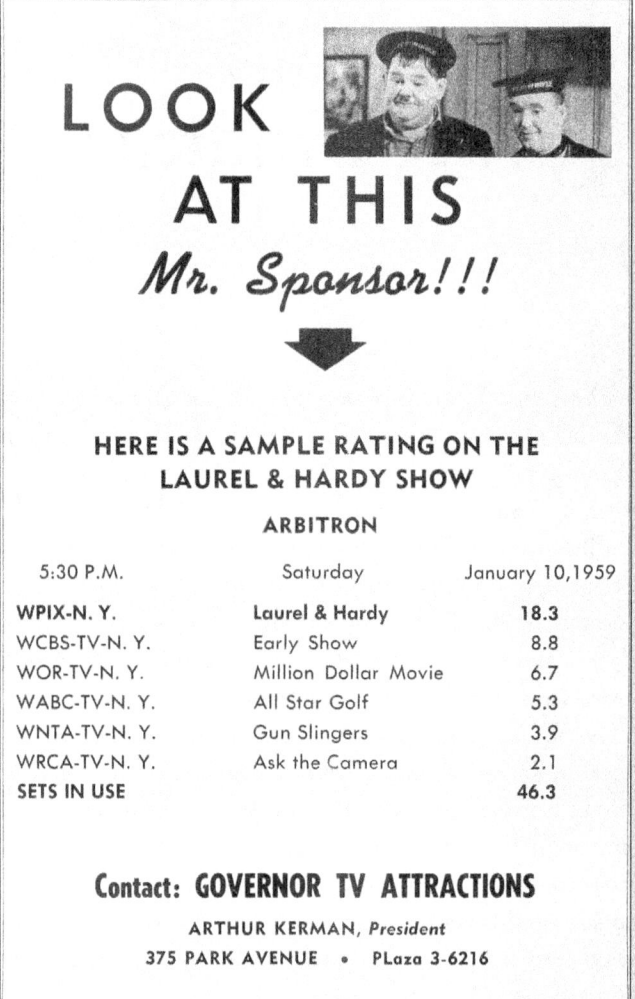

WPIX's Saturday screenings of Laurel and Hardy films in 1959 were clearly out-rating the competition.

March of the Wooden Soldiers is a WPIX Thanksgiving tradition which began in 1963.

Laurel and Hardy films were a mainstay of WPIX programming in the '60s all year long.

– 174 –

his WPIX shows *Laurel & Hardy & Chuck*, *Let's Have Fun*, and *The Chuck McCann Show*.

WPIX had been running Laurel and Hardy shorts on Saturday afternoons since the late 1950s without a host; McCann was a passionate and knowledgeable L&H buff in addition to being a talented writer and comedian, so he was the perfect choice to introduce the films. The films were often stopped for the day before they had reached their conclusion, prompting McCann to wonder, "What's going to happen to Stan and Ollie?" This ensured that viewers would tune in the next day for the answer. Guests on the program included John McCabe, the comedy team's official biographer. *Laurel & Hardy & Chuck*, which prominently featured puppets of Stan and Ollie created by Paul Ashley, ran on weekday and Sunday afternoons from September 7, 1960 through December 31, 1962.

After this, Ashley and McCann performed on *Let's Have Fun*, a four-hour comedy variety show which featured theatrical shorts from Laurel & Hardy, the Three Stooges and Edgar Kennedy along with Abbott and Costello and *Superman* TV episodes, plus the occasional movie serial chapter from Universal or Republic. McCann played a wide variety of zany characters (notably his oversized version of comic strip character *Little Orphan Annie*) and Ashley manned the puppets in other skits. *Let's Have Fun* ran on WPIX from September 18, 1960 through August 15, 1965.

In 1952, WPIX scheduled *First Show*, a movie receiving its first run on New York City television. Each movie would start on Wednesday evening at 7:30 and run for

Chuck McCann, a close friend of Stan Laurel, hosted L&H films on his WPIX programs *Let's Have Fun* and *Laurel and Hardy and Chuck*.

The Laurel and Hardy puppets prominently used on Chuck McCann's WPIX shows were created by Paul Ashley.

When Chuck McCann departed WPIX, he sent this heartfelt tribute to the staff.

WPIX had a powerhouse line-up of kids' show hosts: Captain Jack McCarthy, Chuck McCann, Officer Joe Bolton (who showed Three Stooges films), and Bill Britten as Bozo.

five successive weekdays. On Wednesday, December 24, 1952, Christmas Eve, WPIX presented its first screening of *March of the Wooden Soldiers*, in a 90-minute timeslot. It continued on weeknights through Tuesday, December 30.

At this point, the Laurel and Hardy shorts were being run on rival station WCBS, Channel 2 as part of *Space Funnies*, starring New York actor and radio personality Stan Sawyer as "Captain Jet." Other Hal Roach shorts starring Charley Chase, or Thelma Todd paired variously with ZaSu Pitts or Patsy Kelly, were also part of the show, as were RKO shorts starring Leon Errol. On December 30, 1952, WCBS scheduled the Laurel and Hardy feature *The Bohemian Girl* in a one-hour timeslot, from 5:00 to 6:00 p.m. It must have been brutally cut, since the complete film – without allowing for commercials – runs 71 minutes.

After WPIX ran the film again on April 9, 1955, WCBS acquired it and again subjected it to an editor's scissors, or maybe a hacksaw, by shoving it into a one-hour slot at 5:00 p.m. on December 23, 1956. (It had to make way for the *Hungarian Relief Show*, a telethon with guests Mary Martin, Charles Laughton, Edie Adams and Sammy Davis, Jr.) By 1959, WOR, Channel 9 had added the movie to its library and ran it on December 24 from noon until 1:30. The film was again allowed a 90-minute timeslot by WOR in subsequent broadcasts on December 11 and 17, 1960.

According to former WPIX archivist Rolando Pujol, WPIX began its tradition of running *March of the Wooden Soldiers* on or near Thanksgiving in 1963, on November 28. New York City and the rest of the nation desperately needed some cheer, as President John F. Kennedy had been assassinated in Dallas, Texas only six days earlier. It appears that not every year was graced with a Thanksgiving screening, as in 1964 the movie ran only on Christmas Eve, in a 90-minute slot beginning at 9:30 p.m., perhaps a bit too late for youngsters to view it.

WPIX uncharacteristically cut the film just as WCBS had done years earlier when they ran it in a one-hour timeslot at 3:00 in the afternoon on August 21, 1965. This was followed with a similarly cut broadcast of Laurel and Hardy's 1932 feature *Pack Up Your Troubles*, which was broadcast from 4:00 to 5:00 p.m. (That film in complete form runs 68 minutes.) However, the station atoned for this on November 25, when it ran *March of the Wooden Soldiers* in a two-hour slot from noon until 2:00, as the first of "Two Festive Specials for Thanksgiving Day." It was followed by a "two-hour special of favorite cartoons and children's features" hosted by Officer Joe Bolton and Carol Corbett, who had a weekday show at noon in which she would tell stories, show *Mighty Hercules* cartoons, and eat her lunch on camera.

In 1966, the Thanksgiving screening was sponsored by Hasbro Toys, makers of "Mister Potato Head," and Emenee Industries, which specialized in miniature accordions, trumpets, clarinets and guitars. The annual showings from 1967 through 1970 continued at 1:00 in the afternoon through 2:30, sometimes until 3:00. The station ran the film a second time in 1970 on December 25, from 8:30 until 10:00 in the evening.

Longtime Laurel and Hardy buff Jack Roth, now the Grand Sheik of the New York "Parent Tent" of Sons of the Desert, the international L&H appreciation society, has fond memories of WPIX's screenings in this era. "It was an Auerbach 35mm print," he recalls. "It faded at the end of the titles and faded in at the Mother Goose Toyland number. It was missing Virginia Karns stepping out of the book. Other than that, it was complete. It was the best ever shown on broadcast TV."

Another L&H devotee, Rob Falcone, adds, "As I recall, we never saw the title 'Babes in Toyland' on the book. We never heard Virginia sing the intro, 'When you've grown up, my dears,' et cetera. The action started as she began turning pages, singing the words 'Toyland, Toyland...'"

WPIX did not always air the film on Thanksgiving Day. In 1971, the film was broadcast on the Sunday before Thanksgiving, and in 1972 it was presented on the Saturday after Thanksgiving. From 1976 through 1980 it was run on the Sunday after Thanksgiving, and in 1981 WPIX didn't show the film at all. This prompted a letter from viewer "G.M." of Farmingville, New York, which was printed in the November 14, 1982 issue of *Newsday*: "Every Thanksgiving, our family looks forward to watching 'March of the Wooden Soldiers,' with Laurel and Hardy. Unfortunately, the last few years it was either scheduled after Thanksgiving or not at all. Is it scheduled to be shown this year?" The *Newsday* editors responded, "WPIX/11 used to schedule the fantasy film around the holidays, but according to a spokesperson at WPIX, they won't be able to show the film for a few years because of contractual rights."

Ah, those pesky contractual rights. You will recall that in 1952 Joseph Auerbach sold the television rights for *March of the Wooden Soldiers* to Peerless Television Productions. In 1968, these rights were acquired by Prime TV Films, Inc. This company was run by Alec Campbell, Jr. from offices at 120 West 57th Street in New York. Since its beginning in May 1961, it had syndicated 500 films in 18 packages; many of these were from the Hal Roach Studios, including 13 L&H features and 60 shorts, some of which were portions or abridgments of the team's feature films.

As for *March of the Wooden Soldiers*, Prime TV distributed

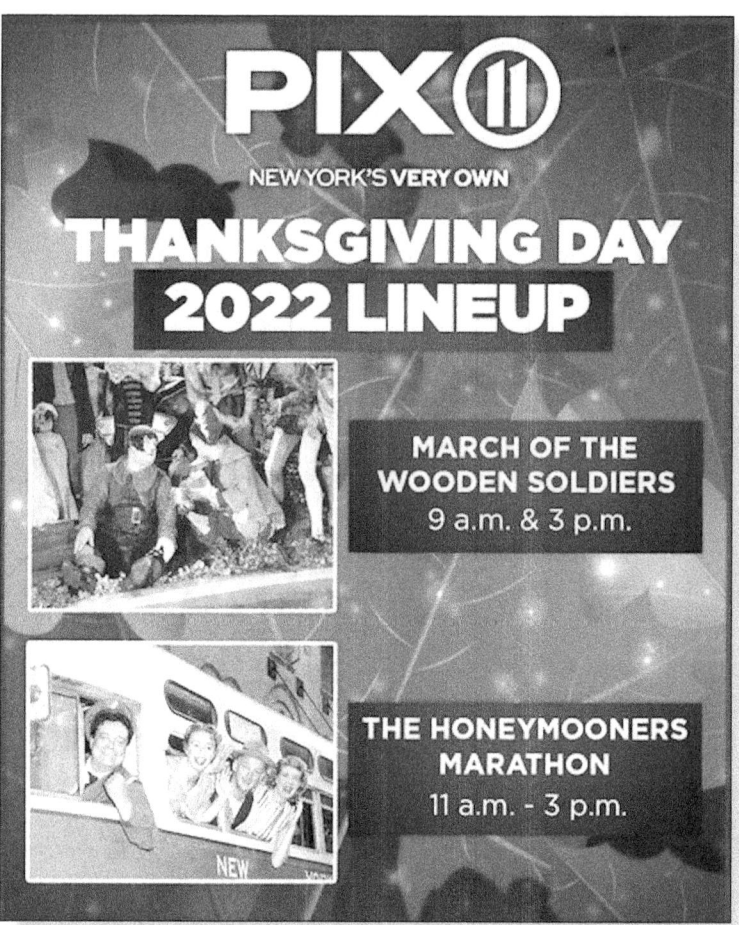

Left: The WPIX tradition continued well into the 1970s. *Right*: In recent years, WPIX has shown the film in both black and white and colorized versions, and on Thanksgiving and Christmas Day.

the Lippert theatrical print made in 1950, which was missing the storybook prologue and the "Go to Sleep" number. Apart from WPIX's longer print, this 73-minute truncated version was the only edition available on television in other markets for the next 23 years.

This would also be the version used for a 35mm theatrical reissue which was distributed starting in November 1971 by the mysterious LBJ Films; the advertising campaign for this used a modified version of Lippert's artwork from 1950. The film had been absent from theaters for a dozen years, because the Walt Disney Company paid Joseph Auerbach to make it unavailable theatrically during the early '60s, so it wouldn't compete with Disney's 1961 feature-film remake.

Then there was the separate and equally thorny issue of copyright renewal.

On November 28, 1934 the Metro-Goldwyn-Mayer Corporation secured a copyright on Hal Roach's film; the United States Copyright Office assigned it the number LP5161. This would be in force for 28 years, or until November 28, 1962, at which time MGM had the option for one further renewal of 28 years. In 1944, when Hal Roach's deal with Ella Herbert Bartlett expired and MGM could no longer distribute the film, the copyright was assigned to Mrs. Bartlett.

The copyright was transferred by the Victor Herbert estate in November 1946 to Boris Morros and William LeBaron's company Federal Films, which subsequently sold the distribution rights, but not the copyright, to Joseph Auerbach, who then made a theatrical distribution deal with Lippert Pictures, Inc. The Lippert theatrical prints of 1950 had new main titles which displayed artwork of the toy soldiers in formation, and included the notice "Copyright

MCMXXXIV by FEDERAL FILMS, INC."

The United States Patent and Trademark Office's website tells us, "Under U.S. copyright law any of the exclusive rights of the copyright owner may be transferred. In general, there are few formal requirements; however, exclusive licenses and assignments of copyright which are regarded as property interests must be in writing."

Some time after 1950, Joseph Auerbach acquired the copyright to the film from what was left of Federal Films. We can assume that this transfer was made in writing, despite Boris Morros' continued preoccupation with working undercover as a counterspy for the FBI.

On October 16, 1962, a renewal was granted to Auerbach Film Enterprises, Ltd, and assigned the number R302938. This was still under the title of *Babes in Toyland*. No copyright was registered for *March of the Wooden Soldiers*.

However, the legal team at MGM had also applied for a copyright renewal on February 2, 1962. Eventually someone there realized that MGM's distribution contract had ended in 1944, with the transfer of the rights to the Victor Herbert estate. On October 29, 1962, the MGM Law Department sent a letter to the Register of Copyrights at the Library of Congress, giving notice that MGM's renewal was in error and adding, "we no longer have any rights in said picture."

MGM subsequently signed a quitclaim to Auerbach Film Enterprises, covering MGM's "right, title and interest in the renewal of copyright and any extension of copyright in the motion picture photoplay entitled BABES IN TOYLAND (also known under the title THE MARCH OF THE WOODEN SOLDIERS) which was originally copyrighted in the name of Metro-Goldwyn-Mayer Corporation." Auerbach paid MGM "the sum of Ten Dollars ($10.00) and other good and valuable consideration" for obtaining any rights that MGM might still have had. All of Auerbach's rights, including copyright, were sold to Prime TV in 1968.

WPIX was not able to run *March of the Wooden Soldiers* at all following the telecast of November 30, 1980, the Sunday after Thanksgiving. Prime TV leased it to the Home Box Office cable network, which ran the film on December 5 and 19, 1982, both screenings running from 7:30 to 9:00 a.m. Eastern time.

After an absence of three years, WPIX was able to return Laurel and Hardy's musical comedy to the holiday schedule, running it on November 25, 1984, the Sunday after Thanksgiving. For the next several years, WPIX ran the film once and sometimes twice at some point during the holiday season, sometimes between Thanksgiving and Christmas, as in 1988 when the film was telecast on December 4.

This continued until 2009, when WPIX management elected not to show the film at all during Thanksgiving week. Since WPIX had run *March of the Wooden Soldiers* at some point during the holidays from 1963 to 1980 and again from 1984 through 2009, it had become a New York City tradition for most of 46 years. The management at WPIX hadn't realized what a cherished institution the annual showing had become.

Continuing its tradition of sports coverage, the station was set to broadcast the NFL Network's coverage of the Denver Broncos-New York Giants game from 8 until 11 p.m. on Thanksgiving night, November 26. Station management decided to replace its regular Thursday daytime programming – and its traditional Thanksgiving Day lineup – with football movies. Instead of *March of the Wooden Soldiers* at its now traditional 9 a.m. slot, WPIX ran *America's Game*, a documentary produced by NFL Films. This was followed by *Knute Rockne, All American*,

The movie made a brief return to theaters around the country in a November 1971 reissue from LBJ Films.

the 1940 Warner Bros. classic starring Pat O'Brien as the famous Notre Dame football coach and Ronald Reagan as his star player, George "the Gipper" Gipp. Next up was *Semi-Tough,* a 1977 comedy starring Burt Reynolds and Kris Kristofferson as football players both in love with Jill Clayburgh. Following this was *Brian's Song,* a 1971 made-for-TV movie starring James Caan as Chicago Bears halfback Brian Piccolo and Billy Dee Williams as his friend and teammate Gayle Sayers, whose friendship grows stronger after Piccolo is diagnosed with cancer. Last before WPIX news and the Pregame show was *Rudy,* a 1993 feature starring Sean Astin as a working-class teenager who yearns to play football for Notre Dame.

Good as these films were, scheduling them instead of the Laurel and Hardy classic on Thanksgiving morning was seen by many New York City viewers as virtually sacrilegious. Viewer D.V. Rice of the Bronx wrote to the opinion section of the *Daily News*: "For the first time in my 42 years on Earth, WPIX Channel 11 will not be showing 'March of the Wooden Soldiers' on Thanksgiving morning. It will be showing football instead. Another tradition – gone."

As soon as the news of the revamped WPIX schedule for Thanksgiving 2009 was made public, the station was deluged with calls and e-mails from angry and disappointed viewers. WPIX director of marketing John Ziegler tried to explain the reason behind the change to *Newsday* reporter Neil Best. "The thought was to make it a celebration all day long," Ziegler said. "We thought it was a little more appropriate than Jerry Springer and Maury Povich." Rather than run the film on Thanksgiving, WPIX chose instead to run it on December 19 and 25. "I don't think we knew how big that was going to be," said Ziegler. "We figured, we'll run this thing Christmas Day and it'll be okay."

This did not appease the viewers who counted on *March of the Wooden Soldiers* as a Thanksgiving Day tradition. A Facebook page was created in protest, allowing viewers to vent their anger and disappointment at "another tradition – gone." On Tuesday, November 24, WPIX tried to patch things up by notifying viewers that a sister station, LATV, which normally broadcast in Spanish, would be showing the film at 9:00 a.m. on Thanksgiving Day, so everyone who needed to see could simply switch from Channel 11.1 to 11.2. (It was also available on Cablevision, Time Warner, Comcast and Verizon channels.) This was the best solution WPIX could provide, as Ziegler noted that it was "way too late to try to manipulate the programming." He concluded, "I think if we would do it all over again, we'd have left 'Wooden Soldiers' at 9 and started the football stuff afterward."

Possibly as a reaction to the potential loss of the annual tradition, James H. Burns wrote an appreciation of the film for *The Village Voice,* published on Christmas Day, 2009. He wrote:

"On an arctic December night in Brooklyn when I was a tot, my family went to visit a local Christmas attraction. It was one of those 'Christmas wonderland' houses, popular at the time, and people lined around the block to take in its colorful lights and seasonal set pieces.

"Atop my mother's shoulder I caught my first glimpse of this candy-cane world and a couple of lifesize, papier mâché soldiers, and asked:

"'Do Laurel and Hardy live here?'"

"No adults laughed at me, but they may have smiled, because they all knew what I was talking about: Laurel and Hardy's *March of the Wooden Soldiers* (originally *Babes in Toyland*), which had already become part of New York's holiday traditions...

"Usually broadcast on Thanksgiving or near Christmas – sometimes both – *March* soon became, for some of us, nearly as significant a seasonal icon as Macy's Thanksgiving Day Parade of the tree at Rockefeller Center....

"Some of us who saw those WPIX showings long ago remember *March of the Wooden Soldiers* like the shimmer of a jingle bell, or with the warmth of the first light reflected off a snowflake. For us, it was part of childhood. And seeing it again after all these years is like a holiday in the heart."

The next year, the WPIX programmers proved that they had learned their lesson, as Neil Best noted in his column of November 21, 2010: "Last year, WPIX enraged viewers by ditching its decades-old Thanksgiving tradition of showing the bizarre, somewhat spooky family film 'March of the Wooden Soldiers' (aka 'Babes in Toyland') in favor of a day of football-themed programming in advance of that night's Giants-Broncos game.

"That in turn caused me to spend my Thanksgiving Eve doggedly hunting down the turkeys at Channel 11 who had made the decision, to seek an explanation. (There wasn't a good one.)

"PIX avoided trouble this year, not only scheduling the movie for 9 a.m. but following it with an eight-hour marathon of 'The Odd Couple,' featuring beloved fictional sportswriter Oscar Madison." (Neil Best is primarily a beloved actual sportswriter.)

In 2018, the station answered many requests from viewers who wanted to see *March of the Wooden Soldiers* in its original black and white form. WPIX had been showing it in a computer-colored version only since 1991. Since 2018, the station has run the black and white original at 9

Left: With the exception of WPIX's annual showings, the film was more available overseas than in the USA during the '60s. This poster promoted a reissue in Yugoslavia. *Right*: A 1960s reissue in New Zealand gave the film yet another title. *Courtesy Steven Thompson.*

a.m. on Thanksgiving Day, and the colorized version at 3 p.m.

Given its many airings on WPIX since 1963, *March of the Wooden Soldiers* has long since become synonymous with Thanksgiving Day (and more recently, also with Christmas) for New York viewers. David Kalmowitz, who began working at WPIX in 1983, remembered it as a cherished tradition. "It becomes something ingrained in the day. You get up, you do what you normally do, except it's Thanksgiving, so you're excited. You're looking for what to do with the day, and you put on channel 11, and *March of the Wooden Soldiers* is on – and you know it's Thanksgiving."

Says viewer Anthony Miranda, "It was a special time here in Brooklyn, New York. Woke up to the smell of turkey and lasagna and watched this with my dad."

Charlie Greenberg adds, "What a fantastically well cast production – and I love the presentation of the music, even if at least half of the score was eliminated, or transitioned to incidental music. Given that I grew up at a time when commercial TV was still constantly absorbing classic films to fill content demands, *Babes in Toyland* runs neck-and-neck for me with 1939's *The Wizard of Oz*."

Notes Phyllis Calzone Frank, "*Babes in Toyland* is so special to me because it was the first time I had ever seen Laurel and Hardy. I was five and I can remember laughing right out loud through the whole movie. I immediately fell in love with these two comic geniuses. As a little kid, I wished I could have this movie in the house so I wouldn't have to wait a year to watch it again. Of course, now I have it on disc and I watch frequently. It never gets old."

Writes Stephan Artist, "I find it a perennial holiday AND Laurel & Hardy favorite. Only a few years ago, I learned that Henry Brandon, whom I knew as Acacius Paige from *Auntie Mame*, was also Barnaby. That was most impressive."

John V. Brennan offers this perspective: "Like MGM's *The Wizard of Oz* and Frank Capra's *It's a Wonderful Life*, the reputation of *March of the Wooden Soldiers* grew by annual repeats on television. During my own childhood, *March of the Wooden Soldiers* was not just another movie, but an event, as important as the annual airing of *The Wizard of Oz*. Thanksgiving was simply not Thanksgiving without Ollie Dee and Stannie Dum. All Laurel and Hardy films are recommended for children, but *Babes in Toyland* is possibly the one L&H film no child should grow up without."

Animator Nancy Beiman provides this memory: "We watched the Laurel and Hardy *Babes in Toyland* every Thanksgiving; it was a tradition. We loved the film despite its obvious staginess. The Boys are charming and funny as always. Felix Knight as Tom-Tom was a delightful singer. We liked Mother Peep and Bo-Peep. The animation delighted us (and now, seeing it as a professional animator, I saw that it is very, very good). But most importantly, we were terrified of Barnaby. There was something dreadfully wrong about him. He had an old man's face on a young man's body and his voice sounded like something nasty sliding down a drain. Something about his agile movements frightened and fascinated us.

"At the time we could not know that 22-year-old Henry Brandon was playing this part. We just feared Barnaby and were genuinely worried when Bo-Peep and Tom-Tom were trapped in the well leading to Bogeyland, which did look scary. We were frightened when Barnaby and his Bogeymen invaded Toyland, but the Bogeymen were not as terrifying as the shot of the huge wooden soldier, marching onward without a head. Years later I met Henry Brandon and told him how much he frightened me when I was a child. His eyes twinkled with pleasure. I watched the film again last year and it is still fun to watch."

Viewer Jason Merrick adds, "I can't think of anything that I don't like about the film. It is one of the very few perfect movies I've seen." Jesse Levy says, "I love this movie: the cat and mouse scenes, any time L&H are onscreen, Barnaby marrying Stan, and Stan mindlessly eating the 'pork' sausage. Utter hilarity." Notes Tom Sito, "Growing up in New York in the '50s and '60s, *March of the Wooden Soldiers* on WPIX was a tradition to watch every Thanksgiving morning. It told us that the holidays were upon us as much as the Macy Parade did." Robert M. Grippo says, "Their best film – no padding at all!" Paula Uruburu notes, "Even though as a small child I had an uncanny sense of the weirdness and outright grotesqueness of so much of it, I would not miss it. Have watched it every Thanksgiving for as long as it has been televised – it was the signal that Christmas season had started."

Steve Churi adds this reminiscence: "*March of the Wooden Soldiers* was the first film I saw featuring Laurel and Hardy. It was in my best friend's basement at a very young age. The first thing I did when my parents picked me up was ask them if they had *March of the Wooden Soldiers* at home, and luckily they did! It was on VHS, taped off WPIX-11 in New York, a holiday tradition every single year here. Since then, this one film has catapulted my love for Stan and Ollie. This film not only means tradition, but the start of a bond that will last forever and ever. This film is everything to me."

Says devoted fan Jonathan DiDonato, "I grew up in New York, so watching WPIX throughout my life, I think of all the traditions the station has put forth. The one that I think of the most has to be *March of the Wooden Soldiers*. I can't think of Thanksgiving morning without watching that movie. I think of all the lines, like Ollie saying 'It's neither pig nor pork – it's beef!' When I showed it to my kids, I explained to them not to be too afraid of the Bogeymen, or Silas Barnaby – and they really enjoy it. They love watching when the wooden soldiers come out; they often will do the little march themselves. I have a picture of Laurel and Hardy in my office, and a gentleman came in and he said, '*March of the Wooden Soldiers*!' I said, 'Absolutely,' and he said, 'I watch that on WPIX every year!'"

Notes Jeff Coe, "I have watched it every year, both in black and white and in color. I think it's the best of the L&H operettas because it keeps Stan and Ollie as the main focus. They never come off as comedy relief in their own film. Their sequences are geared toward children but never talk down to them, and can be fully enjoyed by adults. The Victor Herbert music is brilliant, Charlotte Henry is endlessly charming, Henry Brandon is a wonderfully despicable villain, and I even like Felix Knight. The attack of the Bogeymen is terrifying in the Disney tradition and, of course, in the end, the boys lose even as they win. I have been a Laurel and Hardy loyalist from age six. They have truly been one of the things that have made life worthwhile. There's rarely a day where they don't pop into my head, whether I'm staring into an invisible camera after tripping over something, or silently contemplating how their movie wives could've possibly thought that these two were a catch."

Finally, Rob Falcone offers this eloquent tribute. "Why

do I love *March of the Wooden Soldiers*? As a kid, growing up in 1960s NYC, the annual Thanksgiving Day showing of *March of the Wooden Soldiers* on WPIX was more than tradition. Tradition is far too small a word. I liken it to Jean Shepherd's description of Christmas as the day 'around which the entire kid year revolved.' I looked forward to Christmas and my birthday, but my year was all about making a return trip to Toyland.

"The characters in the movie, from Bo-Peep to the Three Little Pigs, were familiar to me. I knew them from stories and songs related by my mother and other adults. It was fascinating to see them sort of living out their daily lives. The reality they inhabited was charming and so unlike anything I saw living in Brooklyn and, later, Staten Island.

"But, still, they were very firmly anchored to my world by the presence of two of my dearest friends, Stan and Ollie. These were two guys who came to visit and entertain me almost every day via television. And yet, they were also a part of this fairy tale world. As a result, to my mind, so was I.

"I'm sure I wasn't the only kid who made pee-wees out of whittled down pieces of old broom sticks. I'd load 'darts' into a make shift toy cannon. (The cannon was a discarded, empty tube of Christmas wrapping paper balanced on a chair. And the 'darts' were crayons.) I also 'pee-weed' more than a few actual darts into the wall of my father's garage. I think I actually hit the dart board... once.

"But the movie itself seemed to have everything to me. Comedy, music, beautiful sets, real tension and terror. And, oh, that ending.

"I'm hesitant to psychoanalyze myself, but I obsessed over the actual 'march' of the wooden soldiers. There was something about the precision and uniformity of the soldiers that likely appealed to my burgeoning OCD. Everything just perfect. And the fact that Stan and Ollie used anthropomorphic toys to save the day... They were real, formidable soldiers, but they were also just non-sentient toys.

"I don't know. I guess it was a 'secret life of toys' thing that I found so enjoyable. And it never really bothered me that the soldiers were portrayed by both stop-motion figures and real men. Nor did it bother me that the dart-riddled Bogeymen were so obviously padded. I knew that I was being told a tale; that it was just being acted out before me.

"I understand that, in a lot of places, syndicated prints opened with the gates of Toyland opening. (Oddly enough, I think that image is my first conscious memory.) But the WPIX print I grew up watching started with Virginia Karns turning the pages of an already opened book... we were obviously in the realm of the fairy tale.

"Honestly, today, when I feel like watching Laurel and Hardy, *Babes in Toyland* is NOT the first film I'll reach for. That's not because of any flaws in it. It's just that I've seen it so many times, more than any L&H film; probably more than any film period. (And I'm the guy who shocked Richard Donner, when I told him I'd seen *Superman* more than 50 times in theaters alone.) I guess even an obsessive personality like mine needs a bit of variety once in a while.

"Still, when somebody asks me, 'What's your favorite movie?' (a question I find very difficult to answer), *March of the Wooden Soldiers* is always the first thing that pops into my head."

While Laurel and Hardy's fervent fans around the world enjoy *Babes in Toyland* or *March of the Wooden Soldiers*, it's clear that it is especially revered by New York viewers. In 1984, WPIX confirmed its commitment to showing the film by purchasing all rights to the movie. The station has retained its ownership of the film, although WPIX itself has since been acquired by many different hands; it's currently owned by Mission Broadcasting, Inc.

WPIX's purchase of all rights would indirectly lead to a beautiful restoration of *Babes in Toyland* for a new medium: home video.

Chapter 17

Soldiers Marching to Your Home

Long, long ago – say, before 1975 – there was no such thing as home video. If you wanted to see a favorite movie, you had to diligently pore over your local *TV Guide* and hope that some station might deign to show it to you – and even then, it would be interrupted by commercials and usually cut from its original length. This is one reason why WPIX's annual showings of *March of the Wooden Soldiers* became such cherished events. Just as the once-a-year screening of *The Wizard of Oz* on CBS or NBC became the equivalent of a holiday for kids all over the USA, the yearly showing of Laurel and Hardy's operetta was a vital part of the holiday season for kids of all ages in New York City, and often in other cities as well.

An alternative to this situation finally arose in 1975, when Sony introduced its videocassette recorder and player, the Betamax, to consumers. A year later, the Victor Company of Japan unveiled its alternative, the VHS recorder-player. Both companies assumed that their customers would want to record a favorite over-the-air TV show, watch it at their leisure, then erase the tape by recording something else on it. Gradually, they realized that movie buffs would be happy to record and keep – or even rent – tapes of their favorite films.

It was well into the 1980s before the movie studios and video distributors realized that thousands of people wanted to build their own home video libraries, purchasing tapes of their favorite movies and TV shows to keep and watch whenever they wished. (Because children were eager to watch the same films over and over again, the Walt Disney Company soon became a leader in the video-for-sale business.) Instead of selling a few thousand cassettes to rental outlets for $75 each, distributors could sell hundreds of thousands to retailers for around $20 apiece. One happy result of this was that, since old movies were suddenly a new, huge source of "found money," the studios began to take an interest in preserving their libraries. Undoubtedly some movies were rescued in the nick of time, before the decomposition of nitrate film rendered them unusable.

Before the rise of home video, there were a few other ways to acquire at least a portion of your favorite movies. One was through the series of books edited by Richard J. Anobile in the early '70s. Each of these used hundreds of frame enlargements from a given film, accompanied with text of the dialogue. Anobile created books in this format detailing *Casablanca, Psycho, The Maltese Falcon, Stagecoach, Frankenstein,* and *Ninotchka*. He produced several volumes devoted to the Marx Brothers and W.C. Fields, and one book apiece documenting scenes from films starring Abbott and Costello, and Laurel and Hardy.

Another way to own at least part of your favorite movies was through the soundtrack album – a 12" vinyl record (or "LP," short for Long Playing) playing at 33 1/3 rotations per minute or rpms. Most of these only contained the musical scores from the films, although if the film was a musical it would generally include the vocal performances. In 1969, thanks to W.C. Fields' newfound popularity as an "anti-hero" with high school and college students, Decca Records issued an LP of routines from his film soundtracks, narrated by radio personality Gary Owens. Similar albums followed featuring excerpts from the films of the Marx Brothers and Mae West.

In 1973, Mark 56 Records, a specialty label based in Anaheim, California (home to Disneyland) issued an LP, *Laurel & Hardy: Original Motion Picture Soundtracks.* Most copies of this were a picture disc, each side of the record adorned with a portrait of Stan and Ollie. Mark 56 was a one-man operation, and the one man was George Garabedian, who had been in the record business since the late 1950s. Many of his releases were underwritten by corporate sponsors, such as a seven-inch album, *Goofy*

Left: Before home video existed, we were happy to get just an edited version of the soundtrack on an LP record. *Right*: The Mark 56 LP came in a standard black vinyl edition, and in a rare picture disc.

Grape Sings, with Paul Frees as various characters promoting a soft drink mix manufactured by Pillsbury. Garabedian's biggest seller in the early days was a 45rpm single of the theme song to *Engineer Bill*, a children's show broadcast on weekdays by Los Angeles station KHJ-TV. He began releasing LPs of vintage radio shows, ultimately releasing dozens of them. Noting the continuing interest in W.C. Fields, Garabedian got the Coca-Cola company — an ironic sponsor for Fields if ever there was one — to underwrite the cost of an LP featuring Fields' radio broadcasts, with an introduction by his son.

Laurel and Hardy were just as perennially popular as Fields, which prompted Garabedian to make a licensing agreement with Richard Feiner, who was himself a licensee of what was left of the Hal Roach Studios. Garabedian made deals for the use of L&H footage in nationally televised commercials for Hamm's beer and other sponsors, and for a time had a listing for "Laurel and Hardy Products" in the Orange County telephone book.

Garabedian's first L&H LP was very well received, and later in 1973, he released another compilation of dialogue routines from the L&H shorts, *Another Fine Mess*. In 1974, Garabedian released his first soundtrack from a single L&H feature. The *Babes in Toyland* LP was released in two formats — a picture disc (which evidently received very limited distribution, as it's quite hard to find today) and a standard black vinyl record.

The liner notes were written by John McCabe, author of *Mr. Laurel and Mr. Hardy* and as such the team's authorized biographer. They contained some interesting insights:

"'Which one — of all the Laurel and Hardy films — was your favorite?' I asked Stan Laurel one day.

"It was a question he had been asked before and he had a standard answer; he really couldn't pick out any one film as his favorite. He loved special bits and pieces from all that he had done, and he just honestly could not single out one as the apex of them all. I persisted in my questioning, but from another angle. Since he was mercilessly candid about any lacks or faults in his films, which of them all (I asked) had fewer imperfections, which of them all had more continuing and consistent entertainment values? The answer was prompt: *Babes in Toyland*.

"It was for him an ultimate tribute to the world of childhood, a world both Oliver Hardy and Stan Laurel loved. Stan's only regret was that the film had not been filmed in color."

Although the soundtrack had to be edited to about 45 minutes because of space limitations, the Mark 56 LP featured superb sound quality, and gave Laurel and Hardy fans hope that there were better prints available than the 16mm dupes shown by most television stations – with the single exception of WPIX, which had obtained an excellent 35mm print.

The other way in which fans of the film might obtain a copy in those pre-home video days was to buy an actual print. This was expensive, but there were enough old movie fans, and particularly fans of Laurel and Hardy, to create a large customer base for new prints in 16mm and Super 8 during the 1970s and early '80s. Blackhawk Films of Davenport, Iowa was the official licensee of the Hal Roach Studios for Laurel and Hardy in these formats. However, since the Roach studio no longer had any claim to *Babes in Toyland*, Blackhawk never issued it.

Owing to the plethora of rights holders over the years, and because *March of the Wooden Soldiers* was not listed in the Catalog of Copyright Entries, some distributors believed the film was in the public domain. In the early 1970s, Los Angeles-based Thunderbird Films released the Lippert version in Super 8 sound and 16mm prints for the home market. Niles Film Products, located in South Bend, Indiana, also released the film in Super 8 sound and 16mm, and made a special 20-minute edit available for the Super 8 market.

Likely because of these releases, attorney E. Fulton Brylawski wrote on behalf of Prime TV to the Register of Copyrights on November 26, 1975, asking that the assignment be revised to show that "the picture has been reissued and distributed under the title MARCH OF THE WOODEN SOLDIERS."

In 1980, with the emergence of VHS tapes, Prime TV licensed exclusive videocassette rights to Video Tape Network Incorporated, based in New York. *Cash Box*, in its issue of March 22, 1980, reported that "The release of the video will be supported by an extensive advertising, publicity and marketing campaign, including posters and in-store displays, and the 73-minute videocassette will be for sale to the home market and distributed through VTN's closed circuit college network of 650 affiliates." Although VTN had an exclusive license on videocassettes of the film, other distributors still churned out copies, usually of poor quality.

In 1991, CBS executive Ray Faiola, a lifelong Laurel and Hardy admirer, was asked by CBS Fox Home Video's Ken Horowitz to find what they called a "headliner" that they could license to accompany the forthcoming VHS releases of Laurel and Hardy's six features made in the early 1940s for 20th Century-Fox. These films were not highly regarded by most Laurel and Hardy buffs, as Stan Laurel was not permitted to help write, direct or edit the films as he'd done at the Hal Roach studio. The inclusion of a better film would make the whole package more attractive. Faiola suggested that a complete version of *Babes in Toyland* would be an impressive addition if an agreement could be made with the Tribune Corporation, parent company of WPIX, which now owned all rights to the film.

The people at WPIX were amenable to licensing the film for home video, but they had somehow lost access to the virtually complete print that they'd run in the '60s and '70s. Now all they had were multiple prints of the 73-minute Lippert reissue. "Guy Beverlin, the film supervisor at WPIX, told me they had 24 35mm prints of *Soldiers*. All edited," Faiola says. "Several were foreign-language versions."

Faiola made inquiries for a complete print of the film at archives all over the United States and abroad, including the British Film Institute and an Italian archive. Ironically, the best source was in Faiola's home state of New York. Richard May, a Turner Broadcasting executive, suggested contacting The Eastman House archive in Rochester. There Faiola struck gold. The Eastman House held a pristine 35mm nitrate fine grain of the original MGM release, complete in every way. Faiola says, "I didn't find the print, I merely confirmed its being on deposit at Eastman House." Nevertheless, Faiola's work resulted in a new lease on life for *Babes in Toyland*.

Because this film was particularly festive and had become associated with the holiday season, it was decided to put the film through a computer-coloring process. The "new" Hal Roach Studios had begun doing this to several Laurel and Hardy films in 1986, creating gaudy and unpleasant new copies; happily, by 1991 the process had been refined quite a bit and the results were much more pleasing. A license agreement was drawn up, but suddenly the Tribune/WPIX people insisted that CBS pay for the coloring treatment. CBS refused, so the deal was off.

Another party, however, was interested in paying for the colorization, so Tribune/WPIX made a deal with Samuel

Left: Stan Laurel's daughter Lois posed with an original soldier from the animated section of the film, to promote the VHS release in September 1991. *Right*: GoodTimes Video released a colorized version on VHS tapes in 1991.

Goldwyn Home Entertainment. The new, multicolored film now had a new main title that looked like the original *Babes in Toyland* title of 1934 but instead read *March of the Wooden Soldiers*, simply because more people knew the film by that title. It was otherwise complete, and was syndicated to television on the SFM Holiday Network, an "occasional" network which provided special-event programming for Easter, the Fourth of July and other celebratory occasions.

This colorized version was issued on VHS tapes in 1991 by GoodTimes Home Video. At the same time, it was released on laserdisc by Image Entertainment. In 1997, a new and improved home video format, the DVD (for Digital Video – or Versatile – Disc) made its debut, and GoodTimes released its edition of the film in this form in 2001. An entirely different computer-colored version of *March of the Wooden Soldiers* was released by Legend Films on DVD in November 2006. (The choice of colors varied quite a bit from one version to

  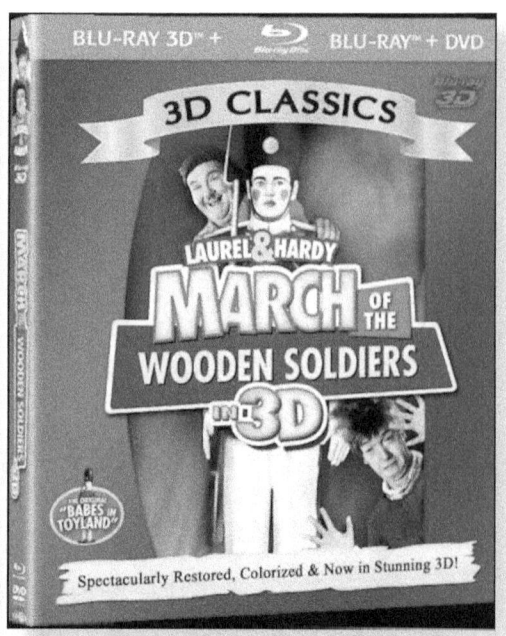

Left: GoodTimes released their colorized edition in 2001. *Center*: The best DVD release is this one from MGM, which delivers a pristine transfer in black and white from the best surviving sources. *Right*: In the Blu-ray era, the Genius Entertainment folks provided a new color transfer, and you could even buy it in 3-D.

the other. Neither one got the colors for the wooden soldiers right; they had black tunics and yellow trousers.)

Those who wished to see that pristine 35mm nitrate fine grain from Eastman House without the "benefit" of added color were rewarded with another DVD in 2008 from MGM – which ironically had now become affiliated with 20th Century-Fox Home Entertainment. Although the packaging billed the film as *March of the Wooden Soldiers*, the transfer was of the original, unaltered *Babes in Toyland*, even including the Production Code seal before the roar of Leo the Lion.

To date, the MGM/Fox DVD is still the best version of the film available, despite the subsequent release in September 2010 of a Blu-ray disc from Legend Films. (Another Blu-ray from Legend, this one presenting the film in a 3-D format, was released in 2014.)

Unauthorized DVDs of the film came from Passport Video in 2003 and Televista in 2007. At least seven different companies released the film in black and white or colorized editions in England between 1999 and 2011, in varying degrees of quality. Kinowelt in Germany issued the film on DVD in 2006 and again in 2009, both editions titled *Rache Ist Suss*, or the long forgotten alternate title *Revenge Is Sweet*.

The film is available through many streaming services on the internet, mostly in the Legend Films colorized edition. The black and white original can also be found, although not in the quality of the MGM/Fox DVD. Besides WPIX, other television outlets continue to broadcast the film, primarily at holiday time, including the Movies! and Turner Classic Movies networks.

Whether it's shown as *Babes in Toyland* or *March of the Wooden Soldiers*, in black and white or in color, Laurel and Hardy's fantasy film has delighted audiences around the world for 90 years, and will assuredly enthrall them for many decades to come.

Chapter 18

Other Productions, 1949-1961

Babes in Toyland remained a popular attraction in dozens of stage performances around the United States during the 1940s and '50s, and the dawn of the television age brought new productions of the property, each with a unique retelling of the story.

Just as television was beginning to supersede radio as America's favorite home entertainment medium, the Mutual Broadcasting System aired an adaptation of *Babes in Toyland* on its *Chicago Theater of the Air* program. This weekly hour-long radio show was devoted to operettas and musical theater; it originated from the 4,200 seat Medinah Temple at 600 North Wabash Avenue over station WGN, and ran from May 9, 1940 until May 7, 1955.

The *Babes in Toyland* broadcast was presented on December 24, 1949 and featured Marie Hadden, Lois Fair and David Polari, with narration by the show's producer, Marion Claire. The production was conducted by Robert Trendler and written and directed by Jack LaFrandre.

This radio adaptation was surprisingly close to the 1903 story, with Alan and Jane being bedeviled by greedy Uncle Barnaby, who lusts after their inherited fortune. (The kids' unsuccessful attempt to calculate the amount of the legacy prompts "I Can't Do That Sum.")

The kids want to sail away to Spain to be away from Barnaby, who says, "If they want to go to Spain, I'll see that they sail. But I'll see that they fall overboard and drown, too! Then their money will be mine! Heh heh heh heh heh!" The kids ask Contrary Mary to talk to Barnaby for them ("Mary, Mary"). Being contrary, Mary refuses to talk to Barnaby, but Alan reminds her that he had asked for her hand in marriage ("Before They Were Married").

Mary accompanies Jane and Alan as they ask Barnaby for some of their inheritance to pay for a sailing trip to Spain; Barnaby agrees, but later calls his henchman, Bobo, to push them off the edge of the pier so they'll drown.

Fortunately, Contrary Mary is just contrary enough to foil Barnaby's plans, so she glides by in a rowboat and saves the kids. Alan and Jane realize that they can't go back home because of Barnaby's evil designs on them, so Mary suggests taking them to a magic land ("Toyland").

Barnaby and Bobo are determined to search Toyland for the kids. "And when we find it," snarls Barnaby, "we'll see that they do not come back alive!" Alan and Jane seem to be hearing threatening voices, but they are very tired ("Go to Sleep, Slumber Deep"). Then they meet a distressed shepherdess ("Never Mind, Bo-Peep"), whose charges are soon located by a friendly Irishman ("Barney O'Flynn"). Bo-Peep, the sheep, and Barney lead the kids to Toyland, where they witness a grand spectacle ("March of the Toys").

Barney then takes them to the workshop of the Toymaker, who is a very nasty fellow indeed; he's working on a secret experiment and doesn't want anyone to see it. Alan is curious and wants to sneak into the workshop, but Jane protests ("Jane"). The toymaker is working on a secret chemical that will impart souls into his toys, so that they will become actual people. Unfortunately, they are even nastier than the Toymaker, and gang up and kill him. The potion soon wears off, and the toys are again inert.

Barnaby surprises Alan – and accuses him of murdering the Toymaker. But Barnaby breaks the beaker containing the Toymaker's potion; the toys return to life and give Barnaby the same fatal treatment. Alan and Jane are at last rid of their evil uncle and realize that it's Christmas Day ("Hail to Christmas"). The Toymaker returns to reveal that not only is he still alive, not only is he really a nice guy, but he is in fact Santa Claus! The finale is a reprise of "Toyland."

This version of the story might well have served as a template for future productions, since it retained much of the 1903 story and presented ten of the show's many songs

– although, surprisingly, not "Castle in Spain," a number almost always included no matter how the story may have been altered. A recording of this broadcast has survived and is readily available on YouTube and, in edited form, on CD.

The first presentation of *Babes in Toyland* made for television aired on NBC on December 25, 1950, as an episode of *Musical Comedy Time*, sponsored by Procter and Gamble. This hour-long series ran from October 1950 through March 1951, alternating on Monday nights at 9:30 with the dramatic anthology *Robert Montgomery Presents*. Other productions included Martha Raye in *Anything Goes*, Jackie Gleason in *No, No Nannette*, and Bert Lahr in *Flying High*.

Dennis King, who starred in this as a new villain, "Dr. Electronic," had lent his splendid baritone and handsome visage to Laurel and Hardy's 1933 feature film *The Devil's Brother*. Now, 17 years later, he still cut a dashing figure but was evidently not well served by the script. Edith Fellows had also appeared in that film as a ten-year-old extra, and now had a featured role.

This show is not known to survive, but period reviews can give us an idea of how its story differed from the original. *Variety* gave this verdict in its issue of December 27:

"As its Christmas Night offering, the Procter & Gamble-sponsored 'Musical Comedy Time' on NBC-TV offered an adaptation of Victor Herbert's 'Babes in Toyland,' endowing it with a cast that included such fine performers as Dennis King, Robert Weede, Edith Fellows, Gil Lamb, Dorothy Jarnac and Robert Dixon, among others. Alexander Kirkland wrote the TV version, transforming the Herbert classic... into a 1950-vintaged musical that took cognizance of such current phenomena as video, Milton Berle and Hopalong Cassidy. Practically everybody and everything, for that matter, was written into the book but Dagmar and Faye Emerson.

"Choice of 'Babes' as the Yuletide offering was understandable, but what was projected over the screen was anything but. Somehow the grownups couldn't make the transition into babes in Toyland. The fantasy was elusive and heavy-handed, the Christmas charm seldom if ever permeated and the resultant hodgepodge never broached the light, melodic tempo of the Herbertian frolic.

"As Dr. Electronic, whose nuclear mind ultimately proved no match for the creator of Toyland, Dennis King had a hapless role. Even the perennially favorite 'March of the Toys' and 'Toyland' tunes didn't come to life in the TV version, though the opportunities for imaginative staging were boundless. Dorothy Jarnac and Gil Lamb projected well in individual specialties; Robert Weede as the season's portender of cheer made the one outstanding musical contribution, but the lengthy number of impressive credits could have labored and brought forth something more rewarding."

Four years later, a much more enjoyable and elaborate production of *Babes in Toyland* graced the NBC airwaves. Max Liebman, who had produced the hit television series *Your Show of Shows* starring Sid Caesar and Imogene Coca, staged a live broadcast which again reworked the story and presented the favorite numbers. It aired from 8:00 to 9:30 p.m. on Saturday, December 18, 1954.

This was one of the earliest programs presented in "compatible color," which meant that viewers with standard black and white sets could also view it. NBC had won FCC approval for its color television process one year earlier and already had a network of 21 cities in the United States that could receive the color signal. The Liebman "spectaculars" were intended to bring viewers over from CBS (which on this night was airing *Two for the Money*, a quiz show hosted by Hoosier humorist Herb Shriner, *My Favorite Husband*, a situation comedy starring Barry Nelson and Joan Caufield, and *That's My Boy*, another sitcom starring Eddie Mayehoff) and from ABC (which likely presented tougher competition with the *Saturday Night Fights*). Even more importantly, the shows were designed to sell color televisions manufactured by NBC's parent company, RCA. These included a brand-new model, the 21-CT-55, with a 21-inch screen; it retailed for $895, a much better set and price than the initial model, the CT-100, which had only a 15-inch screen and sold for $1,000.

The script for Liebman's new *Babes in Toyland*, by a trio of writers including Neil Simon, was sharply funny and the music was well coordinated by Irwin Kostal. A framing device showcased the dry humor of bespectacled Dave Garroway, the popular host of NBC's *Today* show. Garroway played the Santa Claus at the R.H. Macy's department store (where many jolly shoppers at closing time are singing "Hail to Christmas"). Dave is weary from a day of "twelve hundred kids today, all on my left knee." However, there's one more kid, a little girl named Joan (Ellen Barrie), who is lost. Fortunately, she knows her home phone number, so Garroway calls and gets the mother on the line. Mom first has to pick up her little boy, whom she's left at Wanamaker's. To pass the time, Dave tells Joan the story of *Babes in Toyland*.

We are magically transported into Toyland, where we find leading man Dennis Day, finally getting his chance to star in this Victor Herbert evergreen five years after being cast in the failed Boris Morros-William LeBaron attempt.

Left: In the 1954 and 1955 "Spectaculars" produced by Max Liebman for NBC, Dave Garroway – the original host of the *Today* show – was a wryly funny Santa Claus. *Right*: Bombastic comic Jack E. Leonard was a very funny Barnaby, and very different from all who had come before.

This time the handsome hero is not Alan or Tom-Tom Piper, but Tommy Tucker. Dennis/Tommy walks around and sings "Toyland" as we are introduced to its varied residents – Little Boy Blue (who wakes up and then does pirouettes and cartwheels), Little Bo-Peep, Wee Willie Winkie, the Queen and Knave of Hearts, Old King Cole and his three fiddlers, and most impressively Jack B. Nimble, who not only jumps over the candlestick, but does a headstand.

After an elaborate dance number to "Don't Cry, Bo-Peep," the Widow Piper (Mary Mace), who is also the old lady who lives in a shoe (a holdover from the Laurel and Hardy storyline), announces the engagement of Tommy Tucker to her daughter Jane Piper (Jo Sullivan, who had recently starred in a Broadway revival of *Carousel*). In this production, Jane doesn't have a brother named Alan, but she does have a little brother and sister, Peter (Edward Brian) and Ann (Karin Wolfe).

The news of Tommy and Jane's betrothal does not sit well with evil Silas Barnaby, who in this story is not related to Jane and doesn't particularly want any money from her, as he already owns the toy factory and virtually everything else in Toyland. We cut back to Dave Garroway and little Joan; Dave describes Barnaby as having "the Olympic record for open and freestyle villainy....He took first place in such important events as making keys break in sardine cans that were only half-opened, and causing telephones to ring just as people were stepping into showers." Barnaby here is played by rotund, fast-talking insult comic Jack E. Leonard, who – like Garroway – wears 1954-style plastic rimmed glasses. Barnaby wants Jane for himself, and just for spite fires Tommy Tucker from his job at the toy factory. Jane says it doesn't matter, "we can live on love." Barnaby fires back, "If that's a song cue, forget it – there's no such song in this story!"

For some reason, probably a scenery change during this live, all-in-one-take show, a clown (A. Robbins) takes center stage. Accompanied by his high-pitched wail of a laugh, he pulls out all manner of stuff from his oversized topcoat, including a rubbery violin (on which he plays a solo) and bunches and bunches and bunches of bananas.

Peter and Ann are having trouble with their school lessons, so Jane helps them

Dennis Day and (in the 1954 production) Jo Sullivan played Tommy Tucker and Jane Piper.

("I Can't Do the Sum"). Tommy then gives the kids some money to scram while he romances Jane. He fantasizes about having another job and making lots of money ("A Castle in Spain"), prompting a couple to perform a flamenco dance (Rod Alexander and Bambi Linn).

Meanwhile, we see what's happening in the toy factory, now that Tommy Tucker no longer works there. Barnaby's toy-making assistant, Grumio (Wally Cox) has a co-worker, Clyde – played by one of the Bil and Cora Baird marionettes. They dance to "Badinage," which is an orchestral piece Victor Herbert wrote in 1895, eight years before *Babes in Toyland*. Then, a marionette of Bo-Peep cries that she's lost her sheep; three puppet frogs sing "Don't Cry, Bo-Peep," followed by two black sheep, four galloping white sheep, and a fox, which makes them run away. Grumio brings the sheep back to Bo-Peep, which provokes the wrath of Barnaby. "She's supposed to lose the sheep," he barks. "You did the same thing last week, giving Humpty Dumpty a parachute!" Further elaborate choreography by the marionettes is halted when Barnaby rejects a group of eight toy soldiers made by Grumio; Barnaby yells, "Build a soldier to end all soldiers, and end all children!"

Tommy Tucker returns to sing "Barney O'Flynn" for no perceptible reason except that he's Irish. Next comes another specialty number, a "clown concert" performed by a couple of harlequins playing fiddle, trombone, clarinet, bassoon, flute and soprano saxophones. Barnaby tells young Peter and Ann that they're cordially invited to a party on Ice Cream Mountain, but to get there they must count three, say "antidisestablishmentarianism," and go through the Spider's Forest.

This prompts another elaborate dance scene, with big marionettes of a caterpillar and various other bugs, playing musical instruments. Dancers costumed as frogs (four of them) are joined by other hoofers dressed as a skunk, a black cat, a bear, deer, tiger, a guy in a tree suit, and three fellows in a spider suit (with six arms) who ensnare Peter and Ann in a web. Barnaby congratulates the spider for trapping the kids and does a graceful dance with it, twirling away at the finale.

Grumio, Jane and Tommy Tucker enter the Spider's Forest looking for the kids; they're scared and decide to wait until daybreak to continue their search (a cue for "Go to Sleep, Slumber Deep"). Some cute marionette rabbits watch over Tommy, Jane and Grumio, who find Peter and Ann, only to encounter Barnaby – he sprays all of them with "instant sleep," rendering them unconscious. (Again with the spritzing of an evil potion!)

Back at Macy's, Santa Garroway cautions little Joan, "I wanted to spare you from some of the terrible things that happen next – I'll be glad when your mother's here to pick you up. Maybe you're too young to stay up and see the late show." Barnaby has tied and gagged Tommy Tucker, and when Jane again refuses Barnaby's offer of marriage, the evil man straps him to a sawmill. As Jane protests, Barnaby snaps, "What're you squawking about? Think of my electric bill!" Even worse, Barnaby has turned Peter and Ann into dolls and is going to ship them out in tomorrow's Christmas mail. He boasts, "*Time Magazine* will name me the Menace of the Year, unless some politician beats me to it."

Fortunately, one of the marionette bunny rabbits has a spray gun filled with "instant wake up," and awakens Grumio, who foils Barnaby's evil plan by activating the wooden soldiers. Some high-kicking soldiers chase Barnaby out of the toy shop and, after dancing through the Toyland town square put Barnaby's head into a stock. With the villain vanquished and trapped, Tommy Tucker and Jane have a happy wedding. A final chorus of "Toyland" accompanies the closure of the town gates and the end of the story.

Back at Macy's, little Joan says to Santa Garroway, "I want to know how they lived happily ever after." Dave says, "Tommy Tucker organized a band; the fiddle player is always playing 'Love in Bloom.' Grumio became a schoolteacher and now has his own television program." These, of course, refer to Dennis Day's years-long tenure with Jack Benny on radio and TV, and Wally Cox's starring role on NBC's *Mister Peepers*. Joan's mother arrives to

Left: Shirley Temple introduced her NBC production on December 25, 1960 with her children Charles Black Jr., Lori Black and Susan Agar. *Right*: Jonathan Winters put his own spin on the role of Barnaby; Joe Besser as Roderigo, Jerry Colonna as Gonzales and Carl Ballantine as Gonzorgo were his very funny if not too helpful henchmen.

reclaim her kid, and Dave says to us, "Gee, I hope she believed that story. I did." Then, as was his sign-off trademark on *Today*, he raises his right palm to us and simply says, "Peace."

Babes in Toyland was the top-rated show in the Nielsens for its week – it was seen in 14,500,000 homes and achieved a rating of 50.5. This warranted another live broadcast the following year, on Christmas Eve. The repeat performance was largely the same as the original, except Barbara Cook (who took a week off from starring on Broadway in *Plain and Fancy*) took over the role of Jane Piper from Jo Sullivan (who was two months into a six-year off-Broadway run of *The Threepenny Opera*). Dickie Belton replaced Edward Brian as young brother Peter. The "olio" acts were also different this time around. Banana devotee A. Robbins and harlequin musicians Charlie Cairoli and Paul were replaced with clown Jack Powell, who with an assistant did a comedy routine about portrait-painting, which segued into a Punch and Judy show.

Both telecasts were criticized by reviewers for their late start time of 9 p.m. on the east coast, since the kids should have been in bed before the shows were over at 10:30. For the second broadcast, parents thought this would interfere with the Christmas Eve tradition of Santa arriving while the kids were asleep. Producer Liebman told reporters, "I have it on the very best authority that Santa isn't going to start making the rounds this year until after 10:30. He's going to be watching *Babes in Toyland*." Viewers in the rest of the country would have less of a problem, particularly on the west coast, where it ran from 6 p.m. to 8:30.

The 1955 version didn't do quite as well in the ratings, but still had a very respectable national rating of 35.5%, with 11 million sets tuned in. There were rumblings that the show could become an annual television event; Max Liebman noted, "I was discussing the matter with Garroway the other day, and we agreed that if we all could get just a little more money, it would almost be practical for us to put on this show once a year and do nothing else." But the *Max Liebman Spectaculars* were proving too costly, and NBC discontinued

Shirley Temple displayed a surprising flair for outrageous comedy as Floretta the witch.

them in June 1956.

Five years later, on the evening of December 25, 1960, NBC aired another special production of *Babes in Toyland* in color, this time as an entry in *The Shirley Temple Show* – also known as *Shirley Temple's Storybook*. The script was written by Jack Brooks, who had previously written comedy for Fred Allen, Bing Crosby and Phil Harris and had written the lyrics to Hoagy Carmichael's melody for "Ole Buttermilk Sky." His collaborator was Sheldon Keller, who had crafted humor for Sid Caesar, Patti Page, Art Carney and Bing Crosby. (Keller would continue to work into the early 1990s, writing for Dinah Shore, Danny Thomas, Dick Van Dyke, Danny Kaye, Carol Channing, Frank Sinatra, Garry Moore and Bob Hope. He also wrote seven episodes of TV's *M*A*S*H*.)

As you'd expect, the script was heavily weighted toward comedy, and was delivered by an expert cast. Jonathan Winters at only 35 looked much younger as Uncle Barnaby than Henry Brandon had at 22, but he was clearly having so much fun in the role that it wasn't a distraction. The story retained many elements of the original 1903 script. This time, Barnaby had not two, but three bumbling henchmen – Gonzales, Gonzorgo and Roderigo – played respectively by comedy veterans Jerry Colonna, Carl Ballantine and Joe Besser. Again, the story had Barnaby trying to shipwreck or otherwise cause the demise of little Alan and Jane (Michel Petit and Angela Cartwright) in order to gain the large inheritance left by their deceased parents.

Shirley Temple hosted the show in sequences showing her at home with her three children, and played the important role of Floretta, the gypsy witch. She was surprisingly lively and funny, hamming it up outrageously in a way that none of her previous roles had allowed. The tone of the script was surprisingly contemporary, with a reference to a then-current TV commercial, and Winters as Barnaby occasionally making an aside into the camera and saying, "Boy, am I greedy!," or "Why am I always laughing like a boob?"

Victor Herbert's music was given short shrift. The cast included no singers on the order of Felix Knight or Dennis Day. "Toyland" was sung by Shirley at the start of the show and by the entire cast at the end, but in between, "Go to Sleep, Slumber Deep" and "I Can't Do That Sum" were given only one quick chorus. A ballet dance to Herbert's "Toymaker's Shop" melody and Miss Temple's energetic rendition of "Floretta" fared somewhat better, but more emphasis was given to the new songs "Gonzales, Gonzorgo, Roderigo" and "Meantown."

New story elements had Alan and Jane being chased by the bad guys through the Spider Forest and then Meantown, where all of the residents are truly nasty people. And they announce it, too, in song: "Meantown, Meantown, we're citizens of Meantown; we never love, we only hate; we never help, we aggravate. We never, ever hesitate to frown, here in old Meantown." The kids are put into jail for calling a policeman "My good man." (A ready-made cage descends from above to entrap them.) Fortunately, the guard entrusted to prevent their escape (Bobby Jellison) falls asleep; Alan and Jane get the keys and run, soon finding themselves in the much happier environs of Toyland. There, the ruler is the Master Toymaker, a nice guy this time around. He's played by Hanley Stafford, who for years on radio was the frustrated father to Fanny Brice as Baby Snooks.

Barnaby and his three accomplices soon arrive, prompting little Alan to exclaim, "Uncle Barnaby has come to do away with us for our money, which is rightfully ours!" The Toymaker regretfully says that he'll need a witness before he can arrest Barnaby and his cohorts, but suddenly Floretta runs in, happily agreeing to testify against them because Barnaby has only given her a bag of wooden nickels for her previous help. Since she's committed her own share of misbehavior, the Master Toymaker puts Floretta on probation, but allows her to remain in Toyland. Alan and Jane will now have a permanent home there, and Barnaby, Gonzales, Gonzorgo and Roderigo are banished forever to Meantown.

Under Bob Henry's direction, this William Asher production featured inventive sets by E. Jay Krause and lovely costumes by Robert Carlton. Walter Scharf's arranging and conducting served the music well, even if there were too few of Herbert and MacDonough's songs. The show was briskly paced, with Tony Charmoli's staging of the musical numbers never getting in the way of the story.

Variety in its issue of December 28, 1960 gave the show a middling review, saying that it was "hampered by an overabundance of jarring contemporary slang," but praising Herbert's music, the "imaginative choreography" and "a singularly fine portrayal of the miser Uncle Barnaby by comedian Jonathan Winters" – a rather puzzling appraisal, since he had most of those "contemporary" lines.

Walt Disney's association with *Babes in Toyland* went back at least as far as 1933, when RKO asked him to provide an estimate of the cost for an animated feature film of the property. You'll recall that after RKO found Disney's price too high, Walt told his polo-playing pal Hal Roach that RKO was doing nothing with its expensive option, which led Roach to make a deal for buying the rights.

On August 17, 1953, after William LeBaron and Boris Morros had lost their option on the filming rights, Disney announced that he was planning to make *Sleeping Beauty* and *Babes in Toyland*, "both cartoon features." Disney's deal with Glen MacDonough's son Alan and Victor Herbert's children Ella Herbert Bartlett and Clifford Herbert was finalized on October 26, 1953. Nothing more was heard about these projects until April 28, 1954, when *Variety* reported that Disney's next full-length animated films would be *Babes in Toyland* and *Hansel and Gretel*: "Owing to the length of time required by such elaborate projects, 'Babes' will not be released until February 1956, and 'Hansel' until February, 1959."

More time than that was required, as the film was still in the planning stages two and one-half years later. *Variety* reported on October 24, 1956 that the film would begin production early in 1957 "as a live-action Technicolor musical." The Victor Herbert favorites would be "augmented by new music, according to Disney, who has assigned Bill Walsh to produce and Sidney Miller to direct."

Over the next couple of years, three different scripts were developed, each facing the problem of retaining some elements of the original 1903 story while eliminating the gory stuff and making the whole thing more kid-friendly. David Swift, who had recently written and directed two hit features for Disney, *Pollyanna* and *The Parent Trap*, was at one point assigned to do the same for *Babes in Toyland* but left the project because he couldn't create a workable story.

Ward Kimball had joined the Disney studio in March 1934, just after he turned 20. He began as an "in-betweener," soon worked his way up to being a full animator, and by the early 1950s was occasionally working as director and screenwriter. Kimball told writer Paul Amundsen, "About 1958 or '59, Walt called me up to his office and explained he had the rights to *Babes in Toyland*.... There had already been two or three attempts at the Disney studio to write some sort of story, but Walt figured that maybe I would have a different angle on it. I never agreed with the original Victor Herbert plot structure because the relationships between the characters seemed confusing. I forgot about what had been done before and worked out a plot where there was no doubt about what Barnaby was up to. Then I sat down with Joe Rinaldi [a writer and artist who'd been working for Disney since 1940 and *Fantasia*] and we did the storyboards. That's what Walt saw and he liked it.

"Next, I got Mel Leven to write some new 'Gilbert and Sullivan' type lyrics and songs. Walt always thought that a song should advance the plot...That was the big change in *Babes*, and Walt liked it."

Just as there had been friction between the boss and an important, longtime employee on the 1934 Hal Roach-Laurel and Hardy *Babes in Toyland*, a similar rift developed on the new Disney film. Articles in the August 26, 1959 issue of *Variety* and the August 28 edition of *Motion Picture Daily* both noted that while the new film was "being created by Walt Disney," it would be "produced and directed by Ward Kimball." At the time, Disney was in Europe, and these press releases – coupled with the fact that Kimball was auditioning actors and creating designs for the sets – made Disney feel that Kimball was, as Stan Laurel might have said, "bounding over his steps."

"At first, Walt was going to let me direct the whole picture," Kimball explained to Paul Amundsen. "Then the publicity department stepped in. They said they wanted to let the movie colony know that Disney was going to make the film before anyone else started on it. So they start running these ads in *Variety* and *The Hollywood Reporter*: 'Ward Kimball to Direct *Babes in Toyland*.' Walt had only hinted at that, so when he got back, he thought I had run the ad and was a little mad. He called me up to his office and bawled me out, but I told him I had nothing to do with it. It was the Publicity Department's idea. I didn't find out about it until after the fact and would have objected if I had known. Walt didn't seem to understand that and to put me in my place, he decided to get Jack Donahue to direct the picture. He did ask me to direct the parade of the toys and the toy battle, though, and he knew I'd enjoy doing that. I still think it was the best part of the picture."

Ray Bolger as Barnaby Barnicle in the 1961 Walt Disney film had to contend with assistants Henry Calvin (a Hardy-like Gonzorgo) and Gene Sheldon (a Laurelish Roderigo). *Copyright © The Walt Disney Company*

The final script for Disney's new feature was finished on February 14, 1961. The story was written by Ward Kimball and Joe Rinaldi as a team, with Lowell Hawley. Mel Leven was credited for "Lyrics and Libretto." In the film's credits, Kimball, Rinaldi and Hawley were given credit for the screenplay, while Leven received a smaller credit for "Lyrics and Introductory Material." In later years, Leven disputed this. "I wrote that whole thing, not just the music but every bit of dialogue," he said. "There are 16 songs in it, so I get my residuals all right, but I should have gotten paid for the writing, every single word."

The casting gave key roles to then teen-idol Tommy Sands and Disney favorite Annette Funicello, who was poised between her tenure on television's *Mickey Mouse Club* and a series of *Beach Party* comedies co-starring Frankie Avalon. Ray Bolger, limber-legged comic dancer best remembered as the Scarecrow in MGM's 1939 *The Wizard of Oz*, played Barnaby, while legendary comic Ed Wynn portrayed the Toymaker. Tommy Kirk played the Toymaker's timid assistant, Grumio, while Henry Calvin and Gene Sheldon were Barnaby's bumbling henchmen Gonzorgo and Roderigo.

The characters of Alan and Jane are nowhere to be found in this story. Nor is Santa Claus, although the Toymaker worries about meeting a Christmas deadline, and the film was released on December 14, 1961. The new plotline provides yet another variation on the relationships between important characters.

In the original 1903 libretto, Alan (brother of Jane) was in love with Contrary Mary. In the 1934 Laurel and Hardy film, Little Bo-Peep was in love with Tom-Tom Piper. Max Liebman's 1954 and '55 television spectaculars featured Tommy Tucker in love with Jane Piper. *The Shirley Temple Show* edition focused on juvenile siblings Alan and Jane and didn't have any love story. The Disney version presents Tom Piper and Mary Quite Contrary as the young lovers.

Annette Funicello was indeed Mary Quite Contrary in the company of Barnaby's henchmen. *Copyright © The Walt Disney Company*

This time, the story opens on a stage, presumably to justify the theatrical tone of the whole movie. Curtains part to reveal a puppet of a goose – Sylvester J. Goose, to be precise, known to his friends as Silly Goose. Mother Goose (Mary McCarty) then invites us to join the celebration of the engagement of Mary Quite Contrary and Tom Piper. Watching the proceedings from his decrepit shack on a hilltop is Barnaby, dressed permanently in a black suit, cloak and top hat, and sporting a mustache that marks him as the ultimate melodramatic villain.

Just so we in the audience – and especially those of us under five years old – understand his objectives, he looks at us directly and states his evil goals very clearly: "Unbeknownst to Mary, she inherits scads of money when she marries. Thus it carries, that if I'm to get my hands on Mary's money, the person Mary marries must be me! Not Tom, me!"

It's never made clear how Barnaby knows this, nor from whom Mary will inherit that money, but never mind. He enlists Gonzorgo and Roderigo to throw Tom in the sea and drown him, and steal Mary's sheep since they are her only means of support. In case you're puzzled, Mary does have a garden replete with tinkle bells and cockle shells, which we see briefly. She has sheep because one of her three little sisters is Bo-Peep (played by Ann Jilliann). She also has two little brothers, Boy Blue (Kevin Corcoran) and Willie Winkie (Brian Corcoran). Since Barnaby has some money – but always wants more – he figures that he will be a more attractive suitor to Mary.

Barnaby's two compatriots decide instead of killing Tom, they'll sell him to a gypsy camp and somehow will make an even bigger profit. Nevertheless, they relate the news to Mary that Tom has drowned (prompting the new song, "Slowly He Sank into the Sea"). Gonzorgo and Roderigo are suitably soaked while delivering their waterlogged message, and are in danger of drowning themselves by the time they've read Tom's supposed suicide note, in which he supposedly has written that he could never adequately provide for Mary.

Showing a remarkable lack of compassion, Barnaby now reminds Mary that she is deeply in debt to him: "I could seize your home through legal confiscation!" He tries to entice Mary into marriage with a rousing rendition of "Castle in Spain," which instead of being a romantic number has now been shackled to Mel Leven's new, facetious lyric ("In our castle in Spain, you'll be living rent-free; every capital gain you'll share with me.")

Bo-Peep now arrives with the alarming news that the sheep are missing. She conveys the unhappy tidings to Mary with a new lyric set to "Never Mind, Bo-Peep": "My sheep are gone for good; there goes our livelihood." Suddenly, Bobby Shaftoe runs into the scene; he's seen the sheep's tracks going into the Forest of No Return.

Without her sister's sheep (which presumably provide lots of valuable wool), Mary is in deep trouble financially. This prompts a special-effects laden version of "I Can't Do the Sum" in which several brightly colored versions of Mary for some reason leap out of her skin as she's trying to pay her bills.

Barnaby again proposes marriage to her, to which Mary reluctantly agrees only because of her money problems. At a celebration for Barnaby and Mary's impending nuptials, a troupe of gypsies sings and dances, with the most energetic performance given by a wizened old lady named Floretta, describing her talent as a fortune teller and predicting that Mary and Tom will marry and live happily ever after. At the conclusion of her big number she tears away her wig and costume to reveal that "she" is Tom! This is absolutely the best scene in the movie, thanks to a bravura, genuinely funny performance by Tommy Sands, who proves here that he was a talented comedian who should have been given more opportunities to display this ability. He had fond memories of the scene, as he related many years later: "I loved playing an old woman. I had never done anything like that before. I was u-g-l-e-e-e!"

Like Shirley Temple, Tommy Sands displayed a surprising talent for wacky comedy in the film's unquestionable highlight. *Copyright © The Walt Disney Company*

Barnaby's plans to marry Mary are foiled, and she and Tom are blessedly back together. Since this part of the story seems to be prematurely resolved, Tom now helps Mary and her siblings to find the lost sheep. They wander into the Forest of No Return, where a grove of singing trees (shades of MGM's *Wizard of Oz*) warn them to get out. The kids don't find the sheep, and decide instead to "Go to Sleep, Slumber Deep," once again to new lyrics.

Upon the kids' awakening, the trees again warn Mary, Tom and the youngsters that they're on restricted grounds, part of Toyland. This is the cue for a very different arrangement of "Toyland" – no longer a wistful, nostalgic yearning for lost youth, but instead a bright and snappy march led by the talking trees. ("Toyland, Toyland, we're on our way to Toyland; don't know when we'll get there, but we know there's fun in store.")

And now we visit a new locale, the workshop of the Toymaker (Ed Wynn), who is awfully absent-minded, quick to take credit for others' work and equally quick to assign blame for his own failures. His good-natured, brilliant but awkward assistant, Grumio (Tommy Kirk) is about to demonstrate his amazing new, gigantic, toy-making machine, which can create any kind of toy with the proper input. Unfortunately, the Toymaker is so enthused about this amazing contraption that he tries to make too many toys at once, overloading the machine's capabilities, and wrecking it – along with most of the workshop.

Since the Toymaker now despairs of meeting his Christmas deadline, Mary, Tom and the kids offer to help making new toys. They soon become a smoothly running assembly line and create a new inventory – including lots of little wooden soldiers – in record time.

Grumio has invented another device, a ray gun – just

aim it at anything, and the ray will shrink it to a tiny size. Unknown to them, Barnaby, Gonzorgo and Roderigo have been watching this demonstration through a window. When neither the Toymaker nor Grumio can figure out where they'll get more big things to turn into small things, the Toymaker disgustedly throws the ray-gun out a window – and right into Barnaby's clutches.

The Toymaker has gone to his bed, so Barnaby reduces both to miniature size. Gonzorgo and Roderigo are shocked that Barnaby would do this to a human being and decide to have nothing more to do with him. Barnaby's response is to reduce them – and Tom as well, from a strapping six feet tall to shorter than one. Barnaby figures he'll now have Mary (and her money) to himself and orders the Toymaker – who's also the Chief of Police and Mayor of Toyland – to marry them. Tom, however, escapes and uses his new diminutive dimensions to activate the similarly sized toy soldiers. They march out in smart precision. Disney publicity touted this as the studio's new "animotion" technique, although it was simply the same stop-motion animation technique that Roy Seawright and Kenneth Peach used in 1934 and that George Pal would have used in 1950.

The tiny toys are easily defeated – or broken – by Barnaby, and just as he's about to do away with tiny Tom, Mary activates the ray-gun and shrinks Barnaby to the same tiny size. A swordfight follows. and ultimately Barnaby falls to his fate. Grumio then bursts in with yet another invention – of course, it's a restorer ray-gun that will return everyone (except Barnaby) back to their normal size.

All of this has been happening at "half past October" according to the Toymaker's workshop clock. The final scene takes place in winter, with Toyland beautifully bedecked with snow. Tom and Mary, finally wed at last, leave for their honeymoon in a horse-drawn carriage as the denizens of Toyland bid them adieu.

The best adjective to describe this film is "superficial." The objective of the filmmakers seems to have been to create slick, brassy, fast-paced, ultra-colorful entertainment that never becomes too sad or too frightening. (When Tom is hit on the head, the violence is softened by animated blue stars swirling around his cranium.) The sets and costumes are so colorful that they are often gaudy and overdone. The bright lighting, loud orchestrations, and frequent playing directly to the camera make the film seem more like a television variety show.

Since so much of this film is played tongue-in-cheek, we never care about any of the characters. Ray Bolger certainly plays his part with relish and enthusiasm, especially when he makes his asides directly looking at us, but the indelible memory of his performance as the lovable Scarecrow prejudices us. We don't believe him as a villain, and frankly we don't want to see him playing a bad guy. Reportedly, 64 other actors were considered for the role, among them Hans Conried, Vincent Price, David Niven, Christopher Lee, James Mason, George Sanders, Boris Karloff, Claude Rains, Walter Pidgeon and Richard Boone. Any of them would have given more believable menace to the role.

Similarly, Ed Wynn, who could be so lovable, comes across as a jerk who continually steals the credit for Grumio's inventions, but blames him for his own blunders.

The battle between the toy soldiers and Barnaby is not nearly as effective as it should have been, because the soldiers are tiny while Barnaby is still six feet tall, and he breaks most of them, which is a real disappointment. This is not a scene to make an audience stand up and cheer.

While Tommy Kirk deserves some honors for his work as the nerdy assistant Grumio, the best performance comes from Tommy Sands, not only for his remarkable turn as Floretta, but because he's the one actor who plays everything earnestly. Annette tries very hard but doesn't quite have the powerful presence that would have made her scenes more compelling.

Then there are Henry Calvin as Gonzorgo and Gene Sheldon as Roderigo. Their performances are clearly inspired by Laurel and Hardy and were called out as such in many reviews. Henry Calvin made quite a career of imitating Babe Hardy, not only as "Sergeant Garcia" on Disney's *Zorro* television show, but also on a memorable episode of *The Dick Van Dyke Show* and on a couple of Laurel and Hardy records produced by Larry Harmon. Calvin was supposed to supply the voice on Harmon's series of L&H cartoons, a job which ultimately went to Jim MacGeorge – who visually was a doppelganger for Stan Laurel.

Gene Sheldon was also a cast member on *Zorro*, playing the mute servant Bernardo. He doesn't speak at all in *Babes in Toyland*, perhaps inspiring the comedy magicians Penn and Teller. Mel Leven was not impressed with Calvin and Sheldon. "They copied Laurel and Hardy exactly. In fact, Henry Calvin kept quoting Laurel and Hardy. I didn't give a darn what they did! I also didn't want Gene Sheldon to be a mute in the film. That was his idea." Being a "dumb act," one who didn't speak, was an advantage for Sheldon. His stage act, in which he struggled to play a banjo but otherwise made no sound, could play all over the world. In this, he wore a little hat which made him resemble Harry Langdon more than Stan Laurel.

The real Stan Laurel was aware of Disney filming a new *Babes in Toyland*, as he related in a letter of March 21, 1961. He noted that "of course it will be in color," as he

Ray Bolger as Barnaby Barnicle in the 1961 Walt Disney film had to contend with assistants Henry Calvin (a Hardy-like Gonzorgo) and Gene Sheldon (a Laurelish Roderigo). *Copyright © The Walt Disney Company*

had wished for his own film. It's doubtful that he ever saw it; one wonders what his reaction would have been.

Reviewers gave the film mixed reviews, as shown by *Variety's* notice from December 31, 1961: "Walt Disney's first live-action musical, a lavish translation to the screen of Victor Herbert's operetta...is an expensive gift, brightly wrapped and intricately packaged. But some of the more mature patrons may be distressed to discover that quaint, charming Toyland has been transformed into a rather gaudy and mechanical Fantasyland. What actually emerges is *Babes in Disneyland*.... Mel Leven's new libretto and lyrics are clever, but some of the simple charm of the original words, such as in the delightful 'I Can't Do the Sum,' have been sacrificed for purposes of visual trickery."

Time's issue of December 15, 1961 headlined its review with "Nursery Crhymes," and noted, "Children over five who plan to see it will be well advised to take some Berlitz brushup lessons in baby talk... naughty old Barnaby, wielding a wicked snickersneer, does his worst to louse up the proceedings. Unhappily, so does the librettist... So does Director Donohue... And so do Lyricist Mel Leven and Songwriter George Bruns, who...should have restricted the impulse to 'modernize' Victor Herbert's music... Still, *Toyland* has its charms... Singer Sands, who most of the time is about as hard to swallow as a Vaseline sandwich, suddenly pulls on a fright wig and does a brilliant bughouse turn as a batty old bag who reads tea leaves and such."

Wrote critic John L. Scott in the *Los Angeles Times* of December 21, 1961, "It's considerably more showy than either Herbert's stage original or the first film version done in the middle '30s, and older patrons may resent a loss a quaintness and a surplus of fantasy-whimsy... Bolger performs broadly; he's crafty and menacing although none but the small tykes will actually believe his villainy. And he delights with his rubber-legged dance in the "Castles in Spain" number.... Gene Sheldon and Harry [sic] Calvin attempt impersonations of Laurel and Hardy, who starred in the first film version, with just fair results."

Disney's publicity and marketing machinery went into high gear for its *Babes in Toyland*, licensing an onslaught of books, records, dolls, toys and even diapers. The film did not perform as well as hoped at the box office. On a reported budget of $3 million, it took in $4.6 million, only half of what the studio's much less expensive comedy *The Shaggy Dog* had made in 1959. It was never reissued theatrically, but was screened in two parts on NBC's *The Wonderful World of Disney* on December 21 and 28, 1969. It was released on DVD in 2002 and on Blu-ray ten years later. Much bigger versions of the wooden soldiers became a favorite element in parades at Disney theme parks.

Quite likely the best thing about this *Babes in Toyland* was that it taught the creative crew at Disney what not to do when making a live-action musical; they learned from these mistakes when they made their next one, the magnificent *Mary Poppins* (1964).

Tommy Kirk said in 1993, "Actually I think the movie is sort of a klunker, especially when I compare it to the Laurel and Hardy *Babes in Toyland*. It's not a great film but it has a few cute moments. It's an oddity. But I'm not embarrassed about it like I am about some other movies I've made."

In her 1994 autobiography *A Dream Is a Wish Your Heart Makes*, Annette Funicello wrote, "Of all my filmmaking experiences, *Babes in Toyland* is without question my favorite. It was one of those rare times when everything about making the film – from my director, my co-stars, the crew, the costumes, even the scenery – was perfect... It was the first, and unfortunately, I think, the last time I made a movie in which I actually danced something besides the watusi or the swim."

They never did find the sheep.

Chapter 19

Other Productions, 1980-1997

Hal Roach could never let go of his unfilmed story for *Babes in Toyland*. In June 1980, 46 years and six months after he'd written his scenario for Laurel and Hardy, he wrote a 13-page treatment, *Toyland*, essentially the same story with some updated modifications.

"The film opens on a set designer's concept of an office in Hell," notes Roach's script. "The chief demon has a futuristic bank of television screens, and each set is showing pictures of the happy folks on Earth preparing for Christmas." The demon and his crew are sick and tired of all this happiness, but one of them has a plan. He tells his chief, "I know if I can get to Toyland, I can destroy it. Since security is so tight, I will need a very good disguise. You must give me the power to change into a spider at will, and back again when I have to."

The chief demon gives his underling the power to change by simply saying, "I am a spider" or "I am a demon." He also bestows the name of Creep to this chameleonic lackey. In his demon mode, Creep attains the form of a man in a black silk hat and tails; he comes to a "dismal and impoverished orphanage" and begins distributing gifts to the kids. Spying the prettiest girl there, Melody, he induces her to climb up to the roof of the orphanage a few minutes before midnight so that he can have her meet Santa Claus and take a trip to Toyland. She responds with, "Oh yes, Creep, I understand." Just why a little girl places such trust in a stranger named Creep is puzzling, but we must proceed.

Creep and Melody encounter Santa Claus and decide to hide in his sleigh. Because there's so little room, Creep changes back into a spider. Melody is horrified, but Creep says, "You've got it all wrong. I'm going to Toyland to do a very good deed... I'm going to give the toys a soul." Once Santa has finished his Christmas Eve duties, the sleigh – with Melody and Creep secretly aboard – arrives in Toyland. Melody goes to sleep under a tree.

Dawn breaks, revealing a magical city "dominated by Santa's enormous toy factory" and a "Cinderella-style castle." Several Toyland residents begin to fill the streets, among the Simple Simon and the Pie Man. They are puzzled by the presence of this little girl in ragged clothes, who explains, "Creep brought me to Toyland in Santa's sleigh. We've come to give souls to all the toys." This prompts the first big musical number (six pages into a 13-page treatment), which is specified as "'The Toyland March' which is owned by Hal Roach. It should not be confused with 'The March of the Wooden Soldiers,' or more accurately Herbert's 'March of the Toys.'"

They go to the castle to tell the queen that toys will now have a soul; the queen is "somewhat repulsed by Melody's tattered appearance," and has her attendants give her some proper attire. Once she is properly clothed and revealed as "a beautiful young lady in a dazzling costume," the queen commands her to sing and dance. She is uncertain, but handsome Jack Horner comes to her rescue, and they dance and sing a duet.

Creep, in spider form, crawls into Santa's warehouse, "where huge barrels labeled 'Happiness,' 'Love,' and 'Laughter' are arranged in long rows." Creep returns to his semi-human demonic form, heads toward Santa's office and explains to him his plan of giving souls to the toys. He needs a new laboratory to produce the secret formula. All of Toyland helps to build the structure, which "begins to take shape as an impossible Rube Goldberg creation." Creep selects Melody, Simple Simon and the Pie Man as his assistants on his project.

The barrels of liquid are put through a "mass of pipes, coils and tubing" from which eventually emerges a small vial of a very precious fluid. Simple Simon is intrigued by this and tastes it. Says the script, "His face is immediately distorted by the ugliest possible contortion. The Pie Man

"TOYLAND"

A Film Treatment

by

Hal Roach

First Draft
June, 1980

"TOYLAND"

The background for the opening titles should tell the audience that the time is a day or two before Christmas: children excitedly sitting on Santa's lap in department stores; people trimming Christmas trees; children hanging up their stockings. Everyone is laughing and very happy.

The film opens on a set designer's concept of an office in Hell. The chief demon has a futuristic bank of television screens, and each set is showing pictures of the happy folks on Earth preparing for Christmas. He wildly changes the pictures with his remote control, but -- although he gets a different picture -- it too reflects the joy of Christmas.

The chief demon glares at his motley collection of henchmen. "That cursed Toyland is responsible for all of this. Santa Claus! Toys! Wooden soldiers! Dolls! I told you years ago that Toyland must be destroyed. Can't one of you figure out how to get there and blow it up, so we don't have to endure all this happiness every year?"

The demons look at each other helplessly. Finally, one particularly gruesome character (who will become our villain) speaks up.

"Oh powerful master, I have a plan which will work. I know if I can get to Toyland, I can destroy it. Since security is so tight, I will need a very good disguise. You must give me the power to change into a spider at will, and back again when I have to."

TOYALND 2

The Demon points his finger at our villain and a laser-bright flash of light streams forth. "OK, you've got it," the Boss replies. "But remember -- Toyland's destruction is now your problem. Don't bother coming back until it's done!"

"Hey, wait a minute! How does this spider thing work?"

The Demon shakes his head in disgust. "Why do I get all the idiots? Listen, stupid, I made this one easy just for you. When you want to be a spider say, 'I am a spider.' When you don't say, 'I am a demon.' Get it?"

Our villain beams with delight at his new talent. "Can I try it out right now?"

The Demon nods wearily.

Clearing his throat, our villain takes center stage. "OK, here goes. I AM A SPIDER!"

He instantly disappears, and the other demons begin to murmur among themselves. Suddenly, we spot something black and furry on the ground. It is a spider about the size of a tarantula.

A tiny, high-pitched voice breaks the silence. "I AM A DEMON!"

To a round of appreciative applause, the spider instantly returns to his normal form.

"All right, everybody back to work," commands the Boss. To our villain he says, "Remember, Creep, the rest is up to you." He turns back to his wall of TV screens.

"Hmmm. He called me Creep. I like it! And rather appropriate under the circumstances."

TOYLAND 3

The next scene opens on a dismal and impoverished orphanage. The children are making weak attempts at Christmas spirit with a few tattered decorations. Alone in a corner is our heroine, Melody. She is clearly the prettiest of the little girls in spite of her rags, but she has no friends and seems most unhappy.

Suddenly the door bursts open and Creep enters. He is nattily -- and predictably -- dressed in a black silk hat and tails and is carrying a large sack of presents. The children all flock around him, except Melody -- who is much too shy. He quickly distributes the gifts to the gleeful kids, but by the time he sees Melody off in her corner, the sack is empty. Checking to make sure that the other orphans are too busy with their new toys to pay him any more attention, he approaches Melody, who now has big tears rolling down her cheeks.

"Now, now, my dear, don't cry. I haven't forgotten you. In fact, I've saved the best present of all. Tonight, little Melody, you will meet Santa Claus and take a trip to Toyland."

Melody is clearly skeptical. "How could that possibly happen?"

Creep looks around furtively to make sure no one is within earshot. "Tonight, a few minutes before midnight, climb up to the roof. I'll be there to tell you what to do next." He fishes a pretty gold watch out of his pocket and hands it to her. "Are you sure you understand what to do?"

The first four pages of Hal Roach's 1980 script for *Toyland*, which was remarkably similar to the unfilmed story he'd written in 1933.

hurries over to see what's the matter, and Simon smacks him on the nose. Indignant, the Pie Man retaliates, and a short Laurel-and-Hardy, kicking and slapping fight ensues. Melody and Jack break it up and scold them for fighting when they are employed in such a noble endeavor."

A parade of the new toys ready for next Christmas ensues, all of them reaching the queen's castle, where she announces that this is the most special group of toys to be produced in Toyland, since they're the first to receive souls.

Jack Horner and Melody, walking through some woods, find a dilapidated cottage, the abandoned former home of the Rainmaker. Rain has been outlawed in Toyland in favor of permanent sunshine, except for a light dusting of snow on Christmas.

Meanwhile, back at the laboratory, Creep exults over the vial of mysterious liquid, which "is ominously dark, and periodically bubbles, hisses and emits steamy vapors." He orders Simple Simon and the Pie Man to dispose of the surplus barrels of Love, Happiness and Laughter. They go through Toyland, and whenever they encounter a rare unpleasant situation – someone having an argument, or a baby crying – they spray the participants with the liquid Happiness. "The Happiness appears in the form of shimmering silver butterflies, and all is instantly rosy. The baby smiles, the friends embrace, and the oldsters jump up from the park bench and turn handsprings down the street.... By nightfall, the whole town is infected with Happiness, Love and Laughter and there is much celebration."

Sadly, such bliss does not last long, as Creep takes the vial, "which we now discover is really Hate, distilled from his own treacherous spider venom," and sprays it all over rows of tall wooden soldiers in a warehouse. "The transformation is immediate," notes the script. "Their painted smiling faces cloud over and the whole building begins to rumble. En masse, the soldiers start to march, destroying everything in their path. Even Creep gets brutally tossed aside and smashed against a wall."

The soldiers continue their "rampage" through the toy factory and begin a march to Toyland to destroy the whole town. Melody and Jack Horner, sitting under a tree beside a bridge, see the oncoming evil army, but notice that one soldier falls off the bridge and into a stream. His bright colors wash away; the water affects his glued joints, and he falls apart.

Melody and Jack tell Simple Simon and the Pie Man about this, and they all rush to some fire trucks, but these are too small to spray the entire army of soldiers. A huge battle ensues, the Toyland residents besieged by the soldiers. Melody then remembers the abandoned rainmaking machine; she and Jack manage to get it working again, the sky fills with clouds, rain descends upon Toyland, and "the soldiers ooze paint, slow down, and slowly disintegrate in piles of wood along the streets."

Creep is exposed as the villain behind the plan, and "he is duly punished." Melody is celebrated as a heroine by the Toyland townsfolk, and is awarded permanent citizenship.

Again, this is an exceedingly dark story, sacrificing charm and whimsy for extended scenes of grim drama and horror. The heavy emphasis on demons, spiders and liquid Hate does not seem conducive to a movie intended primarily for children. One wonders where the comedy, and where Victor Herbert's music, would have fit.

This project never came to fruition, nor did other ideas Roach had for films well into the 1980s. He had been an uncredited associate producer on *One Million Years B.C.*, a 1966 remake starring Raquel Welch of his 1940 feature *One Million B.C.*, but after that he mainly promoted theatrical reissues or video releases of his great work of the 1920s and '30s.

In 1986, a quarter-century after the release of Walt Disney's feature film, another *Babes in Toyland* was made for television, a German-American co-production. This one went even farther afield from the Victor Herbert original, using only the briefest snippets of "Toyland" and "March of the Toys." It substituted new songs by Leslie Bricusse, who'd had better luck in collaborations with Anthony Newley, among them scores for the stage show *Stop the World, I Want to Get Off* and the movie *Willy Wonka and the Chocolate Factory*.

The story had a framing device reminiscent of MGM's *The Wizard of Oz*. Lisa Piper (Drew Barrymore) is a 12-year-old girl who functions as the parent of her Cincinnati household, since her mother (Eileen Brennan) is lovable but scatterbrained and disorganized. Lisa's older sister Mary (Jill Schoelen) works in a toy store, where she tries to avoid the nasty and flirtatious manager, Mr. Barnie (Richard Mulligan). Her boyfriend Jack Fenton (Keanu Reeves) also works there, as does their friend George (Googy Gress).

After Mr. Barnie makes another unwelcome romantic advance on Mary, Lisa speaks up for her and tells him just what he can do with his toy store; she also warns the customers that a terrible snowstorm is about to engulf all of Cincinnati. Everyone rushes out, and Jack tries to get Lisa, Mary and George home safely in his jeep despite the slippery, icy roads. (They distract themselves by singing a song about the greatness of Cincinnati.) A minor accident sends Lisa flying out of the jeep and sliding down a snowbank, where she hits her head on a tree.

When she awakens, she's in Toyland, where many of the townsfolk have an exact resemblance to her friends. Jack B. Nimble, Junior (Reeves) is in love with Mary Quite Contrary (Schoelen), but evil Barnaby Barnicle (Mulligan) has designs on her. Because he has a mortgage on the shoe in which Mary's mother (Brennan) lives, he forces Mary into a wedding – which is stopped at the last moment because only Lisa is brave enough to tell everyone about Barnaby's blackmail. Mary is really in love with Jack B. Nimble, she announces, no surprise to anyone, especially the couple's best friend, Georgie Porgie (Gress).

Jack works at the Toyland cookie factory, which Barnaby owns. Barnaby exacts his revenge by having his two minions, Zack and Mack – who look like junior versions of Max Schreck in *Nosferatu* – dump the entire inventory of cookies down a secret passageway in the factory floorboards, which somehow leads to his evil lair – a giant black bowling ball. He frames Jack for the theft, but Lisa, Mary and Georgie help him escape.

The friends seek the help of the kindly Toymaker (Pat Morita) in ridding Toyland of Barnaby. The Toymaker wistfully displays his finest creation – a platoon of six-foot-tall wooden soldiers, which nobody seems to want for Christmas. He also shows something very secret, a small black vial of liquid hate (shades of Hal Roach's 1933 story!) which he has extracted from everyone in Toyland and keeps under strict lock and key.

Barnaby learns about this, and he and his minions capture Jack, Mary and Lisa and imprison them in his dungeon. Barnaby now plans to turn the youngsters into his slaves by making them inhale the fumes from the vial of hate. Unable to hold their breaths any longer, Jack, Mary and Georgie begin turning into ogres, but Lisa is immune – because she's not from Toyland, she's from Cincinnati! She teaches the other kids the "Cincinnati" song, and this brings them back to their normal, cheerful selves.

They escape by pretending to still be under Barnaby's evil spell. He lets them out of his prison so they can begin doing their dirty work, but Jack socks him on the jaw and they all make a run for it. A chase around Toyland in miniature cars ensues, to little effect, and Barnaby decides to unleash an army of ogres to destroy Toyland.

Lisa, Jack, Mary and Georgie prevail upon the Toymaker to help defend Toyland against the monsters; the Toymaker sadly reveals that he is powerless, since there is one person in Toyland who doesn't believe in toys because she grew up too fast. It's Lisa, who has always been the adult of her household. However, she remembers that she kept her teddy bear from earliest childhood, and this proves that she believes in the power of toys.

The kids wind up the army of wooden soldiers, and with the help of the giant bunny rabbits, frogs, pigs, puppy dogs and occasional human characters who populate Toyland, they send Barnaby and his ogres into the Forest of the Night, banished there forever by proclamation of the Toymaker. Mary and Jack finally have a happy wedding day – the day of the night before Christmas. Lisa will get back to Cincinnati by hitching a ride on Santa's sleigh, and Santa turns out to be – the Toymaker.

Back home, Lisa wakes up from her dream to find her mother and young friends very concerned about her but relieved that she is well. She recounts her adventures, noting that everyone in Toyland looked just like people she knew, and telling everyone that she's learned the lesson taught to her by the Toymaker, that we must always stay young at heart, be good, and believe.

Filmed in Munich, this was broadcast on NBC on December 19, 1986 in a 145-minute version. It was later cut to 94 minutes, omitting several songs, for overseas release in theaters and worldwide release on home video.

One element retained from the Laurel and Hardy version is Barnaby holding a mortgage against the shoe in which Mother Hubbard lives, a plot point quickly dispensed with. Eileen Brennan is wasted in this microscopic role, and a severely misguided one; at one point she considers selling a few of her many children to pay off the mortgage! Another idea carried over from the 1934 movie is the toymaker creating unwanted six-foot-tall wooden soldiers which eventually vanquish Barnaby's monsters and save Toyland, certainly a much better scene than the miniature misfire in Disney's version.

The sets are uninspiring, except for the Old Woman's shoe – plain buildings painted in bright colors. Since much of the film is shot outdoors in bright sunlight, the film often looks like home movies of Disneyland, especially during the pointless chase around Toyland in the miniature cars, which look like rejects from the Autopia ride. And how does the cookie factory connect to Barnaby's giant bowling ball of a home, which stands alone in Toyland?

The acting is generally flat and lifeless. Richard Mulligan tries hard but needs more color and mystery to go with all of his anger. Only Pat Morita, as the Toymaker, strikes the right tone of theatricality that's needed for a fantasy film.

The original 145-minute version had 12 musical numbers, including two renditions of "Toyland." The 94-minute edition now available has perhaps two minutes' worth of Victor Herbert's music – one quick chorus each of "Toyland' and "March of the Toys." As for the Leslie Bricusse originals, the most memorable song, and not necessarily for good reasons, would be "C-I-N-C-I-N-N-

The 1986 German-U.S. musical film starred Keanu Reeves and Drew Barrymore, with Richard Mulligan as Barnaby Barnicle and Pat Morita as the Toymaster.

A-T-I," a portion of the lyric being, "At first they called it Cincy, but since Cincy is so natty, they named it Cincinnati, so they say.... Cincy's more than merely natty, she's Ohio's Maserati, Cincinnati's at the center of the scene!" By getting Jack, Mary and Georgie to sing this song, Lisa is able to return them from ogres into their normal kindly selves. It may have the reverse effect on some viewers.

Since the corporate successors to the Hal Roach Studios in 1986 had nothing whatsoever to do with the making of this film and at one point considered suing the producers, Bavaria Atelier and The Finegan Company, over similarities to the 1934 movie, it's astonishing that the idea of a vial full of liquid hate shows up in this picture, 53 years after Roach had the same idea. It's not very entertaining here, and accounts for only a few minutes of the running time.

The screenplay was written by Paul Zindel, who created the grim yet Pulitzer Prize winning "kitchen drama" *The Effect of Gamma Rays on Man-in-the-Moon Marigolds*. In 1985, he had written the script for a TV miniseries of *Alice in Wonderland*. This retooled *Babes in Toyland* was directed by London-born Clive Donner, who had been at the helm for well-regarded TV movies of *Oliver Twist* and *A Christmas Carol* for CBS, both starring George C. Scott; it's a pity he couldn't have brought more color, whimsy and life to the performances here.

The reactions to this film are wildly divided; people who saw it on television as kids remember it fondly, while others think of it as a "so bad it's good" movie, or even a "so bad it's bad" movie. I'd say it's just fair, not as relentlessly aggressive or gaudy as the Disney version but far afield from anything Victor Herbert and Glen MacDonough envisioned.

You'll remember that Disney and RKO had flirted with making an animated feature film of *Babes in Toyland* in 1933, and Disney had announced his own feature-length cartoon back in 1953. Neither project was realized (at least not in animated form), but in 1997 a new animated feature film of *Babes in Toyland* was released. Like the 1986 film, this was also an international project. It was produced by Metro-Goldwyn-Mayer Animation with voices recorded in the States, music performed in London, and the animation accomplished in Taipei, Taiwan.

The characters and backgrounds were designed by Toby Bluth, who co-directed with Charles Grosvenor and Paul Sabella. Bluth had worked as a layout artist for Hanna-Barbera in the 1970s and early '80s and also had a prolific career in live theater, performing and often directing close to 100 stage musicals. He often collaborated with his older brother Don, who worked for Disney for ten years before producing his own highly regarded animated features including *The Secret of NIMH*, *An American Tail* and *The Land Before Time*. In 1986, Toby had written and illustrated a children's book which more closely resembled the 1903 play and the 1934 Laurel and Hardy movie than his 1997 film.

This time around, the two "babes" of the title are Jack and Jill. (Why did no one think of that before?) They are orphans, heirs to a large fortune; we meet them on the Toyland Express train, whose conductor is Humpty Dumpty (voiced by Charles Nelson Reilly). The kids are being left in the "care" of their uncle Barnaby Crookedman (whose voice is supplied by Christopher Plummer). Barnaby is evil through and through, and after taking the little bag of coins that the kids have, he locks them in an empty room in his creepy abode, with no food or water. Fortunately, on the train, Jack and Jill have met handsome, blond Tom Piper. He is the creative director at the Toyland Toy Factory, and is smitten with young, pretty Mary Lamb, who has assumed the leadership of the factory after the

Some key characters in the 1997 animated film were Mr. Dumpty (voiced by Charles Nelson Reilly), Barnaby Crookedman (Christopher Plummer), Gonzargo (James Belushi) and Rodrigo (Bronson Pinchot).

death of her father. Jack and Jill manage to sneak out of Barnaby's lair and run to the toy factory.

Santa Claus has just placed an order for 1,000 giant toy soldiers. (He actually wants them to be life-sized this time around.) Mary and Tom despair of making all of these in the next three days, but Jack and Jill offer to help. Alas, Barnaby descends upon the scene, abducts the kids, and locks them in his tower. At that point, two sailors – portly Gonzargo and pint-sized Rodrigo (thus spelled in the credits, and voiced by James Belushi and Bronson Pinchot) – answer Barnaby's advertisement seeking "two vicious cut-throats, object robbery."

Barnaby is not so concerned with Jack and Jill's inheritance; his main goal is to destroy the Toy Factory. He despises toys, laughter and fun, since he had none of these as a child. Gonzargo and Rodrigo disguise themselves as sheep (presumably lost from Bo-Peep's flock) and throw a monkey wrench, literally, into the factory's machinery. Tom holds Jack's hand as he dangles in front of the gears and extracts the wrench. But, alas again, Barnaby once more captures the kids. He orders Gonzargo and Rodrigo to take them to the dark, terrifying Goblin Forest, so they won't interfere with his evil plans.

Humpty Dumpty finds out about this and tells Tom and Mary, who rush to the forest in hopes of rescuing the kids. The Goblins are huge and will eat just about anything or anyone, but they will become paralyzed by light. Fortunately, Tom has a flashlight which wards them off while he and Mary, Jack and Jill make their escape.

Just as Tom and Mary finish Santa Claus's order for the six-foot tall toy soldiers, Barnaby invades Toyland with a huge army of goblins; they set fire to many of the colorful buildings and cause all manner of mayhem, led by the Goblin King. Tom activates the toy soldiers, each of which has a flashlight in its tall black hat. By aiming their beams at the Goblin King, they destroy him, turning him into a puddle of purple goo. Barnaby is incensed at this failure, saying, "To think I trusted you, you pathetic ogre!" This

Also in the 1997 film were Tom Piper (Raphael Sbarge), Mary Lamb (Catherine Cavadini), Jill (Lacey Chabert) and Jack (Joseph Ashton).

angers the hundreds of goblins, who yank Barnaby into their fold and run back to the Goblin Forest, presumably to do away with him.

Finally, just as Christmas Eve is about to begin, Tom has repaired Humpty Dumpty who, during the fracas, had a great fall. Santa Claus arrives and magically shrinks the soldiers down to about one-foot tall (guess he had second thoughts about that order after all), and goes on his way. Tom and Mary are finally about to be wed and will be adopting Jack and Jill.

Originally intended for a theatrical release, the film was instead released directly to DVD by MGM/UA Home Video on October 14, 1997. This shouldn't be seen as an indicator of poor quality: while this is once again far from the Victor Herbert original, on its own terms this *Babes in Toyland* is quite entertaining. At a brisk 74 minutes, it's well paced; the story keeps moving even with the occasional pause for musical numbers. Charles Nelson Reilly is energetic and very funny as Mr. Dumpty, and sings a quick opening chorus of "Toyland" very nicely.

Christopher Plummer provides the best vocal performance of Barnaby since Henry Brandon, imbuing the character with a melodious and menacing delivery. The character design and animation are excellent – although Mary Lamb is a dead ringer for "Belle" from Disney's *Beauty and the Beast*. The sequence where the goblins invade Toyland is truly frightening, much more intense and vivid than anything inflicted by the 1934 Bogeymen. Herbert's music is represented by short renditions of "Toyland," "The Aerial Ballet" and "March of the Toys," with a couple of other compositions given new titles and lyrics by Toby Bluth. Two new songs, "The Worst Is Yet to Come" and "It's You," sport lyrics written by Lorraine Feather, daughter of prominent jazz critic Leonard Feather.

Each of the post-1934 productions has its charms and its flaws. Despite their widely different storylines, they share many responses from viewers on the Internet Movie Database and other sources, proclaiming each one "good, but nowhere near as good as the Laurel and Hardy film." I would agree.

Left: Robert Fennally "Slim" Gragg was a carpenter and model-maker at the Roach studio. In retirement, he carved beautiful miniatures of scenes from Laurel and Hardy movies. He donated them to the Culver City Historical Society. *Top Right*: "Slim" helped to construct the Old Woman's Shoe in 1934, and made a miniature replica of it almost 50 years later. *Both courtesy Jim Kerkhoff.*

At a meeting of the Way Out West Tent (Los Angeles) of Sons of the Desert, tent officers Bob Satterfield and John Duff gleefully hold "neither pig nor pork" sausages, in the company of Dick Jones (Toyland boy), Angelo Rossitto (Little Elmer) and a snarling Henry Brandon (Barnaby). *Courtesy Bob Satterfield.*

Chapter 20

And They Lived Happily Ever Afterward

Despite what Hal Roach and Ella Herbert Bartlett thought of it, the 1934 Laurel and Hardy *Babes in Toyland,* or *March of the Wooden Soldiers* as it is now more popularly known, has shown remarkable staying power in the affections of the public. It has a particularly devoted audience in the New York City area thanks to the annual television screenings on WPIX during the holidays, and remains a favorite with L&H admirers all over the world. What other films from the early 1930s have sustained such popularity?

In addition to television screenings (it's also shown regularly on the Movies! network based in Chicago and Turner Classic Movies out of Atlanta), it's a perennial favorite at Sons of the Desert meetings all over the world at Christmas time. An elaborate tribute was paid to the film and its stars during the fifth annual international convention of the Sons. This was sponsored by the Two Tars Tent in Valley Forge, Pennsylvania from Friday, July 25 through Wednesday, July 30, 1986. (Had it been held a couple of weeks earlier, it would have shared the movie's placement "in the middle of July," as Barnaby notes incredulously.)

Celebrity guests included Thomas Benton Roberts, a long-time prop man and carpenter at the Roach lot who gained immortality as the motorist who has a tomato rubbed into his face by Stan in *Two Tars*. The official Laurel and Hardy biographer and founder of the Sons, John McCabe attended, and surprised the throng by announcing his recent engagement to another guest, Rosina Lawrence, who had played the heroine in L&H's 1937 feature *Way Out West*. Bandleader Vince Giordano and his crew, a 1920s-style dance orchestra called the Nighthawks,

Thanks to the Sons of the Desert, *Babes in Toyland* and its makers were frequently given tribute. Here, L&H enthusiast Steve Randisi greets Virginia Karns (Mother Goose) and Felix Knight (Tom-Tom).

Charlotte Henry Dempsey in later years.

— 209 —

Left: At Valley Forge, 14-year-old Brad Farrell poses with Ollie lookalike Bill Furman. *Right*: Brad's sister Denise strikes a pose with a Stannie lookalike. *Both courtesy Brad Farrell.*

The Toyland set was meticulously recreated at the convention. *Photo by Marcia Opal.*

Henry Brandon displays expert villainy on the Toyland set. *Photo by Brad Farrell.*

Joe Rooney (Stan) and Mike Spack (Ollie) re-enact the "Christmas present" scene. *Photo by Marcia Opal.*

provided the music. Dorothy DeBorba – who had been "Echo" in *Our Gang* comedies from 1930 through '33 was on hand, as was Venice Lloyd, widow of longtime Roach studios (and *Babes in Toyland*) cameraman Art Lloyd. However, perhaps the most special of the guests on this occasion were Felix Knight, Virginia Karns Patterson, and Henry Brandon. A very enthusiastic 14-year-old Laurel and Hardy fan from Dayton, Ohio, Brad Farrell, attended with his family and provides this account of the event:

> The culmination of the fifth international Sons of the Desert convention in Valley Forge (actually King of Prussia), Pennsylvania came on the evening of Tuesday, July 29, 1986. This final banquet was quite a memorable one as it involved not only a recreation of Toyland from the 1934 Laurel and Hardy film, but featured celebrities from the original film itself!
>
> For the first – and last – time at any Sons event I, along with my family, chose to go in costume to one of the costume banquets. If there was one to do it at, it was certainly this one. Nearly all of the convention-goers came as one of the characters from Toyland. My new friend Bob Satterfield, for instance, came as Santa Claus.
>
> My family decided to go simply as town people of Toyland. We had purchased 'antique' clothing at a used clearance store in Kettering, Ohio weeks before the trip. Although I looked absolutely ridiculous in these duds, I felt it my obligation and duty to participate in the family effort.
>
> There were some behind-the-scenes fiascos in getting the fabricated town of Toyland set up, including the giant shoe collapsing as it was being toted down the Pennsylvania highway.
>
> The feature presentation of the evening was to re-create selected scenes from *Babes in Toyland* utilizing look-alikes for Stan and Ollie and other characters, but having Henry Brandon reprise his original role as the evil Silas Barnaby in full regalia!
>
> And to add an even more amazing touch to the evening, Felix Knight, who had played the role of Tom-Tom Piper in the film, got

Henry Brandon, Virginia Karns and Felix Knight reunite at the 1986 Sons Convention in Valley Forge, Pennsylvania. *Courtesy Michael Townsend Wright.*

Mr. Brandon receives some well-deserved, and thunderous, applause. *Courtesy Brad Farrell.*

up and sang a few selected songs from the film. During his performance of "Toyland," Virginia Karns Patterson, who had played Mother Goose in the film, got up and joined him. No matter whether you're a fan of Laurel and Hardy or not, I think you can understand how these were amazing and magical moments in time…and times that can never be recaptured.

What special quality is it that makes *Babes in Toyland*, perhaps more than any other Laurel and Hardy film, a revered treasure for thousands of fans? One longtime admirer, Harold Aherne, offers this assessment:

"*Babes in Toyland* works so well because its comic and semi-serious moments work with, not against, each other. Felix Knight, Charlotte Henry and Henry Kleinbach/Brandon all play their roles just seriously enough for the audience to have a peg on which to hang their emotions, but not so seriously that the film becomes top-heavy. In this revision of the plot, L&H's characters are very nicely integrated into the proceedings, and their routines are consistently funny. (I also have to put in a good word for the 'Go to Sleep, Slumber Deep' sequence, with its shimmering photography and visual effects.) And for any viewers who find the idea of a Toyland-based film too precious, well, the point about one of the Three Little Pigs possibly being pig-napped and turned into sausages provides a suitable hint of morbidity! For running slightly less than 80 minutes, *Babes* has quite a number of moving parts, and it's a credit to the directors and Hal Roach's staff that they all work in harmony."

To this, your friendly author would add that the Laurel and Hardy film possesses one quality in abundance, more than the original 1903 production or any subsequent film or TV versions, and that is charm. Sincere charm, never played facetiously. There's none of the gore or violence of the 1903 edition (or Hal Roach's 1933 script); Glen MacDonough's lyrics are left intact and Victor Herbert's music is presented abundantly in respectful and authentic arrangements; the Mother Goose characters are frequently in view, sustaining the wonder and whimsy of childhood; and the Laurel and Hardy sequences are funny and frequent, but never derail the progression of the story.

How sad it is that in his later years, Hal Roach couldn't remember his own adage that "50 percent of the script will not play," and think of the finished film as the product of the normal process of collaboration and refinement. Far from being "out of the thing completely," he was involved in every aspect of making the film: buying the rights, securing the financing, casting the supporting roles, hiring the writers and the people overseeing the music, finding a talented art director to design the sets and putting dozens of new carpenters to work building them, deciding on the "two unit" procedure to expedite the filming, watching

A poster for *March of the Wooden Soldiers* was on prominent display at Felix Knight's home. *Courtesy Steve Randisi.*

Hal Roach's close associate Richard W. Bann with The Boss at his last public appearance, the Sons' 1992 Las Vegas convention.

Top left: In 1980, cameraman Art Lloyd's widow generously gave the author a "wooden soldier" which Art had brought home in 1934. *Top right*: The soldier was on display at the Hollywood Museum in 2014. *Bottom*: In February 2020, an episode of the PBS television series *Antiques Roadshow* displayed five more soldiers of ten owned by the family of Roach studio executive Lewis A. French.

and criticizing the dailies, and personally delivering the first print to the MGM executives in New York. It was Hal Roach's movie, more than anyone else's.

Babes in Toyland was a remarkable achievement for a small studio like Roach's, the most elaborate and accomplished fantasy film to be made by an American studio until *The Wizard of Oz* by MGM five years later. Generations of fans for more than 90 years have loved this movie and think of it as something very special.

The arguments, "creative differences" and production headaches of 1934 don't really matter anymore. What survives, indelibly, is the magic and humor of the film, which continues to touch the hearts of thousands of people. Stan Laurel was surprised in his years of retirement that the Laurel and Hardy films were still so amazingly popular with audiences young and old. He said, "I guess people see how much love we put into them." Yes, we see the love, and we in turn love *Babes in Toyland*.

Who's Who in Toyland
The Cast

— The Major Characters —

Tweedledum and Tweedledee
Agreed to have a battle;
For Tweedledum said Tweedledee
Had spoiled his nice new rattle.
Just then flew down a monstrous crow,
As black as a tar-barrel;
Which frightened both the heroes so,
They quite forgot their quarrel.

Stan Laurel (Arthur Stanley Jefferson) – Stannie Dum – Born on June 16, 1890, Ulverston, Lancashire, England. Died on February 23, 1965 at 74 in Santa Monica, California of a heart attack. Stanley was born into a theatrical family; his father, Arthur Jefferson (1862-1949), was an actor, playwright, director and theater manager. His mother (1860-1908) was an actress, going under the stage name of Madge Metcalfe (her maiden surname). He had an older brother, George Gordon Jefferson (1885-1938), and three younger siblings: Beatrice Olga Jefferson (1894-1976), Sydney Everitt Jefferson (April 30-September 10, 1899) and Edward Everitt "Teddy" Jefferson (1901-1933).

The family moved to Glasgow, Scotland, where Stan spent much of his youth. He was enamored of the boy comedians such as "Nipper Lane" (later Lupino Lane) who appeared in his father's theaters, and worked up his own act as "Stan Jefferson, Boy Comedian," making his debut at 16 in 1906 at the Panopticon Music Hall in Glasgow. His father wasn't thrilled about Stan pursuing a career as a comedian but got him a job with the Levy and Cardwell touring company of *Sleeping Beauty*; Stan played a "Golliwog," or a large stuffed doll. Eventually he worked with the Fred Karno Company, where he understudied and roomed with the star comedian, Charlie Chaplin. The company came to America in 1910 and again in 1912, and Stan decided to stay in the States and work in vaudeville.

The sketches in which he toured the country from 1912 through 1922 included *The Rum'uns from Rome* (as one-half of "The Barto Brothers"), *The Nutty Burglars*, *The Crazy Cracksman*, *The Keystone Trio* (in which he imitated his former roommate, Chaplin, who had by this time become the most popular comedian in the world), *Raffles the Dentist*, and *No Mother to Guide Her*, the last two with professional and personal partner Mae Charlotte Dahlberg. Stan realized that "Stan Jefferson" had 13 unlucky letters, and a shorter name would guarantee larger billing on a marquee; Mae found a book in their dressing room one day that depicted a Roman general wearing a wreath of laurel, and the team's new surname was set.

Stan began working sporadically in films in 1917, and after 1922 was able to work exclusively in pictures. He had three tours of duty with Hal Roach, the first in 1918, the second in 1923-24, and the last from 1925 through late 1939. His teaming with Oliver Hardy occurred gradually through 1926 and '27, but by the end of the year they were an established and popular team. They easily made the transition to sound films in 1929, making shorts through 1935 and winning an Academy Award for *The Music Box* in 1932. Their first feature-length film, *Pardon Us*, was released in 1931 and after 1935 they made features exclusively.

After *Babes in Toyland*, Laurel and Hardy made *Bonnie Scotland* for Roach, which caused further friction between the producer and star over the story. This caused Stan to be suspended from the studio, which happened again after *Way Out West* (1937) and *Block-Heads* (1938). Despite their quarrels, Roach needed Laurel and Hardy as their films were virtually the only pictures his studio produced which could reliably return a large profit.

Stan's private life was tumultuous. After Mae Laurel returned to her native Australia in 1926, Stan married Lois Neilson in August of that year. They had a daughter, Lois Junior, in December 1927, but divorced in October 1933. Stan married Virginia Ruth Rogers in April 1934, a union which ended on December 31, 1937. The next day, Stan married the high-spirited and hot-tempered Russian singer Vera Ivanova Shuvalova, known professionally as "Illeana." Despite the couple going through three wedding ceremonies, the marriage resulted in lots of damaging headlines thanks to Vera's heavy drinking and roisterous behavior; they were divorced by 1941, when Stan remarried Virginia Ruth. This marriage lasted only a few months, although the divorce wasn't finalized until April 1946. Later that month, Stan married another Russian, Ida Kitaeva Raphael. Fortunately, Ida (pronounced as EE-da) was a much more congenial partner, and this marriage lasted happily until Stan's passing 19 years later.

Laurel and Hardy left Roach after *Saps at Sea* (released 1940), but soon regretted the move to 20th Century-Fox and MGM, as they had no creative control and were forced to perform material written by others which was unsuitable for their established characters. After their last Fox feature, *The Bullfighters* (released in 1945), they performed onstage in music halls in England, Scotland, Denmark, Sweden, France and Belgium in 1947-48, 1952, and 1953-54. Stan and Babe also made one last film, *Atoll K*, in France in 1950-51; Stan's health problems caused a lengthy delay in filming, and the result was not as good as the team had hoped. They were surprised by host-producer Ralph Edwards as the subjects of television's *This Is Your Life* on December 1, 1954, which was their only appearance on live TV; a planned series of *Laurel and Hardy's Fabulous Fables*, in the same spirit as *Babes in Toyland*, was shelved after Stan suffered a mild stroke on April 25, 1955. He recovered quite well, but Babe Hardy then had a debilitating stroke on September 14, 1956 which put an end to the team's hopes of performing again.

Stan spent his final years in Santa Monica, residing from June 1958 at the Oceana Apartment and Hotel complex. He was visited by luminaries such as Marcel Marceau (whose work he had publicized during the making of *Atoll K*), Dick Van Dyke, Dick Cavett, Peter Sellers, Charlton Heston, Dana Andrews and many others, but he was just as happy to welcome just plain folks into his apartment for conversation and reminiscences. He was a very active correspondent, and hundreds of his letters have been collected on the website lettersfromstan.com.

He suffered a mild heart attack on February 23, 1965 and was joking with the male nurse who attended him in his apartment, saying "You know, I'd lot rather be skiing." When the nurse asked, "Do you ski, Mr. Laurel," Stan replied, "No, but I'd lot rather be skiing than this." He suffered a final, fatal attack soon after. Dick Van Dyke gave the eulogy at his memorial service, held at Forest Lawn in the Hollywood Hills.

Later in 1965, Laurel's biographer, John McCabe, founded Sons of the Desert, which has grown to be an international organization with hundreds of "tents" or chapters all over the world. Information about joining is available online at sonsofthedesertnyc.org.

**Oliver Hardy** (Oliver Norvell Hardy) – Ollie Dee – Born on January 18, 1892, Harlem, Georgia. Died on August 7, 1957 at 65 in North Hollywood, California of cancer and heart failure, after a stroke. Young Hardy's given name was Norvell, which was his mother Emily Norvell Tant's maiden surname. His father, Oliver Hardy, was a Civil War veteran, a county tax collector and hotel manager who died when Norvell was only ten months old. Emily had two daughters and two sons from her prior marriage to Thomas Samuel Tant, who had died of a heart ailment at 34 in February 1887. Norvell's half siblings were Thomas Samuel Tant, Junior (1879-1909), Mary Elizabeth Tant (1882-1964), Emily Tant (1887-1940) and Henry Lafayette Tant – later known as "Bardy Hardy" (1887-1938). Emily took care of her five kids by starting her own hotel, The Hardy House, near the train depot in Madison, Georgia.

In 1903 the family moved 45 miles south to Milledgeville, where Emily took over the management of the Milledgeville Hotel – later named the Baldwin – an impressive three-story structure. Norvell attended the Georgia Military College just across the street (which had students ranging from first grade to junior college), and at 18 became the projectionist and man of all work at the town's first movie theater, the Palace, which was just across another street from the hotel. Norvell was so appalled at some of the supposed acting in the comedies he screened that he decided he couldn't be any worse than they were. He headed for the then-burgeoning movie capital of Jacksonville, Florida late in 1913. He sang in cabarets at night and made himself known at the many studios during the day. He helped the prop men at the Lubin studios without being asked and without payment – but sure enough, one day they needed a fat boy for a comedy. Hardy's first film appearance, in a Lubin split-reeler called *Outwitting Dad*, was released on April 21, 1914.

Hardy had married a young pianist, Madelyn Saloshin, in November 1913. He was soon able to support her with plenty of work at Lubin and subsequently for Vim Comedies, which lasted through 1917. For a time, he was teamed with diminutive Billy Ruge as "Plump and Runt," and also directed and starred in several shorts, now billed as Babe Hardy. He acquired this name from a neighborhood Italian barber – described by Hardy as "a boy who liked boys" – who enjoyed patting talcum powder into his chubby cheeks and saying "Nice-a babe-ee, nice-a babe-ee." A bit later, the young actor took the professional billing of Oliver N. Hardy, adopting the name of his late father, but he would be "Babe" among friends to the end of his days.

By 1918 he was working with Chaplin imitator Billy West, who took many of the Vim veterans to Bayonne, New Jersey, and then to Hollywood. Hardy developed a reputation as a funny and reliable "heavy" or comic villain, and supported Jimmy Aubrey (who was, like Stan Laurel, a veteran of the Fred Karno Company) and Larry Semon in two-reelers for Vitagraph. Just as Hardy's school and the movie theater where he worked were across the street from his Milledgeville home, in 1921 Hardy lived right across from the Vitagraph studios, at 1719 Talmadge Avenue. By 1926, Hardy was a contract player at the Hal Roach studios, and during late 1926 and all through 1927 he developed his character as half of a team with Stan Laurel.

While Stan spent almost all of his time away from the cameras working on stories for the films or helping to cut the pictures with editor Bert Jordan, Babe enjoyed betting on the horse races at Agua Caliente and later at Santa Anita, and thereby lost much of his earnings. He was much more successful at golf, to which he'd been introduced by Larry Semon; he won many tournaments and was renowned as one of the best golfers among the movie colony.

Hardy's first marriage to Madelyn Saloshin ended in divorce in November 1921; soon after, he married Myrtle Lee Reeves, a Georgia girl who had been working in comedies at the Balboa studio in Long Beach. Sadly, by the late 1920s, Myrtle had developed a severe drinking problem, which nearly caused the dissolution of the marriage in 1932. The Hardys reconciled, but Myrtle continued to drink. Hardy found solace with Viola Morse, a widow with a young son. Myrtle's many stays at the Rosemead Sanitarium to dry out were unsuccessful, and Babe reluctantly divorced her in 1937.

In 1939, while working with Stan on *The Flying Deuces* for independent producer Boris Morros, Babe fell in love with the script girl, Virginia Lucille Jones, and they married in Las Vegas on March 7, 1940. This was a blissfully happy union – they were married at 4 o'clock on a Thursday afternoon and celebrated their anniversary with a kiss, a drink or a phone call at that time every week. It lasted for 17 years, until Babe's death.

Having finally achieved a happy home life, Babe shared Stan's frustration with the substandard scripts they were given at 20th Century-Fox and MGM. Lucille recalled that at night, when he'd be learning his lines for the next day's filming, he would often find one that was unsuited to his character; he'd turn to her and say, "Now, you know I wouldn't say that." The European tours of 1947 through 1954 were exciting, however, and confirmed that Laurel and Hardy were still beloved in other countries even if they were being ignored by Hollywood.

Babe weighed nearly 350 pounds in December 1954 when the team was saluted on TV's *This Is Your Life*, and he was determined to finally lose weight. He went on a strict diet, eating nothing but beets, and by June 1956 he was down to around 200 pounds, less than he had weighed in his adult life. This may have been too drastic and too rapid a loss, as Babe suffered a major stroke on September 14, 1956. He was unable to walk or talk and was mostly bedridden for the next 11 months. He was further diagnosed with cancer, and on August 7, 1957, as Lucille said, "his heart just stopped beating." Stan was very much affected by Babe's death and resolved to never perform again.

Unlike his often self-important screen character, Babe in private was a quiet and humble man. He told his biographer, John McCabe, "There's very little to write about me...as for my life, it wasn't very exciting and I didn't do very much outside of doing a lot of gags before a camera and play golf the rest of the time." Stan, however, had a different view: "Whatever I did was tops with him. There was never any argument between us, ever. I hope wherever he is now that he realizes how much people loved him."

Little Bo-Peep has lost her sheep
And doesn't know where to find them.
Leave them alone and they'll come home,
Bringing their tails behind them.

**Charlotte Henry** (Charlotte Virginia Henry) – Bo-Peep – Born on March 3, 1914, Brooklyn, New York. Died on April 11, 1980 at 66 in La Jolla, California of cancer.

Charlotte was modeling and appearing on the stage from the age of five and made her Broadway debut at 14 in the drama *Courage* at the Ritz Theatre on October 8, 1928; it ran for 280 performances, through June 1929. Her mother brought her to Hollywood, and Charlotte's film debut came late in 1929 with *Harmony at Home* (released January 12, 1930), a Fox comedy feature starring Marguerite Churchill and Rex Bell, with Charlotte third billed as "Dora Haller." She was prominent in the Warner Bros. film of *Courage* (1930) and in *Huckleberry Finn* (1931) with Jackie Coogan and Junior Durkin. Charlotte attained a starring role as *Lena Rivers* in a 1932 feature for Tiffany. She was enrolled at Lawlors, a school for professional children (where her classmates included Anita Louise, Frankie Darro and Betty Grable) and continued to work in films. She had a good role in *Forbidden* (1932) with Barbara Stanwyck, and co-starred in RKO's *Man Hunt* (1933) with Junior Durkin, who suggested that she try out for *Growing Pains*, a play in which he'd been cast at the Pasadena Playhouse. A Paramount talent scout saw her there and arranged a screen test for the leading role in *Alice in Wonderland*. While this all-star feature was not entirely successful, Charlotte's star was on the ascendant, and during 1934 she was a standout with George Arliss in *The Last Gentleman*

for 20th Century, and in *The Human Side* with Adolphe Menjou for Universal. *Babes in Toyland* was Charlotte's 16th film, and she made a further 16, although these tended to be smaller parts in major studio releases (such as *Charlie Chan at the Opera*, made in 1936 for 20th Century-Fox) or leading roles in pictures made by small studios (*The Return of Jimmy Valentine*, 1936 for Republic; *Young Dynamite*, 1937 for Conn Pictures).

She made no films from 1938 through mid-1941, focusing on modeling and stage work in productions of the Federal Theatre Project. She returned to pictures in two films for Paramount and two for Monogram, but now she was billed close to last and playing small roles as nurses and secretaries. At this point, as she later said, "I simply lost interest."

She worked for a time in stock companies but relocated to San Diego. There she ran an employment agency with her mother before becoming the executive secretary to Charles F. Buddy, the Roman Catholic Archbishop of San Diego, for 15 years. She married dental surgeon Dr. James J. Dempsey, and continued acting in stage productions at San Diego's Old Globe Theatre. Charlotte was well aware of the affection in which she was held by fans; prominent Sons of the Desert member Rick Greene was able to contact her not long before she passed away. She enjoyed a joke about "Alice Through the Looking Glass" with a personalized license plate on her car which read ECILA.

Tom, Tom, the piper's son,
Stole a pig, and away did run;
The pig was eat, and Tom was beat,
And Tom went crying down the street.

Felix Knight (William Felix Knight) – Tom-Tom Piper – Born November 1, 1908, Macon, Georgia. Died June 18, 1998 at 89 in the Bronx, New York City. Felix was the youngest of eight children born to Julia and Thomas Knight; his father was a cotton farmer who died in a hunting accident in October 1913, just before Felix turned five. In 1920, the family moved to Pensacola, Florida, and 12 year old Felix learned to play the guitar, earning money by playing and singing at dances and in clubs. He had a local radio show when he was 17, and by 1929 he had moved to California. There he found a vocal coach and another radio berth. He won a scholarship sponsored by the Atwater Kent radio manufacturing company which paid for further vocal training in New York.

Felix returned to Hollywood and sang *La Traviata* with Lily Pons at the Hollywood Bowl, and performed on CBS radio with Raymond Paige's orchestra. This led to some movie work – a bit part as a Gypsy singer in the Charles Boyer-Loretta Young romantic drama *Caravan* (1934), and a prominent number in the RKO comedy *Down to Their Last Yacht*, where Felix, bronzed as a Hawaiian native, sang a rather inane ditty, "Malakamokolu." The *Babes in Toyland* Campaign Book tells us, "He spends at least two hours every day in the gymnasium, not only for athletic pleasure but to keep his voice in condition. He is a fast handball player and a good boxer. For amusement he likes to watch prize fights and midget automobile racing, both popular sports in Southern California."

After the L&H film was released, Knight won a contract with MGM, but made no films for them; instead, he was loaned to Warner Bros. for two Technicolor shorts, *Springtime in Holland* (1935) and *Carnival Day* (1936). His two remaining films were both at the Roach studio; he sang "Then You'll Remember Me" as a strolling gypsy in *The Bohemian Girl* (1936) and sang and danced to "I've Got It Bad" in *Pick a Star* (1937). Knight moved to New York in 1937, where he made records for Victor, performed on NBC radio, played on Broadway in *It Happens on Ice*, and sang in *The Merry Widow* at Carnegie Hall. In addition to continuing his radio and recording work, in November 1946 Felix made his debut with the Metropolitan Opera in New York, in *The Barber of Seville* as Count Almaviva; he would essay this role, and that of Arturo in *Lucia di Lammermoor*, repeatedly in his Met career, which continued through 1950. He continued with television work, singing on *Your Show of Shows* and *The Jack Paar Show* and his own twice-weekly program. He also toured the country, appearing with the Philadelphia and Detroit symphony orchestras, and playing in summer stock theaters and nightclubs.

In the late '60s, tired of constant travel, he focused on becoming a vocal teacher, which he remained for the rest of his life. During the filming of *Babes in Toyland*, Felix fell in love with Alice Moore, who had a tiny role as the Queen of Hearts ("Boys! Boys!"). They married in Yuma, Arizona on October 17, 1935, but divorced on March 14, 1939. He remarried, to radio actress Ethel Blume, on June 21, 1940. They remained happily wed for the rest of Felix's life, and produced a son, William Felix Knight II, who during his childhood was popular on television's *Juvenile Jury*. Felix was a frequent and welcome guest at Sons of the Desert meetings in New York, and at the conventions of 1986 (in Valley Forge, Pennsylvania) and 1990 (in Clearwater, Florida). He died at Calvary Hospital in the Bronx and is buried at the Woodlawn Cemetery.

There was a crooked man, and he walked a crooked mile.
He found a crooked sixpence upon a crooked stile.
He bought a crooked cat, which caught a crooked mouse,
And they all lived together in a little crooked house.

Henry Brandon (Heinrich von Kleinbach) – Silas Barnaby – Born on June 8, 1912, Berlin, Germany. Died on February 15, 1990 at 77 in Los Angeles of a heart attack. Young Heinrich's family – Hugo R. Kleinbach, wife Hildagard, and older siblings Hugo O. and Maria – emigrated to the United States and arrived at Ellis Island on October 22, 1912; soon after, they had settled in Los Angeles. The newly rechristened Henry became active in school plays in elementary school and at Benjamin Franklin High School in Glendale. Henry attended Stanford University from 1928 to 1931 and continued in school plays.

By January 1932 he was performing at the Pasadena Playhouse in productions of *Berkeley Square* and *Peer Gynt*; in the latter show, Henry played "A Buttonmoulder" and "A Voice in the Darkness" in a cast that included future notables Lee J. Cobb, Douglass Montgomery and Gloria Stuart. In July 1933 Henry began a long run as the villainous Squire Cribbs in *The Drunkard* at the Theatre Mart in Los Angeles, which led to his being cast as Barnaby in *Babes in Toyland*. He continued to appear in the play at night after working on the film during the day, eventually giving 132 performances in the role through early 1935. He changed his surname to Brandon in 1936, a shorter version of his mother's maiden name, Brandonburg.

Brandon appeared in 101 movies, playing everything from Chinese villains to Native American warriors. He made a return to the Roach studio for *Our Gang Follies of 1938*, playing a character very similar to Barnaby, this time as an opera impresario who signs Alfalfa to a lifetime contract in a dream sequence.

His other notable films include *Trail of the Lonesome Pine* (1936), in which his character accidentally kills Spanky McFarland. Others are *Black Legion* (1937) with Humphrey Bogart, the serial *Drums of Fu Manchu* (1940), *The Paleface* (1948) with Bob Hope, and *Scared Stiff* (1953) starring Martin and Lewis. Brandon further proved his versatility in *The Searchers* (1956) starring John Wayne, as Commanche chief Scar, and *Auntie Mame* (1958) as iconoclastic teacher Acacius Page. He had a starring role in the 1974 adventure film *When the North Wind Blows*, one of his personal favorites.

His 84 television credits include episodes of many popular series, among them *Wagon Train, Gunsmoke, 77 Sunset Strip, The Outer Limits, F Troop, Mister Ed, Get Smart, Mission: Impossible,* and *Murder She Wrote*. He continued his stage work, in plays as varied as *Medea* (with Judith Anderson) and *Once More with Feeling*, including two revivals of *The Drunkard* in 1983 and 1987.

Having been a cherished guest at many meetings, banquets and conventions of the Sons of the Desert, the Laurel and Hardy appreciation society, Henry passed away from a heart attack at 77 during the night of February 15, 1990, at his home on 1033 North Spaulding Avenue in West Hollywood. Only a month before, he had given several bravura performances as "The Old Man of the Sea," attired in a bright green leotard and snarling with great exuberance, in an English-style "Christmas Pantomime." This was staged at North Hollywood's Mayflower Club by Tony Hawes, who was married to Stan Laurel's daughter, Lois. Henry's connection with Laurel and Hardy and *Babes in Toyland* continued to resonate until the very end of his life. Although he had been married for a brief time, he was survived by his longtime partner, Mark Herron, and a son, Rick. The full story of this astonishingly versatile actor can be found in the book *Henry Brandon: King of the Bogeymen* by Bill Cassara and Richard S. Greene, published in 2018 by BearManor Media.

> There was an old woman who lived in a shoe.
> She had so many children, she didn't know what to do.
> She gave them some broth without any bread;
> Then whipped them all soundly and put them to bed.

Florence Roberts – Mother Peep – Born March 16, 1861 on the Isle of Man. Died on June 6, 1940 at 79 in Hollywood of a heart attack. Born on an island between England and Ireland, Florence was brought to New York with her family at a very young age and gave that as her birthplace on subsequent documents.

She began her career at 19, in 1880, in *Hoop of Gold* at the Brooklyn Opera House. In Philadelphia, she became the leading lady of the stock company at the Fourpaugh Theatre; she played Bo-Peep in *The Moth and the Flame*. Miss Roberts next joined the Denman Thompson stage troupe, and eventually got to Broadway in four plays between 1907 and 1917. She toured the Orient, then joined the Henry Duffy company and toured Australia. She formed her own stock company in Philadelphia and ran it for 15 years.

She appeared in seven films from 1917 through 1925 (including the 1917 Universal comedy short *A Wise Dummy*, starring Max Asher), but her film career truly began when Mack Sennett saw her in 1930, on the stage in the comedy *Your Uncle Dudley*, starring Taylor Holmes. Sennett cast her in an Andy Clyde two-reeler, *Grandma's Girl* (1930); the next year Florence appeared in seven films, with particularly notable roles in *Everything's Rosie* (RKO, starring Robert Woolsey) and *Fanny Foley Herself* (RKO, with Edna May Oliver). She was busily employed in movies for the rest of her life, playing lovable grandmothers, faithful servants, and society dowagers.

Besides *Babes in Toyland*, she made three other appearances in Hal Roach films. In the Charley Chase short *The Cracked Ice Man*, she was the mother of leading lady Betty Mack; in Chase's *Four Parts*, she played the mother of Charley and his three identical brothers; and in *Nobody's Baby* (1937), she played "Mrs. Mason," landlady to Patsy Kelly and Lyda Roberti. She was also "Lady Flora" in Cecil B. DeMille's *Cleopatra* (1934), "Toussaint" in *Les Miserables* (1935) with Fredric March and Charles Laughton, and reprised her stage role as "Janet Dixon" in the 1935 film of *Your Uncle Dudley* starring Edward Everett Horton, whom she considered her adopted son. She also worked with Horton on stage in *The Unsuspected Husband* at the Hollywood Playhouse. (She had been married to actor Walter Gale, who predeceased her, and had her own son, Robert Gale.)

Beginning in 1936, she co-starred in 16 *Jones Family* features for 20th Century-Fox, with Jed Prouty, Spring Byington, Shirley Deane and Russell Gleason. She finished the last entry, *On Their Own*, and embarked on a vacation in Panama. On June 6, 1940, three weeks after her return, she was stricken with a heart attack at her Hollywood home. Edward Everett Horton delivered the eulogy at her memorial service.

> Old Mother Goose, when
> She wanted to wander,
> Would ride through the air
> On a very fine gander.

Virginia Karns (Jessie Virginia Karns) – Mother Goose – Born May 30, 1907, Dayton, Ohio. Died on June 21, 1990 at 83 in Dayton, Ohio.

Virginia studied music at the Cincinnati Conservatory and voice at Chicago Musical College. She began her professional career playing Shubert theaters in a stock company presenting *The Student Prince*. She toured with musical comedy companies from 1925 to 1932, at which point she came to Los Angeles and supplemented radio work with stage appearances. Virginia was a television pioneer, performing on experimental broadcasts in 1932.

An appreciation of her talent is in this review from the *Hollywood Filmograph* of September 17, 1932, when she was playing the Paramount Theatre in Los Angeles: "Virginia sang 'Lover, Come Back to Me' and this little lady has one of the finest voices we have ever heard at the Paramount.... Eddie Stanley, held over from last week, tells a few gags and introduces Virginia Karns in another vocal rendition of 'Ain't It Romantic?' [possibly a comedy version of Rodgers and Hart's "Isn't It Romantic?"] for solid applause."

As for movie work, Virginia provided the singing voice in films for actresses who couldn't, among them Norma Shearer, and was in the chorus for several MGM musicals. She's onscreen in four films, all made at the Roach studio and released in 1934: *Four Parts* with Charley Chase as a Nurse; *Soup and Fish* with Thelma Todd and Patsy Kelly as "daughter"; the musical short *Music in Your Hair*, singing "Lover, Come Back to Me"; and *Babes in Toyland* as Mother Goose. Virginia returned to Dayton in 1935 for the premiere broadcast of radio station WMSK, and in July of that year married lawyer Robert William Patterson.

Laurel and Hardy embarked on a stage tour which ran from December 17, 1941 to February 19, 1942; they played the Colonial Theater in Dayton from January 23 to 29, and on Sunday, January 25, they attended a party in Bill and Virginia's home, where Stan was captivated by the couple's twin babies, Ryan and James (and their older sister, Anne). Virginia was the radio hostess of *Welcome Wagon* on WING, and in 1950 appeared on television for WLWD. The next year, she moved to WHIO-TV, and hosted *The Virginia Patterson Show* through 1957. Her husband became mayor of Dayton in 1958 and held that office through 1961. Virginia retired from show business and ran a business, Services Unique, through 1967, but continued singing as a soloist in her church's choir. She was a special guest at meetings of Dayton's Sons of the Desert chapter (the A-Haunting We Will Go Tent), and at the group's conventions in 1986 and 1988.

William Burress (William Rosenberry Burris) – The Toymaker – Born August 19, 1867 in Newcomerstown, Ohio. Died on October 30, 1948 at 81 in Los Angeles. William's father, also named William, was a farmer and died at 24 a year after young William was born. His mother Victoria remarried to Joseph Hayworth (28 years older than she) and the family relocated to a farm on Newton, Ohio.

William became an operator for the Pennsylvania Railroad before embarking on a stage career, working in vaudeville and in stock companies for several producers and theater managers: Charles Frohman, Klaw and Erlanger, and Lee, Sam and Jacob Shubert. He got to Broadway in 1900 with the musical *Little Red Riding Hood*, and would appear in 14 Broadway shows through 1920, the most notable being *A Chinese Honeymoon* (1902-1903), *It Happened in Nordland* (1904-1905) and *The Spring Maid* (1910-11). He also toured the country in the comedy *A Gilded Fool* (1904) and played in vaudeville with *The New Song Birds*

(1913), which featured music by Victor Herbert.

He began working in films in 1915, with an Essanay comedy, *A Bunch of Keys*. By 1916 he was working steadily and prominently in features for Fox such as *End of the Trail, Bitter Roots,* and *The Scarlet Pimpernel*. After a 1922 Universal feature, *The Girl Who Ran Wild*, Burress made no more films for five years, touring with a stage comedy, *Kosher Kitty Kelly*. He returned to films briefly in 1927 in a feature for FBO, *Yours to Command*, and a two-reeler for Hal Roach, *Fluttering Hearts*, starring Charley Chase. He then resumed stage work until 1931, after which he concentrated on films, ultimately appearing in more than 70 of them.

Hollywood Filmograph indicates that the actor playing the ill-tempered, snarling Toymaker was a fine actor in its August 25, 1934 issue: "To William Burress, grand old trouper, Sunday, August 19 was the birthday of one of the dearest personalities in pictures. The staff of *Filmograph* wishes to extend to William Burress their heartiest congratulations and best wishes. William Burress has played many parts on the stage and on the screen, but the loveliest part he plays is his sweet, quiet self, with always a good word for everybody, and a helping hand to the discouraged. He is indeed a credit to his profession, and we wish him many more years of good health and contentment."

He was steadily employed through 1937 in movies such as *Blonde Crazy* (1931) with James Cagney; *The Little Colonel* (1935) starring Shirley Temple; and the Paramount comedy *Wild Money* (1937), starring Edward Everett Horton. He made only one film each in 1938 and 1939, doing uncredited bit parts, and by 1940, age 73, he was living in Islip, New York, at the Percy Williams Home for retired actors. In her column of November 6, 1948, Hollywood reporter Hedda Hopper wrote: "William Burress, old-timer of stage and screen, had been living at an actor's home back East, until last week when he was transferred to the Motion Picture Relief Fund Home. It had been his dream to live in California. Last Friday, when he arrived, he was met by his daughter and grandchildren, and had a wonderful reunion with them. But the excitement was too great. He died the following day."

> His eyes — how they twinkled! his dimples, how merry!
> His cheeks were like roses, his nose like a cherry!
> His droll little mouth was drawn up like a bow,
> And the beard of his chin was as white as the snow;
> The stump of a pipe he held tight in his teeth,
> And the smoke it encircled his head like a wreath;
> He had a broad face and a little round belly
> That shook, when he laughed, like a bowl full of jelly.
> He was chubby and plump, a right jolly old elf,
> And I laughed, when I saw him, in spite of myself.

Ferdinand Munier – Santa Claus – Born December 3, 1887 in National City, California. Died on May 27, 1945 at 57 in Hollywood of a heart attack. After graduating from Stanford University, Munier joined a stock company in San Diego. He continued his stage career after moving to New York in 1910; he remained there through 1915, marrying actress Charlotte Treadway along the way; they toured in vaudeville on the Orpheum circuit from 1916 through 1918. Munier continued to work in stock companies and had his own for two years, with his wife as featured star. He dabbled in films during the silent era, making three pictures (with a featured role in the 1926 feature *The Dixie Flyer*), but his part as "Senator Pillsbury" in the 1931 Will Rogers feature *Ambassador Bill* established him in pictures. Many of his appearances in 113 known films were uncredited. However, he received billing for *The Count of Monte Cristo* (1934), *Clive of India* (1935) and *Tovarich* (1937).

He was prominent in two Clark and McCullough two-reelers at RKO, *Kickin' the Crown Around* (1933) and *Love and Hisses* (1934). In fact, he was prominent everywhere; a 1932 Fox press release described him as "probably the fattest man in motion pictures, weighing 287 pounds, height five feet, nine inches." Besides *Babes in Toyland*, he made three other films at the Hal Roach Studios, all in 1935: *Okay, Toots!*, a Charley Chase short; *Top Flat*, a two-reeler starring Thelma Todd and Patsy Kelly; and the Robert Young-Evelyn Venable feature *Vagabond Lady*. One of his last film roles was again as Santa Claus, this time with Bing Crosby and Bob Hope in *Road to Utopia* (1945).

> Old King Cole was a merry old soul
> And a merry old soul was he;
> He called for his pipe, and he called for his bowl
> And he called for his fiddlers three.
> Every fiddler he had a fiddle,
> And a very fine fiddle had he;
> Oh there's none so rare, as can compare
> With King Cole and his fiddlers three

Kewpie Morgan (Horace Allen Morgan) – Old King Cole – Born February 1, 1892 in Anna, Texas. Died September 24, 1956 at 64 in McKinney, Texas from a peptic ulcer and peritonitis. Horace's father was a railroad ticket agent, and with wife Sara also produced four sisters – Blanche, Bessie, Nellie and Grace. Horace was a meat cutter for a retail market when he was 18; he served for three months in the Navy before the World War. From May 1 to August 20, 1918, he served in the Army, attaining the rank of Corporal at Camp Funston in Kansas.

By that time, he'd already been in the movies for at least three years, working as an electrician in the studios before making his first onscreen appearance in *Teasing a Tornado* (1915), a Western short for Lubin. By 1917 he was working regularly in short comedies and features for Universal. Before and after his Army service, he performed in 12 movies in 1918, most of them "Clover Comedies" in which he co-starred with Bud Duncan and Dot Farley. In 1920 he worked for Fox in Western features and two-reel comedies starring Chester Conklin and Clyde Cook.

Early in 1921, Kewpie made his first short for Mack Sennett, *A Small Town Idol* starring Ben Turpin, and became a mainstay of the Sennett studio. He was a memorable heavy in more than 30 shorts such as *Nip and Tuck* (1923) with Billy Bevan, and the features *Bow Wow* (1922) starring Louise Fazenda, and *The Shriek of Araby* (1923) with Ben Turpin. Away from Sennett, Kewpie supported Buster Keaton in his features *The Three Ages* (1923) and *Sherlock Jr.* (1924).

Starting in 1926, Kewpie freelanced. He appeared in *The Better 'Ole* (1926) for Warner Bros. with Syd Chaplin, as well as Larry Semon's last feature *Spuds* (1928), and some Lloyd Hamilton two-reelers for Educational such as *A Home-Made Man* (1928). Morgan also made the occasional dramatic feature, such as *Beggars of Life* (1928) – in which he played "Skinny" – with Wallace Beery and Louise Brooks, directed by William A. Wellman for Paramount.

With the coming of talkies, he returned to his job as a studio electrician until director Roy Del Ruth gave him a good part in *The Aviator*, a Warner Bros. comedy feature starring Edward Everett Horton. He had a prominent role as "Frolov" in the MGM operetta *The Rogue Song* (1930), which also included Laurel and Hardy in the cast. He appeared in only 15 sound films, one of the last being the Hal Roach-Charley Chase short *The Count Takes the Count* (1936). In 1940, Kewpie moved to Dallas, and then back to his hometown of Anna, where he started a business as a contractor. His 1926 marriage to Alice Lucille Johns ended in divorce, but his 1950 marriage to Hassie Katherine Lawrence lasted until his death.

> Hey diddle diddle,
> The Cat and the fiddle,
> The Cow jumped over the moon,
> The little Dog laughed to see such sport,
> And the Dish ran away with the Spoon.

Pete Gordon (Pietro Armandi) – The Cat – April 22, 1887 in Naples, Italy. Died on May 25, 1943 at 56 in Los Angeles. Pete's association with Stan Laurel dated to at least 1918, when he appeared with Stan and Mae Laurel in support of Larry Semon in the Vitagraph two-reelers *Huns and Hyphens* and *Bears and Bad Men*. Continuing with Larry Semon, Gordon also appeared with Oliver Hardy in *The Bakery* and *The Rent Collector* (both 1921), and *The Show, Golf* and *The Gown Shop* (all 1922).

Pete adopted the new name of Eddie Gordon for a series of 11 starring two-reel comedies, produced by Abe and Julius Stern's Century Film studio and released by Universal. His onscreen output slowed dramatically with the coming of the talkies (possibly he still had an Italian accent), although we get to hear him say "Naughty, naughty!" to Stan and Ollie just before he rides his bicycle into a pond in 1929's *Men o' War*.

He appeared in nine films after *Babes in Toyland*; six of them were unbilled bit parts (in *The Live Ghost* as a Chinese waiter, in *Swiss Miss* as a townsman), but he was billed – again as Eddie Gordon – in his last three pictures: *Sunset Murder Case* (1938) starring fan-dancer Sally Rand; *Ride 'em Cowgirl* (1939) starring female Western star Dorothy Page; and *Lady of Burlesque* (1943), as "Officer Pat Kelly" in support of Barbara Stanwyck.

— The Other Characters —

Frank Austin (George Francis Austin) – Justice of the Peace – Born on October 9, 1877 in Mound City, Missouri. Died on May 13, 1954 at 76 in Los Angeles. He was billed as George Austin in his earliest films, such as his first, the 1917 Western short *The Secret of Black Mountain*. In 1925 he played "Rigo" to Lon Chaney's "Dr. Ziska" in MGM's *The Monster* (1925). In the silent era, he had several roles large enough for him to receive billing, often in Westerns such as *The Circus Cyclone* (1925) and *Clicking Hoofs* (1926). He portrayed Leonardo da Vinci in a dramatic short starring Hedda Hopper, *Mona Lisa* (1926), and played Abraham Lincoln in a 1928 Columbia feature starring Jack Holt, *Court-Martial*. Austin often played butlers, as in *The Terror* (1928, Warner Bros.), and memorably in *The Laurel-Hardy Murder Case* and the Spanish-language equivalent, *Noche de Duendes*, as well as the German-language *Spuk um Mitternacht* (all 1930). He also buttled for the *Taxi Boys* in the Roach two-reeler *Strange Innertube* (1932). (He was considered for the role of the butler in Laurel and Hardy's 1933 short *Dirty Work*, a part that went to Sam Adams.)

In the later 1930s, he appeared in his fair share of B-Westerns, but also did bits in more prestigious films such as Frank Capra's *You Can't Take It with You*, *Mr. Smith Goes to Washington* and *State of the Union*. He was still receiving onscreen credit for low-budget comedy features such as *Jiggs and Maggie in Court* (1948) and Westerns including *Arizona Territory* (1950) when he retired at 73. In *Babes in Toyland*, he is the Justice of the Peace who has the unhappy task of wedding Barnaby to Bo-Peep – or so he thinks.

Eddie Baker (Edwin King Baker) – Dunker – Born on November 17, 1897 in Davis, West Virginia. Died on February 4, 1968 at 76 in Hollywood of emphysema. Eddie has one of his less memorable roles in *Babes in Toyland*, being one of the masked men who operates the crane which serves the express purpose of "ducking" Toyland miscreants before banishing them to Bogeyland.

His father, Edwin, ran a stock theatrical company with wife Georgianna as leading lady, so Eddie at 12 was living in a boarding house in Los Angeles. By the time he was 15, in 1913, he was working for the Biograph film company as a prop boy; he got in front of the cameras in 1916 and amassed more than 300 film and television credits in a career that ran until 1967.

He appeared in comedy shorts for Vitagraph in the late Teens, notably the 1918 *Huns and Hyphens* with Larry Semon and Stan Laurel; he also lent support to comedienne Gale Henry in several two-reelers for Reelcraft. Starting in 1922, he was very busy at the Hal Roach Studios, appearing in dozens of shorts starring Paul Parrot (later director James Parrot), Snub Pollard, Stan Laurel and Charley Chase.

From 1925 through 1929, he performed in comedies produced by Al Christie, starring Neal Burns and Jimmie Adams, but returned to the Roach lot in mid-February 1929 to play a sheriff in Laurel and Hardy's *Bacon Grabbers*. From 1930 through 1936 he was a freelancer; in 1934 he became the treasurer of the newly formed Junior Screen Actors' Guild, specifically reserved for extras and bit players.

He played cops, and specifically motorcycle cops, so frequently that early in 1937 he left the movies to become a real member of the California Highway Patrol. He appeared in only seven films and two TV episodes from 1945 through 1954 – two of them as a motorcycle cop – but resumed his acting career in 1955 and worked mostly in television, often as a courtroom spectator on *Perry Mason*. He amassed a further 102 credits through 1967, bringing his total known film and television appearances to about 310.

Scotty Beckett (Scott Hastings Beckett) – Toyland Boy – Born October 4, 1929 in Oakland, California. Died on May 10, 1968 at 38 in Hollywood, California from an overdose of barbiturates. Scotty's family moved to Los Angeles when the boy was three years old. Soon after, his father needed hospital attention and Scotty entertained him by singing. A casting agent noticed him and thought he had movie potential.

In 1933, Scotty appeared in his first film, *Gallant Lady*, starring Ann Harding. The next year he was signed by Hal Roach to appear in *Our Gang* comedies; Roach thought Scotty resembled Jackie Coogan and gave him a cap and oversized turtleneck sweater, similar to what Jackie had worn in *The Kid* (1921). Scotty became a sidekick to Spanky McFarland in 15 shorts over the next two years. (He returned to the gang in 1939 at MGM for *Dog Daze* and *Cousin Wilbur*.)

Unlike most child actors, Scotty remained very active through his teenage years and worked in dozens of films, including *Heaven Can Wait* (1943), *The Jolson Story* (1946, portraying Al as a boy), and *A Date with Judy* (1948). A drinking problem and some serious encounters with the law derailed his career in 1952. He rebounded in 1954 and played sidekick "Winky" to *Rocky Jones, Space Ranger* in 33 episodes of the TV series and did a few uncredited bits for movies in 1957, but from this point on, his life was a sad story of alcoholism, drug abuse, divorce and jail time. He checked into the Royal Palms Hotel in Hollywood and was found dead two days later, leaving behind a note, his third wife, and his son, Scott, Jr.

Georgie Billings (George Malcolm Fraser Billings) – Toyland Boy – Born March 3, 1924 in Toronto, Ontario Canada. Died on November 13, 2009 at 85 in Los Angeles, California. Georgie began his movie career at age five, appearing as "Davey Compton" in the 1929 drama *Woman to Woman*, starring Betty Compson, which was filmed in England. His next appearance was a bit as a shepherd in the *Our Gang* comedy *Shivering Shakespeare* (1930). Among his 75 films are nine at the Hal Roach lot, including *Choo-Choo!* (1932) and *Fish Hooky* (1933) with *Our Gang*, and *Hasty Marriage* (1931) with Charley Chase. He also appeared in *Mr. Deeds Goes to Town* (1936) with Gary Cooper, *The Adventures of Tom Sawyer* (1938), *My Little Chickadee* (1940) with W.C. Fields and Mae West, and *Knute Rockne All American* (1940) with Pat O'Brien. His

film career came to a halt in 1942, after *Code of the Outlaw* with Bob Steele. He probably entered the military; in any event he worked in only two more films, *Living in a Big Way* (1947) and *My Blue Heaven* (1950).

Billy Bletcher (William Bletcher) – Chief of Police – Born September 24, 1894 in Lancaster, Pennsylvania. Died on January 5, 1979 at 84 in Los Angeles. Billy's father Harry was a printer; his older brother Donald was a salesman in a hat store at 17, while 15 year old Billy sold newspapers and mother Dora kept the family together. Billy did a tour in vaudeville, singing a special song written by Bobby Heath and Charley O'Donnell, who had written the 1909 smash "Pony Boy." Unfortunately, as Billy said in 1975 about the ditty he got, "Oh, that was a lousy song!"

At his full height, Billy was only 5'2", which stood him in good (if short) stead as a silent movie comedian. He began appearing in comedies for Vitagraph in 1914, and made another pact by marrying Arline Harriet Roberts in Brooklyn, New York on December 7, 1915; they remained a devoted couple for the rest of Billy's life. In early 1916 they moved to Jacksonville, Florida, where both of them appeared in *Plump and Runt* comedies starring Babe Hardy and Billy Ruge, for the Vim Comedy Film Company. Billy starred in many silent comedies after moving to Hollywood, many for the Al Christie and Universal studios, sometimes billed as Billy Fletcher. One particularly notable film was *The Fresh Lobster* (1928), which used stop-motion animation to illustrate Billy's bad dream after eating the title delicacy as a midnight snack.

He was very active in talkies and particularly busy as a voice actor for cartoons, starting with his role as a donkey in the 1930 Mickey Mouse short *The Cactus Kid*. For Disney he played the Big Bad Wolf in *Three Little Pigs* (1933), and Pegleg Pete from 1934 to 1944. He did dozens of Warner Bros. cartoons, playing father Fritz Owl in *I Love to Singa* (1936), the wolf bedeviled by Bugs Bunny in *Little Red Riding Rabbit* (1944), and the long-suffering Pa Bear in *What's Brewin', Bruin?* (1948), among others. At MGM he gave voice to Barney Bear and Spike the bulldog in Tom and Jerry cartoons.

He was frequently visible in live-action films at the same time, sometimes doing bits (he's the man crushed in a deck chair in 1931's *Monkey Business* with the Marx Brothers), and sometimes getting a featured role. Billy was particularly busy at the Hal Roach Studios from 1931 through 1936, starting with a bit as "Recruit 11" in Laurel and Hardy's *Beau Hunks* and graduating to larger supporting roles in Roach's *Taxi Boys* series, and comedies with Thelma Todd and ZaSu Pitts or Patsy Kelly. Roach teamed him with Billy Gilbert as "the Schmaltz Brothers" (Gilbert was Louie, Bletcher was Meyer) in a series of musical comedies such as *Keg o' My Heart*, released November 11, 1933.

Billy continued working into the early 1970s, amassing more than 530 credits; one particularly nice later appearance was a 1971 commercial for Shasta Root Beer in which Billy played a Keystone Kop (and also the desk sergeant) while a messy street fight ensued, with root beer foam substituting for pie filling.

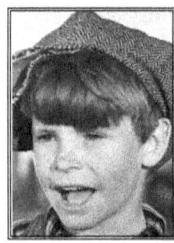

Tommy Bupp – Toyland Boy – Born February 10, 1924 in Norfolk, Virginia. Died on December 24, 1983 at 59 in Santa Ana, California of cancer. Tommy made his debut in the movies in the *Our Gang* comedy *Hi'-Neighbor!*, released March 3, 1934. Later that year, Tommy would play W.C. Fields' 10-year-old son ("Uncle Beeeeean died!") in *It's a Gift*. He had featured roles in *The Hoosier Schoolmaster* (1935), which also starred Charlotte Henry. He appeared in a number of B-Westerns, such as *Roarin' Guns* with Tim McCoy and *Roarin' Lead* with the Three Mesquiteers (both 1936). Tommy joined Tex Ritter for three pictures made for Grand National in 1937 and '38. In 1942 he left movies to join the Navy; he was a gunner's mate on the *USS Tennessee*. In later life, he married, fathered four sons, and worked in the wholesale electrical business.

Here comes the Sandman, stepping so lightly,
Creeping along on the tips of his toes.
As he scatters the sand with his own tiny hand,
In the eyes of the sleepy children.

Bobby Burns (Robert Paul Burns) – Sandman – Born on September 1, 1878 in Philadelphia, Pennsylvania. Died on January 16, 1966 at 87 in Woodland Hills, California of lymphoma. Burns was active on the stage and on Broadway – he was the giant spider in the original 1903 company of Victor Herbert's *Babes in Toyland* – before going into the movies with the Selig Polyscope Company in 1908. By 1912 he was in Jacksonville, Florida, appearing in comedies for the Lubin company. From May 1915 through December 1917, he co-wrote, co-directed and co-starred with Walter Stull in a series of *Pokes and Jabbs* comedies (Burns was "Pokes"), sometimes supported by Babe Hardy. In the early '20s he starred in comedies made by firms including Schiller Productions and King Cole Comedies; later in the decade he was frequently seen in Educational comedies produced and directed by Jack White.

With the coming of sound films, Burns became a mostly uncredited bit player, but provided memorable moments as Professor Fuller to would-be artists the Three Stooges in *Pop Goes the Easel*, and with Laurel and Hardy in *Below Zero*, as a blind man who isn't. He also brightened *The Laurel-Hardy Murder Case* (as an agitated relative), *Helpmates* (as a man watering his lawn and doing a spectacular fall), *Any Old Port* (as a Justice of the Peace who gets the back of his head shorn by an electric fan), and *The Chimp* (as a music-loving boarder).

Burns worked less frequently in the '40s, although he managed to again join the Three Stooges in *I'll Never Heil Again*, *Loco Boy Makes Good* and *Gents Without Cents*. He also made one last appearance with Laurel and Hardy, attending a lecture in a school gymnasium in *Air Raid Wardens* (1943). His last known credits were two 1958 episodes of the TV series *Adventures of the Sea Hawk*, starring John Howard.

Rock-a-bye baby, on the treetop,
When the wind blows, the cradle will rock,
When the bough breaks, the cradle will fall,
And down will come baby, cradle and all.

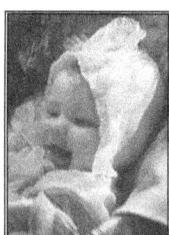

Ricardo Lord Cezon – The Rock-a-Bye Baby – Born July 18, 1932 in Los Angeles. Died on July 7, 2001 at 68 in Reseda, California. Certainly the youngest member of the *Babes in Toyland* cast, young Cezon managed to compile 20 film credits before retiring from the screen just before he turned 11. He was two years old when he played the baby, complete with cradle, in the treetop. He may be most memorable as the little boy who stares at Robert Benchley in the MGM one-reeler *A Night at the Movies* (1937). He was also prominent in another Benchley short, *How to Raise a Baby* (1938). Other credits include *The Prisoner of Zenda* (1937) starring Ronald Colman; *The Old Maid* (1939) with Bette Davis and Miriam Hopkins; *The Big Store* (1941) with the Marx Brothers; and his last appearance in *The Moon Is Down* (1943), a World War II drama with Cedric Hardwicke, Henry Travers and Lee J. Cobb. His older sister, Consuelo Lord Cezon (1925-2004), was featured in many Three Stooges comedies as Connie Cezan.

Old Mother Hubbard
Went to the cupboard,
To give the poor dog a bone:
When she came there,
The cupboard was bare,
And so the poor dog had none.

Alice Cooke (Alice Bailey Hamilton Cooke) – Mother Hubbard – Born July 12, 1882 in New York City. Died on June 6, 1985 at 102, in Los Angeles. Alice appeared in vaudeville during the early 1900s, partnered in the early Teens with her husband Baldwin, whom she married in 1913. From 1915 through 1917, the Cookes teamed with Stan Laurel in a vaudeville act called *The Crazy Cracksman*. Although the act broke up, the Cookes remained friendly with Stan, and both appeared in Hal Roach comedies. Alice was a secretary in *Chickens Come Home* (1931), a gypsy in *The Bohemian Girl* (1936) and a nightclub patron in *Our Relations* (1936). Her husband was more active at the Roach lot. Alice and Baldy also acted as chaperones for Stan and his second wife, Ruth, during the time when they'd been married in Mexico but the marriage was not yet recognized as legal in California, pending a final decree of divorce from Lois.

Baldwin Cooke (Baldwin Gardiner Cooke) – Policeman – Born March 10, 1888 in New York City. Died on December 31, 1953, at 65 in Los Angeles of pneumonia. Baldy – who still had some hair on his head well into the 1940s – served in the New York National Guard, 22nd Regiment. He was in vaudeville during the Teens (as noted above) but thanks to his continuing friendship with Stan Laurel, he worked frequently at the Hal Roach Studios, starting in 1928 with the L&H comedy *Two Tars*. He worked in 94 films, 89 of them for the Roach lot. (The rest were at MGM, except for one-time jobs at Paramount and RKO.) He was a bit player for the most part; of his 31 films with Stan and Ollie, he's most notable in *Berth Marks* as a train passenger; *Perfect Day* as the friendly, then combative, next-door neighbor; *Be Big!*, as a persuasive fellow lodge member; and *Twice Two* as an obstinate soda jerk. His last film for Roach was the 1941 streamliner *Niagara Falls*, starring Slim Summerville and ZaSu Pitts; his very last was the MGM musical comedy *Ship Ahoy* (1942) with Eleanor Powell and Red Skelton.

Ellen Corby (Ellen Hansen Corby) – Townswoman at Tom-Tom's Trial – Born June 3, 1911 in Racine, Wisconsin. Died on April 14, 1999 at 87 in Woodland Hills, California. Ellen spent much of her youth in Philadelphia. She came to Hollywood in 1932 to be "a movie glamor girl" but became a script supervisor for 11 years. She married director and cameraman Francis Corby in 1934, and worked frequently at the Roach studio; with Laurel and Hardy, she worked on three features and several shorts. (She can be seen briefly as an extra during the party sequence in *Sons of the Desert*.) She also worked on *Hopalong Cassidy* features and claimed to have written scripts for two of the films.

She divorced Francis Corby in 1944, and the next year began working steadily as a film actress, racking up 26 uncredited roles (often as a maid) before finally getting a good part as "Aunt Trina Halvorsen" in the Irene Dunne drama *I Remember Mama* (1948). She not only received her first onscreen credit, she was also nominated for an Academy Award as Best Supporting Actress. Although she lost to Claire Trevor in *Key Largo*, she began getting more prominent roles, as in the women's prison drama *Caged* (1950); she also had brief but memorable moments in George Stevens' *Shane* (1953), Billy Wilder's *Sabrina* (1954) and Alfred Hitchcock's *Vertigo* (1958).

Ellen began working in television in 1950 and found her niche in memorable supporting roles for *The Adventures of Ozzie and Harriet*, *The Andy Griffith Show*, *The Lucy Show* and dozens of other series. In 1972 she found her lasting fame as Grandmother Esther on *The Waltons*, which ran on CBS through 1980. Although a stroke curtailed her activities, she managed to make appearances in *Waltons* TV movies through 1997.

While working on that series in 1974, she told reporter Jerry Buck, "I can't go anywhere without meeting someone I worked with. I think people get tired of me saying, 'That reminds me.' But when the kids on the show found out I was with Laurel and Hardy, I was in."

> Little Miss Muffet
> Sat on a tuffet,
> Eating her curds and whey;
> Along came a spider,
> Who sat down beside her
> And frightened Miss Muffet away

Alice Dahl (Alice Norberg) – Little Miss Muffet – Born on January 7, 1913 in Petersburg, Alaska. Died on May 8, 1977 at 64 in Chula Vista, California. Alice got into movies at 19, with unbilled bits in *The Phantom Express* (1932), a B-picture for Monogram, and in Warner Bros.' prestigious musical *42nd Street* (1933). By 1934, she was prominent, and receiving onscreen credit, in B-Westerns such as *Deadwood Pass* and *Twisted Rails*, but also doing microscopic bits such as her role in *Babes in Toyland*. She had a bit as a dance hall girl in the 1935 Three Stooges two-reeler *Horses Collars*. In 1936, she changed her screen name to Terry Walker and this seemed to work, as she was prominent in Paramount's 1936 drama *And Sudden Death* and in another Paramount drama, *Blonde Trouble*. Before long, she was back to Westerns, such as *Billy the Kid in Texas* (1940) and *The Medico of Painted Springs* (1941). She left the picture business after one last role in a Bela Lugosi chiller for Monogram, *Voodoo Man* (1944).

> Curly Locks, Curly Locks, will you be mine?
> You shall not wash dishes, nor yet feed the swine.
> You'll sit on a cushion and sew a fine seam,
> And feed upon strawberries, sugar and cream.

Jean Darling (Dorothy Jean LeVake) – Curly Locks – Born on August 23, 1922 in Santa Monica, California. Died September 4, 2015 at 93 in Rodermark, Germany. When Jean was five months old, her mother separated from her father, and changed her surname to Darling as well as that of her daughter. At the age of six months, Jean was registered with Central Casting, and made her movie debut around February 1923. This was followed by theater appearances with her mother in three Sam Harris Broadway productions.

Late in 1926, they had moved back to Hollywood, where the wife of Roach Studios executive L.A. French saw Jean in a candy store. Conveniently, the studio was having try-outs for new *Our Gang* members that same day; Jean started as a "per diem" player at the Roach lot on October 6, 1926. On April 18, 1927, Jean was placed under contract as the new leading lady of the gang, receiving $35 a week, which was raised to $50 per week on December 19. She appeared in 32 *Our Gang* comedies and one Charley Chase short (*Are Brunettes Safe?*), making the transition to talkies not long before leaving the series with *Bouncing Babies* in July 1929.

The next four years saw Jean appearing in vaudeville theaters all over the United States, finally settling in Los Angeles to perform on radio shows from station KHJ. Near the end of 1933, Roach cast her in *Babes in Toyland*. Much publicity was made of the "reunion" of Jean with fellow Gang member Bobby Downs, but they had made only three films together: *Bring Home the Turkey*, *Seeing the World* and *Chicken Feed* (all 1927).

More vaudeville followed *Babes in Toyland*, but by 1938 Jean and her mother had returned to New York, where Jean commenced training for opera, working with Clemente DiMachi in his Carnegie Hall studio.

In 1942, she was on Broadway in the short-lived musical *Count Me In* (October 8-November 21). She alternated New York stage work with USO Camp Show tours during the war, but early in 1945 won the plum role of "Carrie Pipperidge" in Rodgers and Hammerstein's Broadway show *Carousel*. She stayed with the show through March 1947, completing 806 performances. March 1948 saw her again on Broadway, in *Hold It!* with Johnny Downs; she also began working in television in New York and Los Angeles.

In June 1954, Jean married Reuben Bowen, whose stage name was Kajar the Magician. Jean continued working in television until 1964, when her husband joined a touring revue, *Magicadabra*. They left the USA for South Africa and would move to Dublin, London, Antwep, Fiji and again South Africa; Jean separated from Reuben in 1972 and moved to Dublin, where she began a writing career. She would pen many short stories, several of them published in *Alfred Hitchcock's Mystery Magazine*. By 1980 she was writing scripts and appearing as a personality on RTE Radio in Dublin, where she became known on a children's show as "Aunty Poppy." Her writing and broadcasting continued well into the 21st century. She also published two memoirs, *A Peek at the Past* and *Buttercakes and Banana Oil*. In her last years, she attended many Sons of the Desert events in the USA and also spoke and sang at Italy's Pordenone Silent Film Festival.

Little Boy Blue, come blow your horn,
The sheep's in the meadow, the cow's in the corn.
Where is the boy who looks after the sheep?
He's under a haystack, fast asleep.

Johnny Downs (John Morey Downs) – Little Boy Blue – Born on October 10, 1913 in Brooklyn, New York. Died June 6, 1994 at 80 in Coronado, California of cancer. Johnny's father, Lieutenant Morey Downs, was a Navy aviator and was transferred from New York to San Diego when Johnny was eight. Already stage-struck, Johnny learned how to sing, dance and play the violin and made his stage debut at San Diego's Colonial Theater. Adding humorous patter to his repertoire, Johnny won several prizes at the Colonial's amateur contests. His mother then gave him a haircut modeled after Jackie Coogan's and took him around to many studios; he appeared in the *Reg'lar Kids* series for Winkler Pictures and worked in at least one of the Educational Juvenile Comedy series produced by Jack White for Educational Pictures. After a few shorts for Hal Roach as a "per diem" actor, he was signed to a long-term contract for $50 a week on December 29, 1924. He appeared in 26 films for Roach (ultimately making $75 a week) through late 1927, becoming a regular *Our Gang* member until he turned 14.

After appearing in MGM's *The Crowd* and *The Trail of '98* in 1928, he turned to vaudeville; he appeared in a 1931 Vitaphone short, *The High School Hoofer*, and made his Broadway debut on May 4, 1933 with Jimmy Durante in *Strike Me Pink*. Further Broadway roles came with *Ragged Army*, *Take a Chance* (with Olsen and Johnson) and *The Tingel Tangel Revue*.

His role in *Babes in Toyland* prompted a return to movie work, and he was signed to a long-term contract with Paramount in 1935. After more than 60 film appearances, including a return to the Roach lot for a riotous performance, mostly in drag, in *All-American Co-Ed* (1941), he moved back to New York for the Broadway shows *Are You With It?* with Dolores Gray (November 10, 1945-June 29, 1946; 264 performances) and *Hold It!* with Buddy Rogers and Red Buttons (May 5, 1948-June 12, 1948; 46 performances).

He alternated stage, film and television work for the next few years before returning to San Diego in 1953 and starting *The Johnny Downs Show*, a very popular children's program over Channel 10 (originally KFSD, then KOGO). Johnny entertained the kids in the studio audience between *Little Rascals* shorts and Popeye cartoons. The show lasted through 1971. In his later years, Johnny sold real estate and was also a well-regarded amateur tennis player. Married to the former June Draper since 1941, he was father to four daughters and a son.

John George (Tufei Fatella) – Barnaby's Henchman – Born on January 21, 1898 in Aleppo, Syria. Died on August 25, 1968 at 70 in Los Angeles of emphysema. Tufei left Syria in 1911 to join his mother and sisters in Nashville, Tennessee. He came to Hollywood and made his debut playing a tenement dweller in *Bobbie of the Ballet*, 1916, starring Lon Chaney, for Universal. George had a handsome and distinctive face and expressive eyes, but his stature of 4'2" ensured that he would often be cast as "dwarf" or "hunchback."

He received onscreen credit (a rarity) for his role as "Ali Bara" in *Black Orchids* (1916), and as "Grishka" in the 1924 Agnes Ayres feature *When a Girl Loves*. He became part of a stock company for director Rex Ingram, but during the filming of *Mare Nostrum* (1926) in France, Ingram reportedly became so annoyed with George's obsession with gambling that he paid his way back to the States. He then appeared in *Bachelor Brides* (1926) as a circus midget; *Don Juan* (1926) as a hunchback; *The Night of Love* (1927) as a Jester; and had what may be his most prominent role in *The Unknown* (1927) as Cojo, henchman to Lon Chaney's character of Alonzo.

With the coming of talkies, he appeared in the English and Spanish editions of *Dracula* (1931) as Van Helsing's assistant, and had unbilled bits in several horror classics, among them *Chandu the Magician* (1932), *Island of Lost Souls* (1932, as one of the half-man, half-animal creatures), *The Black Cat* (1934), *Bride of Frankenstein* (1935), *Mark of the Vampire* (1935), *The Hunchback of Notre Dame* (1939) and *The Creeper* (1948). He returned to the Roach studio in 1940 for a bit as a sailor in the Victor Mature swashbuckler *Captain Caution*.

George continued to be very active in the 1940s and '50s, featured in the serials *Mesa of Lost Women* (1949) and *The Lost Planet* (1953). He had a continuing part in the TV series *The Adventures of Fu Manchu* (1956). Henry Brandon remembered him fondly and recalled that he had a shoeshine stand to augment his income from movie work.

Little Jack Horner
Sat in the corner,
Eating a Christmas pie;
He put in his thumb,
And pulled out a plum,
And said "What a good boy am I!"

Sumner Getchell (Sumner Winfield Getchell) – Little Jack Horner – Born October 20, 1906 in Oakland, California. Died September 21, 1990 at 83 in Sebastopol, California. This chubby, baby-faced actor appears to have only one shot and one line in *Babes in Toyland*: as Little Jack Horner, he dutifully sticks his thumb into a Christmas pie and pulls out a plum, but instead of saying "What a good boy am I," he instead squeals, "Wheeeeeeeeee!!" His first five films were entries in Universal's two-reel series *The Collegians*, released in 1926 and '27. In 1929-30, he co-starred in a similar series, joining Ann Christy and Joan McCoy as *The Sporting Youth*. After 1930 he freelanced but worked steadily, always able to provide a funny moment in various features and shorts. He did receive onscreen credit in yet another collegiate series, the Universal serial *The Adventures of Frank Merriwell*, starring Donald Briggs as a school sports star turned adventurer; Getchell played sidekick "Harry." Getchell had a day job on the staff of the Academy of Motion Picture Arts and Sciences. He served in World War II from 1942 through December 1944, returning to films in 1946 with a bit in Jean Renoir's *Diary of a Chambermaid*, and a hefty part as "Tank Tinker" in the Columbia serial *Hop Harrigan, America's Ace of the Airways*. He continued to appear in movies and television (*The Silver Theatre, The Ford Television Theatre*) through 1953, the last in a credited role as "Lieutenant Cord" in William Wellman's *Island in the Sky*, starring John Wayne. After that, Getchell made only one known final appearance in 1957, in the Paramount Jerry Lewis feature *The Sad Sack*.

Charlie Hall (Charles Hall) – Townsman – Born on August 19, 1899 in Birmingham, England. Died on December 7, 1959 at 60 in North Hollywood, California. Charlie left England in January 1920 to take a job in a canning factory in New York, but soon decided to move to the warmer climes of Hollywood. He found work as a carpenter at the Roach studio, but soon made his debut as an extra in the Stan Laurel two-reeler *Mother's Joy*, released on December 23, 1923. (He was never, as is often stated, a member of the Fred Karno troupe of comedians, but he became friendly with Fred Karno Jr., who was working at the Roach lot in 1923; at one point they did a brief vaudeville tour together.)

By 1924, Charlie was alternating his carpentry work with regular appearances in comedies starring Laurel, Will Rogers, Charley Chase and *Our Gang*. He ultimately appeared in more than 300 films, 175 of them produced at the Roach studio. He worked in 55 Laurel and Hardy films (including eight of the foreign-language editions), more than any other actor. His roles ranged from barely seen extra to featured player. He's an annoyed taxi driver in *Double Whoopee* (1929), an obstreperous ice cream vendor in *Come Clean* (1931), a mostly helpful postman in *The Music Box* (1932) and a combatant with Stan and Ollie in *Them Thar Hills* (1934) and *Tit for Tat* (1935).

His last film for Roach was the streamliner comedy *Niagara Falls* (1941), but he continued to work, mostly at RKO and often in shorts starring Leon Errol or Edgar Kennedy. He returned to the Roach lot for television appearances on *My Little Margie*, *Topper* and *The Abbott and Costello Show*, and was a contestant on Groucho Marx's *You Bet Your Life*, sporting an outrageous Cockney accent and claiming to be a cab driver who was trying to break into the movies. In his last years, he worked in the prop department at Warner Bros., and his last film was a Warners Joe McDoakes short, *So You Want to Play the Piano* (1956).

Jack Hill (Lawrence Young Hill) – Townsman – Born on September 12, 1887 in Marion, Virginia. Died on November 22, 1963 at 76 in Los Angeles. Jack has 126 known film appearances, but there are certainly others, as he's often in the middle of a crowd or far in the background. His distinctive large ears, long nose and pencil mustache make him easy to spot, however. He has 36 known appearances with Laurel and Hardy, including three foreign-language pictures. Jack has one line in *Pack Up Your Troubles* (1932), as a doughboy in the trenches who tells Ollie, "Been a raid!" He's a nightclub doorman in *Their Purple Moment* (1928), and later a patron inside; he's the motorist whose rolled-up mattress keeps falling off of his car in *Two Tars* (1928); he's the sawmill worker kicking a barrel of shellac in *Busy Bodies* (1933).

Jack had a colorful background. His father, John, was a dentist; his mother's name was Arkansas Missouri Paxton Hill, but she was called "Cannie." In 1912 Jack was living in Los Angeles, working as a laborer, and unmarried. That would change, as by 1917 he was married and working at the Keystone Film Company as a mechanic and actor. He considered himself a full-time actor by 1920, and was still married to wife Leta; she would be followed by Virginia (1920s), Reba (1929-1937), Doris (1938-1940), Josephine (1942-?) and Freda (1949-1963).

Jack's earliest known film appearance (but probably not his first) is in the 1922 Hal Roach short *Hook, Line and Sinker*, starring Snub Pollard. He would appear in 107 known films for Roach, finishing with Laurel and Hardy's *Saps at Sea* (1940). He also worked as Charley Chase's stand-in and stunt double. Most of his work outside of the Roach lot was in Columbia two-reelers, including 13 shorts with the Three Stooges. Jack died on the day John F. Kennedy was assassinated; his mother was born on the day Abraham Lincoln died.

Fred C. Holmes (Frederick Clifton Holmes) – Balloon Man – Born on September 10, 1876 in Cambridge, Massachusetts. Died on December 24, 1940 at 64 in Los Angeles, of kidney disease and pneumonia. Another of those nearly-invisible performers, Fred was portly, bald, often wore spectacles, and was expert at playing clerks and doctors. His first known film is evidently the 1924 Harold Lloyd feature *Hot Water*, in which he had a small bit; however, he received onscreen credit for larger roles in four silent features from 1925 to 1927.

Of his 25 known appearances, 13 were at the Roach studio. With Laurel and Hardy, he was a motorist in *Two Tars* (1928), a stableboy in *Wrong Again* (1929), a courtroom spectator in *Going Bye-Bye!*, the balloon man in *Babes in Toyland* (1934) in which he get to hear him shout, "Balloons! All colors of the rainbow!," and a bailiff in *Our Relations* (1936). He received onscreen credit as "Wilson" in his final film, *The Courageous Dr. Christian* (1940), starring Jean Hersholt.

Payne Johnson (Payne Breazeale Johnson) – Jiggs (First Pig) – born June 2, 1930 in Los Angeles. Quoting from a history of his family in Mr. Johnson's collection, "In 1920, Sidney K. Johnson moved his young family from Jennings, Louisiana to resettle in Los Angeles, California. After her arrival in California, Payne's mother began her career as a reporter for the *Los Angeles Times*, as well as a freelance writer and screenwriter. In 1923, she sold a movie script, titled *Desert Destiny*, to Harry Carey, an early cowboy movie star, and Carey asked that Payne's oldest sister, Cammilla, play the role of his child in that movie. Mr. Carey also convinced Payne's mother to enlist all her children as actors in the movie industry.

Payne's father, Sidney K. Johnson, enjoyed a career at the *Los Angeles Times*, as a financial manager, and Payne himself would later become editor-publisher of a regional magazine. Since each of Payne's older siblings: Kenneth, Richard, Cammilla, Seessel-Ann, Carmencita, and Cullen, had been working as child actors in dozens of movies long before his birth, it was a natural transition for the new baby to become an actor. Payne was in movies practically from birth, appearing in the MGM drama *Paid*, starring Joan Crawford, when only a few months old. He never received onscreen credit but managed to appear in 102 films before retiring from the screen at 16. His six siblings were also child actors.

At the Hal Roach Studios, he also appeared in the 1937 *Our Gang* shorts *The Pigskin Palooka* and *Our Gang Follies of 1938*, as well as six 1938-39 *Our Gang* shorts at MGM. He's in some impressive films: *At the Circus* (1939) with the Marx Brothers; *Road to Singapore* (1940) with Bing Crosby and Bob Hope; *Santa Fe Trail* (1940) with Errol Flynn and Olivia de Havilland; *The Pride of the Yankees* (1942) with Gary Cooper; *Joan of Paris* (1942) with Paul Henreid and Alan Ladd; and his last, *The Strange Love of Martha Ivers* (1946) with Barbara Stanwyck, Van Heflin and Kirk Douglas.

Payne graduated from Los Angeles High School in 1948. In 1950 he enlisted in the Air Force and flew as an Arial Gunner on a B-50 bomber during the Korean War. He earned a Bachelor of Science Degree in Marketing from USC in 1957, and a Master's Degree in Mass Communications from San Diego State University in 1976. Payne is also a renowned photographer, specializing in views of Machu Picchu in Peru. In later years, he has run his own travel and touring agency, and has been a welcome guest at many Sons of the Desert functions. Payne's older brother Cullen (1926-2009) appeared in 27 films from 1927 to 1944, three at the Roach lot, and reportedly is one of the many *Babes in Toyland* children.

Dickie Jones (Richard Percy Jones, Jr.) – Toyland Boy – Born February 25, 1927 in Snyder, Texas. Died July 7, 2014 at 87 in Northridge, California, after a fall. Dickie's first film appearance came with the Al Jolson Warner Bros. musical *Wonder Bar* (1934). He then played a schoolboy in two entries of the Mascot serial *Burn 'em Up Barnes*, starring Jack Mulhall. Dickie appeared in the *Our Gang* two-reeler *Washee Ironee* (1934), just before working in *Babes in Toyland*; later he would be in the cast of *Our Gang Follies of 1936*, *The Pinch Singer*, *The Pigskin Palooka* and *Our Gang Follies of 1938*. He has a memorable moment in *Babes in Toyland* during the battle of the Bogeymen as the boy holding on to the lower leg of a wooden soldier (a human one, of course) and riding on his flat shoe. In 1939, he had a good role as a pageboy who shows Jimmy Stewart around Congress in *Mr. Smith Goes to Washington*, and during that year, he gave voice to the creation of Geppetto – and Walt Disney – in *Pinocchio* (released in 1940). He remained active in films and television into the mid-1960s, starring in two Western TV shows, *The Range Rider* (1951-53) and *Buffalo Bill Jr.* (1955-56).

Ham Kinsey (Hamilton Richard Kinsey) – Townsman – Born on February 21, 1900, Walterboro, South Carolina. Died December 9, 1967 at 67 in Los Angeles. Ham was the great utility player at the Hal Roach Studios, serving as Stan Laurel's stand-in and stuntman, a bit player and a prop man. The youngest of six children, Ham spent much of his youth in Savannah, Georgia. During the first World War, he served as an engineer until being discharged in January 1919. He worked in a shipyard as a rivet inspector for a time, then moved to Los Angeles.
By 1921, he was working at the Roach studio; his first known film appearance is in that year's Harold Lloyd short *Never Weaken*, but he was mainly working as a prop man. In 1923 he married Helen Olivia Johnson, with whom he would have a son, Richard Hamilton Kinsey, in 1924. That year he worked as an assistant director to Jay Howe on Roach's *Spat Family* series.
He's in 20 Laurel and Hardy films, including two of the foreign-language pictures, most prominently as Jean Harlow's cab driver in *Double Whoopee* (1929) and as a telegram boy in *Pack Up Your Troubles* (1932). He served as Stan Laurel's stand-in for films in which he does not appear, among them *The Flying Deuces* (1939). In the gag reel *That's That* (1938), Ham is dressed in Stan Laurel's costume for *Way Out West*, and delivers the Gettysburg Address, revealing his southern drawl.
Ham occasionally worked at other studios and can be seen in Buster Keaton's *The Cameraman* (1928) at MGM, the RKO Wheeler and Woolsey feature *The Nitwits* (1935) and the comedy Western *Destry Rides Again* (1939), made at Universal. Ham also worked as a salesman for the Terminix pest-control company.
He enlisted for service in the Army on May 20, 1942, and suffered a wound to an arm while overseas in August 1944. During Ham's service, his wife Helen died of polyneuritis and chronic alcoholism on October 16, 1943. Ham was discharged in April 1945; he remarried to Virginia Wise Lewter (1903-1995) in August 1948 and worked as a salesman for the Carnation Milk Company. He is buried at the Los Angeles National Cemetery.

Alice Lake – Townswoman – Born on September 12, 1895, Brooklyn, New York. Died on November 15, 1967 at 72 in Hollywood, of a heart attack.
Alice's career is, sadly, representative of many silent stars who became casualties of the talkies. She may have been in films as early as 1912 but was definitely appearing in Vitagraph comedies starring Wally Van, Sidney Drew and Billy Quirk by 1914. She was the leading lady in a dozen Fatty Arbuckle-Buster Keaton "Comique" two-reelers made in New York and then Hollywood. She graduated to starring roles in features but mostly for small companies such as the Aywon Film Corporation (*The Law and the Lady*, 1924) and Irving Cummings Productions (*Broken Hearts of Broadway*, 1923).
Her star was waning at the dawn of the talkie era; she's eleventh billed in *Twin Beds* (1929), for First National, starring Jack Mulhall and Patsy Ruth Miller. She's known to be in 15 films after this, mostly in uncredited bits; her last filmed scenes, for *Hollywood Boulevard* (1936, Paramount) were cut from the film. Years later, she is reported to have said, "All gone – fame, fortune and false friends. I guess they went in that order!"

Joy Lane (Joy Irene Wurgaft) – Toyland Girl – Born September 19, 1927 in Santa Monica, California. Died on February 25, 2018 at 90 in Laguna Woods, California.
Joy's film career consisted of four appearances, three of them at the Hal Roach lot: *Mike Fright* (1934), where she did an impressive backflip; *Our Gang Follies of 1936* (1935), where she sang "The Object of My Affection" to Alfalfa; and *Babes in Toyland*, as one of the many children. She also appeared in *Freckles* (1935) with Tom Brown and Virginia Weidler at RKO. She graduated from Anaheim High School and worked as a singer with the orchestras of Ted Fio Rito and Ray Anthony. Her marriage to Jo Van Ronkel ended in divorce in March 1976. In later years, she attended theatrical screenings of *Babes in Toyland* as a special guest.

Gus Leonard – Candle Snuffer – Born February 4, 1859, in Marseilles, Bouches-du-Rhone, France. Died on March 27, 1939 at 80 in Los Angeles of a stroke. Some sources give his birth name as Amedee Theodore Gaston Lerond; he used Gustave R. Lerond consistently on documents. He grew up in San Francisco and was already on the stage at six. In 1878, at 19, he was still there, but working as a frame-maker. He played in vaudeville for many years; in 1904 and '05 he was billed as "The Great Herrmann the Second," presenting a monologue in a German accent, performing magic tricks, and playing musical instruments described by reviewers as "comical" and "complicated."
He began alternating vaudeville with films in 1914. His first was *St. Elmo*, a dramatic feature produced by the Balboa Amusement Producing Company, based in Long Beach, California. In 1916 he was performing in short comedies at Kalem, many starring Lloyd Hamilton and Bud Duncan and directed by William Beaudine.
December 31, 1916 marked the release date of his first film for Hal Roach: *Luke's Shattered Sleep*, a one-reeler starring Harold Lloyd as Lonesome Luke, with Bebe Daniels and Snub Pollard. Gus worked on more than 200 films, 103 of them for Roach. Through 1920, they were mostly shorts with Lloyd; he appeared in many of Lloyd's features before and after he formed his own company. Gus was in three of the five one-reelers Stan Laurel made for Roach in 1918 and '19 (*No Place Like Jail*, *Do You Love Your Wife?* and *Hoot Mon*).
He began working for other studios in the early '20s, appearing in shorts for Al Christie and features starring Charles Ray. Gus continued to freelance for the rest of his career, returning to the Roach lot for two Harry Langdon shorts in 1930 (*The Head Guy* and *The Fighting Parson*), and the two *Our Gang* films for which he is best remembered, *Mush and Milk* (1933) and *The Lucky Corner* (1936). He also appeared in two Charley Chase shorts in 1936, *Life Hesitates at 40* (as the father of twins) and *Neighborhood House*. His last known film appearance is a bit as a concierge in the Jeanette MacDonald-Nelson Eddy romantic musical *Maytime* (1937), for MGM. He was survived by his wife, actress Minnie Jacobs Mintzer, whom he'd married in 1910 at age 51; she died about nine months after Gus, on January 3, 1940.

Jack "Tiny" Lipson (Jacob Seymour Lipschitz) – Nobleman – Born on January 17, 1901 in Denver, Colorado. Died on November 28, 1947 at 46 in Los Angeles of transverse myelitis. Jacob's father Louis Lipschitz and mother Sarah Goldfarbin Lipschitz were from Russia. The family included Jacob's sister Adeline, born in 1903, and brother Milton, born in 1910. They moved to Cheyenne, Wyoming when Jacob was 15; Louis got a position as a draftsman for a land surveyor, and the family changed their surname to Lipson. Jack attended business college and served in the World War as a private in the 164th Depot Brigade at Camp Funston in Fort Riley, Kansas. He returned to Cheyenne and in 1920 worked as a salesman, but moved to Los Angeles a few years later.

At about six feet tall and weighing over 300 pounds, "Tiny" was a natural to play strong men and heavies in short comedies. (Jack's wife Millie, whom he married in 1925, also appeared in movies.) He made his film debut in the 1927 Larry Semon two-reeler *The Stunt Man*, for Chadwick Pictures. Lipson appears in eight films with the Three Stooges, notably as a boxing spectator who is pummeled by enthusiastic fan Dorothy Granger in *Punch Drunks* (1934). He can also be seen with the Marx Brothers in *A Night at the Opera* (1935) as an engineer's assistant in Groucho's crowded stateroom; with W.C. Fields in *Never Give a Sucker an Even Break* (1941) as a Turkish airplane passenger ("You a big nose have it!"); and most prominently as King Vultan in chapters five through 13 of *Flash Gordon*, a 1936 Universal serial starring Buster Crabbe.

He has bits in six Hal Roach films, most visibly as a sailor in Laurel and Hardy's *The Live Ghost* (1934). In the 1940s, he supplemented his movie income by managing the Hollywood Café at 6916 Santa Monica Blvd. in Hollywood. He worked steadily through the '40s, compiling more than 100 appearances, and had uncredited bits in four films awaiting release at the time of his death. While many sources state that he died of a heart attack in Madera County, California, he actually died from inflammation of the spinal cord at the Veterans Administration Center in Los Angeles.

Sam Lufkin (Samuel William Lufkin) – Townsman – Born on May 8, 1891 in Salt Lake City, Utah. Died on February 19, 1952 in Los Angeles at 60, of uremia.

Sam's father, Samuel Henry Lufkin (1863-1920) was at one point a piano mover – shades of *The Music Box*. Sam's mother, Martha Alice Yates Lufkin (1866-1944), gave birth to three children. Sam had an older sister and a younger brother; the sister died at age three from malnutrition and the brother died in a drowning accident at age five. Lufkin spent some time in reform school after a teenage prank, and worked as a bellboy, a salesman for the Wilshire Oil Company, and a laborer for a city surveying crew before getting into the movies at the Roach studio.

Among his close to 180 films are 89 for Roach ranging from 1921 (*The Corner Pocket* starring Snub Pollard) through 1943 (the streamliner comedy *Nazty Nuisance*). He's in many Columbia two-reelers, 20 of them with the Three Stooges. Sam appeared in 38 films with Laurel and Hardy, most notably as the homeowner in *The Finishing Touch* (1928), a pedestrian and later a mustachioed, bowler-wearing motorist in *Two Tars* (1928), and the cop who wants "that other monkey" in *The Music Box* (1932).

Aside from short comedies, many of Lufkin's other appearances were uncredited bits in Westerns, as in his last known film, *Law of the Badlands* (1951), for RKO, starring Tim Holt. He married Gladys Slater in 1912; this marriage appears to have ended in divorce, as did his 1931 union with Libby Drahos, by whom he had a son, Samuel Jr. In October 1951, he married Maude Anderson, four months before his death.

Edward Earle Marsh – Willie (Third Pig) – Born on December 20, 1929 in Santa Barbara, California. Died on May 29, 2004 at 74 in Las Vegas, Nevada. Like Payne Johnson, Marsh was only four years old when he played Willie, the third little pig. He only appeared in a few films as a young actor, notably *Born to Dance* (1936) starring Eleanor Powell and James Stewart, and *The Rains Came* (1939) with Myrna Loy and Tyrone Power; in each of these, he was a boy pianist. By the 1960s, he was producing shows at nightclubs, and also writing, directing, editing and appearing in adult films under the name Zebedy Colt.

Scotty Mattraw (Winfield Scott Mattraw) – Town Crier – Born on October 19, 1880 in Evans Mills, New York. Died on November 9, 1946 at 66 in Hollywood of a heart attack. Short and stout, Mattraw's movie career consisted mostly of unbilled bits in crowd scenes that required a fat man. He was a theater manager at an opera house in Watertown, New York before his film debut in Douglas Fairbanks' *The Thief of Bagdad* (1924).

He received onscreen credit for six silent Western features made for Universal from 1927 through 1929 (including *The Border Cavalier*, directed by William Wyler). Of his nearly 50 film appearances, five were for Hal Roach (including a bit as a tavern patron in Laurel and Hardy's *The Devil's Brother*). One of his more notable roles was as the voice of Bashful for Walt Disney's *Snow White and the Seven Dwarfs* (1937). He was again given credit for his role as "The Beef King" in 20th Century-Fox's 1938 musical drama *In Old Chicago*. He appeared in two more films after this, the last as a migrant worker in *The Grapes of Wrath* (1940). He left a widow, Edna, whom he'd married in 1902, and children Ada, Rosalind, and Scott, Jr.

> The Queen of Hearts,
> She made some tarts,
> All on a summer's day;
> The Knave of hearts,
> He stole those tarts,
> And took them clean away.

Alice Moore (Alice Mary Moore) – Queen of Hearts – Born on November 23, 1915 in New York City. Died on May 7, 1960 at 44 in Washington, DC of an internal hemorrhage. Alice has one of the more notable (or at least noticeable) small roles in *Babes in Toyland*, as the Queen of Hearts. She's bearing a tray full of tarts, but instead of having them stolen by a Knave, she scolds a couple of boys who presumably should be in school.

Alice was part of movie royalty. Her parents were Tom Moore and Alice Joyce, both very popular in the silent era, her uncle was actor-director Matt Moore, her aunt was Mary Pickford, and her stepfather was MGM director Clarence Brown. Despite this advantage, Alice appeared in only six movies, the first being *Down to Their Last Yacht* (1934), an RKO comedy feature which also included Felix Knight in the cast, as a bronzed Hawaiian singer. Knight and Moore had a more extended working relationship on *Babes in Toyland* which developed into their marriage in Yuma, Arizona on October 17, 1935. Unfortunately, they divorced on March 14, 1939.

Alice had a bit as "Miss Centerville" in the 1937 Hal Roach feature *Pick a Star*; possibly her most prominent role was in *Fighting Lady* (1935), a low-budget drama for Fanchon Royer Pictures, in which she played "Betty Davis"! She married twice more, to Air Force Colonel Nicholas DeTolly (a former Disney animator) and then to Stanley Miller, who worked with the US Information Agency; Alice is buried in the Arlington National Cemetery. Her grave marker inexplicably gives the death year as 1950, although it occurred a decade later.

Bob O'Connor (Roberto O'Conor) – Townsman – Born November 18, 1893 in Nuevo Laredo, Tamaulipas, Mexico. Died on May 1, 1974 at 80 in Laredo, Texas.

The O'Conor family was partly of Irish origin but had roots in Spain and Mexico dating to the 1760s. Bob's father, Don Tomas O'Conor, was at one time the British Consul to Mexico. Bob appears to have joined the Hal Roach Studio in 1916 and worked in "Lonesome Luke" one-reelers starring Harold Lloyd. He was billed as H.L. O'Connor in his earliest films. He worked regularly in bit roles at the Roach studio through 1943, making 82 known appearances there. (He's notable as "Voitrex," a French prison official, in Laurel & Hardy's 1927 short *The Second 100 Years*.)

His fluency in English and Spanish was particularly valuable when the studio made Spanish-language versions of its films. He worked as the dialogue coach for Stan and Babe and other actors, and was prominent in their 1930 films *Ladrones* as a police desk sergeant, *Tiembla y Titubea* as a policeman whose wallet has unknowingly been acquired by Stan and Ollie, and *Noche de Duendes* as a train conductor.

When the Roach studio began making fewer films in the later '30s, Bob branched out to other studios. At Columbia he supported the Three Stooges in *Cookoo Cavaliers* (1940); in Abbott and Costello's *The Naughty Nineties* (1945) he's a croupier; in *It's a Wonderful Life* (1946) he's a bar patron, and in his last known role, for Bob Hope's *The Lemon Drop Kid* (1951) he's a bartender. He relocated to Laredo, Texas and became the proprietor of a tile company. He was survived by his wife Frances (1904-1980) and son Robert, Jr.

Gene Reynolds (Eugene Reynolds Blumenthal) – Toyland Boy – Born April 4, 1923 in Cleveland, Ohio. Died February 3, 2020 at 96 in Burbank, California, of heart failure.

Gene made his film debut in *Babes in Toyland*; subsequently, he was with the Gang as a football player in *Washee Ironee* (1934) and was one of Miss Jones' students in *Teacher's Beau* (1935). He was a busy young actor in feature films, appearing in *Boys Town* (1938) with Spencer Tracy and Mickey Rooney; *In Old Chicago* (1938) with Alice Faye; and *Santa Fe Trail* (1941) with Errol Flynn and Olivia de Havilland.

He moved to television work in 1949, appearing on *The Lone Ranger*, *Dragnet*, *Highway Patrol* and *I Love Lucy* before creating the Western series *Tales of Wells Fargo*. After this, he became a much-in-demand director of many top-rated series, especially *My Three Sons* and *Hogan's Heroes*. That military comedy many have sparked some ideas when he became a writer-director-producer of *M*A*S*H*, a show on which he contributed from its inception in 1972 through 1977. He left that series after creating *Lou Grant*, for which he was the producer and occasional writer and director from 1977 through 1982. He continued to direct and was executive producer of the teen comedy *Blossom* through 1999.

Angelo Rossitto – Elmer (Second Pig) – Born on February 18, 1908 in Omaha, Nebraska. Died on September 1991 at 83 in Los Angeles, California, after complications from surgery.

He only stood 2'11", but he was a very prolific actor, appearing in more than 100 movies and television shows from 1927 to 1987. (Nevertheless, because he usually averaged two film jobs a year, he kept his day job running a newsstand.) John Barrymore reportedly discovered him; Rossitto's first known film credit is as "Beppo, the Dwarf" in Barrymore's costume drama *The Beloved Rogue*, released on March 12, 1927. This is one of the few roles for which he received screen credit.

His other credits include director Tod Browning's horrific story of the sideshows, *Freaks* (1932); *The Wizard of Oz* (1939), *Spooks Run Wild* (1941) and *Scared to Death* (1946) both with Bela Lugosi, who considered Rossitto a good luck charm and "my greatest free advertisement." Later films were *Samson and Delilah* (1949) and *The Greatest Show on Earth* (1952), both produced and directed by Cecil B. DeMille; *Jungle Moon Men* (1955); the Rodgers and Hammerstein musical *Carousel* (1956); and *Doctor Dolittle* (1967).

His television work includes episodes of *The Fugitive, Gunsmoke, The Man from U.N.C.L.E.*, many episodes of Sid and Marty Krofft's series *H.R. Pufnstuf* (as Seymour Spider and Clang) and *Lidsville* (as Mr. Big and the lead singer of the Hat Band). He was frequently featured as newsstand operator Little Moe on Robert Blake's detective drama *Baretta* from 1975 through 1977. His last credit was an episode of *Star Trek: The Next Generation*. In addition to playing Elmer in *Babes in Toyland*, Angelo was the first-seen "sandman" during the "Go to Sleep" number.

Tiny Sandford (Stanley John Sandford) – Dunker – Born on February 26, 1894 in Osage, Iowa. Died on October 29, 1961 at 67 in Woodland Hills, California of colon cancer. Stanley spent much of his youth in Seattle, Washington. His father, Charles G. Sandford, was a poultryman, raising chickens. Stanley at 16 worked as an elevator operator, and later was a farmer and tractor mechanic.

By 1917 he had moved to Los Angeles, and made his first known film appearance in 1919, as "Goliath" in *After His Own Heart*, a Metro feature comedy starring Hale Hamilton. (He was not in Chaplin comedies for Mutual, as is frequently reported.) Tiny was a reported 6'2" and 270 pounds, making his nickname an ironic jest, as it was for Jack "Tiny" Lipson. Other early appearances were in *Rubes and Boobs* (1921) a two-reeler starring Billy Bletcher, and *Be Reasonable* (1921) for Mack Sennett with Billy Bevan. He worked in other short comedies at Universal and FBO.

Of his nearly 150 known film appearances, 57 are for Hal Roach, starting with the 1925 Charley Chase one-reeler *Plain and Fancy Girls*. He's in 29 films with Laurel and Hardy, including several of the foreign-language pictures. He's prominent in *From Soup to Nuts* (1928) as the reluctant husband to social climber Anita Garvin; in *Big Business, Double Whoopee* and *The Hoose-Gow* (all 1929) as policemen; and *The Chimp* (1932), as "Destructo," the circus strongman.

His films away from the Roach lot include the 1929 Douglas Fairbanks feature *The Iron Mask*, in which he played Musketeer Porthos; *The Timid Young Man* (1935), a Buster Keaton two-reeler for Educational; *Modern Times* (1936), as a factory worker with Charlie Chaplin who turns to burglary; and one of his last films, *A Trailer Tragedy* (1940), an RKO Edgar Kennedy short which also included Charlie Hall in the cast.

Sandford married Lyda Virginia Harris on February 24, 1917 in Hollywood, but this union was short lived. His lasting marriage was to Edna May Rolling, on April 10, 1920 at St. Stephen's Church in Los Angeles. In February 1921 they welcomed son Robert S. Sandford, and in 1923 daughter Edna L. Sandford. In the '30s he could afford living in Beverly Hills (at 800 North Westbourne Drive and later at 934 Havenhurst). He had a "day job" in the 1920s as a contractor and house remodeler, and returned to this in 1940, making one last appearance as a cook in a 1943 MGM musical short, *Shoe Shine Boy*. In later years he was a furniture refinisher.

Margaret Seddon (Marguerite Hungerford Whiteley Sloan) – Mother Peep in early filming – Born November 18 1872 in Washington, DC; died at 95 on April 17, 1968 in Philadelphia, Pennsylvania. Margaret was the first of five children born to Charles and Josephine Whiteley. She married civil engineer Frank Howard Sloan in 1896 and had three children, two of whom, Frank Jr. and Josephine, died in infancy; her third,

Marguerite, was born in 1901 and lived until 1981. Her husband died of fever while working in South America in 1919.

After a career on the stage, which included the Broadway shows *Modern Marriage* (1911) and *The Things That Count* (1913), Margaret began working in films in 1915, ultimately making more than 100. Her debut came with the Mary Pickford feature *The Dawn of a Tomorrow*. Other notable performances were in *Headin' Home* (1920) as Babe Ruth's mother; *Little Johnny Jones* (1923), starring comedian Johnny Hines, as Johnny's mother; and *Gentlemen Prefer Blondes* (1928), as the mother of Lorelei Lee, who was played by Ruth Taylor. Obviously, she specialized in "mother" roles.

She continued to work in talkies and on radio dramas in the 1930s and '40s, making a notable contribution to Frank Capra's *Mr. Deeds Goes to Town* (1936), as one of the "pixilated" sisters with Margaret McWade. They made such an impression that they were teamed again as "Aunt Pitty" (Seddon) and "Aunt Patty" (McWade) in the 20th Century-Fox musical *Danger – Love at Work* (1937), starring Ann Sothern and Jack Haley. Seddon and McWade also did a vaudeville tour together.

Margaret is the matron in the fancy automobile that W.C. Fields attempts to repair in *The Bank Dick* (1940); her chauffeur is played by Eddie Dunn, a mainstay of the Roach studio. Her last known credit is a television episode of *The Loretta Young Show* from September 1953, in which she worked when she was 80. Her only other film at the Roach studio is *The Nickel-Hopper* (1926), starring Mabel Normand, with Oliver Hardy in a supporting role. She may have been replaced on *Babes in Toyland* because she was working in MGM's *David Copperfield* (1935).

Jackie Lynn Taylor (Jacqueline Devon Taylor) – Toyland Girl – Born on June 29, 1925 in Compton, California. Died on May 5, 2014 at 88 in Citrus Heights, California of Alzheimer's disease.

Jackie won a children's beauty pageant in Long Beach, California and began working in movies after her mother, who was a nurse, brought her to a casting call. Jackie reportedly had bit parts in 75 movies; her most prominent roles were in eight films for the Hal Roach Studios, five *Our Gang* shorts (*Hi'-Neighbor!, For Pete's Sake, The First Round-Up, Washee Ironee,* and *Shrimps for a Day*), along with the Laurel and Hardy features *The Devil's Brother* and *Babes in Toyland* and a 1948 Roach "streamliner," *Here Comes Trouble*. Her true medium was television, where she started in 1950 as a host and interviewer for KTTV-Los Angeles.

Marriages to actor and drama teacher Ben Bard, and to Eugene Valencia, ended in divorce. She moved to Salinas, Calfornia in 1965 and worked as a TV news anchor. Relocating to Sacramento, she met TV newsman Jack Fries. They married in 1966 and this union endured until Jackie's death. Jackie became a very popular personality in San Diego and for a time hosted *Little Rascals Family Theater* there. In 1970 her book was published, *The Turned-On Hollywood 7: Jackie Remembers Our Gang*.

In the late '70s, the couple left television news and became ministers in the nondenominal Unity Church, leading congregations in Southern California and Nevada before retiring in 1993 to Sacramento; both continued to work as chaplains in retirement communities. They also taught vocal classes; at Sierra College. She was an inductee of the "Silver Circle" of the National Academy of Television Arts and Sciences, and was also honored for her broadcasting work by the San Diego Press Club.

Jerry Tucker (Jerome Harold Schatz) – Toyland Boy – Born on November 1, 1925 in Chicago, Illinois. Died on November 23, 2016 at 91 in Stony Brook, New York of natural causes.

Jerry's father, Leonard Schatz, managed a boxing club in Chicago. During one match, Leonard brought Jerry into the ring, where he recited "Gunga Din" from memory. Paramount Pictures executive Albert Kaufman was in attendance; he thought that young Jerry might have a future in movies, so the family moved to Hollywood. Jerry made his film debut at the age of five, in the MGM Buster Keaton feature *Sidewalks of New York* (1931). His next film was the first of 18 for Hal Roach, the *Our Gang* two-reeler *Shiver My Timbers* (1931). He was particularly memorable as Percy, the spoiled rich kid with a fire engine in *Hi'-Neighbor!* (1934).

Jerry was signed to a Paramount contract – the youngest performer to be given a contract by that studio – and appeared in *Blonde Venus* (1932) with Marlene Dietrich, *The Phantom President* (1932) with Jimmy Durante, Claudette Colbert and George M. Cohan, and *Sitting Pretty* (1933) with Jack Oakie. He ultimately worked in more than 70 films, among them *Captain January* (1936) at 20th Century-Fox with Shirley Temple, and *San Francisco* (1936) at MGM with Clark Gable and Jeanette MacDonald.

By 1939, Jerry's father had died, and Jerry and his mother relocated to New York. Here, the youngster became a busy radio actor, appearing in the programs *Hilltop House, King Arthur Jr.,* and *Jones and I*. With the coming of World War II, Jerry in 1942 joined the Navy at 17. He was part of the demolition team aboard the destroyer USS Sigsbee. During the Battle of Okinawa in 1945, Jerry caught some shrapnel in his leg during a kamikaze attack on his ship, which gave him a permanent limp and a Purple Heart.

Jerry married Myra K. Heino in 1944. The couple moved to Copiague, New York and had two daughters, Karen and Renee; they remained married until her death on August 2, 2012. Jerry studied electrical engineering at the State University of New York, Stony Brook and became an engineer for RCA Global Communications until retiring in 1981. He was very active in the Veterans of Foreign Wars, and in June 2015, a portion of St. Ann's Avenue was renamed Jerry Schatz Place in honor of his service. He died at the Long Island State Veterans Home in Stony Brook. Jerry enjoyed his time in the movies, but was proudest of his Navy career. "Jerry Tucker died at the age of 16, and Jerry Schatz was reborn in the Navy," he said in 2016. "It's not that being in the movies was anything that was bad. That's just not my life."

May Wallace (May Collins Ludlow Maddox) – Townswoman – Born on August 23, 1877 in Russiaville, Indiana. Died on December 11, 1938 at 61 in Los Angeles, California of heart disease.

May married at 18 in September 1895 to Charles H. Ludlow, three years her senior. In June 1900, they were living in Monroe, Indiana, where Charles was a physician and surgeon. They had three children: Clara, age five; Warren, three; and Mary, one. By 1910, it appears that this marriage had ended. May remarried in December 1915 to Thomas Whitmer Maddox, also born in 1877 and a veteran of the Spanish-American War. In 1918 they were living at 4416 Calumet Avenue in Chicago. Thomas, who worked as a decorator, had children Edith and Allen from his prior marriage to the former Sarah Durnham.

At some point, May performed in vaudeville; her film career appears to have begun with *The Cup of Life* (1921), a dramatic feature starring Hobart Bosworth and Madge Bellamy, produced by Thomas H. Ince. She soon appeared in comedies starring Mr. and Mrs. Carter DeHaven, and had a good role as "Auntie Meyrick" in **The Reckless Age** (1924), starring Reginald Denny, for Universal. By 1930, May and Thomas were living at 1857 North Gramercy Place in Hollywood; Thomas was now a house painter, while May gave her occupation as "actress, stage and screen."

Of her nearly 70 known film appearances, about 40 were for Hal Roach. She's in several Charley Chase silents, starting with *One of the Family* (1924), and had bits in eight films with Laurel and Hardy, most notably as the jolly head nurse in *County Hospital* (1932) and as the voice of Ollie's sister in *Twice Two* (1933). Undoubtedly, she's best remembered for her work with *Our Gang*, where she played the mother of one of the kids, as in *Love Business* (1931) and *The Kid from Borneo* (1933).

While the Roach studio provided most of her employment, she

occasionally worked at other studios, receiving onscreen credit for her appearances in two of her last films, *Midnight Madonna* (1937) for Paramount, and *Smashing the Spy Ring* (1938) for Columbia. Her final appearance was an unbilled bit as a townswoman in Oliver Hardy's solo feature *Zenobia*; this was released on April 21, 1939, four months after her passing, of a heart attack while en route to a hospital. Husband Thomas lived until January 14, 1941; he and May are buried at Forest Lawn in Glendale.

Marie Wilson (Katherine Elizabeth Wilson) – Mary Quite Contrary – Born on August 19, 1916 in Anaheim, California. Died on November 23, 1972 at 56 in Hollywood, California of cancer.

When Marie was seven months old, her parents divorced; she was raised by her stepfather, Frank White. Her father, Wally Wilson, died when Marie was five and left her a trust fund of $11,000, which she used to further her dramatic studies. She graduated from Anaheim High School – where she was affectionately known as Maybelle – and then attended the Hollywood Cumnock School for Girls. In 1933, she was working as a salesgirl in a department store and occasionally getting extra work, as in RKO's *Flying Down to Rio* and *Down to Their Last Yacht*, which included Felix Knight and Alice Moore in its cast.

She chanced to meet film director and writer Nick Grindé in 1934 when he stopped to help her after her car stalled. They soon became close personally and professionally. She was 18 when she appeared in *Babes in Toyland*, on which Grindé worked as a screenwriter. Marie has only one line in *Babes in Toyland*; as a very contrary Mary, she's rather angrily digging in her miniature garden and, knowing that Bo-Peep's sheep are missing, she snaps, "No, I haven't seen them!" Owing to her later fame on radio and in films and television, she was prominently listed in the cast on posters for the 1950 Lippert reissue of *March of the Wooden Soldiers*, just after Charlotte Henry and Felix Knight.

In 1935, Marie was in Grindé's RKO two-reel comedy *My Girl Sally* starring Sterling Holloway, and was an extra in his Mascot Pictures feature *Ladies Crave Excitement* (1935). She won a contract with Warner Bros. that year and made her debut for the studio in *Stars Over Broadway*, appearing in 22 films there through 1939. Most of them were B-pictures, but she occasionally got a chance to shine in better films such as *Colleen* (1936) and *Boy Meets Girl* (1938).

She made a few films in the '40s but primarily worked as a foil to the star of *Ken Murray's Blackouts*, at the El Capitan Theatre on Vine Street in Hollywood. She remained with this show for the entire Los Angeles run, some 2,300 performances from 1942 through 1949. Radio writer and producer Cy Howard saw Marie in *Blackouts* and cast her in the leading role of a new show, *My Friend Irma*, which became a hit and ran on CBS from April 11, 1947 to August 23, 1954. There were also two Paramount films based on the show, and a television version from 1952 through 1954.

After this, she performed in summer stock and dinner theaters, with *Born Yesterday* and *Gentlemen Prefer Blondes* being perennials for her. She made occasional television appearances, providing the voice for "Penny McCoy" in Hanna-Barbera's cartoon series *Where's Huddles* in 1970. Her last appearance was on an episode of ABC's comedy series *Love American Style*, which aired on October 6, 1972, seven weeks before her death.

Marie and Nick Grindé had announced their engagement in August 1938, but never married. She married actor Allan Nixon on April 27, 1942, but they were divorced on December 29, 1950. She married actor-producer Robert Fallon on December 15, 1951 and they remained married until her death.

Who's Who in Toyland
Behind the Camera

THE PRODUCER

Hal Roach (Harry Eugene Roach) – Producer – Born January 14, 1892 in Elmira, New York. Died November 2, 1992 at 100 in Los Angeles, California of pneumonia. After a colorful youth in which Roach worked with six-horse pack teams in Alaska, drove an ice-cream truck in Seattle, and worked with a construction company in Los Angeles, Roach saw a newspaper advertisement offering one dollar, carfare and lunch to anyone who owned Western-style clothes and wanted to work in movies as an extra. Roach put on his Stetson hat and cowboy boots and took the bus to the 101-Bison Company offices.

He struck up friendships with young actor Harold Lloyd and future director George Marshall, working as a $30-a-week dress extra at Universal. With the help of a modest inheritance, was soon producing one-reel comedies starring Lloyd as "Willie Work" and then "Lonesome Luke." Roach ultimately produced more than 1,200 films, most of them shorts starring Lloyd, Our Gang, Charley Chase, Laurel and Hardy and other comedians. He moved into feature-film production in the later '30s and in the '40s concentrated on 40-minute "streamliners." The studio was very successful in TV production early in the '50s, but after turning the reins over to his son, Hal Junior, in 1955, the financial misdeeds of young Roach's business partner forced the studio into bankruptcy in 1959; it was demolished in August 1963.

Roach remained vital and active in his last years, planning new projects, hunting quail, swimming each day, smoking Winston 100s and granting interviews to dozens of film students who were taking classes at UCLA, near his home in Bel-Air.

THE WRITERS

Frank Butler (Frank Russell Butler) – Screenwriter – Born on December 28, 1889 in Oxford, Oxfordshire, England. Died on June 10, 1967 at 77 in Oceanside, California. Frank worked for the Canadian Pacific Railway early in the 1910s, but after military service in the World War, he moved to Hollywood. There he found a niche playing British aristocrats in silent features, and starred for Hal Roach in a series of two-reel comedies, *The Spat Family*, from 1923 through 1925. When talkies arrived, Frank was busy writing screenplays at MGM for films such as *When a Feller Needs a Friend* (1932) with Jackie Cooper, and at Paramount for *College Humor* (1933) with Bing Crosby. After another tenure at the Roach lot as head of the scenario department, Butler spent most of his next 15 years writing at Paramount, contributing to scripts for Bob Hope and Bing Crosby, together and separately. Butler and Frank Cavett won Oscars for their screenplay for *Going My Way* (1944), starring Crosby and directed by Leo McCarey.

Nick Grindé (Harry Andrew Grindé) – Screenwriter – Born on January 12, 1893 in Madison, Wisconsin. Died on June 19, 1979 at 86 in Los Angeles. Nick graduated from the University of Wisconsin at Madison in 1915. He was in Hollywood by 1920, where he was an assistant director on films such as *Riders of the Dawn* for Zane Grey Pictures. Within a year, he'd worked on pictures for Triangle, Universal and Selznick. He was at MGM in 1925, where he was an assistant director on big pictures such as *Excuse Me* starring Norma Shearer, and a director on more modest efforts like the Tim McCoy Westerns *Riders of the Dark* and *Beyond the Sierras* (both 1928). From mid-1928 through early 1931, he directed MGM musical shorts and a feature, *The Bishop Murder Case* (1929), starring Basil Rathbone. He made another MGM short, the Oscar-winning *How to Sleep* (1935) with Robert Benchley, but found his niche making B-picture features for Warners, Columbia, Paramount, PRC and Republic, directing a total of 65 films through 1945.

THE DIRECTORS

Gus Meins (Gustave Peter Ludwig Luley Meins) – Director – Born March 6, 1893 in Butzbach, Wetteraukreis, Hesse, Germany. Died August 1, 1940 at 47 in La Crescenta-Montrose, California of carbon monoxide poisoning. Meins drew cartoons for the Los Angeles *Evening Herald*, which led him to becoming a scenario writer for Fox in 1919. In 1922 he was writing and co-directing shorts for Mack Sennett, but late in 1925 he began directing the *Buster Brown* series, starring nine-year-old Arthur Trimble (with Pete the Pup as Tige).

He began working at the Roach studio late in 1932, directing the two-reeler *Sneak Easily* with ZaSu Pitts and Thelma Todd. He would direct 38 films for Roach, 16 of them with *Our Gang*, from 1934 (*Hi'-Neighbor!*) through 1936 (*Second Childhood*). He also directed the Patsy Kelly starring features *Kelly the Second* and *Nobody's Baby*, although a dispute during the production of that picture caused Meins to leave the studio. Meins directed one feature in 1937 for producer Sol Lesser, *The Californian*, starring Ricardo Cortez, but found a new home at Republic, where he made 14 features, seven of them starring James, Lucile and Russell Gleason as *The Higgins Family*.

On July 31, 1940, Meins was having dinner with his wife and son in their home at 3839 Carnavon Way in Los Angeles, when police arrested him, charging him with sexual offenses against three boys aged 10 to 15. He was released on $5,000 bond and vehemently denied the charges. On August 4, Meins' body was found in his car, in the Montrose Hills residential suburb; he had committed suicide by inhaling carbon monoxide, with a hose leading from the exhaust pipe to the car's interior. Clearly, Meins could not bear being brought up in court on a morals charge. It's worth noting that, with Meins' close proximity to children in so many of his films, not one of them in later years ever mentioned any improper behavior from the director.

Charlie Rogers (Charles Alfred Rogers) – Director – Born January 15, 1887 in Birmingham, England. Died on December 20, 1956 at 69 in Los Angeles after an auto accident. Charlie (which is how he wrote it, not "Charley") had worked onstage in England and in America before getting into the film industry; he has 39 known film credits as actor overall, dating to the first feature length American film, *Oliver Twist* (five reels), made by General Film in 1912, in which he played the Artful Dodger. He starred in a Vitaphone one-reeler, *The Movie Man*, released June 2, 1928, so he made a sound film before Laurel and Hardy did.

At the Roach studio he was primarily a gag man, always on the set to provide ideas to replace what wasn't working in the script. He was also a fully-fledged writer; despite Hal Roach's recollection to the contrary, Rogers received credit for story, screenplay or adaptation on six of the Roach L&H features. He also earned writing credits on two L&H features made outside of the Roach lot, the 1939 RKO release *The Flying Deuces* and MGM's *Air Raid Wardens* (1943).

Charlie is credited as director with Laurel and Hardy of *Me and My Pal*, *The Devil's Brother* (co-directed with Hal Roach), *Going Bye-Bye!*, *Them Thar Hills*, *Babes in Toyland* (co-directed with Gus Meins), *The Live Ghost*, *Tit for Tat*, *The Fixer Uppers*, and *The Bohemian Girl* (co-directed with James Horne). In later years he wrote for television and built and rented stores.

Ray McCarey (Raymond Benedict McCarey) – Planned Director – Born September 6, 1904, Los Angeles. Died December 1, 1948 at 44 Los Angeles, of an overdose of sleeping pills. Ray seemed destined to live in the shadow of his older and more famous brother Leo, but he still had a respectable career. He started as a laborer at Paramount, then became a prop boy. At 16, he gave his occupation as "artist, motion pictures." At 21, he was an assistant director on the Mack Sennett lot, working in two-reel comedies such as *Hubby's Quiet Little Game* (1926) with Billy Bevan and *The Pride of Pikeville* (1927) starring Ben Turpin.

At the Hal Roach lot, he directed the first *Our Gang* film with Spanky McFarland, *Free Eats* (1932), and the Laurel and Hardy short *Scram!* and their feature *Pack Up Your Troubles* (both 1932). He was hired by Hal Roach to direct *Babes in Toyland*, but a dispute over the story with Charlie Rogers caused McCarey to walk out. At Columbia he piloted the Academy Award-nominated Three Stooges short *Men in Black* (1935), but began directing B-picture features for Paramount RKO and Republic, making about 30 of them through 1948.

He married the former Grace Thomas on July 1, 1924, and they produced daughters Patricia and Sharon. On December 1, 1948, after Grace had filed for divorce, he was found dead in his Wilshire Boulevard apartment, now living alone; two empty bottles of sleeping pills were beside his body.

THE CAMERAMEN

Art Lloyd (Arthur Raymond Lloyd) – Cinematographer – Born on October 17, 1896 in Los Angeles. Died on November 25, 1954 at 58 in Los Angeles of a heart attack. Art was interested in photography from an early age, and by 1918 he was a cameraman for the Vitagraph Film Company. He was also married to the former Fay North, and they had a son, Richard George Lloyd. He evidently freelanced in the early '20s, as he was one of many cameramen on the 1921 Metro feature *The Four Horsemen of the Apocalypse*, starring Rudolph Valentino. He had arrived at the Hal Roach studio by February 1924; his first credit is on the Will Rogers two-reeler *The Cake Eater*, released March 2.

Art remained at the Roach lot exclusively through late 1939, photographing just over 200 films. He worked mostly on *Our Gang* comedies in the late '20s, his only L&H credit during this time being *They Go Boom* (1929). Starting with *Laughing Gravy* in 1931, Art filmed 37 of the team's movies, while continuing to photograph entries in the *Our Gang*, Charley Chase, Todd & Kelly and *Taxi Boys* series. He called it a wrap on his theatrical film career when Laurel and Hardy left Roach in December 1939, having finished *Saps at Sea*.

With the entry of the United States into World War II, Art enlisted and became Captain Art Lloyd in the Signal Corps, teaching cinematography at the Army's Training Film Production Center at Fort Monmouth in New Jersey, and the Photographic Center in Astoria, New York. Art suffered a paralyzing stroke in the late '40s and was confined to the Birmingham Veterans Administration Hospital in Van Nuys until its closure in 1950. He died of a heart attack in his Hollywood home, survived by Venice and son Richard.

Francis Corby (Francis Marian Corby) – Cinematographer – Born June 23, 1893 in Omaha, Nebraska. Died August 5, 1960 at 67 in Los Angeles. Corby's family was in the oil business, and young Francis ran his own gas station at age 20 in 1917. However, by 1920, he was a cameraman at Universal, and in 1923 was filming comedies for Jack White, produced by Earle W. Hammons' Educational Film Exchange. By 1925, Corby had moved to the director's chair, and made 87 two-reelers through 1929 for producers Samuel Van Ronkel (the *Andy Gump* series), Abe and Julius Stern (*The Newlyweds and Their Baby*), and Joe Rock (*The Three Fat Men*).

Corby came to Roach in 1933, working as a cinematographer for the first time since 1924 on the Charley Chase two-reeler *Midsummer Mush*. He photographed 40 films for Roach, mostly Charley Chase, *Our Gang* and Todd and Kelly shorts. For Laurel and Hardy, his only other credits are the 1934 two-reeler *Going Bye-Bye!* and the 1936 feature *The Bohemian Girl*. For *Babes in Toyland*, he shot the "plot" footage with Gus Meins directing, while Art Lloyd, Laurel and Hardy's preferred cameraman, filmed the L&H scenes under Charlie Rogers' direction.

He left the Roach lot in 1936, and his film career after that was sporadic. The year 1944 saw the end of his ten-year marriage to Ellen Hansen Corby – later known as an actress in the TV series *The Waltons* – who had worked as a script clerk at the Roach lot. His father Edward and brother Grant had worked in the petroleum industry, so perhaps it was inevitable that Francis was also involved in it; he ended his working life as he began it, working 60 hours per week as a gas station attendant.

Roy Seawright (Roy William Seawright) – Animation – Born on November 19, 1905 in Los Angeles. Died on April 30, 1991, at 85 in Hermosa Beach, California of pneumonia, after a stroke. Roy started at the Roach studio at age 14, as Hal's office boy. Showing a talent for drawing, he became the studio cartoonist and animator. He also worked as a prop man with the various Hal Roach companies, being on hand for Laurel and Hardy's classics *Two Tars* (1928) and *The Music Box* (1932).

He contributed some split-screen shots and an animated mouse for *Brats* (1930), as well as devising the amusing animated titles for several shorts. In *The Chimp* (1932), two clowns hold a trampoline, which rips away to reveal each new title; in *The Midnight Patrol* (1933), a windshield wiper sweeps each title away; *Busy Bodies* (1933) has each title swept away by a circular saw; and *Dirty Work* (1933) shows test tubes overflowing to reveal each new credit.

Besides the stop-motion animation for *Babes in Toyland*, Roy contributed the "pull away" scene transitions for *Thicker Than Water* (1935), the split-screen work that allowed Stan to talk to his lookalike sister in *Twice Two* (1933), more split-screen work for the twin Laurels and Hardys in *Our Relations* (1936), and the animated bubbles bursting from a pipe organ in *Swiss Miss* (1938). He was nominated for Academy Awards for his optical effects on *Topper Takes a Trip* (1939), *One Million B.C.* (1940), and *Topper Returns* (1941), devising the "ectoplasm" effect for the ghosts in the *Topper* pictures.

When the Roach lot was taken over by the U.S. Government in 1942, Roy became a Major in the US Army Air Force's First Motion Picture Unit. He continued to create optical effects at "Fort Roach" for its military training films. After the war, Roy created effects for several notable film noir pictures, such as *The Gangster* (1947) and *Port of New York* (1949).

In 1948, he and fellow Roach alumnus Barney Carr leased space on the lot for their new company, Cascade Pictures of California, pioneering the field of animated television commercials. In later years, Roy served as a Hermosa Beach city councilman and police commissioner; he was also a cherished and frequent guest as Sons of the Desert meetings, banquets and conventions.

Kenneth Peach (Kenneth Donald Peach) – Special Effects – Born March 6, 1903, El Reno, Oklahoma Territory. Died on February 27, 1988 at 84 in Los Angeles, California. Working in the film industry at age 20, Peach was a director of photography at 23. His specialty was optical effects and "process shots," and in the '20s and early '30s he worked in this capacity for Tiffany, Warners, Columbia and RKO (assisting on *King Kong* in 1933). His six-year tenure at the Roach lot began in 1933. Much of his work was in special effects with Roy Seawright, but he was a cinematographer on 16 Hal Roach films in 1933-34, including L&H's *Dirty Work* and *Sons of the Desert*. During World War II, Peach served in the Navy. In the late '40s he worked at RKO. With the coming of TV, Peach became a very busy director of photography, starting in 1951 with *The Cisco Kid* and ending with *Taxi* in 1983.

THE FILM EDITORS

Bert Jordan (Albert Adrian Jordan) – Film Editor – Born on May 5, 1887 in Hackney, London, England. Died September 10, 1983 in Los Angeles at 96 of pneumonia. Bert got into the film industry in 1913, for the Lion's Head studio in Croydon, England. He worked in a darkroom and ran a machine which would punch these into the unexposed film stock, and then he would load the film magazines. He soon became a cinematographer. On March 27, 1915, he married Lillian Catherine Little (known as Lily), and they departed for America on October 23, arriving in New York on November 1. Bert was an assistant cameraman on D.W. Griffith's *Intolerance* in 1916.

He almost certainly was working at Roach's in 1925 and likely began working with Laurel and Hardy after the departure of editor Harry Lieb, who had cut many of the team's silent pictures, in early 1929. However, Bert didn't receive credit for editing the L&H films until supervising editor Richard Currier left the studio in 1932. From *County Hospital* (1932) through *A Chump at Oxford* (1940), Bert worked on 22 Laurel and Hardy pictures, becoming Stan Laurel's favorite editor.

Jordan remained with the Roach studio through the 1950s, editing Roach's television series *My Little Margie, Screen Director's Playhouse* and *Oh! Susanna*. With the demise of the Roach studio in 1959, he immediately went to work for producers Irving and Norman Pincus on their hit series *The Real McCoys*, starring Walter Brennan. He retired in 1962.

William Terhune (William Hilton Terhune) – Film Editor – Born February 18, 1899 in Kokomo, Indiana. Died on December 15, 1940 at 41 in Cheviot Hills, California of a heart attack. William was interested in magic, and his skill at legerdemain made him a popular student at Kokomo High School. He served in the World War at 19, then attended and graduated from Indiana University. He followed his interest by performing by managing a Chautauqua company, with which he toured the country.

He got into the film industry in 1924, at the Universal lot. By 1926, he was at the Roach studios and worked on more than 70 films through 1938. He was editor or co-editor on the Laurel and Hardy films *Liberty, The Devil's Brother, Wild Poses, Babes in Toyland, The Bohemian Girl* and *Way Out West*. He also served as unit manager, overseeing the entire production, of *Our Relations* and *Way Out West*.

Terhune suffered a heart attack in June 1940 and was bedridden from that point; he had a second attack and passed away in the home which, in December 1928, he had rented to the Roach lot to be used as Jimmy Finlayson's house in Laurel and Hardy's classic *Big Business*.

THE SOUND ENGINEER

Elmer Raguse (Elmer Roy Raguse) – Recording Engineer – Born May 9, 1901 in Springfield Massachusetts. Died March 2, 1972 at 71 in Palm Beach, Florida. In 1917, Elmer at age 16 built an amateur radio station in his room. By 1919 he worked as a wireless operator aboard a steam ship.

With the advent of commercial radio, Elmer got a position at WEAF-New York, in the studio and also taking equipment for remote broadcasts. He proved his versatility by next working for the Bell Telephone Labs, where he essentially created the electrical recording equipment that replaced the acoustic horn method, installing this at Columbia Records and its rival, the Victor Talking Machine Company.

In 1928, he began working full-time for Victor, designing and building portable field-recording equipment for the company to use in Argentina, Canada, Japan and England. When Hal Roach convinced the Victor executives to install sound recording equipment in his studio, Elmer came out from Victor's headquarters in Camden, New Jersey, the head engineer with a crew of five (three more were recruited from Southern California).

In December 1931, Raguse was terminated from the Roach studio by cost-cutting executive Henry Ginsberg. Ginsberg soon realized how valuable Raguse had been, because Elmer was back at the Roach lot in January 1934. He stayed at the Roach lot for eight years and nine months, leaving only when the U.S. Army took over the studio to make training films late in 1942. After a year at Paramount and 19 months at the Samuel Goldwyn Studios, Elmer came back to the Roach lot in November 1945, continuing through the studio's transition to television production, and recording the sound for series such as *Racket Squad, Amos 'n' Andy* and *The Life of Riley*. In 1957, Elmer moved to Desilu and in 1961 transferred to 20th Century-Fox, where he remained through 1967.

THE MUSICAL DIRECTOR

Harry Jackson (Harry Asbury Jackson) – Musical Director – Born November 15, 1896, in Columbus, Kansas. Died on July 16, 1961, in Wadsworth, Kansas, at 64. At age 11, Harry began learning to play the violin, and he soon organized a nine-piece orchestra with the neighborhood kids. In 1917, he was working professionally as a violinist.

By 1925, radio was booming in Los Angeles, and Harry soon began playing regularly with his "Maxwell House Coffee String Quartette" over KFI. He became a popular bandleader at Los Angeles social events, and in 1928 began a long-running series of broadcasts over KFWB, sometimes with his quartet, and others leading a full band, Harry Jackson's Entertainers. In November 1932, Harry began leading the orchestra for *Hollywood on the Air*, emanating from Los Angeles station KECA and broadcast coast-to-coast by NBC. He began to work with the Hollywood elite, and his orchestra was also selected to play at prestigious functions. One such event was Hal Roach's 20th Anniversary Party, held at the studio on December 7, 1933; Harry waved the baton while Laurel and Hardy, Charley Chase, Thema Todd and Patsy Kelly spoke on a half-hour broadcast, which was carried by NBC. On January 9, 1934, the *Los Angeles Times* announced that Hal Roach had signed broadcasting executive John Swallow as technical director for the music in *Babes in Toyland*, and engaged Harry Jackson's orchestra to perform it.

Jackson continued leading orchestras for radio programs for the next several years. On November 14, 1942, Harry enlisted in the U.S. Coast Guard, and was a Boatswain's Mate, First Class, until his honorable discharge on November 4, 1944. The next year, he became a co-owner of a recording studio in New York for radio commercials and airchecks; this occupation lasted into the 1950s.

Credits
1903-1997 Productions

BABES IN TOYLAND Grand Opera House, Chicago, June 17 – early October 1903. A musical in three acts. Produced by Fred R. Hamlin. Directed by Julian Mitchell. Music by Victor Herbert. Book and Lyrics by Glen MacDonough. Scenic Design by John H. Young and Homer Emens. Conducted by Max Hirschfeld.

With William Norris (Alan), Mabel Barrison (Jane), George W. Denham (Uncle Barnaby), Hattie Delaro (The Widow Piper), Amy Ricard (Contrary Mary), Bessie Wynn (Tom-Tom), Dore Davidson (The Master Toymaker), Gus Pixley (Inspector Marmaduke), Charles Barry (Giorgio), Elmer Tenley (Roderigo), Hulda Halvers (Hilda, the Maid), Francis Marié (Gertrude), Nellie Daly (Jill), Nella Webb (Bo-Peep), Charles Guyer (Grumio), Susie Kelleher (Red Riding Hood), Irene Cromwell (Miss Muffett), Virginia Foltz (Simple Simon), Bertha Krieghoff (Peter), Doris Mitchell (Tommy Tucker), Albertina Benson (The Moth Queen), Grace Field (Mima), Robert Burns (The Giant Spider).

The production moved to the Majestic Theatre in New York. It opened on October 13, 1903 and achieved 192 performances before closing on March 19, 1904. The cast and crew were essentially the same, although Frank Hayes now played Roderigo.

The production returned to the Majestic Theatre on January 2, 1905; a total of 21 performances were given before closing on January 21. William Norris as Alan was replaced by Ignacio Martinetti, while Amy Ricard as Contrary Mary was replaced by May de Souza. Gonzorgo and Roderigo were now played by James Rome and George Stone.

BABES IN TOYLAND Jolson's 59th Street Theatre, New York, December 23, 1929-January 11, 1930; 32 performances. A musical in three acts. Produced by Jolson Theatre Musical Comedy Company. Music by Victor Herbert. Book and Lyrics by Glen MacDonough. Staged by Milton Aborn.

With Frank Gallagher (Alan), Betty Byron (Jane), William Balfour (Uncle Barnaby), Jane Waterous (The Widow Piper), Leotabel Lane (Contrary Mary), Marcella Swanson (Tom-Tom), Mary Thurman (Jack), Wee Griffin (Jill), Margaret Byers (Bo-Peep), Chester Herman (Grumio), Ethel Lynne (Red Riding Hood), Helen Etheridge (Miss Muffett), Frances Baviello (Simple Simon), Helen Rae (Peter), Evelyn Brown (Tommy Tucker), Dean Raymond (The Master Toymaker), W.J. McCarthy (Inspector Marmaduke), Barry Lupino (Gonzorgo, Bobby Shaftoe, The Baby Bear), Rupert Darrell (Roderigo), Mona Moray (Hilda, the Maid), Joseph Schrode (The Giant Spider), Frank Yanelli (1st Dandy, Max), Donald Catlin (2nd Dandy), Louis Diamond (Santa Claus), Dene Dickens (Boy Blue, a Fairy), Martha Gale (Curly Locks), Eleanor Gilmore (Sallie Waters), Frances Moore (Frances), Helen Rae (Peter), Bernie Sager (The Brown Bear), Adele Savoye (Adele).

BABES IN TOYLAND Imperial Theatre, New York, December 20, 1930-January 1931; 33 performances. A musical in three acts. Music by Victor Herbert. Book and Lyrics by Glen MacDonough. Staged by Milton Aborn. Choreographed by Virginie Mauret.

With Charles Barnes (Alan), Betty Byron (Jane), William Balfour (Uncle Barnaby), Jane Waterous (The Widow Piper), Dorothy Kane (Contrary Mary), Ruth Gillette (Tom-Tom), Betty Hayden (Jack), Ethel Lynne (Jill), Margaret Byers (Bo-Peep), Joseph Knight (Grumio), Gertrude Waldon (Red Riding Hood), Lillian Morris (Miss Muffett), Frances Baviello (Simple Simon), Florence Little (Peter), Lydia Lucke (Tommy Tucker), Leslie Stowe (The Master Toymaker), Bert Matthews (Inspector Marmaduke), Jack Cameron (Gonzorgo), Robert Darrell (Roderigo), Mary Wilson (Hilda, the Maid), Bernie Sager (The Giant Spider), Frank Yanelli (1st Dandy, Max), Mabel Thompson (Bobby Shaftoe), Edward Bird (Santa Claus), Billie Williams (Boy Blue), Dene Dickens (A Fairy), Dorothy May (Curly Locks), Eleanor Gilmore (Sallie Waters), Frances Moore (Frances), Florence Little (Peter), Harry Knabenshue (The Brown Bear), Betty Flanigan (Betty).

BABES IN TOYLAND Hal Roach Studios Production F-5. Original story written by Hal Roach, December 1933. Sets and stop-action sequences prepared, January 1934. Shooting scheduled to start Thursday, February 15. Production suspended Monday, February 26; no filming (except screen tests). New story and screenplay, June 1934; final script (Number 13) completed Saturday, July 28. Filmed Monday, August 6 through Thursday, August 16; production suspended. Filming resumed Monday, September 24, finished Wednesday, October 17. Edited during late October; previewed Friday, November 9. Copyrighted November 28, 1934 by MGM (LP 5161). Released November 30. 79 minutes. Reissued as *March of the Wooden Soldiers*, *Revenge Is Sweet* and *Toyland*, often cut to 73 minutes.

Produced by Hal Roach. Music by Victor Herbert. Book and Lyrics by Glen MacDonough. Directed by Gus Meins and Charles Rogers. Screenplay by Frank Butler and Nick Grinde. Photographed by Art Lloyd, ASC and Francis Corby, ASC. Edited by William Terhune and Bert Jordan. Recording Engineer, Elmer Raguse. Musical Director, Harry Jackson. *Uncredited assistance*: Camera operator, Jack Roach. Makeup by Jack Casey and James Collins. Barnaby costume designed by Corliss McGee. Masks by Robert Cowan. First assistant director, Gordon Douglas. Second assistant director, Chet Brandenburg. Props, Ed Brandenburg, Charles Oelze. Draughtsman, Chris Christensen. Stop-motion animation and photographic effects, Roy Seawright and Kenneth Peach. Stunt double for Stan Laurel, Ham Kinsey.

With Stan Laurel (Stannie Dum), Oliver Hardy (Ollie Dee), Charlotte Henry (Little Bo-Peep), Felix Knight (Tom-Tom Piper), Florence Roberts (The Widow Peep), Henry Kleinbach/Brandon (Silas Barnaby), Virginia Karns (Mother Goose), William Burress (The Toymaker), Ferdinand Munier (Santa Claus), Kewpie Morgan (Old King Cole), Billy Bletcher (Chief of Police), Alice Dahl (Little Miss Muffett), Charlie Rogers (Simple Simon), Frank Austin (Justice of the Peace), Marie Wilson (Mary Quite Contrary), Sumner Getchell (Little Jack Horner), Alice Moore (Queen of Hearts) Alice Cooke (Mother Hubbard), Pete Gordon (The Cat and the Fiddle), Fred Holmes (Balloon man), Johnny Downs (Little Boy Blue), Robert Hoover (Bobby Shaftoe), Russell Coles (Tom Tucker), Jean Darling (Curly Locks), Angelo Rossitto (Little Pig Elmer/First Sandman), Payne Johnson (Little Pig Jiggs), Edward Earle Marsh (Little Pig Willie), John George (Barnaby's minion), Ricardo Lord Cezon (Rockabye Baby in treetop), Gus Leonard (Candle snuffer), Jack "Tiny" Lipson (Nobleman), Tiny Sandford, Eddie Baker (Dunkers), Richard Alexander (King Cole's guard), Anne Brown (Sally Waters), Charles Bimbo, Buster Brodie (Jack in the Box), Baldwin Cooke, Arthur Lovejoy (Policemen), Scotty Mattraw (Town crier), Jack Hill, Ernie Alexander, Bobby Burns, Charles Dorety, Edward Earle, Bobby Hale, Charlie Hall, Ham Kinsey, Sam Lufkin, Bob O'Connor, Richard Powell, John Wood (Townsmen), Ellen Corby, Alice Lake, Margaret Nearing, May Wallace (Townswomen), Scotty Beckett, Georgie Billings, Carl R. Botefuhr, Tommy Bupp, Marianne Edwards, Dickie Jones, Joy Lane, Jacqueline Taylor, Jerry

Tucker (Children) Eddie Borden, Jack Raymond (Bogeymen).

Music cues, all compositions by Victor Herbert and lyrics by Glen MacDonough unless otherwise noted: Overture, Ku-Ku (Marvin Hatley), Overture, Toyland [sung by Virginia Karns and Chorus], Rock-a-Bye Baby (Traditional), Toyland, Who's Afraid of the Big Bad Wolf? (Frank Churchill-Ann Ronnell), Toyland, Never Mind Bo-Peep [Sung by Felix Knight, Charlotte Henry and Chorus], Melodramatic, Birth of the Butterfly, I Can't Do That Sum, Melodramatic, I Can't Do That Sum, Toymaker's Workshop, Never Mind Bo-Peep, Toyland, Country Dance, Toymaker's Workshop, Jane, Melodramatic, I Can't Do That Sum, Melodramatic, I Can't Do That Sum, Melodramatic, I Can't Do That Sum, Ducking Scene (Myrl Alderman), Never Mind Bo-Peep, I Can't Do That Sum, Birth of the Butterfly, Never Mind Bo-Peep, I Can't Do That Sum, Birth of the Butterfly, I Can't Do That Sum, Jane, I Can't Do That Sum, Our Castle in Spain [Sung by Felix Knight], Melodramatic, Who's Afraid of the Big Bad Wolf? (Frank Churchill-Ann Ronnell), Melodramatic, Who's Afraid of the Big Bad Wolf? (Frank Churchill-Ann Ronnell), Toyland, I Can't Do That Sum, Never Mind Bo-Peep, Melodramatic, The Spider's Den, Go to Sleep - Slumber Deep [Sung by Felix Knight], I Can't Do That Sum, Melodramatic, The Spider's Den, I Can't Do That Sum, The Spider's Den, March of the Toys.

CHICAGO THEATRE OF THE AIR: BABES IN TOYLAND A radio production presented on December 24, 1949 from 9 to 10 p.m. by the Mutual Broadcasting System, through originating station WGN-Chicago. Performed at the Medinah Temple, Chicago. Produced by Marion Claire. Written and directed by Jack LaFrandre, based on the book by Glen MacDonough. Orchestra conducted by Robert Trendler. Music by Victor Herbert. Lyrics by Glen MacDonough.

With Marie Hadden, Lois Fair, David Polari. Probable other performers: John Barclay, Everett Clark, Mary Frances Desmond, Sondra Gair, Norman Gottschalk, Jonathan Holt, Carl Kroenke, Butler Manville, Elmira Ressler. Narration by Marion Claire. Opening recitation by Colonel Robert R. McCormick, editor and publisher of the *Chicago Tribune*.

MUSICAL COMEDY TIME: BABES IN TOYLAND A television production presented on December 25, 1950 from 9:30 to 10:30 p.m. by the National Broadcasting Company. Episode seven in the series. Sponsored by Procter and Gamble (Camay soap, Tide laundry detergent). Adapted by Alexander Kirkland from the original book by Glen MacDonough. Music by Victor Herbert. Lyrics by Glen MacDonough.

With Dennis King (Dr. Electron), Edith Fellows (Jane Piper), Dorothy Jarnac (Video/Telewoman), Robert Weede (Santa Claus/The Toymaker), Gil Lamb (Sambo), Helen Wood (Mam'selle Flighty), Robert Dixon, the Ken Christie Singers, the Kevin Jonson Dancers, Harry Sosnik's Orchestra.

MAX LIEBMAN PRESENTS: BABES IN TOYLAND A television production presented in compatible color on December 18, 1954 from 8 to 9:30 p.m.by the National Broadcasting Company. Produced and Directed by Max Liebman. Music by Victor Herbert. Book and Lyrics by Glen MacDonough. Adaptation by William Friedberg, Neil Simon, Will Glickman, Fred Saidy, Bill Jacobson. Book Staged by Milton Lyon. Dances and Musical Numbers staged by Rod Alexander. Musical Conductor, Charles Sanford. Arrangements by Irwin Kostal. Music Adaptation, Mel Pahl. Choral Director, Clay Warnick. Associate Producer and Director, Bill Hobin. Supervising Producer, Hal Janis. Unit Manager, Rick Kelly. Production Stage Manager, Sterling Mace. Assistant Director, Marcia Kuyper. Art Director, Frederick Fox. Costumes by Paul Dupont. Produced at NBC Studios, Rockefeller Center, New York.

With Dave Garroway (Santa Claus), Dennis Day (Tommy Tucker), Jo Sullivan (Jane Piper), Wally Cox (Grumio), Jack E. Leonard (Silas Barnaby), Karin Wolfe (Ann Piper), Edward Brian (Peter Piper), Ellen Barrie (Joan), Mary Mace (Widow Piper), Bambi Linn and Rod Alexander (Featured Dancers) A. Robbins; Charlie Cairoli and Paul (Clowns), Bil and Cora Baird and their Marionettes, Lee Bowman (Host), Don Pardo (Announcer).

Another live performance of this production was telecast in compatible color by NBC on December 24, 1955 from 8 to 9:30 p.m. The crew, cast and songs were the same, except for the substitutions of Barbara Cook as Jane Piper, Dickie Belton as Peter Piper, and Jack Powell as the Clown.

THE SHIRLEY TEMPLE SHOW: BABES IN TOYLAND A television production presented in color on December 25, 1960 from 7 to 8 p.m. by the National Broadcasting Company.

Music by Victor Herbert. Lyrics by Glen MacDonough (uncredited). Written for Television by Sheldon Keller and Jack Brooks (including new song, "Meantown"). Adapted from the book by Glen MacDonough (uncredited). Produced by William Asher. Directed by Bob Henry. Musical Numbers Staged by Tony Charmoli. Music Scored and Conducted by Walter Scharf. Theme Music by Vic Mizzy. Story Editor, Lois Green. Music Coordinator, Nat Farber. Unit Manager, Don Van Atta. Art Director, E. Jay Krause. Costumes by Robert Carlton. Associate Director, Dick Bennett. Production Assistant, Jean Messerschmidt. Assistant to the Choreographer, Dick Beard. Technical Director, Robert Finch. Lighting, Jim Kilgore. Audio, Hal Flood. Make-up, John Chambers. Senior Video, Jerry Smith. Executive Producer, William H. Brown, Jr. Color Coordinator, Henri Jaffa (uncredited). Filmed at NBC Studios, 3000 West Alameda Avenue, Burbank, California.

With Shirley Temple (Herself/Floretta), Linda Susan Agar (Herself, Co-host), Charles Black, Jr. (Himself, Co-host), Lori Black (Himself, Co-host), Jonathan Winters (Barnaby), Jerry Colonna (Gonzales), Joe Besser (Roderigo), Carl Ballantine (Gonzorgo), Michel Petit (Alan), Angela Cartwright (Jane), Hanley Stafford (The Toymaker), Ray Kellogg (The Mean Officer), Bob Jellison (The Mean Jailer).

BABES IN TOYLAND Presented by Walt Disney. Based on the Operetta by Victor Herbert and Glen McDonough [sic]. Directed by Jack Donohue. Screenplay by Ward Kimball & Joe Rinaldi, and Lowell S. Hawley. Choreographer, Tom Mahoney. Choral Arrangement, Jud Conlon. Orchestration, Franklyn Marks. Lyrics and Introductory Material, Mel Leven. Music Adapted and Conducted by George Bruns. Director of Photography, Edward Colman, A.S.C. Color by Technicolor. Art Direction, Carroll Clark, Marvin Aubrey Davis. Film Editor, Robert Stafford, A.C.E. Set Decoration, Emile Kuri, Hal Gausman. Costumes Designed by Bill Thomas. Assistant to the Producer, Lou Debney. Unit Manager, Arthur J. Vitarelli. Assistant Director, Austen Jewell. Special Effects, Eustace Lycett, Robert A. Mattey. Toy Sequence, Bill Justice, Xavier Atencio. Animation Effects, Joshua Meador. Matte Artist, Jim Fetherolf. Music Editor, Evelyn Kennedy. Special Art Styling, A. Kendall O'Connor. Sound Supervisor, Robert O. Cook. Costumes, Chuck Keehne, Gertrude Casey. Make-up, Pat McNalley. Hair Stylist, Ruth Sandifer. Released December 14, 1961. 106 minutes.

With Ray Bolger (Barnaby Barnicle), Tommy Sands (Tom Piper), Annette Funicello (Mary Quite Contrary), Ed Wynn (Toymaker), Tommy Kirk (Grumio), Kevin Corcoran (Boy Blue), Henry Calvin (Gonzorgo), Gene Sheldon (Roderigo), Mary McCarty (Mother Goose), Ann Jillian (Bo-Peep), Brian Corcoran (Willie Winkie), Jack Donohue (Sylvester J. Goose), James Martin (Jack), Ilana Dowding (Jill), Jerry Glenn (Simple Simon), John Perri (Jack-be-Nimble), David Pinson (Bobby Shaftoe), Bryan Russell (The Little Boy), Robert Banas (Russian Dancer), Marilee Arnold, Melanie Arnold (Twins), Leon Alton, Don Anderson, Tex Brodus, Boyd Cabeen, Joe Evans, Bess Flowers, James Gonzalez, William Meader, Joe Ploski, Bernard Sell, Tim Taylor, Judith Woodbury (Villagers), Candy Candido, Thurl Ravenscroft (Voices of Trees), Eileen Diamond (Dancer), Jeannie Russell (Singer).

BABES IN TOYLAND A Co-Production of The Finnegan/Pincher Company and Bavaria Atelier Gmbh. Distributed by Orion Television. Televised by the National Broadcasting Company on December 19, 1986 (145-minute version). Released theatrically in West Germany December 17, 1987 and on home video beginning in 1990 (94-minute version). Executive Producers, Sheldon Pinchuk, Pat Finnegan, Bill Finnegan. Supervising Producer, Anthony Spinner. Produced by Tony Ford and Neil T. Maffeo. Based on the stage production *Babes in Toyland*, Music by Victor Herbert, Lyrics and Book by Glen MacDonough. Screen Story and Screenplay by Paul Zindel. Directed by Clive Donner. Music and Lyrics by Leslie Bricusse. Music Supervised and Conducted by Ian Fraser. Costume Designer, Evangeline Harrison. Supervising Editor, David Saxon A.C.E. Editor, Susan Heick. Production Designer, Robert Laing. Director of Photography, Arthur Ibbetson B.S.C. Casting by Jose Villaverde, C.S.A. Production Supervisor, Leonard Gmuer. Unit Manager, Michael Waldleitner. First Assistant Director/Second Unit Director, Bert Batt. Second Assistant Director, Udo Alter, Hans Schonherr. Art Director, Helmut Gassner. Choreographer, Eleanor Fazan. Animals Created by Vin Burnham. Sound Recordist, Edward Parente. Makeup and Hairstyling, Rudiger Von Sperl.

With Drew Barrymore (Lisa Piper), Richard Mulligan (Barnie/Barnaby Barnicle), Eileen Brennan (Mrs. Piper/Widow Hubbard), Keanu Reeves (Jack Fenton/Jack-be-Nimble), Jill Schoelen (Mary Piper/Mary Contrary), Googy Gress (George/Georgie Porgie), Pat Morita (The Toymaster/Santa Claus), Walter Buschoff (Justice Grimm), Shari Weiser (Trollog), Rolf Knie (Zack), Gaston Haeni (Mack), Pipo Sosman (Jack in the Box), Chad Carlson (Joey), Jean Moake (News Announcer), Bill Marcus (Weather Announcer), Mona Lee Goss (Mrs. Goosefoot), Elizabeth Schot (Raggedy Ann), Ray Samberg (Town Crier), Andrew Steitz (Tree Monster #3), John Westhoff (Tree Monster #7), Tony Barton, Wanda Burke, Annissa Hewson, John Kanarowski, Jean Leroy, Veronica Loomis, Stanley I. Walker, Jr. (Cookie Factory Workers).

BABES IN TOYLAND A Metro-Goldwyn-Mayer Animation Production. Executive Producer, Don Mirisch. Produced by Paul Sabella, Jonathan Dern, Kelly Ward, Mark Young. Associate Producer, Robert Winthrop. Screenplay by John Loy. Based on the Operetta by Victor Herbert and Glen MacDonough. Directed by Charles Grosvenor, Toby Bluth, Paul Sabella. Score by Mark Watters. Production Designer, Toby Bluth. Voice Directors, Maria Estrada, Kelly Ward. Animation Director, Shivan Ramsaran. Supervising Editor, Michael Brakey. Editor, Tony Garber. Casting Director, Maria Estrada. Orchestra Leader, Peter Manning. Released by MGM Home Entertainment on VHS videocassettes and on laserdiscs October 14, 1997 and on DVD in 2004.

With the voices of Charles Nelson Reilly (Mr. Dumpty), Christopher Plummer (Barnaby Crookedman), James Belushi (Gonzargo), Bronson Pinchot (Rodrigo), Catherine Cavadini (Mary), Raphael Sbarge (Tom Piper), Joseph Ashton (Jack), Lacey Chabert (Jill), Lindsay Schnebly (Goblin King), Susan Silo (Scat), Newell Alexander, Tom Amundsen, Jackie Gonneau, Luisa Leschin, Mitch Carter, Ike Eisenmann, Edie Mirman, Elisa Pensler Gabrielli, Philece Sampler ("LA Mad Dogs" ADR Group), Jeff Bergman (Additional Voice ADR).

Video and Audio Releases

DVD AND BLU-RAY RELEASES:

Video releases are often out of print, but can be found online as used copies on eBay or Amazon.

The 1934 film is on DVD in a variety of sources, but the best is the black and white (only) release from Metro-Goldwyn-Mayer, distributed by Twentieth Century-Fox Home Entertainment in 2007. The packaging bills the film as *March of the Wooden Soldiers*, as do all DVD releases of the L&H film. However, this transfer, from a pristine 35mm source, has the original *Babes in Toyland* main title.

An early computer-colored version of the film was available on DVD from GoodTimes Entertainment Limited in 2001.

A different computer-colored edition was released on DVD in 2006 by Legend Films, and on Blu-ray in 2010. These also included a black and white version. Bonus features include the original trailer, and Christmas-themed cartoons, trailers and commercials. Information can be found at www.legendfilms.com. This version of the film is also available from several online streaming services.

The 1954 and 1955 Max Liebman NBC productions, originally broadcast in color, survive in black and white kinescopes, but are still very entertaining. A DVD release with both productions was released in 2012 by Video Artists International, 109 Wheeler Avenue, Pleasantville, NY 10570; www.vaimusic.com.

The 1960 *Shirley Temple Show* version was released on DVD with another episode, Winnie the Pooh. It was also released in 2006 by Legend Films.

Disney's 1961 feature film is available in Blu-ray, DVD and Digital formats; information is online at movies.disney.com/babes-in-toyland.

The 1986 Drew Barrymore-Keanu Reeves movie was released on Blu-ray in November 2023 by Kino Lorber. It contains only the 94 minute version, but presents this in the original 4x3 television aspect ratio and a 1.78:1 theatrical widescreen ratio. The theatrical trailer is also included. Ordering information is online at kinolorber.com.

The 1997 Toby Bluth animated feature was released on VHS on October 14, 1997. It returned on DVD in 2004 as a standalone title, and as part of a four-movie "MGM Movie Collection" of "Holiday Kids Movies" in 2010.

CD RELEASES:

Many different performances of Herbert's score, or part of it, have been issued. An edited version of the 1949 *Chicago Theater of the Air* production is available in a 1997 CD on the AEI label, which also includes vintage recordings performed by Victor Herbert and his Orchestra, the Victor Light Opera Company, and Bessie Wynn of the original cast.

In 1946, Decca released an album of five 78rpm records with most of the songs, performed by tenor Kenny Baker (who had been a singing sidekick on Jack Benny's radio show before Dennis Day inherited the part) and Karen Kemple. This was combined with selections from Herbert's *The Red Mill* and released on CD in 2002. It's available online at https://www.deccabroadway.com/releases

A compact disc of instrumental selections ("Hang March," "Birth of a Butterfly," etc.) was released by Naxos of America in 1999. The recording, made in September 1996, features the Razumovksy Symphony Orchestra – a group of Slovakian musicians assembled expressly for recordings – under the direction of Keith Brion.

A very lengthy recording of the score was conducted by John McGlynn for EMI in London in 2001, but remains unreleased. McGlynn also conducted this in a live concert performance with the St. Paul Chamber Orchestra and Minnesota Chorale. Both performances may be found online.

Sources

Books:

Basinger, Jeanine and Sam Wasson. *Hollywood: The Oral History*. New York: HarperCollins, 2022.

Bluth, Toby. *Babes in Toyland*. Nashville, Tennessee: Ideals Publishing, 1986.

Bogdanovich, Peter. *Who the Devil Made It*. New York: Alfred A. Knopf, 1997.

Calman, Craig. *100 Years of Brodies with Hal Roach*. Albany, Georgia: Bear Manor Media, 2014.

Cassara, Bill and Richard S. Greene. *Henry Brandon – King of the Bogeymen*. Albany, Georgia: Bear Manor Media, 2018.

Gill, Jonathan. *Hollywood Double Agent*. New York: Abrams Press, 2020.

Gould, Neil. *Victor Herbert – A Theatrical Life*. New York: Fordham University Press, 2008.

Guiles, Fred Lawrence. *Stan – The Life of Stan Laurel*. New York: Stein and Day, 1980.

Harmetz, Aljean. *The Making of The Wizard of Oz*. Chicago: Chicago Review Press, 2013.

Louvish, Simon. *Stan and Ollie, The Roots of Comedy: The Double Life of Laurel and Hardy*. New York: St. Martin's Press, 2001.

MacDonough, Glen and Anna Alice Chaplin. *Babes in Toyland*. New York: Fox Duffield and Company, 1904.

MacDonough, Glen. *Babes in Toyland – A Musical in Three Acts* [1903 Libretto]. Theatre Arts Press, 2018.

MacGillivray, Scott. *Laurel and Hardy: From the Forties Forward* (2nd Edition). Bloomington, Indiana: iUniverse, 2009.

Maltin, Leonard. *The Disney Films*. New York: Disney Editions, 2000.

Marriot, A.J. *Laurel – Stage by Stage*. Hertfordshire, England: Marriot Publishing, 2017.

Marriot, A.J. *Laurel and Hardy – The U.S. Tours*, Revised Second Edition. Alicante, Spain: Marriot Publishing, 2019.

McCabe, John. *Babe – The Life of Oliver Hardy*. London: Robson Books, 1989.

McCabe, John. *Mr. Laurel and Mr. Hardy*. New York: Grosset & Dunlap, 1966.

McCabe, John. *The Comedy World of Stan Laurel*. Beverly Hills, California: Moonstone Press, 1990.

Morros, Boris and Charles Samuels. *My Ten Years as a Counterspy*. New York: The Viking Press, 1959.

Roberts, Richard M. with Robert Farr and Joe Moore. *Smileage Guaranteed – Past Humor, Present Laughter, Musings on the Comedy Film Industry 1910-1945 Volume One: Hal Roach*. Phoenix, Arizona: Practical Press, 2013.

Scarfone, Jay and William Stillman. *The Road to Oz*. Guilford, Connecticut: Lyons Press, 2019.

Sherman, George and Mary Carey. *Walt Disney's Babes in Toyland*. New York: Golden Press, 1961.

Skretvedt, Randy. *Laurel and Hardy: The Magic Behind the Movies*. Aliso Viejo, California: Bonaventure Press, 2016.

Stone, Rob. *Laurel or Hardy – The Solo Films of Stan Laurel and Oliver "Babe" Hardy*. Temecula, California: Split Reel Books, 1996.

Ward, Richard Lewis. *A History of the Hal Roach Studios*. Carbondale: Southern Illinois University Press, 2005.

Watz, Edward. *Wheeler & Woolsey – The Vaudeville Comic Duo and Their Films, 1929-1937*. Jefferson, North Carolina: McFarland & Company, Inc., 1994.

The online Lantern Media History Digital Library (lantern.mediahist.org) provided access to the following film industry trade papers and magazines:

American Cinematographer, Broadcasting, Cinelandia, Cinemundial, Exhibitors Herald World, The Film Daily, Harrison's Reports, Hollywood, Hollywood Filmograph, Hollywood Lowdown, Hollywood Reporter, Independent Exhibitors Film Bulletin, International Photographer, Modern Screen, Motion Picture, Motion Picture and the Family, Motion Picture Daily, Motion Picture Herald, Motion Picture Reviews, Movie Classic, Movie Mirror, Movie Review News, The New Movie, Philadelphia Exhibitor, Photoplay, Picture Play, Picturegoer, Ross Reports, Screenland, Silver Screen, Sponsor, Television Digest and *Variety*.

The online search engine Newspapers.com provided access to the following newspapers:

Asbury Park (New Jersey) *Press, Baltimore Sun, Bradford* (Pennsylvania) *Evening Star and Daily Record, Brooklyn Times-Union, Buffalo News, The Chicago Tribune, Daily Sentinel* (Grand Junction, Colorardo), *Detroit Free Press, Evening Sun* (Baltimore, Maryland), *Honolulu Star-Bulletin, Indianapolis Times, Jersey Journal* (Jersey City, New Jersey), *Los Angeles Times, New York Daily News, Newsday, Pittsburgh Press, Press of Atlantic City, Salt Lake Tribune, Santa Rosa* (Democrat) *Press Democrat, Tacoma Daily Ledger, Tampa Tribune, The Gazette* (Cedar Rapids, Iowa), *The Village Voice* (New York City), *Washington D.C. Evening Star*.

The author's interviews include Henry Brandon, January 21, 1981; Richard Currier, August 26, 1980; Marvin Hatley, October 12, 1979; Payne Johnson, December 17, 2022; Bert Jordan, April 5, 1980; Felix Knight, January 31, 1981; Venice Lloyd, July 9, 1980; George Marshall, September 21, 1974; Hal Roach, January 21, 1981 and February 20, 1981; Roy Seawright, August 16 and 24, 1980, and Anita Garvin Stanley, January 28, 1981.

The University of Southern California Cinematic Arts Library provided access to the 1934 Hal Roach Studio payroll ledgers. The Margaret Herrick Library at the Fairbanks Center for Motion Picture Study provided several documents, including the correspondence pertaining to the 1934 script and film being accepted by the Production Code Administration.

Acknowledgements

Continued thanks to Richard W. Bann, preeminent historian of Hal Roach and his studio, in this case for making available a mountain of documents pertaining to the 1934 film, and also quite a few regarding the 1986 production.

Thanks to Robert M. Grippo, Jonathan Di Donato and Rob Falcone for rare and welcome information about WPIX and its amazing history. Kevin Butler is a scholar of locally generated children's TV shows and provided a great deal of material about the WPIX personalities of the '60s.

Grateful thanks to Larry Rochman, Noreen Lark and Liz Esquirol at WPIX and Rolando Pujol, former WPIX archivist and continued historian.

Ray Faiola is a swell guy and dedicated historian of the 1934 film. He did all of us a wonderful favor by locating the pristine 35mm materials at Eastman House, which were used for the best available DVD. Ray has a superb website devoted to the film, which you can find at www.chelsearialtostudios.com/toyland/toyland.htm

Thanks to Bob Satterfield, and the San Diego Saps at Sea Tent of Sons of the Desert, for facilitating my interview with Payne Johnson, who played Jiggs, smartest of the Three Little Pigs.

Rick Greene, Bob Duncan, Lori Jones McCaffery and Jim, Jimmy and Kris Wiley of the Way Out West Tent of Sons of the Desert gave continued support. The Sons have many tents or chapters around the world, and you may find information about the organization and how to join it online here: sonsofthedesertinfo.com.

Many thanks to Alyce Mott of the Victor Herbert VHSource website (www.vherbert.com) for illustrations, confirmations and corrections.

Thanks to Sandra M. Garcia-Myers at the University of Southern California Cinematic Arts Library. Thanks also to Ned Comstock, formerly with the library; for years, my yardstick as to whether a film history book was worth reading or not was to look in the acknowledgements for a paragraph of glowing appreciation for Ned, who would not only find what you wanted, but would suggest many items you hadn't thought of which would prove to be vitally important. Ned went the extra mile and then some for hundreds of film researchers, and although he has retired from USC, he was still very helpful to this volume, so I'm happy to add my thanks to his many well-deserved accolades.

Genevieve Maxwell at the Margaret Herrick Library of the Academy of Motion Picture Arts and Sciences was helpful in providing rare documents pertaining to the Production Code Administration.

Russell Babidge, Trevor Dorman and Patrick Vasey in the U.K. graciously contributed dozens of original photographs. Dave Lord Heath's website *Another Nice Mess* (lordheath.com) is an amazing resource for information about Hal Roach's films. This book would be much the poorer without their generosity.

Benedetto Gemma and Andrea Ciaffaroni in Italy sent some remarkable graphics of advertising artwork and other memorabilia. Grazie, signori, di tutto!

Gratitude to Steve Randisi for 1980s pictures of Felix Knight and Virginia Karns.

Particular thanks to David Koenig for his encouragement, his design and layout skills, his valuable suggestions in the editing, his friendship of over 45 years, and for agreeing to publish this book.

Grateful acknowledgement to all of the following: Harold Ahern for information about Nick Grindé; Stephan Artist, Steve Churi, Jeff Coe, Phyllis Calzone Frank, Charlie Greenberg, Jason Merrick, Anthony Miranda, Jack Roth and Tom Sito for memories of WPIX holiday screenings; Mark Bale and William Cairns for background on Sumner Getchell; Nancy Beiman for an animator's perspective on the stop-action sequences; Jesse Brisson for biographical background about Ham Kinsey; Craig Calman for information about Hal Roach's planned 1945 remake; Bill Cassara for the illustration of the 1915 re-creation of Toyland; Charlie Christ for amazing detective work; Michael Ehret for rare photos; Brad Farrell for his first-hand account of the 1986 Valley Forge Sons of the Desert convention and accompanying photos; Russel Fehr, Keith Scott, John Tefteller and Steven Thompson for information about orchestra leader Harry Jackson; Jorge Finkielman and Wes Heath for amazing photo restoration; Richard Finegan for rare photos of Thelma Todd's niece, Shirley Todd; Jim Kerkhoff for wonderful first-hand remembrances of Virginia Karns and Slim Gragg; Kevin Mulligan for the scans of the MGM "advertising and analysis" document; Frank Muni for further information about the Valley Forge convention; Mike Nemeth for rare photographs; Marcia Opal for wonderful photos documenting the 1986 convention and so many Sons of the Desert events; Scott T. Rivers for photos, articles and information; Jack Taylor for providing rare articles and graphics; Steven Thompson and Rene King Thompson for tbe Tiny Sandford death certificate; Charles Tranberg for material about Marie Wilson; Ed Watz for permission to quote from his interview with Dorothy Lee.

Extra special thanks to Jordan R. Young, Edgar Bullington and my wonderful mother, Zelda Skretvedt, for reviews of the work in progress and keen observations; and to my life partner, Rob Ray, for putting up with me for 37 years and counting.

Index

Abbott, Bud, 165, 175, 184, 228
Air Raid Wardens, 55
Alice in Wonderland, 37, 39, 61-62, 66, 81-82, 103, 127, 153, 159-160, 205, 217
Allen, Fred, 173, 194
Amundsen, Paul, 195
Anobile, Richard J., 184
Arbuckle, Fatty, 44-45
Aristophanes, 68, 73
Ashley, Paul, 174-175
Astaire, Fred, 16, 22, 61, 128, 163
Aubrey, Jimmy, 30
Auerbach, Joseph, 167-172, 177-179
Babes in Toyland (1930's RKO film), 15-22, 37, 162
Babes in Toyland (1934 film), 4, 37, 42-45, 55, 57-68, 70-162, 167-188, 209, 212-233
Babes in Toyland (1940's Morros film), 162-167, 177
Babes in Toyland (1949 radio), 189
Babes in Toyland (1950 TV), 190
Babes in Toyland (1954/1955 TV), 190-193
Babes in Toyland (1960 TV), 193-196
Babes in Toyland (1961 Disney film), 195-200, 203-205
Babes in Toyland (1986 TV), 203-205
Babes in Toyland (1997 animated film), 205-207
Babes in Toyland (stage), 5, 7-14, 16, 21-22, 36-37, 163-165, 167, 189
Bann, Richard W., 27, 56, 64, 85, 161, 213
Barrymore, Drew, 203, 205
Bartlett, Ella Herbert, 6, 16, 26, 37, 59, 143-144, 163-164, 167, 207-208, 217, 245, 265
Battle of the Century, 34
Baum, L. Frank, 5, 37
Benchley, Robert, 56
Benny, Jack, 165-166, 192
Best, Neil, 180
Big Business, 34
Bletcher, Billy, 71, 89, 98, 138, 144, 122, 228
Block-Heads, 60, 62, 216
Bluth, Toby, 205, 207
Bohemian Girl, The, 74, 88, 111, 117, 218, 223, 232

Bolger, Ray, 196, 199-200
Bolton, Joe, 174, 176-177
Bonnie Scotland, 88, 160
Boy Friends, The, 112
Brandenburg, Chet, 94, 104
Brandon, Henry, 75-77, 79, 82, 88, 94, 96-97, 99, 102-105, 109-110, 114, 118, 122-124, 127, 134-135, 140, 142, 182, 194, 207-208, 211-213, 218-219, 224
Breen, Joseph, 73, 156
Burns, Robert "Bobby," 10, 12, 32, 117, 122, 222
Burress, William, 88, 114
Busch, Mae, 70-71
Butler, Frank, 58-59, 74, 78, 81, 89, 92, 102-103, 127, 141, 231
Caesar, Sid, 190, 194
Calvin, Henry, 196-197, 199-200
Carnegie Hall (film), 164-167
Casey, Jack, 77-78, 114-115, 119
Cassidy, Hopalong, 169, 190
Cawthorn, Joseph, 17-18, 20
Chaplin, Charlie, 25, 30-31, 36, 42, 44-45, 68, 123, 128, 216-217, 220, 228
Chase, Charley, 26, 28-30, 36, 55, 58, 60, 80-81, 97, 101-102, 105, 127, 177
Christie, Al, 23, 26, 56-57
Cobb, Irvin S., 69-70, 72, 75, 80-81, 98, 101, 126-127
Cohn, Sam W.B., 95-96, 113-114, 116, 119, 140, 143-144
Cook, Clyde, 30
Cooke, Baldwin, 89, 98, 107
Corby, Francis, 88, 93, 127
Costello, Lou, 165, 175, 184, 228
Cowan, Bob, 95-96, 114
Cox, Wally, 192
Crawford, Joan, 61, 96
Crosby, Bing, 142, 162, 194
Currier, Richard, 25
Dancing Masters, The, 55
Darling, Jean, 87, 89, 91, 97, 119, 139
Davidson, Max, 29
Day, Dennis, 165-166, 190, 192-193
Dean, Priscilla, 29, 60
DeMille, Cecil B., 42, 75, 77, 219, 228
Denham, George W., 9, 11
Devil's Brother, The, 22, 36, 42, 44, 57-58, 70, 88, 113-114, 122, 126, 142, 161, 190

Disney, Walt, 22, 26, 55, 58, 70, 82-85, 93, 95, 120, 150-152, 155, 178, 184, 195, 200, 203, 205, 226-227
Dixiana, 16-20, 22, 153
Do Detectives Think?, 33
Douglas, Gordon, 94, 99, 104
Downs, Johnny, 87, 89, 97-98, 142
Drunkard, The, 74-79, 94, 99-100, 118, 218
Duck Soup, 33
Dunne, Irene, 17-18, 21, 173
Ellis, Patricia, 60, 62
Errol, Leon, 13, 56, 82, 177
Faiola, Ray, 186
Falcone, Rob, 177, 182
Farrell, Brad, 210-212
Fellows, Edith, 190
Fields, W.C., 37, 75-76, 81, 102, 162, 184-185, 221-222, 227, 229
Finishing Touch, The, 41
Finlayson, James, 29, 33-34, 233
Flying Deuces, The, 162-163, 171, 217, 226, 230, 232
Flying Elephants, 33
Fra Diavolo (see *Devil's Brother*)
Funicello, Annette, 196-197, 200
Gable, Clark, 61, 140, 229
Garabedian, George, 184-185
Garroway, Dave, 190-193
Garvin, Anita, 26, 29
George, John, 89, 114, 119
Ginsberg, Henry, 60, 62-63, 66-68, 71, 93-94, 127
Going Bye-Bye!, 70-71, 225, 232
Goldwyn, Samuel, 37, 173
Gordon, Pete, 66, 89, 105, 132, 221
Granger, Dorothy, 112
Grant, Cary, 37, 162
Graves, Stax, 109, 130
Grindé, Nick, 74, 78, 89, 91, 115, 127, 141, 230-231
Hall, Charlie, 29, 71, 89, 225, 228
Hamlin, Fred R., 5, 7, 9-10
Hardy, Lucille, 162-163, 237
Hardy, Myrtle Reeves, 63-64, 70, 227
Hardy, Oliver, 4, 10, 12, 22, 29-58, 60, 62-73, 79, 81-82, 84, 86,

88, 101-114, 117, 120-133, 136, 140-171, 174-175, 177, 208-209, 212-213, 215-217, 219-223, 225-229, 231-233
Harlow, Jean, 58, 73, 226
Hatley, T. Marvin, 40, 45, 142
Hearst, William Randolph, 18, 63
Helpmates, 36, 222
Henry, Charlotte, 37, 39, 61-62, 64-66, 79, 81-82, 88, 93, 98, 103-106, 108, 110, 116, 126-127, 132, 142, 153, 182, 209, 213, 217-218, 220, 222, 230
Hepburn, Katharine, 62
Herbert, Clifford, 37, 195
Herbert, Victor, 5-10, 13-19, 21, 37, 55, 60, 62, 82-83, 86, 90, 92, 95, 108, 117, 121, 129, 141, 143, 146, 149-153, 155, 163-165, 167, 170, 178-179, 182, 190, 192, 194-195, 200-201, 203-205, 207, 209, 212, 220, 222
Hog Wild, 36, 112
Hollywood Party, 66, 160
Hope, Bob, 105, 162, 194
Hutton, E.F., 70, 72
Jackson, Harry, 39, 58, 60-61, 82, 233
Jefferson, Arthur, 9
Jitterbugs, 55
Johnson, Payne, 95-96, 114, 225, 227
Jolson, Al, 14, 19
Jones, Dickie, 98, 119-121, 208
Jordan, Bert, 122-126, 217, 233
Karno, Fred, 31, 44-45
Karns, Virginia, 79-80, 82, 89, 106-109, 170, 177, 183, 209, 212-213, 216, 219
Kaye, Danny, 105, 194
Keaton, Buster, 36, 44-45, 57, 81, 96, 220, 226, 228-229
Kelly, Patsy, 60, 64, 69-72, 80-81, 101, 105, 127, 160, 177
Kennedy, Edgar, 41, 56, 75
Kennedy, John F., 15, 177
Kerkhoff, Jim, 106-107, 208
Kimball, Ward, 195-196
King, Dennis, 22, 36, 57, 190
Kinsey, Ham, 68
Kirk, Tommy, 196, 198-200
Kleinbach, Henry (see Brandon, Henry)

Knight, Felix, 59, 62, 81-82, 88, 93, 100, 103-105, 108-111, 113, 116, 122, 127, 130, 140, 142, 153, 182, 194, 209, 212-213, 218, 227, 230
Lahr, Bert, 74, 190
Lamb, Gil, 190
Laurel-Hardy Murder Case, The, 112, 221-222, 231
Laurel, Lois (daughter), 39, 63-64, 110, 187
Laurel, Lois (wife), 63-69, 98, 105
Laurel, Mae, 31, 33, 216, 221
Laurel, Stan, 4, 9, 12, 22, 25, 30-31, 33-58, 60, 62-73, 79, 81-82, 84, 86, 88, 101-114, 117, 120-133, 136, 140-171, 174-175, 177, 208-209, 212-213, 215-217, 219-223, 225-229, 231-233
Laurel, Virginia Ruth, 42, 68, 71, 95, 128-129, 216, 223
LeBaron, William, 15-18, 20-21, 162, 164-168, 178, 190, 195
Lee, Dorothy, 18, 20, 22
Leno, Dan, 9, 129
Leonard, Jack E., 191
Leven, Mel, 195-196, 198-200
Lewis, Jerry, 41, 44-45, 105, 225, 218
Liberty, 113, 233
Liebman, Max, 190-191, 193, 196
Lippert, Robert, 168-171, 178, 186
Live Ghost, The, 126, 221, 227, 232
Lloyd, Art, 60, 88, 122, 124, 127, 130, 212, 232
Lloyd, Harold, 24-25, 36, 55, 70, 95, 225-226, 228, 231
Lloyd, Venice, 88, 124-125, 212, 232
Loew, Arthur, 42-43, 95, 101
Long, Walter, 70, 126
Lucky Dog, The, 33
Lysistrata, 68, 73, 81
*M*A*S*H*, 119, 194, 228
MacDonough, Glen, 5, 7-10, 13-14, 44, 92, 195, 205, 213
Mackinnon, Douglas, 91-93, 102, 127
Macpherson, Jeanie, 24, 42
March of the Wooden Soldiers (reissue), 4, 116, 168, 170-174, 177-184, 186-188, 209, 213, 230
Marshall, Everett, 16-20, 22
Marshall, George, 24, 40, 42, 45, 231
Martin, Dean, 105, 218
Marx Brothers, 95, 222, 225, 227
Marx, Chico, 95
Marx, Groucho, 225
McCabe, John, 40-41, 58, 175, 185, 209, 216-217

McCann, Chuck, 174-176
McCarey, Leo, 26, 29, 33-34, 40, 45, 71, 231-232
McCarey, Ray, 71-72, 74, 82, 98, 232
McFarland, Spanky, 46, 52-55, 60, 66, 71, 106, 119, 160, 218, 221, 232
McGee, Corliss, 76, 78
McManus, Louis, 123, 126
Me and My Pal, 70, 232
Meins, Gus, 71, 79, 82, 88, 93-94, 98-99, 102-103, 106, 109, 118, 122, 141-142, 231-232
Méliès Geoge, 121, 167
Men O' War, 44, 221
Midnight Patrol, The, 70, 232
Mitchell, Julian, 5, 7-9, 13
Moore, Alice, 83, 89, 98, 104, 218, 227, 230
Morgan, Kewpie, 88, 107, 111-112, 114, 137, 220
Morita, Pat, 204-205
Morros, Boris, 162-168, 171, 178-179, 190, 195, 217
Mother Goose Goes to Hollywood, 49, 55
Mulligan, Richard, 203-205
Munier, Ferdinand, 88, 114, 138, 220
Music Box, The, 36, 216, 225, 227, 232
Navarro, Ramon, 60-61
Normand, Mabel, 33, 97, 239
Novis, Donald, 59, 61-62
O'Brien, Fitz-James, 8
O'Brien, Pat, 115, 180, 221
Oliver the Eighth, 60, 62, 70
Our Gang, 25-26, 28-29, 55, 66, 71, 81-82, 86, 88, 96-97, 101, 105-106, 113-114, 119-120, 125-126, 212, 218, 221-226, 229, 231-232
Pack Up Your Troubles, 36, 42, 71, 177, 225-226, 232, 241
Pal, George, 164, 166, 199
Pardon Us, 36, 42, 160, 216
Parrott, James, 43, 69, 221
Parsons, Louella, 63-64
Patterson, Bill, 107-108
Patterson, Joseph, 173
Peach, Kenneth, 55, 60, 62, 101, 121, 199, 233
Perfect Day, 36, 223
Pickford, Mary, 75, 85, 97, 172, 227, 229
Pinza, Ezio, 164-166
Pitts, Zasu, 61, 127, 177, 222-223, 231
Plummer, Christopher, 205, 207
Pollard, Snub, 22, 55, 225-227
Pujol, Rolando, 177

Putting Pants on Philip, 44
Rains, Claude, 165, 199
Randisi, Steve, 120, 209, 213
Rathbone, Basil, 74, 173, 231
Rée, Max, 16, 18, 22
Reed, Luther, 17-20, 22
Reeves, Keanu, 203, 205
Reilly, Charles Nelson, 205, 207
Revenge Is Sweet, 169-170, 172, 188
Reynolds, Gene, 119, 228
Rinaldi, Joe, 195-196
Rio Rita, 16-18
Roach, Hal, 22-31, 33-47, 49, 53-86, 88-90, 92-102, 104-106, 109-114, 116-117, 119, 122-130, 140-146, 149-151, 153, 156, 160-161, 164-165, 167, 169, 177-178, 185-186, 190, 195, 201-205, 209, 212-213, 215-216-229, 231-233
Roach, Hal Jr., 60
Roach, Margaret, 60, 97
Roach, Marguerite, 57, 60, 66, 70, 97
Roberts, Florence, 102-104, 110, 142, 219
Roberts, Thomas Benton, 209
Rock, Joe, 30, 33, 232
Rogers, Charlie, 39-43, 45, 64, 70-71, 79, 82, 88-89, 91, 94, 98, 102, 105, 109, 122, 136, 141-142, 231-232
Rogers, Ginger, 22, 128
Rogers, Will, 25-26, 28, 55, 57-58, 69, 80-81, 220, 225
Roosevelt, Franklin D., 74, 144-145
Rossitto, Angelo, 95, 114, 122, 228, 208
Roth, Jack, 177
Sailors, Beware!, 33
Sanders, George, 171, 191
Sands, Tommy, 196, 198-199
Sarnoff, David, 15
Satterfield, Bob, 208, 212
Sawyer, Arthur H., 24-25
Schallert, Edwin, 58, 62, 74, 81-82, 85
Scram!, 71, 232
Seawright, Roy, 26, 55, 121, 123, 125, 199, 232-233
Second 100 Years, The, 34, 228
Seddon, Margaret, 88, 96, 102, 228-229
Seiter, William, 68
Semon, Larry, 30, 33, 217, 220-221, 227
Sennett, Mack, 23, 26, 57, 61, 85, 101, 111, 219-220, 228, 231-231
Shearer, Norma, 74, 80, 219, 231
Sheldon, Gene, 194, 196-197, 199-200
Shipman, Ben, 64, 144

Slipping Wives, 34, 60
Smith, Pete, 56, 74
Sons of the Desert (film), 36, 42, 60, 66, 68, 126, 223, 233
Spat Family, The, 25, 30 58, 226, 231
Stanwyck, Barbara, 73, 96, 217, 221, 225
Steiner, Max, 18, 22
Stevens, George, 26, 124, 223
Sullivan, Jo, 191-193
Swallow, John, 60, 62, 82
Tati, Jacques, 44-45
Temple, Shirley, 193-194, 196, 198, 220, 229
Terhune, William, 92-94, 102, 122, 233
Terry, Frank, 42, 70-71, 104
That's My Wife, 34
Their Purple Moment, 34, 225
Them Thar Hills, 71-72, 81, 225, 232
They Go Boom!, 44, 232
Three Stooges, 56, 82, 174-175, 222-223, 225, 227-228, 232
Todd, Shirley, 80-81
Todd, Thelma, 22, 28, 36, 55, 61, 69-72, 80-81, 101, 105, 177
Towed in a Hole, 40
Toyland, 201-203
Tryon, Glenn, 30
Two Tars, 34, 44, 223, 225, 227, 232
Ulmer, Edgar, 164-165
Valentino, Rudolph, 33, 58, 232
Vallee, Rudy, 59-61
Velez, Lupe, 66
Way Out West, 209, 216, 226, 233
We Faw Down, 34
Weede, Robert, 190
Weintraub, Charles, 171-172
West, Billy, 30, 32, 217
West, Mae, 151, 157, 162, 184, 221
Wheeler, Bert, 16-18, 20-22, 226
White, Jules, 56
Wilson, Marie, 89, 114, 116, 230, 138
Wizard of Oz, The (film), 181-182, 184, 196, 198, 203, 215, 228
Wizard of Oz, The (stage), 5-9, 13
Wizard of Oz, The Wonderful (book), 5, 13, 37
Woolsey, Robert, 16-18, 20-22, 219, 226
Wrong Again, 40, 225
Wynn, Bessie, 9, 14
Wynn, Ed, 196, 198-199
Young, Jordan R., 40
You're Darn Tootin', 41
Ziegler, John, 180
Zorro, 199

www.ingramcontent.com/pod-product-compliance
Lightning Source LLC
Chambersburg PA
CBHW080742250426
43671CB00038B/2717